The Evolving Role of the Public Prosecutor

The modern public prosecutor is a figure both powerful and enigmatic. Legal scholars and criminologists often identify "three essential components" of criminal justice systems: police, courts and corrections. Yet increasingly, the public prosecutor occupies a distinct role independent from any of these branches. Acting outside of the court, and therefore largely out of the public eye, the prosecutor's control over whether and what charges proceed to court can limit judicial discretion on sentencing, open pathways to alternative measures and even deny entry into the criminal justice system entirely. In this sense the prosecutor serves as a true "gatekeeper" to the criminal process.

This book addresses key aspects of the evolving role of domestic and international prosecutors in common law and civil law systems in the twenty-first century, and the challenges posed by this evolution. This collection of chapters from respected scholars takes an international, comparative approach and explores how these different legal systems have borrowed theorisations and articulations of the prosecutorial role from each other in adapting the office to changing conditions and expectations. The volume is structured around four main themes relating to the role of the modern prosecutor: the nature of the prosecutor's office, the role of the prosecutor in investigations, prosecutorial discretion and how it is exercised, and politicisation and accountability of prosecutors.

This book is essential for scholars and students in criminal justice, pre-law/legal studies, criminology, justice studies and political science, and is useful as a resource for those interested in legal change around the world.

Victoria Colvin is a lecturer at the School of Law, University of Wollongong. She completed her doctorate at the TC Beirne School of Law, University of Queensland, in 2017. From 2001–2009, she was a prosecutor with the Criminal Justice Branch of the Attorney General of British Columbia, Canada.

Philip Stenning is an Adjunct Professor in the Griffith Criminology Institute at Griffith University in Brisbane, Australia, a Visiting Professor in the Law School at Leeds University in the UK and an Honorary Professor in the School of Applied Human Sciences at the University of KwaZulu-Natal in South Africa. His published books include *Appearing for the Crown: A Legal and Historical Review of Criminal Prosecutorial Authority in Canada* (1986), *The Modern Prosecution Process in New Zealand* (2008) and, with David Bayley, *Governing the Police: Experience in Six Democracies* (2016).

Directions and Developments in Criminal Justice and Law

The ways in which crime is constructed in society is of time-honoured interest to criminologists across the globe. The ever-changing landscape of what is criminal and what is not affects scholars and policymakers in their approach to the body of law defining prohibited conduct, how that law evolves, and the modes by which it is administered. Rule of law cannot exist without a transparent legal system, strong enforcement structures, and an independent judiciary to protect against the arbitrary use of power. Critical consideration of the mechanisms through which societies attempt to make the rule of law a reality is essential to understanding and developing effectual criminal justice systems. The *Directions and Developments in Criminal Justice and Law* series offers the best research on criminal justice and law around the world, offering original insights on a broadly defined range of socio-legal topics in law, criminal procedure, courts, justice, legislation, and jurisprudence. With an eye toward using innovative and advanced methodologies, series monographs offer solid social science scholarship illuminating issues and trends in law, crime, and justice. Books in this series will appeal to criminologists, sociologists, and other social scientists, as well as policymakers, legal researchers and practitioners.

1 **Criminal Law and Precrime**
Legal Studies in Canadian Punishment and Surveillance in Anticipation of Criminal Guilt
Richard Jochelson, James Gacek, Lauren Menzie, and Kirsten Kramar

2 **Manufacturing Crime**
The Market's Role in Crime Control
John Brent and Peter Kraska

3 **The Evolving Role of the Public Prosecutor**
Challenges and Innovations
Edited by Victoria Colvin and Philip Stenning

www.routledge.com/Directions-and-Developments-in-Criminal-Justice-and-Law/book-series/DDCJL

The Evolving Role of the Public Prosecutor

Challenges and Innovations

Edited by
Victoria Colvin and Philip Stenning

Routledge
Taylor & Francis Group
NEW YORK AND LONDON

First published 2019
by Routledge
605 Third Avenue, New York, NY 10017

and by Routledge
2 Park Square, Milton Park, Abingdon, Oxon, OX14 4RN

Routledge is an imprint of the Taylor & Francis Group, an informa business

Library of Congress Cataloging-in-Publication Data
Names: Colvin, Victoria., editor. | Stenning, Philip C., editor.
Title: The evolving role of the public prosecutor: challenges and innovations/edited by Victoria Colvin and Philip Stenning.
Description: New York, NY: Routledge, 2019. | Series: Directions and developments in criminal justice and law; 3 | Includes bibliographical references and index.
Identifiers: LCCN 2018029326| ISBN 9781138606791 (hardback) | ISBN 9780429467547 (ebook)
Subjects: LCSH: Public prosecutors.
Classification: LCC K5425.E93 2019 | DDC 345/.01262-dc23
LC record available at https://lccn.loc.gov/2018029326

ISBN: 978-1-138-60679-1 (hbk)
ISBN: 978-0-429-46754-7 (ebk)

Typeset in Times New Roman
by Wearset Ltd, Boldon, Tyne and Wear

DOI: 10.4324/9780429467547

Philip Stenning wishes to dedicate this book to the memory of the late Professor John Ll. J. Edwards (1918–1994), mentor, colleague and friend, whose scholarship and encouragement first sparked his interest in the topic of the book.

Victoria Colvin wishes to dedicate this book to her parents Eric and Julia Colvin, in love and gratitude for their support, guidance and inspiration.

Contents

Contributors

Adedeji Adekunle is a Senior Advocate of Nigeria and Professor and current Director General of the Nigerian Institute of Advanced Legal Studies. Prior to his appointment he served the Federal Government in various capacities as delegate to various national and International Expert Working Groups and Special Adviser to Nigeria's Attorney General and Minister of Justice advising on various aspects of law and policy. He also served as Secretary of the 2004 Law Revision Committee. Among several other publications, he has authored a Guide to Judicial officers on Nigeria's Administration of Criminal Justice Act 2015 and several other monographs.

Cecilia Blengino, Ph.D. in Philosophy of Law and Sociology of Law, is Assistant Professor in Sociology of Law in the University of Turin, Italy. She is also Director of Prison and Rights Legal Clinic and Human Trafficking Clinic, activated by the Law Department of Turin. Her field of research mainly deals with the selectivity of criminalisation processes, justice management, access to justice and clinical legal education. She is author of several publications and coordinator of research projects in these fields.

Simon Bronitt is a Professor, Deputy Head of School and Deputy Dean, Research at the TC Beirne School of Law, University of Queensland, Australia. He also worked as a legal academic at the Australian National University (1991–2009) and Griffith University (2009–2014) where he served as Director of the Australian Research Council Centre of Excellence in Policing and Security (2009–2014). He has published more than 100 articles, book chapters and edited collections across criminal law, criminal justice, evidence and policing. He is co-author of two leading textbooks, *Principles of Criminal Law* (2017, with McSherry) and *Law in Context* (2012, with Bottomley).

Victoria Colvin is a lecturer at the School of Law, University of Wollongong. She completed her doctorate at the TC Beirne School of Law, University of Queensland, in 2017. From 2001–2009, she was a prosecutor with the Criminal Justice Branch of the Attorney General of British Columbia, Canada. Her research focuses on the role of the prosecutor, accountability, and the law of evidence with a particular interest in miscarriages of justice.

Heather Douglas is a Professor of Law at the School of Law at The University of Queensland, Australia, an Australian Research Council Future Fellow, Fellow of the Australian Academy of Law and Fellow of the Australian Academy of Social Sciences. Heather researches in the areas of criminal justice and domestic violence and has published widely on these issues. She was the lead researcher and project co-ordinator on the development of Australia's National Domestic and Family Violence Bench Book. Her current work explores the way women engage with the legal system as part of their response to domestic violence.

Jane Goodman-Delahunty, JD Ph.D., is a Research Professor at Charles Sturt University, Australia, and member of the New South Wales Civil and Administrative Tribunal. Her recent books include *Legal Psychology in Australia* (2015, Thomson Reuters), *Juries and Expert Evidence in Criminal Trials* (2017, Oxford University Press) and *Trends in Legal Advocacy: Interviews with Leading Prosecutors and Defence Lawyers Around the Globe* (2017, CRC Press). She led three projects for the Royal Commission into Institutional Responses to Child Sexual Abuse.

Robyn Holder is a Postdoctoral Research Fellow at Griffith Criminology Institute, Griffith University, Australia. Her work examines the relationship between victimised peoples and communities, and the state, especially along axes of gender and race. Current work compares institutional design of international and domestic criminal justice, and the place of third parties. She completed doctoral studies at the Regulatory Institutions Network, ANU, in 2014 after 20 years professional practice in the UK and Australia.

Julia Jansson is a Ph.D. researcher at the University of Helsinki, Finland. She holds a Master's in Social Sciences and a Licentiate in Laws. Her Doctoral thesis analyses how the threat of terrorism has historically affected the protection offered to political offenders. She has also researched the history of prosecution in Finland, the accountability of Europol, and is finalising a book on the history of police training and education in Finland.

Michael Jasch, Dr. jur., is a Professor at the University of Applied Science of the Federal State of North Rhine Westphalia, Germany. He teaches courses on criminal law and criminology for police officers in higher education. His scholarship focuses on criminal law policy and policing in Europe. Jasch has been a research assistant at the Centre for Criminological Research of the University of Oxford (GB) and at the Universities of Frankfurt and Rostock.

Natalie Martschuk, Dipl-Psych, is a Research Associate at Charles Sturt University, Australia. Her research focuses on witness credibility and reliability, investigative interviewing strategies and jury decision-making. In 2018 she will complete her Ph.D. at the University of Giessen, on the reliability of elderly eyewitnesses. Previously, she practised as a psychologist at the State Hospital for Forensic Psychiatry in Stendal, Germany.

Justine Medrano is a Ph.D. student in criminology at the University of Texas at Dallas, USA.

Melanie O'Brien, Ph.D., is Senior Lecturer in International Law at the University of Western Australia, teaching International Humanitarian Law, Public International Law and Supervised Research. She is 2nd Vice-President of the International Association of Genocide Scholars (IAGS) and co-convened the 2017 IAGS conference at University of Queensland. Melanie is an admitted legal practitioner who has previously worked at several Australian universities; the National Human Rights Institution of Samoa; and the Legal Advisory Section in Office of the Prosecutor at the International Criminal Court. She is the author of *Criminalising Peacekeepers: Modernising National Approaches to Sexual Exploitation and Abuse* (2017, Palgrave).

Martine Powell, Ph.D., is a Professor in the Griffith Criminology Institute, and Founding Director of the Centre for Investigative Interviewing at Griffith University, Australia. She has over 20 years of experience conducting research on investigative interviewing, particularly in the area of child abuse and sexual offences. Martine has worked extensively with police and prosecutors within Australia and internationally.

Kent Roach, C.M., F.R.S.C., is a Professor of Law and Prichard-Wilson Chair of Law and Public Policy at the University of Toronto Faculty of Law, Canada. His 13 books include *Due Process and Victims' Rights* (short-listed for the Donner Prize), *The 9/11 Effect: Comparative Counter-Terrorism* (winner of the Mundell Medal) and (with Craig Forcese) *False Security: The Radicalization of Canadian Anti-Terrorism* (winner of the Canadian Law and Society Association best book prize). He teaches a course on wrongful convictions and was the research director of an inquiry examining wrongful convictions and has litigated cases involving prosecutorial conduct.

Philip Stenning is an Adjunct Professor in the Griffith Criminology Institute at Griffith University in Brisbane, Australia, a Visiting Professor in the Law School at Leeds University in the UK and an Honorary Professor in the School of Applied Human Sciences at the University of KwaZulu-Natal in South Africa. His research interests include policing, governance of the police, the prosecution process, Indigenous justice, firearms abuse and gun control, and gender-based violence. His published books include *Appearing for the Crown: A Legal and Historical Review of Criminal Prosecutorial Authority in Canada* (1986), *The Modern Prosecution Process in New Zealand* (2008) and, with David Bayley *Governing the Police: Experience in Six Democracies* (2016).

Kellie Toole has a background in legal aid criminal defence practice, and has had an academic position at the Adelaide Law School in South Australia since 2011. She teaches criminal law, evidence law, Aboriginal People and the Law, and military disciplinary law. Her research interests are at the intersection of criminal law and human rights law. Her current projects include empirical research on the connection between military service and criminal offending, and a Ph.D. on prosecutorial decision-making.

Rasmus H. Wandall is a Senior Research Fellow at the Faculty of Law, University of Lund. He was the General Counsel for the International Association of Prosecutors (2015–2018) and works with prosecution services worldwide. Wandall also worked as senior advisor to the Director of Public Prosecutions (2007–2011) and to the Prosecutor General in Ethiopia (2012–2015). He was Hauser Global Research Fellow at the NYU Law School (2004–2005), Robbins post-doctoral fellow at the UC Berkeley (2005), visiting scholar at the University of Oxford (2005), research professor at the University of Copenhagen (2005–2007) and senior research fellow, University of Bergen (2012–2015). Wandall researches and publishes widely on comparative and empirical criminal law and procedure.

Penelope Weller is a Professor and Director of the Juris Doctor Program in the Graduate School of Business and Law at RMIT University, Australia. Her research focuses on health law, mental health law and human rights. Weller is an internationally recognised expert on the Convention on the Rights of People with Disabilities. She is a former Deputy Directory of the Centre for the Advance of Law and Mental Health (Faculty of Law, Monash University, Australia). She is an editorial board member of the *International Journal of Mental Health and Capacity Law*.

Nina Westera, Ph.D., served as an officer in the New Zealand Police before moving to academe. She was a Research Fellow in Criminology and a key member of the Centre for Investigative Interviewing, Griffith University, Australia. Nina's research focused on investigative interviewing, interviewer training, eyewitness testimony, investigation and prosecution of sexual and violent offences. Sadly, Nina passed away in May 2017.

Andrew P. Wheeler is an Assistant Professor of Criminology in the School of Economic, Political, and Policy Sciences at the University of Texas at Dallas, USA. His research focuses on the spatial analysis of crime at micro places and practical problems faced by crime analysts. His recent work has been published in the *Journal of Quantitative Criminology*, *Cartography and Geographic Information Sciences*, the *International Journal of Police Science and Management*, the *Security Journal* and the *Journal of Investigative Psychology and Offender Profiling*.

John L. Worrall is a Professor of Criminology at the University of Texas at Dallas, USA. He has published articles and book chapters on a variety of topics ranging from legal issues in policing to crime measurement. He is also the author of several books, including the popular *Crime Control in America: What Works?* (3rd edn, Pearson). He currently serves as editor of the journal *Police Quarterly* and Executive Director of the Academy of Criminal Justice Sciences.

Introduction

Philip Stenning, Victoria Colvin and Heather Douglas

The modern public prosecutor is a figure both powerful and enigmatic. Legal scholars and criminologists often identify three essential components of criminal justice systems: police, courts and corrections. Yet increasingly, the public prosecutor occupies a distinct role independent from any of these branches. In common law jurisdictions, the prosecutor's special power and influence derives mainly from his or her extensive and well recognised discretionary decision-making authority. Although discretion has not been traditionally associated with the prosecutorial office in continental European civil law systems, in recent decades discretionary decision-making authority has increasingly been recognised as a feature of the prosecutor's role in these jurisdictions as well. Acting outside of the court, and therefore largely outside the public eye, the prosecutor's control over whether, and if so what, charges proceed to court can limit judicial discretion on sentencing, open pathways to alternative measures and even deny entry to the criminal justice system entirely. In this sense the prosecutor serves as the true "gatekeeper" to the criminal process.

Because so much of the prosecutor's discretionary authority is exercised "backstage" and out of public view and oversight, the prosecutor's office is in need of much greater attention, analysis, transparency and public discussion than has been the case up to now. Well-developed research literatures exist on police, courts and corrections but, with some exceptions (e.g. Tonry, 2012; Luna and Wade, 2012), comparatively little work has been done about the role of prosecutors. Brian Forst (2011) has described the prosecutor as one of the most powerful and least understood members of the criminal justice system (see also Sallman, 1984, p. 4; Schonteich, 2001, p. 9). Barcow (2009, p. 871) has noted both the power and the lack of scrutiny of federal prosecutors in the U.S. He wrote:

> It is hard to overstate the power of federal prosecutors. The number of federal criminal laws has exploded in recent decades, and the punishments attached to those laws have increased markedly … Federal prosecutors control the terms of confinement in this vast penal system because they have the authority to make charging decisions, enter co-operation agreements, accept pleas, and recommend sentences. In the current era dominated by pleas instead of trials, federal prosecutors are not merely law enforcers.

> They are the final adjudicators in the vast majority of cases. It is only in the rare 5% of federal cases that go to trial that an independent actor reviews prosecutorial decisions.[1]

This lack of scrutiny from within the system makes scholarly scrutiny particularly pressing. The central goal of this book is to address this deficiency by shedding light on the role of the prosecutor through an international comparative lens.

The Origins of the Modern Public Prosecutor in Common and Civil Law Jurisdictions

Modern prosecution scholars owe a considerable debt to John Langbein (1973) for explaining the origins of the modern public prosecutor within the English common law system, and to Esmein's (1913/2000) and Hodgson's (2005) accounts of the origins of the public prosecutor within the French civil law system. We do not need, of course, to dwell at length here on these accounts, but a very brief summary of their explanations will be helpful, for two reasons.

In the first place, Langbein's account is useful in dispelling what he refers to as lawyers' assumption that the modern system of lawyer-prosecutors in criminal cases "goes back to some sort of antiquity" in English common law (1973, pp. 315–316). He points out that in fact the public prosecutor was "an historical latecomer" in this system (1973, p. 313), and that the confusion arises from the fact that historians have failed to distinguish between the famous State Trials that were typically prosecuted by one of the law officers of the Crown (the Attorney General or his deputy, the Solicitor General) (Edwards, 1964)), and "ordinary felony" cases in which lawyers did not participate on either side (prosecution or defence) until very late in the eighteenth century, and even then by no means always (Beattie, 1986).

Perhaps more importantly, Langbein demonstrates in his very well-documented account that many of the investigative and forensic functions we associate with public prosecutors today were assumed from private complainants by the lay Justices of the Peace (nowadays usually called magistrates in the UK). This office was originally established in the fourteenth century, and the assumption of this role was not confirmed in legislation until the passage of the Marian bail and committal statutes, passed in 1554 and 1555 respectively. The role of the J.P.s did not supersede prosecution by citizens, in a tradition of "gratuitous citizen prosecution" (Langbein, 1973, p. 318), but rather complemented it. It was not until the creation of "the new police" in the early nineteenth century, and the office of the Director of Public Prosecutions in 1879, that the prosecutorial responsibility was finally entrusted entirely to state officials. A state institution of lawyer-prosecutors (the Crown Prosecution service) was finally established in 1986 in England and Wales.[2]

Esmein's (1913/2000) account of the origins of the public prosecutor in France tells a contrasting story. He makes it clear that the office of public prosecutor in France dates back at least to the late thirteenth/early fourteenth century. He indicates that up to this time, the feudal inquisitorial procedure founded on Roman and Canon law "did not acknowledge the principle of representation in courts of law" (1913/2000: 114); only those with a direct interest in the case could appear before the courts. But this rule did not apply to the king, who was represented by a "procurator", or to lords who could be represented by their "procurators fiscal" (ibid.).[3] The king's procurators initially played a prosecutorial role similar to that of the law officers of the Crown in England in the most serious criminal cases involving the sovereign. The procurators fiscal played a role like that of the Justices of the Peace in England with respect to "ordinary offences" at that time, initially supplementing, rather than taking over, the role of private prosecutors. But they gained a monopoly over the prosecution of all criminal cases (albeit in collaboration with inquisitorial investigating magistrates as *juge d'instruction*) long before England had any public prosecution service with such a monopoly. Following the French Revolution in 1789, this monopoly was consolidated, and the procuracy represented the Republic rather than the King, as it had under the *ancien regime*, eventually coming to be known as the "parquet", responsible to a Minister of Justice, but administratively located within the magistry (Hodgson, 2005, pp. 14–22). These parallel histories illustrate how public prosecutors' offices directly reflect the different constitutional and political contexts in which they develop.

The second reason to pay attention to the history of public prosecutors in common law and civil law jurisdictions has to do with the influence of each system over development of public prosecutors in the other system over the centuries. Langbein (1973) disputed the Victorian historian William Holdsworth's claim that the assumption of prosecutorial functions by Justices of the Peace in England could be explained as "a 'reception' of Continental inquisitorial ideas", a "foreign graft" (Langbein, 1973, p. 324). He argued that rather than being seen as "a foreign graft" this development in England could better be explained by relevant developments in criminal justice administration in England itself, specifically a desire to ensure that it remained local and community-informed, and the fact that neither sufficient funds nor personnel to staff a separate prosecution service were at hand (ibid., pp. 334–335).

Given that England had been conquered and governed by Norman (French) kings in the eleventh, twelfth and thirteenth centuries, and continued to have substantial economic, political and military involvement in continental jurisdictions well into the sixteenth century, it is hard to accept that there would not have been two-way influences over conceptions of governance in general, and the administration of justice in particular. Whatever may be the truth about this, however, there can be no doubt, as much recent literature confirms (see e.g. Di Federico, 2005), that there has been significant conceptual and practical cross-fertilisation with respect to the administration of criminal justice in general, and the role of prosecutors in particular, between common law and civil law jurisdictions during the late twentieth and early twenty-first centuries. This trend can be seen not only with inter-jurisdictional influence, but also with the establishment of international criminal tribunals and the International Criminal Court.

The Modern Public Prosecutor

Globally, the role of the modern public prosecutor has been evolving in recent decades. As noted above, legally trained public prosecutors working in organised public prosecution offices are relatively recent institutions in most common law jurisdictions. To this day, the great majority of "routine" non-indictable cases, which comprise up to 90 per cent of criminal prosecutions in most common law jurisdictions, are still prosecuted by police officers, most of whom are not trained or qualified lawyers. However, the United States of America, Canada and Scotland are notable exceptions in this respect; in those countries, legally trained public prosecutors took charge of prosecutions in the eighteenth and nineteenth centuries.

Just as there is no one single institutional architecture for the office of the prosecutor throughout the common law world, prosecution systems in continental European "civil law" systems display no uniformity. Each is the product of a particular political, constitutional and legal history. As we have noted, however, it is certainly true that legally trained public prosecutors have a much longer history in civil law systems than in most common law jurisdictions (see e.g. Di Federico, 2005; Hodgson, 2005).

Comparing civil law prosecution offices with their common law counterparts is especially complicated by two key matters. First, in many, if not most, civil law jurisdictions public prosecutors have been (and still are) institutionally associated with the magistracy rather than the executive. Second, and equally importantly, the kinds of authority and powers associated with public prosecutors are, in many civil law jurisdictions, as much, if not more, vested in supervising investigating magistrates (for example *juges d'instruction* in France) as in public prosecutors (Merryman and Perez-Perdomo, 2007). This allocation of investigative and prosecutorial authority and functions to magistrates rather than to "independent" public prosecutors and police is recognised as a foundational feature of the "inquisitorial" process, in contrast to the "adversarial" or "accusatorial" process that underpins common law systems.[4] Hodgson (2005, Ch. 1) has argued that the post-revolution Napoleonic *Code d'instruction criminelle* of 1808 conceived of prosecutions as the exclusive responsibility of a strong state that represented "the people", upholding the public interest. By contrast, in her chapter in this book, Julia Jansson argues that the office of public prosecutor in the "old cities" in Finland dates back to the 1600s.

During the last 30 or 40 years, the role of public prosecutors in civil law jurisdictions has been evolving just as much as has the role of public prosecutors in common law jurisdictions. However, there has been relatively little discussion (at least in English language scholarship) of the major reforms that have been introduced in many civil law jurisdictions in the latter half of the twentieth century, or of the effect of those reforms (Hodgson, 2005 and 2010 writing about France, and Di Federico, 1998 and 2005 writing about England, France and Italy, are notable exceptions; see also Goethals, Fijnaut and Parmentier, 2000; and Gilliéron, 2013).

Globalisation and economic pressures during the last decades of the twentieth century and the early twenty-first century have led to transformations and innovations in the role and practices of prosecutors in many countries, as well as a gradual breaking down of traditional distinctions between prosecution systems and practices in common law and civil law jurisdictions, as each has drawn on ideas, experiences and reforms from the other. In the European context, scholars have argued that the development of jurisprudence under the *European Convention on Human Rights*, as well as various treaties favouring "the Europeanisation of criminal justice", have had a major influence in this respect (Hodgson, 2005, pp. 6–9), to the point that there are now proposals for the establishment of a European Prosecutor (Monar, 2013).

There are a number of areas where the role of the public prosecutor needs greater scrutiny. Despite the significant expansion of their discretionary decision-making authority during the last half of the twentieth century, this very critical feature of prosecutors' authority was for a long time treated as an almost taboo topic, if not outright denied, especially in civil law jurisdictions where it was considered incompatible with the prevailing "principle of legality" (Davis, 1969; Pizzi and Marafioti, 1992; Fionda, 1995). The controversial practice of "plea bargaining", which came to light during the last three decades of the twentieth century, has played a part in bringing prosecutorial discretion onto the academic and public agenda in common law jurisdictions. However, while there has been plenty of (often critical) literature on plea bargaining (e.g. Flynn, 2011), and there have been efforts to "guide" and structure the exercise of prosecutorial discretion (e.g. through official published prosecution guidelines), there is still very limited empirical evidence of how the discretion is exercised in practice, and with what consequences and implications. There have been some notable exceptions (e.g. Grosman, 1969 and Klein, 1976, in Canada; Baldwin and McConville, 1977 and McConville and Baldwin, 1981, in the UK; Ma, 2002 and Sklansky, 2018 in the USA.), but prosecutors have frequently been found to be unwilling to give researchers access to "backstage" negotiations with defence lawyers, or even to redacted and anonymised records of them. This is out of concern that allowing such scrutiny would undermine expectations of confidentiality, could inhibit candour in such negotiations, and/or could reveal information that could be used to critique past and future decisions, potentially exposing inequities that would be incompatible with the principle of equality under the law.

Beyond the transformations in the role and practices of prosecutors around the world, their relationships with the governments under which they serve have also been the subject of growing interest. Issues of political independence and accountability have led to demands for reform in both established and emerging democratic states in recent decades. Finding the right balance between desirable political independence and growing expectations of effective public accountability and transparency of decision-making in a democratic polity has become the subject of increasingly robust public and academic discussion. Yet scholarship on this topic, like most scholarship on prosecutors, has primarily been focused on individual jurisdictions (e.g. Corns, 2014) rather than exploring lessons that might be learned from comparative research (although see e.g. Edwards, 1984; Di Federico, 2005; Stenning, 2010, 2013; and Yang, 2013).

The great majority of the academic attention that has been paid to prosecutors has focused on prosecution systems in North America and the UK, and to a lesser extent on systems in continental European countries, particularly France and Italy. The processes and nature of adaptation of these systems that accompanied their export to other parts of the world through colonisation, and their impact on local populations and legal traditions, are less well explored in the literature (see e.g. Woods, 2002), while scholarship on prosecution systems in "closed" political systems such as modern China is very limited (e.g. Qian, 2003).

Introducing the Book

This book addresses key aspects of the evolving role of domestic and international prosecutors in the twenty-first century, and the challenges posed by this evolution. The collection takes an international, comparative approach to the subject. Chapters explore how different legal systems have "borrowed" theorisations and articulations of the prosecutorial role from each other in adapting the office to changing conditions and expectations. While some of the authors focus on their own jurisdictions as case studies for the particular issues they explore, their analyses can be extrapolated across jurisdictions.

The volume is structured around four closely related main themes relating to the role of the modern prosecutor: the nature of the prosecutor's office, the role of the prosecutor in investigations, prosecutorial discretion and how it is exercised, and politicisation and accountability of prosecutors.

Part I: The Office of the Modern Public Prosecutor

The first theme, explored in this part, is the question of the nature and impact of the prosecutors' office and powers, both within the criminal justice systems in which they operate, and within the wider society. The power of the prosecutor, which has expanded significantly in recent decades, does not exist in a vacuum. Prosecutors themselves hold views about their power and how to exercise it responsibly. It is influenced by broad societal values, the prosecutor's relationship to victims of crime, and the need to address particular forms of crime. How, in what ways, and why has the power of prosecutors has increased and expanded so significantly in the last two (or in some cases three) decades? What are the effective limits of their power?

Based on interviews with former Australian Directors of Public Prosecutions, Robyn Holder explores how these prosecutors talk and think about their role and status within the criminal justice system. She notes their discourse demonstrates how they function as a powerful elite due to their ability to define public and community interest while acting for the state and in the name of the sovereign. Cecilia Blengino discusses the impact on prosecutors of the introduction of New

Public Management principles and practices in Italy, arguing that its primary effect has been to enhance the power and status of prosecutors in that country. Simon Bronitt addresses the emerging practice of "deferred prosecution", through which typically large corporations avoid prosecution by negotiating settlements with prosecutors in high profile cases. He raises concerns about how the role of the prosecutor in such agreements challenges the concept of due process of law and the divide between the criminal and civil law. Rasmus Wandall describes how, through their exercise of prosecutorial discretion and advocacy, prosecutors in Denmark have recently had a substantial influence and constraint over the sentencing authority of judges, as well as over public sentencing policy. He argues that currently dominant common law theorisations of the respective roles of legislatures, judges and prosecutors with respect to sentencing do not adequately account for such developments in European civil law jurisdictions.

Part II: The Role of Prosecutors in Investigations

Part II focuses on the role of prosecutors in investigations. In many common law jurisdictions involvement in criminal investigations is not part of the prosecutor's role; investigations are considered as being within the exclusive purview of police. But in some jurisdictions prosecutors either oversee or actually direct criminal investigations by police. The issue is complicated, as the police may also exercise prosecutorial authority in the vast majority of less serious ("summary conviction") cases, the role of separate prosecution offices being confined to prosecuting the minority of more serious cases on indictment. By contrast, in civil law jurisdictions prosecutors typically share oversight and direction of police investigations, as well as prosecutorial decision-making, with investigating magistrates. This part considers the explanations and rationales that have been offered in different jurisdictions for these very different approaches to the role of prosecutors in investigations, and for changes in their role in particular jurisdictions over time.

Julia Jansson reviews the historically changing role of legally trained prosecutors, and their relationships with police, with respect to the investigation of criminal offences in Finland. She reviews current and ongoing debates over this role and these relationships. She and Philip Stenning also present a possible theoretical and methodological framework within which to explore and understand variations, both historically and currently, in this respect in different common law and civil law European jurisdictions. Penelope Weller discusses how these roles and relationships are shaped by the special challenges presented by the prosecution of offenders with disabilities. Melanie O'Brien discusses the unique challenges of investigations in the context of international criminal tribunals and the International Criminal Court, where prosecutors, unlike their domestic counterparts, do not have any international police force at their disposal to undertake investigations. She explores the roles of lawyers and the limited investigative resources that are available to them in undertaking such investigations, concluding that international prosecutors are functioning in a way distinct from their domestic counterparts.

Part III: The Nature and Extent of Prosecutorial Discretion

The focus of Part III is on the extent and exercise of prosecutorial discretion, particularly in charging, sentencing and diversion. The growing role of prosecutorial discretion has manifested itself in at least three distinct ways in different jurisdictions. One is through pre-trial charging decisions, the effect of which is to constrain judges and magistrates with respect to sentences that are available to them on a conviction. Another is by the use of procedural rules in sentencing hearings whereby prosecutors are entitled to make arguments on sentencing to magistrates and judges. The most substantial source of prosecutorial power in this domain, however, has been the growth of prosecutorial authority to divert cases away from the regular prosecution process in courts to alternative processes for the disposition of cases such as restorative justice, "community prosecution" processes, and deferred prosecution agreements. These diversionary processes are typically negotiated and magistrates and judges may or may not have a role. What implications does prosecutorial power over criminal justice outcomes have for the role of the prosecutor? Is a prosecutor who influences or controls the process usurping the role of the judge?

Victoria Colvin develops a theoretical framework for understanding the exercise of prosecutorial discretion at a nexus of competing interests. Heather Douglas discusses current debates over the role of victims with respect to the exercise of prosecutorial discretion in domestic violence cases in Australia. She argues that a balance needs to be struck between public policy with respect to reducing offender impunity in such cases through "no drop" charging practices, and the protection of vulnerable victims of domestic violence. Jane Goodman-Delahunty, Natalie Martschuk, Martine Powell and Nina Westera examine the development of Australian prosecutorial policy regarding child sex abuse and outline a proposed empirical method to systematically test the influence of legal and extra-legal factors on the exercise of police and prosecutorial discretion in these cases. John Worrall, Andrew Wheeler and Justine Medrano discuss the emerging practices of "community prosecution" in the United States, in which community representatives play an increasingly significant role in the exercise of prosecutorial discretion with respect to charging, diversion and alternative dispositions of criminal cases. They present the first place-based evaluation of community prosecution, and suggest that it may have a beneficial effect of improving quality of life for community members in targeted areas.

Part IV: Prosecutors, Politics and Accountability

Part IV focuses on the issue of the governance and the potential politicisation of prosecutorial offices, and the related question of how the prosecutor can effectively be held accountable for decision-making without compromising the desired political independence of the office. Prosecutors who make key decisions regarding criminal justice matters have varying degrees of independence from political direction and from the undesirable influence of politicians who appoint them, determine their working conditions and the resources that are provided to them, as well as determining their career progression. How, and how adequately and effectively, are prosecutors held politically and publicly accountable for their decisions and conduct, for the outcomes of their decisions, and for the ways in which they allocate the resources provided to them? What barriers and impediments are there to effective and acceptable prosecutorial accountability? Can these be overcome without compromising the independence of prosecutors or the privacy rights and reputations of those who are affected by their decisions?

Michael Jasch discusses the increasingly difficult situation of public prosecutors in Germany with regard to criminal cases with political implications, and the challenges they face in navigating the respective influences of politicians, the public and the media. He reviews current German initiatives and debates about legal and administrative options available to increase the independence of public prosecutors from political interferences, which he surmises result from the increasing recognition of prosecutorial discretion in Germany in recent decades. He argues that in some cases formal legislative decriminalisation should be preferred over prosecutorial discretion to maintain an acceptable balance between public sentiment and the law in prosecutorial decision-making. Adedeji Adekunle considers the constitutional position of prosecutors in the criminal prosecution system in Nigeria, arguing that an independent prosecution system is no guarantee for an efficient criminal justice system where autonomy is not complemented with effective accountability. In particular he addresses current suggestions that the politically sensitive office of the Minister of Justice should be separated from that of the Attorney General (as chief prosecutor), and the need for mechanisms such as budgetary and funding arrangements which protect prosecutorial independence as well as objective oversight mechanisms to provide accountability. Kellie Toole considers international trends to greater accountability for prosecutorial decision-making in the Australian context. She argues that the structural features of prosecution systems in Australia reduce opportunities for inadvertent misuse of prosecutorial discretion, and incentives and legislative tools for its deliberate misuse are limited compared to other jurisdictions. She cautions against uniform adoption of accountability mechanisms without considering the unique context of the Australian system. Finally, Kent Roach explores the role of prosecutors in directly and indirectly contributing to wrongful convictions, and discusses the relative merits of "hard" sanctioning approaches versus "softer" remedial approaches in addressing this problem.

The book ends with a short chapter by editors Victoria Colvin and Philip Stenning. The main themes about the future role of prosecutors and of the prosecution process that have emerged from the chapters in the book are briefly reviewed. Some broad conclusions are drawn about the kinds of research that will be required in the future to further our understandings of the evolving role of prosecutors.

Acknowledgements

The chapters in this book were originally presented in the form of discussion papers at a workshop on "The Evolving Role of the Prosecutor, Domestically and Internationally", held on 28–29 July 2016 at the International Institute for the Sociology of Law in Oñati, Spain, chaired by Professors Heather Douglas (University of Queensland, Australia) and Professor Philip Stenning (Griffith University, Brisbane, Australia). We wish to express our sincere thanks to the Institute and its staff, especially Sra. Malen Gordoa Medizabal, for providing the venue for this workshop, and for their great administrative assistance in holding it. We also wish to acknowledge with gratitude the support we received from Griffith University and the University of Queensland, without which neither the workshop nor this book could have been realised. We wish to express our great appreciation for the support, encouragement and assistance the editorial staff at Routledge, especially Ellen Boyne, provided to us in the process of preparing and editing the manuscript of this book for publication. Finally, Philip Stenning and Victoria Colvin wish to express our deep gratitude to our colleague, Professor Heather Douglas, for all her hard work in preparing the proposal for the workshop, organising and co-chairing it, and contributing to the preparation and early editing of this book.

Notes

1 More recently, Davis (2017) and Wright (2017) have commented on the "unfettered" power, and lack of effective accountability for their discretionary decisions, of elected prosecutors in the United States.

2 Such public prosecutors (called Procurator Fiscals) had, however, been established in Scotland at the beginning of the eighteenth century, and given complete responsibility for prosecution of all criminal cases in 1867. Public prosecutors were established in the United States in the late eighteenth century (Steinberg, 1984) and in Canada (Stenning, 1986) in the mid nineteenth century (Stenning, 1986).

3 Esmein notes that these were "originally merely men of business" (Esmein, 1913/2000, p 114) entrusted with taking care of the King's financial and business affairs (hence the word fiscal in their title). It is noteworthy, however, that the King's Attorneys in England at the same period had similar responsibilities, but in the fourteenth century one of them came to be referred to as the King's "Attorney-General", and eventually came to be responsible for representing the King as prosecutor in criminal cases, such as treason, directly affecting the King's interest (Edwards, 1964).

4 Goldstein and Marcus (1977), however, have argued that this theoretical distinction, which they refer to as "the myth of judicial supervision", does not accurately reflect most prosecutorial practices in the three inquisitorial jurisdictions (France, Germany and Italy) that they discuss. See also Hodgson, 2005, p. 5.

References

Baldwin, J. and M. McConville (1977) *Negotiated Justice: Pressures to Plead Guilty* (London: Martin Robertson).

Barcow, R. (2009) "Institutional Design and the Policing of Prosecutors: Lessons from Administrative Law" *Stanford Law Review* 61(4): 869–921.

Beattie, J. (1986) *Crime and the Courts in England, 1660–1800* (Princeton, NJ: Princeton University Press).
Corns, C. (2014) *Public Prosecutions in Australia: Law Policy and Practice* (Pyrmont, NSW: Law Book Co.).
Davis, A. (2017) "The Prosecution of Black Men" – in Davis, A. (ed.) *Policing the Black Man: Arrest, Prosecution and Imprisonment* (New York: Pantheon Books), pp. 178–208.
Davis, K. (1969) *Discretionary Justice: A Preliminary Inquiry* (Baton Rouge, LA: Louisiana State University Press).
Di Federico, G. (1998) "Prosecutorial Independence and the Democratic Requirement of Accountability in Italy: Analysis of Deviant Case in a Comparative Perspective" *British Journal of Criminology* 38(3): 371–387.
Di Federico, G. (2005) "The Independence and Accountability of the Public Prosecutor in Search of a Difficult Equilibrium: The Cases of England, France and Italy" *Mediterranean Journal of Human Rights* 9(2): 93.
Edwards, J. (1984) *The Attorney General, Politics and the Public Interest* (London: Sweet & Maxwell Ltd. – Reprint: New York: Wm. W. Gaunt & Sons, Inc., 1992).
Edwards, J. (1964) *The Law Officers of the Crown* (London: Sweet and Maxwell).
Esmein, A. (1913/2000) *A History of Continental Criminal Procedure with Special Reference to France* (Boston: Little, Brown and Company) – translation by John Simpson, published by the Lawbook Exchange Ltd., Union, NJ, in 2000 – accessible online at https://books.google.co.uk/books?hl=en&lr=&id=dBubbTnqKXQC&oi=fnd&pg=PP1&ots=x2QbrsT-Os&sig=vx_cuVffl17mViWJdvTxxMprE70&redir_esc=y#v=onepage&q&f=false.
Fionda, J. (1995) *Public Prosecutors and Discretion: A Comparative Study* (Oxford: Clarendon Press).
Flynn, A. (2011) "Fortunately We in Victoria Are Not in That UK Position: Australian and United Kingdom Legal Perspectives on Plea Bargaining Reform" *Deakin Law Review* 16(2): 361–404.
Forst, B. (2011) "Prosecution" – in Wilson, J. and J. Petersillia (eds) *Crime and Public Policy* (Oxford: Oxford University Press), pp. 437–467.
Gilliéron, G. (2013) *Public Prosecutors in the United States and Europe* (Zurich: Springer International Publishing).
Goethals, J., C. Fijnaut and S. Parmentier (eds) (2000) "Preface" Special Issue: The Future of the Public Prosecutor's Office in the European Union: Proceedings of the Leuven Conference on 25 May 2000 *European Journal of Crime, Criminal Law and Criminal Justice* 8(3): 149–153.
Goldstein, A. and M. Marcus (1977) "The Myth of Judicial Supervision in Three 'Inquisitorial' Systems: France, Italy and Germany" *Yale Law Journal* 87(2): 240–283.
Grosman, B. (1969) *The Prosecutor* (Toronto: University of Toronto Press).
Hodgson, J. (2005) *French Criminal Justice: A Comparative Account of the Investigation and Prosecution of Crime in France* (Oxford/Portland, OR: Hart Publishing).
Hodgson, J. (2010) "The French Prosecutor in Question" *Washington & Lee Law Review* 67(4): 1361–1411.
Klein, J. (1976) *Let's Make a Deal: Negotiated Justice* (Toronto: D.C. Heath Co).
Langbein, J. (1973) "The Origins of Public Prosecution at Common Law" *The American Journal of Legal History* 17(4): 313–335.
Luna, E. and M. Wade (eds) (2012) *The Prosecutor in Transnational Perspective* (Oxford: Oxford University Press).

Ma, Y. (2002) "Prosecutorial Discretion and Plea Bargaining in the United States, France, Germany, and Italy: A Comparative Perspective" *International Criminal Justice Review* 12(1): 22–52.

McConville, M. and J. Baldwin (1981) *Courts, Prosecution and Conviction* (Oxford: Clarendon Press, 1981).

Monar, J. (2013) "Eurojust and the European Public Prosecutor Perspective: From Cooperation to Integration in EU Criminal Justice?" *Perspectives on European Politics and Society* 14(3): 339–356.

Merryman, J. and R. Perez-Perdomo (2007) *The Civil Law Tradition: An Introduction to the Legal Systems of Europe and Latin America* (Stanford, CA: Stanford University Press).

Pizzi, W. and L. Marafioti (1992) "The New Italian Code of Criminal Procedure: The Difficulties of Building an Adversarial Trial System on a Civil Law Foundation" *Yale Journal of International Law* 17(1): 1–40.

Qian, S. (2003) "On the Prosecution Reform in China" *Cass Journal of Law* 6. – accessible online at http://en.cnki.com.cn/Article_en/CJFDTotal-LAWS200306000.htm.

Sallman, P. (1984) (Editorial) "Improving the Prosecution Process" *Australian and New Zealand Journal of Criminology* 17(1): 4.

Schonteich, M. (2001) *Lawyers for the People: The South African Prosecution Service* ISS Monograph #53 (South African Institute of Security Studies) – accessible online at: www.issafrica.org/pgcontent.php?UID=1564.

Sklansky, D. (2018) "The Problems with Prosecutors" *Annual Review of Criminology* 1: 451–469 – accessible online at www.annualreviews.org/doi/pdf/10.1146/annurev-criminol-032317-092440.

Steinberg, A. (1984) "From Private Prosecution to Plea Bargaining: Criminal Prosecution, the Districty Attorney and American Legal History" *Crime & Delinquency* 30(4): 568–592.

Stenning, P. (1986) *Appearing for the Crown: A Legal and Historical Review of Criminal Prosecutorial Authority in Canada* (Cowansville, PQ: Brown Legal Publications Inc.).

Stenning, P. (2010) "Prosecutions, Politics and the Public Interest: Some Recent Developments in the United Kingdom, Canada and Elsewhere" *Criminal Law Quarterly* 55(4): 449–478.

Stenning, P. (2013) "Prosecutions, Politics And The Law: The Way Things Are" – in Chirwa, D. and L. Nijzink (eds) *Accountable Government in Africa: Perspectives from Public Law and Political Studies* (Cape Town: University of Cape Town Press), pp. 105–126.

Tonry, M. (ed.) (2012) *Prosecutors and Politics in Comparative Perspective – Crime and Justice: A Review of Research*, Vol. 41 (Chicago: University of Chicago Press).

Woods, G, (2002) *A History of Criminal Law in New South Wales: The Colonial Period, 1788–1900* (Anandale, NSW: Federation Press).

Wright, R. (2017) "Elected Prosecutors and Police Accountability" – in Davis, A. (ed.) *Policing the Black Man: Arrest, Prosecution and Imprisonment* (New York: Pantheon Books), pp. 234–254.

Yang, K. (2013) "Public Accountability of Public Prosecutions" *Murdoch University Law Review* 20(1): 28–75.

Part I

The Office of the Modern Public Prosecutor

1 Decoding Hegemony

Exploring the Discourse of a Prosecuting Elite

Robyn Holder[1]

Introduction

The institutions of criminal justice have an extraordinary degree of power and authority over ordinary citizens. Whereas police and the courts are sharper in focus, prosecutors conduct their business largely unseen by the public eye. This chapter explores their hidden power through the discourse of a prosecuting elite. As "high mandarins" they do not produce case law and are parsimonious in their production of "treatise literature" (Gordon, 1984, p. 120). Rather they produce, apply and interpret law in liminal spaces through definitional authority and the exercise of discretion. This capacity allows prosecutors to represent "reality", delineate what is possible and what is not, and to decide who is and is not a legitimate subject of the law's application. This chapter traces the contours of prosecution thinking with appreciation of their enormous responsibility. Nonetheless the chapter situates the discourse within a political frame that highlights prosecution as a state organ.[2] From this standpoint the seeming benevolence of the mandarin administrator demands more forensic illumination.

Looking at Public Prosecutors

While comparatively under-studied, in recent years prosecution has attracted growing scholarly interest. One body of work describes prosecution forms, functions and authority.[3] Another has examined the outcomes that flow from prosecution decisions and the effects on criminal justice and criminal policy (Tonry, 2012). These especially focus on the exercise of prosecution discretion regarding different offences, characteristics of the accused or victim, and criminal justice decision-making more generally.[4] Others have examined the interactions between prosecutors and other criminal justice actors in shaping institutional practices and forming organisational cultures.[5] The burgeoning institutions of international criminal justice have generated considerable attention to the office of the prosecutor (Reydams, Wouters and Ryngaert, 2012). In combination, studies describe an organisation that is critical to the functioning of criminal justice systems, its efficiency and its calibration with social and legal norms.

Yet those who work as prosecutors, who they are and what they think, are an unknown. One recent United States (U.S.) study considered diversity amongst prosecutors and between prosecution offices. Researchers interviewed over 200 prosecutors from nine locations. The study found differences in the "social architecture" of offices, their sense of "balance", and their "sense of belonging to the wider legal community". These differences related in part to whether prosecutors were "rookies" or "veterans" (Wright, Levine and Miller, 2014, pp. 28, 35, 41). The latter were less trial-oriented and more collegiate with defence counsel. They saw themselves and their views situated within a system of checks and balances.

Chief Prosecutors,[6] however, are slightly more visible. They share surface similarity and network through transnational organisations such as the International Association of Prosecutors.[7] Yet different histories, different legal and social environments, and different political and legislative mandates unsettle comparisons. For example, in the U.S., where state chief prosecutors are elected and federal attorneys are appointed, there is more visibility in terms of career aspiration, career trajectory and leaders' impact (Eisenstein, 1978; Boylan, 2005; Bandyopadhyay and McCannon, 2014). However, in other common law countries Chief Prosecutors rarely give a public account of themselves.

This is not to say that Chief Prosecutors do not speak in public. Rather, their public appearances tend to be formal affairs in which they present their legislative mandate, set out their function, and elaborate prosecution policy (Bugg, 2007). They barely hint at "changes in social conditions" that may influence a Director's decision-making (Hetherington, 1987, p. 10). The occasional memoir has illuminated working contexts. Every day, said one ex-Director, almost every decision "would make somebody unhappy" (Cowdery, 2012a, p. 220). Another reflected on her many disappointing encounters with the powerful (Del Ponte, 2011). These individual accounts speak to the highly political environments in which Chief Prosecutors work.

Conversations with "High Mandarins"

This chapter acknowledges that environment by styling prosecution leaders as mandarins. The narrative of six ex-Directors of Public Prosecution (DPP) in Australia is used as "mandarin materials" to de-code institutional logic (Gordon, 1984, p. 120). Elites such as these come with the usual problem of accessibility to researchers, but present additional challenges by virtue of their expertise. They are masters of specialised forms of knowledge "embedded in processes of modernisation". Public service elites such as the DPP are also highly attuned to the political nature of their utterances. Through the research interview they actively shape the creation of knowledge. Yet their disciplinary and institutional settings impose "cognitive and social norms" that are habituated and routinised in their professional lives (Meuser and Nagel, 2009, pp. 17, 20). In their professional lives the ex-Directors can be viewed both as agents and as acted upon; but in their aggregated discourse they are more than individuals.

For this research approaches were made to people who had been (but were no longer) a DPP in Australia. Ex-Directors are not only expert but were further assumed to have greater latitude to speak freely about the challenges to the role. There are nine criminal jurisdictions in the Australian federal system.[8] From these, 15 potential respondents were identified through a key informant and an internet search. Eight persons were approached directly with a request for an interview and six accepted the invitation. The six had practiced as Directors in six different criminal jurisdictions. Between them they had over 51 years of prosecuting experience and all were still active in other legal roles at the time of interview. Interviews were conducted in 2011 and comprised over ten hours of conversation in total. The interviewees were assured that no personal or professional characteristics would identify them. All were interviewed in a professional setting; surroundings that created a meta-narrative of authoritative ease.

Discourse analysis treats individual reflections as a whole and as connected to the production and reproduction of power (Chouliaraki and Fairclough, 1999). In single narrative form the interviews identify and map institutional orthodoxies. Interview quotations are de-identified but differentiated numerically from A1 to A6. In the first section, the ex-Directors narrate depictions of their mandarin status. The discourse is then briefly situated within the evolution of prosecution in the Australian context. Following sections then amplify core "codes" to the institutional logic of public prosecution embedded within the discourse.

Mandarin: Administrative and Doctrinal

A mandarin denotes a high official or bureaucrat in imperial China. This image of mandarin presents prosecution administrators as "just one cog in the process" (A3). They are pragmatic actors who prosecute "because you have a case" (A1). Theirs is a modest role to act "professionally with the body of evidence and wherever that and the law and the guidelines take him or her" (A3). This managerialist picture distances prosecution from the exercise of substantive authority.

For the mandarin administrator, criminal law is a piece of equipment – a "mechanism" (A1, A4) and a "brake" (A5). Sometimes it is "more like a sledge hammer than a jeweller's pliers" (A1) and "pretty blunt" (A5). Law is a means to various ends.[9] It is a mechanism "for keeping order ... for controlling the power of other public officials ... for protecting the community ... for publicly expressing the community view of what ought to or ought not to be permitted ... And essentially in its day-to-day activities it is a mechanism by which persons accused of things are prosecuted and dealt with" (A1). As an instrument, the criminal law is explained as a means "to ensure that the society can be managed in a way that allows people to get the benefits from the society" and "to regulate and promote positive interaction" (A4). These are administrators who are responsible and unsentimental.

Ideas of delivering justice in daily practice are articulated as being "professional" because "on a day-to-day basis you run the case that you are doing ...

the process takes over and you hope in some sort of way ultimately that it gets to, in general terms, a just result" (A1). As professionals they do "the best we can with the tools we have" (A2) to "achieve a generally acceptable outcome" (A3). Doing the best one can is scrutinising the case "as closely as you can" because "justice can't be perfect" (A2). Not doing this means not being "properly prepared" and being unable or unwilling to make an "effort at persuasion" (A2). Justice is a bureaucratic "mission" (A6) not "some abstract concept" (A1).

Abstract notions do emerge through statements that, as Directors, they are "ministers of justice" (A4, A5).[10] Pressed to describe *justice* in this guise and "I suppose you come out with a few basic things like convict the guilty and acquit the innocent, fairness, fair trial, sentences that were proportionate" (S4). At this end of their representational spectrum prosecutors take this "responsibility really really seriously" (A2). They will typically refer to their "duty" (A1, A4, A5, A6) and "obligation" (A1, A4) and invoke higher, if vague, principles. As doctrinal mandarins, prosecutors model constraint (A4). Being fair and just is "broad overall consistency", "equality of treatment" (A5), "dealing with the individual fairly" (A6) and ensuring that "the same test applies to you and to me but not one for the high-profile cases and not for others" (A2).

From their position as "minister of justice" ex-Directors emphasise criminal law's normative expression of "what ought to or ought not to be permitted" (A1) and as drawing "the lines within which the community can comfortably live" (A4). It is "the first and most basic system of norms" that any society – democratic or despotic – requires (A5). Furthermore, these norms involve "moral wrongdoing easily recognised and readily acceptable throughout the world" (A5). Law's multiple relationship(s) to peoples range from it as a "subservient construct on society" (A4) to it as a "guard" (A2).

These pictures of the administrative and the doctrinal mandarin appear to suggest a disjuncture between the mundane and the lofty. However, the combination of administrative practice and their claim to buttress social stability is the precise feature that generates real and discursive authority. Discretionary decision-making directs attention "to the low-lying details of how law makes itself felt" on a day-to-day basis (Gordon 2012, p. 205); *and*, as high officials, prosecutors "project a discourse of inevitability and naturalness" (Harris 1997, p. 110). The ex-Directors associate law with an arc of social and political enlightenment, and appropriate and reformulate certain historical moments as inevitable modernisation.

A Civilising Trajectory

In England and Wales that modernisation rests on a long history of private initiation and carriage of proceedings,[11] and a couple of centuries' debate about establishing a comprehensive Crown Prosecution Service (Rock, 2004). However, the assertion of an organic and grounded evolution made in relation to the English common law and its lay institutions becomes something different during the dramatic rupture of a militarised penal and later settler colony of

Australia (Godfrey and Dunstall, 2005). The profound differences in social, economic and political practices including dispersed populations and Indigenous warfare (Hughes, 1986) caution against too many assumptions of commonality with English developments.

Yet contemporary ex-Directors assert that "we came to this country with the Magna Carta in our back pockets" (A5) and "inherited the English system lock, stock and barrel in the beginning" (A3). At the same time, both colonial and contemporary changes are seen to have shaped differences (A3). Over time the systems of thought "drift [...] apart" (A3) and, at the same time, remain "closely aligned" (A5). There is clearly elasticity to tradition. But the trends towards institutionalising, centralising and standardising of criminal practice and procedure that commenced in the nineteenth century and accelerated in the twentieth in England were similar if not more pronounced in Australia (Neal, 1991). Yet it would not be until the 1980s and 1990s that independent prosecuting authorities were legislated in the Australian states and territories.[12]

Although public prosecution offices were latecomers to the architecture of criminal justice, the discourse of ex-Directors attached to a larger narrative about the civilising trajectory of English legal history. The association of criminal law with the taming of human societies gains power not simply through its air of inexorability but in depictions of a history – claimed as Australia's inheritance (A1–A6) – "that occurred over hundreds and hundreds of years" (A5). Successive efforts from the twelfth century to introduce "the concept of offences being a breach of the King's peace" are given as foundational to the present idea of criminal offences being committed against "the public" rather than against individual members of that public (Kearon and Godfrey, 2007, pp. 19–20). The origin of British criminal law, it is claimed, "was to prevent victims from taking the law into their own hands" (A1). Without law "a society ... is anarchic, out of control" (A1). Indeed, law both accompanies and assists the move out of "the realm of stone-age thinking" (A5). Vengeance was the past; public ownership of criminal law is the civilised present.

The construction of a history that is "generally enlightened, humanitarian and progressive" (Emsley, 2005, p. 2) emerges from an image of medieval brutishness (A1), to claim liberty against autocracy (A3), then the disinterested professionalising of a "flawed" process (A4), and finally to provide stern independence of decision-making against the venality and arbitrariness of a politician – Attorney General or other (A2, A3, A5). Moreover, through the flow of history, criminal law is said to claim "a common core of values" that reaches back to the Babylonian era and is found infused in the world's major religions (A5).

These statements about the criminal law invariably draw on an account of social, legal and political historical change that steadily progresses towards liberal democratic capitalism and which systems of laws naturally and properly enable. Emphasised variously as a civilising process (Elias, 1939) as "the solidarity project" (Garland, 2001), and as "the Enlightenment project" (Lacey, 2001), these changes are posed as following a linear path with an air of inevitability: "as time progressed" (A1) informal or fragmentary rules would "gradually solidify" in "an evolutionary process" (A4). In the discourse, these historical references constitute markers in a "chain of legitimation" (Bourdieu, 1987, p. 824).

Contemporary Guardians of Core Prosecution Concepts

As markers, these provide a kind of reconstructed logic to the appearance of public prosecution in Australia. But the new, modern prosecution office is also "organized around a body of internal protocols and assumptions, characteristic behaviours and self-sustaining values" (Terdiman, 1987, p. 806). The legislative framework and published guidelines for public prosecution share certain classifying concepts such as independence, representing community and public interest.[13] It is through these core concepts, as internal and institutionalised patterns of knowledge, that the remainder of the chapter arranges ex-Directors' discourse.

Independence

Prosecutorial independence is a prized attribute and signifier. Independence is maintained against a number of influences: from politics, police and the public. Its special significance is claimed in the first instance against politicised interference in the form of actions (or inactions) of recent and long past Attorneys General (A2, A3, A5, A6). Prosecution was "in private hands probably until the 1880s, 1890s when the first DPP was appointed. It was in political hands in this country for a very long time. The Attorneys General used to do it … they are basically politicians." This came to be "regarded as quite wrong [...] that they should be making decisions about persons [where] they might be beholden" (A6).

Independence from political intrusion is also pragmatic. Directors tend to say to Attorneys General, "don't try and second guess us because once you do that you buy into the argument and then you have to make the decision. One of the points about having a DPP is to have someone else making the decision and wear the opprobrium" (A4). It also recognised that prosecution is an intrusive power – "it is the line that protects everybody because one day, who is to say that a weakened and futile prosecution ought to be run this week but not next week?" (A2).

While police have a more extensive history in prosecuting (Corns, 2000), prosecution independence from investigators assumed greater significance over the twentieth century. In England and Wales, this is claimed in relation to a succession of miscarriages of justice (McConville and Wilson, 2002, p. 155) and, in Australian jurisdictions with police prosecutors, to more generalised concerns about probity (Krone, 2003). Here the argument is that police seek to "win at all costs" whereas the obligation of justice institutions is to abide "by your oath to act according to the law" (A1). Nonetheless, there is a continuum from, at one end, an ethical stance about the "appropriate moral censure" a prosecutor seeks (Young and Sanders, 2004, p. 194), to understanding, at the other end, "that every prosecutor ever born wants the person to be found guilty" (A6).[14]

Finally, argument about independence finds traction in the day-to-day decision-making of prosecutors. Here, independence is not being told what to do, whoever was expressing a preference. Discretionary decision-making both indicates independence and enacts it. A noble rationale is that discretion "is a tool indispensable for the individualisation of justice" (Davis, 1975). More prosaically it "allows for compromise and expediency" (Findlay, Odgers and Yeo, 2010, p. 114). Without discretion it is said "our system would grind to a halt" (A5). While there are different perspectives on discretion and the independent role (Sarat and Clarke, 2008), there is a shared view of what it is not; that is, being directed by an individual what to do – it is "quite wrong to [prosecute] because the victim wants to" (A1). Rather, it is a matter of "professional judgment" (A1) framed by "extensive" guidelines (A3, A6).

Contemporary prosecutors assert their independence in a charged environment. Some claim "there was a period when what the Director said was not questioned, it was accepted publicly and by politicians" (A2). There is unanimity (A1–A6), however, that the "rantings of the shock jocks and the media tabloids and all the rest of it" (A3) have produced a tense contemporary atmosphere where public prosecutors can see themselves as misunderstood if not assailed from all sides. For them, the central challenge is perceived to be "to protect the prosecution process from all external pressures, whether blatant or subtle, which can arise in a divided society" (Cowdery, 2012b, p. 18).

Representing Community

In its assertions of independence, public prosecution commonly refers to founding statutes supported by judicial decision.[15] These provide the constitutional footing to prosecutorial independence and their status as part of the apparatus of the state. Beyond constitutional legality, public prosecutors claim normative roots in the privilege to "represent community" (A2, A3, A4). That is, to prosecute "on behalf of society" (Myjer, Hancock and Cowdery, 2009, p. 1) – "the whole community" (A3). The normative and legal dissimilarity between the concepts and forms of Crown, state and community appear unacknowledged.

The term "community" evokes a ductile, more exposed assortment of publics – "those who can't protect themselves", "the weak and vulnerable" (A2) who should be kept safe "from aggression" (A4). At the same time, and linked with the curse of "expectations", communities can become something wielded as a kind of threat (A1) but also in entreaty (A4). It is a source of those blatant and subtle external pressures. As a word *community* can obscure the fact that it "is made up of many disparate groups and individuals with widely divergent views" (A5) and there is some cynicism in the perception that it can "mean whatever a politician wants [it] to mean at a particular time" (A1). In the discourse, therefore, the idea of community is modelled as "figments of fiction, of imagination" (A4). An answer to the question "what's the cut of community" is that "it's the greater community interest" for "the greater good" (A2). It is a circular argument. Ultimately the prosecutor is left to "take a holistic view of what's in the interests of the community" (A4).

Conceptualising the subjects of victim and accused as members of community is both abstracted for the former, and generally situated in rights discourse for the latter. The individual accused as rights-bearing is uncontested – "we do bend over backwards to be fair" (A6). Public prosecutors will easily turn to say, "we have to ensure that the accused is treated fairly" (A5, A6).[16] There is equal readiness to reach for stories that act as exemplars for certain representations of victim. On the one hand, for example, there's the image that the victim is "hysterical, out of control" (A1) and, on the other hand, those who "have hope and optimism" (A2). As rights-bearing individuals in the community, victims "don't have any rights. No, certainly not" (A6).[17] Recognition of the imbalance in power and resources vis-à-vis the state is confined to the accused civilian only (Dal Pont, 2009).

As an alternative term, "public" can allude to a harsher critic. In this guise, the public guardian role depends on a distinct characterisation of a public in which criminal law and justice are required "to guard against anarchy and vigilantism" (A2) and contain "unrestrained passions, vengeance, criminal acts" (A5). Here the criminal law is simply "to protect the society from the bad people" (A6). The prosecutor protects an excited public from itself.

Public Interest

Ideas of protecting the community thread through prosecutors' projections of what is the "public interest" – an indeterminate and malleable term that is also extraordinarily normatively resonant. It is claimed as "the underlying philosophy" (A2) to prosecution guidelines. These then specify a long list of criteria that may be taken into account when deciding what is in the public interest: "if you are looking for a peg to hang your coat on you might find one there" (A3). The policy frameworks conclude that, "in many cases, of course, the interests of the public will only be served by the deterrent effect of an appropriate prosecution".[18] In practice, however, thinking will turn to ask, "are there reasons as to why in the public interest nevertheless the case should not be prosecuted?" (A3, A6). In this ambivalent and media-saturated space it is suggested that "the thing that Directors are most criticised for is not prosecuting" (A2). With the core two-part test through which the assessment is made, it will either be on the sufficiency of evidence or the public interest to which that criticism is directed.

When weighing up the public interest, and linked to prosecutorial ethics, it is said that a prosecutor should apply "the highest standards to which the community would or should aspire if it were aware of all the facts and were equipped to make an objective and informed decision" (Crispin, 1995, p. 181). At the same time this weighing requires consciousness of "several audiences" (A5) and different dimensions: it "requires you to look back, to look out and to look forward". Ultimately, "acting in the public interest is taking that continuum, that historical continuum and balancing all the factors that are operating now in a way that will serve that continuum satisfactorily" (A3).

The public interest concept is fluid and contested in application: "we have interests that countervail the public interest in all sorts of things" and there are "no simple right answers" – "not always, not always" (A5). Figuring out the conceptual nuance and the delicacy to practice is largely confined to internal discussants – "colleagues, their supervisors, with senior people" (A3). That is, "informed by some shared understanding … within the legal community" (A4). Engaging with the actual public on the nature and scope of their interests is formal – through speeches and presentations – and unidirectional (A2, A3, A4, A5, A6).

How public interest is more generally vernacularised in prosecution discourse does vary – in part because of the multiplicity of formal criteria – but there is a shared view of what it is not. That is, prosecution is a decision made free of any sectional or representational interests in the name of "the public" (A1–A6), never "simply because it might get the media off my back" (A2), or "in some atavistic interest of somebody who is pressuring you into doing something" (A1). An individual, asking where they as a member of the public fit in the conception, might "often think that the public interest is at one with theirs". Consequently, prosecutors see little that is constructive arising from such "inflammatory" discussion (A2). The preference is to conceive "an independent statutory authority casting his or her mind over the entirety of the case" (A5) as properly arriving at a decision about the public interest in a particular circumstance that is "buyable by the community" (A4). Ultimately it is the prosecutor's prerogative to decide what is in the public interest at a crucial decision-making point within that machinery. "Their decision has to be final … I don't know of any other public official with quite the same role" (A4). As such, claiming a decision "in the public interest" has a unique capacity to silence questioning.

Accountability

With this degree of decision-making power, questions of accountability are grave. Ex-Directors acknowledge that "the community generally has [no] high regard for the operational workings of our criminal justice system" (A5). But with this recognition public prosecutors walk a conceptual tightrope – they represent community as a greater, a holistic, an almost incandescent ideal; are responsive to community norms as they see it, and yet are extremely sensitive to contentions of accountability from community, or from sections of community. Responsiveness to changing community norms, for example in prosecuting offences such as domestic violence and child abuse as serious public concerns[19] or indeed responsiveness to regional and local circumstances (Hetherington, 1989, p. 79), is set in contrast to perceived obligations to resist a punitive public (A1, A3, A6) and to resist notions of direct answerability to the public or specific publics. The prosecution is conceived as distant as well as responsive.

Accountability is a layered notion. When viewed "in a unitary mode that if you are accountable then you are beholden in some way or subservient or at the direction or at the behest of the person" then "most prosecutors" would "run a mile" (A4).[20] Consequently "there [is] no mileage in explaining" prosecution decisions (A1). At another level, formal accountability as a state agency rests in "superintendence" by the Attorney General, annual reports, court rules and providing reasons for decision "in certain circumstances" (A3). A mid-way between these points might accept that, where persons might be "heavily invested in something, they are entitled to a proper explanation as best we can give them" (A2). Notwithstanding, "many prosecution decisions made by independent prosecutors are not reviewable by the Courts" (Bugg, 2007, p. 7). However, with the spectre of invested others directing prosecutorial decision-making there is little to no specificity to depictions of accountability in the everyday prosecutorial world. It is unbound by any enforceable standard.

Further, and central to debate about accountability, is the separation of private and public interests (A2). Contemporary prosecutors strongly assert that "the Crown is acting for the public, the people, the State" (A1) as if these are indivisible. The institutional depiction is that "when you come to the court room there are only two parties, one is the community or the Crown (the prosecutor) and the other is the accused. There is no place at the bar table for the victim in our system" (A3). The rejection of the interests and involvement of particular publics on the grounds that these are private (and therefore not legitimate) is emphatic. It is an institution with "a great deal of power" (A3).

Concluding Discussion

The discourse of legal elites may be "an imagination of an ideal social order" (Gordon, 2012, p. 209). In the fog of law, much of it is "unworkably vague" (Plater, 2011, p. 166). Elites may also be credited with "disproportionate influence" (Gordon, 1984, p. 122) especially where the routine minutia of the mandarin is "almost totally commonplace". At the same time, public prosecution "is legally approved but generally unchecked, [and] legally exceptional" (Sarat and Clarke 2008, p. 411).[21] Like sovereigns of old, prosecuting authorities assert "monopolistic control" through daily decisions to whom the law will or will not apply (Cardemas, 1986, p. 361). They are sovereign, state, public and community in one. Theirs is a "presumption of legitimacy" (Chomsky, 1969, p. 9). "Trust me" (P6) says the prosecutorial mandarin.

As an ideology, the discourse codes are a kind of "institutional fundamentalism" (Sen, 2009, p. 83) that emphasise order, objectivity and subordination to prosecution decisions. These are the voices of "benevolently competent authority" (Duff, 2001, p. 8) where exclusivity is sustained by an "official-centric" jurisprudence (Marcus and Waye, 2004, p. 114) and resonant historic references. However, an ideology "does not passively exist as a form of dominance. It has continually to be renewed, recreated, defended, and modified" (Williams, 1977, p. 112). The affirmation and reaffirmation of prosecutors' custodianship of core concepts maintains discourse fluidity that is sufficiently robust to respond to political challenges to institutional independence,[22] as well as malleable enough for interacting with different public groups on decision-making.

The skill of the modern bureaucratic state is to portray moderation – to look competent, appear benign and to nestle in neutral phraseology that "is capable of compelling universal acceptance" (Bourdieu, 1987, p. 818). Mandarin pronouncements on the body of ideas, beliefs and claims that comprise liberal legal ideology consecrate particular norms and practices. Hegemony is the capacity to fashion a field according to this world view as well as capacity to require it.[23] Prosecution mandarins not only define what is within the purview of the law, but can compel conformity with that vision. Their capacity and authority to act unbound reveals where power resides in criminal justice.

Notes

1 I wish to thank the individuals interviewed for this chapter for their generosity and wisdom. Aspects were originally published in Robyn Holder (2018), "Mapping Institutional Discourse About Justice", in *Just Interests: Victims, Citizens and the Potential for Justice*, Chapter 4, Cheltenham, UK and Northampton, MA, USA: Edward Elgar Publishing Ltd, 75–99.

2 It is "political" in that there are "issues of the moral value or human desirability of an institution or practice whose decisions affect a large number of people" (Young, 1987, p. 73).

3 The edited collection from Luna and Wade (2012) provide sections on prosecution in particular countries, in transnational perspective, and comparing contemporary challenges. For discussions about similarities and differences between prosecution in the US and Japan see Johnson (2002) and in relation to Switzerland, France and Germany see Gilliéron (2014).

4 There are many examples to draw from in this category. For example, for Europe see Jehle and Wade (2006); for the US see Sarat and Clarke (2008); for England see King (2000); in international criminal justice see Brubacher (2004); and for Australia see Lievore (2005).

5 In the US see, for example, Mellon, Jacoby and Brewer, (1981), and in England see Rock (2004).

6 The Head of a Public Prosecution Office is known by different names in different countries. In this chapter Chief Prosecutor and Director of Public Prosecutions are used interchangeably.

7 The Association (IAP) was established in 1995 to respond to the problem of transnational crime. It also works to set and raise the standards of conduct and ethics for prosecutors. See www.iap-association.org/.

8 Within the Australian federation each State and Territory and the Commonwealth has an independent Office of Public Prosecution thus making nine offices. In most States and Territories police prosecutors operate in summary proceedings and an independent DPP conducts indictable prosecutions.

9 These sentiments echo realist approaches to law. Karl Llewellyn, for example, posed law as a functional system doing "law-jobs" (Wacks, 2006, p. 94).

10 For argument that the notion of the prosecutorial "Minister of Justice" is outdated see Plater (2011), and overstated see Young and Sanders (2004).

11 Although the sovereign absorption of criminal law occurred early in England, its enforcement and prosecution remained substantively in private hands well into the eighteenth and nineteenth centuries (Langbein, 2003).

12 In 1896 the first police prosecution department was established in Van Diemen's Land (now Tasmania). Directors of Public Prosecution began in 1973 with Tasmania (established by statute later in 1986), Victoria (1982), Queensland and the Commonwealth

(1984), NSW (1986), the ACT (1990), Western Australia and the Northern Territory (1991) and South Australia (1992). To date, only in the Commonwealth, Tasmania and the ACT is the Director of Public Prosecutions responsible for both summary and indictable matters.

13 In Australia each prosecuting authority publishes its own guidelines. However, there is broad commonality between them.

14 Professional and scholarly literature also discusses representations of prosecutors as zealots or moderates (Plater, 2011, pp. 2–3).

15 Deane, J. in *R v. Whitehorn* affirmed that "prosecuting counsel in a criminal trial represents the State", (1983) 152 CLR 657; and see Plater (2011, p. 139).

16 Fairness to the accused is prominent in the prosecution policy of all Australian Directors of Public Prosecution, and is protected in the United Nations Declaration of Human Rights and in the International Covenant on Civil and Political Rights. It is claimed that the protection of the accused person's right to a fair trial is a core if not *the* defining element to the prosecution's role as a Minister of Justice (Plater, 2011, pp. 31–32).

17 Some argue that the idea of victims' rights should more properly "be assessed on general principles" (Ashworth and Redmayne, 2010, p. 49).

18 The criteria across Australian prosecuting authorities are mostly the same. The reference here is from the ACT DPP (1991), *Prosecution Policy* at 2.6, viewed 28 February 2018, www.dpp.act.gov.au/publications/prosecutions_policy.

19 Interviewees commented on the way their guidelines "move" (A1) in relation to social mores. For further discussion on this point, see Hetherington (1989, p. 139).

20 Barristers have a duty to the administration of justice and to their clients. However, the barrister in a prosecution role has no client but has a duty to the court (ABA, 2010, pp. 1, 16). The prosecutor owes no enforceable duty of care to either the victim or the accused (Plater, 2011, p. 27).

21 Scope for review of prosecution decisions is extremely narrow. In Australia, see *Maxwell v R* [1996] HCA 46; (1996) 184 CLR 501 (15 March 1996). A decision to prosecute is reviewable by courts but the decision not to is "largely immune from public or even judicial scrutiny and review" (Australian Law Reform Commission 1980, p. 61). In contra, judicial review is extensively available in the UK across government entities especially where there is a serious abuse of power (von Berg, 2014). Note also a new initiative of the UK CPS on victims' right of review located at www.cps.gov.uk/victims_witnesses/victims_right_to_review/index.html [retrieved 4 October 2016].

22 I thank Professor Pierre de Vos for this point when he reflected on the challenges facing South Africa's National Prosecuting Authority (Prosecution Workshop, International Institute for the Sociology of Law, Onati, Spain 29 July 2016).

23 Here I rely on Raymond Williams' exposition of "hegemony" as a dynamic process as much as it is a system of dominance. Hegemony is adaptive and not necessarily total (Williams, 1977, chapter 6).

References

Ashworth, A. and Redmayne, M. (2010) *The Criminal Process* 4th edn (Oxford University Press, Oxford).

Australian Bar Association (ABA) (2010) *Barristers' Conduct Rules* Sydney.

Bandyopadhyay, S. and B. McCannon (2014) "The Effect of the Election of Prosecutors on Criminal Trials" *Public Choice* 161(1–2): 141–156.

Bourdieu, P. (1987) "The Force of Law: Towards a Sociology of the Juridicial Field" *The Hastings Law Journal* 38: 814–853.

Boylan, R. (2005) "What do Prosecutors Maximize? Evidence from the Careers of US Attorneys" *American Law and Economics Review* 7(2): 379–402.

Brubacher, M. (2004) "Prosecutorial Discretion within the International Criminal Court" *Journal of International Criminal Justice* 2(1): 71–95.

Bugg, D. (2007) "The independence of the Prosecutor and the Rule of Law" Speech to the conference: Rule of Law: Challenges in a Changing World, Brisbane.

Cardemas, J. (1986) "The Crime victim in the Prosecutorial Process" *Harvard Journal of Law and Public Policy* 9: 357–398.

Chouliaraki, L. and N. Fairclough (1999) *Discourse in Late Modernity: Rethinking Critical Discourse Analysis* (Edinburgh: Edinburgh University Press).

Chomsky, N. (1969) *American Power and the New Mandarins* (New York: Pantheon Books).

Corns, C. (2000) "Police Summary Prosecutions in Australia and New Zealand: Some Comparisons" *University of Tasmania Law Review* 19: 280–310.

Cowdery, N. (2012a) "Reflections of a (re) tired DPP" *Australian Journal of Forensic Sciences* 44(3): 219–226.

Cowdery, N. (2012b) "Challenges to Prosecution Discretion" *Commonwealth Law Bulletin* 39(1): 17–20.

Crispin, K. (1995) "Prosecutorial Ethics" – in Parker, S. and C. Sampford (eds), *Legal Ethics and Legal Practice: Contemporary Issues* (Oxford: Clarendon Press).

Dal Pont, G. (2009) *Lawyers' Professional Responsibility in Australia and New Zealand* 4th edn (Sydney: Lawbook Co).

Davis, K. (1975) *Police Discretion* (Eagan, MN: West Publishing Company).

Del Ponte, C. (2011) *Madame Prosecutor: Confrontations with Humanity's Worst Criminals and the Culture of Impunity* (New York: Other Books).

Duff, R.A. (2001) *Punishment, Communication, and Community* (Oxford: Oxford University Press).

Elias, N. (1939/2000) *The Civilising Process* (Oxford: Blackwell).

Emsley, C. (2005) "Filling in, Adding up, Moving on: Criminal Justice History in Contemporary Britain" *Crime, History and Societies* 9(1): pp. 117–138.

Eisenstein, J. (1978) *Counsel for the United States: US Attorney in the Political and Legal Systems* (Baltimore, MD: Johns Hopkins University Press).

Findlay, M., Odgers, S. and Yeo, S. (2010) *Australian Criminal Justice* 4th edn (South Melbourne: Oxford University Press).

Garland, D. (2001) *The Culture of Control: Crime and Social Order in Contemporary Society* (Oxford: Oxford University Press).

Gilliéron, G. (2014) *Public Prosecutors in the United States and Europe: A Comparative Analysis with Special Focus on Switzerland, France and Germany* (New York: Springer International Publishing).

Godfrey, B. and Dunstall, G. (eds) (2005) *Crime and Empire – 1840–1940: Criminal Justice in Local and Global Context* (Devon: Willan).

Gordon, R. (1984) "Critical Legal Histories" *Stanford Law Review* 36(57): 57–125.

Gordon, R. (2012) "Critical Legal Histories Revisited: A Response" *Law and Social Inquiry* 37(1): 200–215.

Harris, J.W. (1997) *Legal Philosophies* 2nd edn (London: Butterworth).

Hetherington, T. (1987) "Prosecutor and the Public Interest" *The Bracton Law Journal* 19: 7–11.

Hetherington, T. (1989) *Prosecution and the Public Interest* (London: Pergamon Press).

Hughes, R. (1986) *The Fatal Shore* (London: Vintage).

Jehle, J. and M. Wade (2006) *Coping with Overloaded Criminal Justice Systems* (Heidelberg: Springer).
Johnson, D. (2002) *The Japanese Way of Justice: Prosecuting Crime in Japan* (Oxford: Oxford University Press).
Kearon, T. and B. Godfrey (2007) "Setting the Scene: A Question of History" – in Walklate, S. (ed.) *Handbook of Victims and Victimology* (Portland, OG: Willan Publishing).
King, P. (2000) *Crime, Justice and Discretion in England 1740–1820* (Oxford: Oxford University Press).
Krone, T. (2003) "The Limits of Prosecution Authority" Regulatory Institutions Network (RegNet) Working Paper 18, The Australian National University, Canberra.
Lacey, N. (2001) "In Search of the Responsible Subject: History, Philosophy and Social Sciences in Criminal Law Theory" *The Modern Law Review* 64: 350–371.
Langbein, J. (2003) *The Origins of the Adversary Criminal Trial* (Oxford: Oxford University Press).
Lievore, D. (2005) *No Longer Silent: A Study of Women's Help-Seeking Decisions and Service Responses to Sexual Assault* (Canberra: Australian Institute of Criminology.
Luna, E. and M. Wade (eds) (2012) *The Prosecutor in Transnational Perspective* (Oxford: Oxford University Press).
McConville, M. and G. Wilson (eds) (2002) *The Handbook of the Criminal Justice Process* (Oxford: Oxfored University Press).
Marcus, P. and V. Waye (2004) "Australia and the United States: Two Common Criminal Justice Systems Uncommonly at Odds" *Tulane Journal of International & Comparative Law* 12(1): 27–116.
Mellon, L., J. Jacoby and M. Brewer (1981) "The Prosecutor Constrained by his Environment: A New Look at Discretionary Justice in the United States" *The Journal of Criminal Law and Criminology* 72(1): 52–81.
Meuser, M. and U. Nagel (2009) "The Expert Interview and Changes in Knowledge Production" – in Bogner, A., B Littig, N. and W. Menz (eds) *Interviewing Experts* (London: Palgrave Macmillan).
Myjer, E., B. Hancock and N. Cowdery (eds) (2009) *Human Rights Manual for Prosecutors* (Nijmegen: Wolf Legal Publishers).
Neal, D. (1991) *The Rule of Law in a Penal Colony: Law and Power in Early New South Wales* (Cambridge: Cambridge University Press).
Plater, D. (2011) "The Changing Role of the Modern Prosecutor: Has the Notion of 'Minister of Justice' Outlived its Usefulness?" doctoral thesis, University of Tasmania, viewed 28 February 2018, http://eprints.utas.edu.au/10743/2/David_Plater_whole.pdf.
Reydams, L., J. Wouters and C. Ryngaert (eds) (2012) *International Prosecutors* (Oxford: Oxford University Press).
Rock, P. (2004) "Victims, Prosecutors and the State in Nineteenth Century England and Wales" *Criminal Justice* 4(4): 331–354.
Sarat, A. and C. Clarke (2008) "Beyond Discretion: Prosecution and the Logic of Sovereignty, and the Limits of Law" *Law and Social Inquiry* 33(2): 387–416.
Sen, A. (2009) *The Idea of Justice* (Cambridge, MA: Harvard University Press).
Terdiman, R. (1987) "The Force of Law: Translator's Introduction" *Hastings Law Journal* 38: 805–813.
Tonry, M. (ed.) (2012) *Prosecutors and Politics: A Comparative Perspective* (Chicago, IL: University of Chicago Press).
Wacks, R. (2006) *Philosophy of Law: A Very Short Introduction* (Oxford: Oxford University Press).

Williams, R. (1977) *Marxism and Literature* (Oxford: Oxford University Press).
Wright, R., K. Levine and M. Miller (2014) "The Many Faces of Prosecution" *Stanford Journal of Criminal Law and Policy* 1(27): 27–47.
Young, I. (1987) "Impartiality and the Civic Public" – in Benhabib, S. and D. Cornell (eds) *Feminism as Critique* (Minneapolis, MN: University of Minnesota Press).
Young, R. and A. Sanders (2004) "The Ethics of Prosecution Lawyers" *Legal Ethics* 7(2): 190–209.

2 New Public Management, Citizens' Fears and Calls for Justice

The Prosecutor's New Role in Italy

Cecilia Blengino

Prosecution and the Interpretation of the Law

Reforms to the Italian judicial system in the past decade offer an interesting opportunity to reflect on both the paradigm of judicial interpretation and the role of the judiciary and prosecutors in this function.

Founded on Montesquieu's metaphor of the judge as "*la bouche de la loi*", the European legal paradigm of modernity[1] imagines a judicial power that is completely subordinate to the legislator.[2] The idea that magistrates are mere interpreters of the law seeks to guarantee the separation between powers proclaiming both the ethical indifference and the political neutrality of legal interpretation.

In the perspective of legal positivism, the primacy exerted by the legislature on the judicial power arises from the idea that laws have pre-constituted meanings that the court is called to apply. Within this theoretical position, both judicial reasoning and decisions are designed as deductive syllogisms, where any legal problem can be addressed through a series of logical steps that lead to the sole possible solution and the judgement is conceived as the result of an entirely rational process (Catellani, 1992, p. 115).

Furthermore, the criteria on which magistrates must decide are defined by "*rules of recognition*",[3] a second-level rule system that defines interpretation methods and procedures. The Italian Constitution and the Code of Criminal Procedure are the most important *rules of recognition* for prosecution. They provide for the subordination of the magistrate to the law,[4] the mandatory prosecution principle,[5] but even the public prosecutor's duty to investigate in the suspect's favour.[6] Consequently, the new Italian "cross-examination model" assigns to the public prosecutor a quite hybrid role.[7]

Furthermore, after the snail's pace of the Italian judicial system was condemned by the Court of Strasbourg in 1999, the Italian Parliament approved a major constitutional reform[8] that provides that a "fair trial" is no longer guaranteed solely by the cross-examination principle, but it is also related to its speed in responding to the call for justice. The introduction of the concept of the efficiency of justice breaks with some pillars of the legal modernity concept of interpretation of the law, which is traditionally founded on the rule of law, a bureaucratic judiciary.[9]

The ideological nature of the dogmatic representation of the primacy of the law has been explored in depth by studies that deal with the real ways through which legal practitioners take their decisions. These studies underline that, rather than proceeding from the general and abstract rule, as required by the legal paradigm of modernity, judicial reasoning proceeds from the particular to the general (Hruschka, 2009). Empirical psychological research on magistrates' reasoning highlights that this reasoning is essentially "problem solving" (Catellani, 1992, p. 112). Both the need to resolve situations and a lack of detailed information needed to create solutions lead magistrates to adopt decision-making procedures or cognitive shortcuts that constitute systematic deviations from the theory-inspired regulatory approach (Bona and Rumiati, 2013, p. 147).

The law cannot be represented as a closed and independent system, consisting exclusively of formal rules (Ehrlich, 1976). In fact, the law involves both legal rules and norms that regulate social life and requires observation of the manner in which the formal rules are applied within what Llewellyn calls "the area of contact between judicial (or official) behaviour and the behaviour of laymen" (1930, pp. 455–456).

Furthermore, the adoption of the new criteria of "reasonable duration of the judicial action" as a constitutional principle highlights the distance between judicial interpretation *in the books* and judicial reasoning *in action*.[10] Several empirical studies have observed that judicial reasoning systematically uses "preconceptions" (Esser, 1983), "mundane reason" (Pollner, 2010) and criteria based on probabilistic calculation and inferential reasoning (Catellani, 1992, p. 150). These simplified methods of reasoning emphasize that judicial thinking is influenced by many variables other than the law, such as preconceptions, the organization of the office, and the resources of the court. Then, constitutionalizing the objective of judicial efficiency could improve the function of categorization devices as simplification tools of the cognitive process (Sudnow, 1965; Blumberg, 1967; Hester and Eglin, 1992). Strategies adopted to speed judicial action mainly found on categorizations, aimed to simplify judicial reasoning when prosecutors meet the cases. It reveals why the efficiency of justice is not a neutral objective, but could be strongly linked to judicial policies and to labelling processes of specific types of crimes and criminals (Sarzotti, 2007; Blengino, 2011). The criminal justice system relies on a broader use of categorizations to lighten the judicial machine's workload (Blumberg, 1967). Stereotypes and categorizing crimes as "ordinary crimes" or "normal affairs" (Sudnow, 1965) then, could become a standardization factor for organizational practices in the courts (Quassoli, 1999) and Public Prosecutor's Offices (Sarzotti, 2007)[11] to speed up their work.

Another argument challenging the dogmatic view of the judiciary is the political role it plays outside of proceedings. The trial is not the only space in which magistrates express their beliefs. The judiciary interacts with both the political system and the media system. Recent decades have seen an explosion in the power of the judiciary, and correspondingly with the media coverage of it.

On several occasions, the judiciary has played a role as an agent of reform of civil and political life in Italy, encroaching on the legislature's political power and assuming an unprecedented role regarding public morality (Pizzorno, 1998). In the 1970s, the so-called "alternative use of the law"[12] led some magistrates to believe that they were justified in using legal procedural instruments for progressive and liberating tasks. In the 1980s, terrorism and the Mafia were fought through a gradual expansion of the magistrate's role. In the 1990s, the "Mani Pulite" (literally "Clean Hands") investigations conducted by a group of magistrates in the Milan Public Prosecutor's Office highlighted the corruption of numerous members of the ruling parties, and served as a crucial stage in the process representing the public prosecutor magistrate as the guardian of public morality. This investigation was one of the first manifestations of a relationship between the judiciary and the media that continues to place judicial activity under the constant glare of the public spotlight (Giglioli, Cavicchioli and Fele, 1997). More recently, the role of the judiciary as an agent of reform has been exercised through speeches inaugurating judicial years (Sarzotti, 2004) whose communicative significance is heightened through the media coverage they receive. The scream "*Resist, resist, resist*!" launched by the Head Prosecutor of Milan during the judicial year inauguration in 2002 continues to echo today as a symbol of the conflict between the Italian judiciary and the government that reached its peak at the time of the "Berlusconi governments".

Rules and the Working of Judicial Action in Italy

The combination of the Italian Prosecutor's obligation to prosecute all crimes – with no formal possibility of choice or priority – and the steady increase in criminal complaints significantly obstructs the possibility of implementing the Constitutional principle to expedite criminal justice. Furthermore, it creates tensions on the equality and efficiency principles.

The implementation of the constitutional reform of "due process" has been accompanied by a series of strategies aimed at improving the efficiency of the justice system. Although these strategies were intended to be compatible with mandatory prosecution, they have shown how the organizational issue in Italian justice does not produce neutral effects in terms of judicial policy.

Selectivity of the criminalization process has emerged with respect both to criminal trials and prosecution. Regarding trials, it has meant a crisis of the judicial ritual and the rise of alternative procedures, with cross-examination tending to be reserved for those trials where the accused are assisted by competent lawyers and enjoy all procedural guarantees (Sudnow, 1965; Hester and Eglin, 1992). A second level of justice risks being reserved for accused parties who are poor or socially and culturally weak, involving them in alternative processes or standardized proceedings that do not provide all procedural guarantees (Cottino and Fischer, 1995; Cottino and Sarzotti, 1995; Mosconi and Padovan, 2005).

As regards prosecution, new expressions of selectivity have resulted in new managerial tasks being assigned to the Chief Prosecutor. In the new conception of justice as a "flow" (Garapon, 2012, p. 38), the most recent judiciary reform laws assign a duty to the Chief Prosecutor to promote efficiency, instructing him to reorganize the Prosecutor's Office, delegate staff to manage homogeneous types of crimes, and identify types of offences that could be handled by automatic mechanisms.[13]

These managerial tasks introduce significant transformations into the concept of judicial interpretation, with a new element of discretionality in the key phase of preliminary investigations, starting with the moment at which the Prosecutor receives *notitiae criminis* and assigns them to his staff. The Prosecutor's managerial role also introduces a new political role of the judiciary in Italy. Indeed, judicial action straddles the executive and the judiciary, because prosecutors not only play a crime repression function but also a judicial function as guarantors of legality. By assigning managerial tasks to Prosecutors, the responsibility of compounding mandatory prosecution with the efficiency scope is decentralized from the legislator to the local offices. This requires an awareness of the organizational dimension of judicial action. Although the dogmatic perspective sees judicial interpretation as an individual cognitive act, it must be considered a collective process related to the organization of work that involves many actors and offices.

The Chief Prosecutor is required to coordinate not only the deputy public prosecutors but also the administrative line and the judiciary police assigned to its office.[14] The coexistence of different professionals in the same office characterizes Italian Public Prosecutor Offices (Blengino, 2007). It also produces some consequences with respect to formal distinction of roles and functions. To understand judicial activity "in action", we need to consider both the relationships within the Public Prosecutor's Office and the links between that office and external actors. The growing autonomy of the Chief Prosecutor interacts with the availability of human, material and technology resources. The progressive restriction of resources at a time of growing demand for justice has highlighted the issue of the sustainability. Furthermore, an entire system of laws, regulations and administrative rules governs the judicial working office. However, a practical organization exists alongside the formal organization, one that is forged every day by the behaviour of individuals, through the ways they apply and practice the rules (Di Federico, 1994; Nelken and Zanier, 2006; Blengino, 2007; Sarzotti, 2007). Administrative workers, police and magistrates create specific workgroups (Eisenstein and Jacob, 1991) whose cooperation or disunion can achieve or fail to achieve the organizational goals primarily on the basis of the leader's ability to engage his or her employees.

The managerial style adopted by the strategic apex (Mintzberg, 1979; Kotter 1995) plays a crucial role in determining both the procedures and praxis in the office. Organizational differences between local offices are the result of both the way the Chief Prosecutors perceive their target audience – since the main standard of reference in their decision-making orientation may be the legitimacy of the administration of justice, or accounting for the performance of their office (Piana, 2010, p. 124) – and their leadership ability to involve all organization staff in achieving their objectives. Prosecutors who are inspired strictly by the principle of formal legality tend to adopt a laissez-faire leadership style that does not concern itself with office output times or means. On the contrary, a Prosecutor's efficiency-oriented organizational culture creates timely internal procedures and specialized groups. Where Prosecutors exercise a charismatic role, all the workers in their office tend to share goals and work together to realize them. When a laissez-faire leadership style is adopted, informal niches of power (Crozier, 1997) and praxis tend to arise with unpredictable effects that could counteract the Chief Prosecutor's instructions (Sarzotti, 2007; Blengino, 2011).

This becomes clear when we observe a concrete procedure in which two different Italian Public Prosecutor's Offices deal with the Chief Prosecutor's function of assigning *notitiae criminis* to his delegates.[15] In one case, the aim is to avoid obstacles in the judicial flow, so a specific group composed of a magistrate with police and administrative staff is put in charge of reading daily *notitiae criminis*, immediately assessing them and deciding whether they should be archived or prosecuted, and if they are to be prosecuted, deciding to which specialized pool they should be assigned. Although this Prosecutor function is actually performed primarily by administrative staff, a strong awareness and sharing of his aims is observed and the staff has learned to reason as the Prosecutor would, so the entire *notitiae criminis iter* continues coherently with the Prosecutor's organizational directives. In the second case, a perceived constraint to respect the rule of law prevails, leading the Prosecutor to neglect the way in which cases are assigned by his administrative staff, giving his people substantial power to both evaluate criminal records and address *notitia criminis* in one procedural direction or another, with anarchic and unpredictable consequences both in terms of procedural times and inhomogeneity of the treatment of similar cases (Blengino, 2007, p. 152ss).

The Local Dimension of Judicial Action

The characteristics of the local institutional context play a decisive role in the judicial interpretation process.

Both the ways in which Public Prosecutor's Offices are designed and the tasks that are assigned to them underscore the local dimension of the response to crime (Fabri, 1997; Blengino, 2007; Zanier, 2011). In turn, both the Prosecutor's leadership style and the organization of the work in the Public Prosecutor's Office are linked to the variable of the *local legal culture*.[16] Judicial thinking is placed within a network of extrajudicial variables that shape every single Prosecutor's office. Consequently, the flexibility of the mandatory prosecution principle differs in every *local juridical field* (Sarzotti, 2007, Blengino, 2011[17]).

As a complex "system of concrete action" (Crozier, 1997), every Prosecutor's Office works as an open organization characterized by specific relationships both with 'institutional' and 'non-institutional' actors that play a role influencing the decision-making processes. Prosecutors' managing strategies take into account juridical rules, but also the environment in which they operate (Sarzotti, 2007). Input, constraints and directives may come from the Ministry of Justice, the

Superior Board of Magistrates, the local courts, the Bar and police forces. Judicial activity then may also be influenced by input and interactions with local governments, social services, neighbourhood committees, associations and the media. When "social problems"[18] are perceived by the components of the organization, mutual interaction between the Public Prosecutor's Office and the external environment leads to new organizational decisions (Friedberg, 1996). Furthermore, every new legal, political or social input, and new juridical and social actors in the local juridical field, can influence a change in the working strategies of judicial action. For example, in recent years, Italian Prosecutors have been called to radically revise organizational procedures as a result of the pardon law voted in 2006 for people who have or would have been sentenced to less than three years[19] and of new criminalization or decriminalization laws.[20] Moreover, the laws that have reduced the number of judicial offices in the country, which accelerated the retirement of employees or required Prosecutors to leave their offices after a number of years, forced the judicial offices to implement organizational changes (Blengino, 2011).

Local legal culture also implicitly influences prosecutors' ideas and preconceptions about legal rules and crimes, and forms the basis of the criteria on which Prosecutors account for their action to the public opinion and the political system (Pizzorno 1998; Piana 2010). Thus, they are inevitably influenced by the perception of criminal emergencies and the local demand for justice.

Considering the variable of local legal culture, we can understand the different ways in which Prosecutor's Offices have reconciled the need to expedite the process with mandatory prosecution (Fabri, 1997; Sarzotti, 2007; Blengino, 2007; Montana, 2009; Zanier, 2011). Some immediately responded to requests to reform due process, setting up organizational models inspired by *New Public Management* (Barzelay, 2001) to speed up justice, while inevitably sacrificing some guarantees. On the other hand, other prosecutors chose to maintain the principles and guarantees of the Procedural Code to the detriment of procedural speed (Blengino, 2007; Sarzotti, 2007).

Within the same concept of local legal culture, we can explain the Prosecutor' availability to allow external input to permeate his tasks to organize internal procedural and distribute human and financial resources in the office. Local calls for justice and public opinion may explain, for example, the Public Prosecutors' different choices to assign human resources to a specialized pool charged to solve famous "cold cases" in Turin, to a specific economic affairs pool in Milan (Blengino, 2011), to the protection of the artistic heritage in Rome, and to prosecute environmental crimes in Naples (Piana, 2016).

The open relationship in the local legal field between the Public Prosecutor's Office and local players can also be seen in the rise of a new collective governance model in response to specific types of crime, in partnerships with other institutional or social actors. These are, for example, strategies devised by some Public Prosecutor's Offices to fight violence against children and women with the collaboration of local police, health and social services, and NGOs that provide psychological support to victims, or the construction of statistical surveys and observatories to identify and prosecute occupational deaths (Blengino, 2011, p. 74) and diseases (Blengino and Torrente, 2013) with the cooperation of welfare and health services.

Calls for Justice, People's Fears and the Organization of Judicial Action

The shift of Prosecutors' accountability from the role of "guardian of the rules" to that of "defender of the people" (Blengino, 2011) introduces a strong new connection between the Prosecutor's perception of crime and local citizens' demand for justice. This affects his choices regarding the definition of – formal or informal – priority criteria in the *notitiae criminis* procedure. Prosecutors have begun to play a crucial role in receiving and reflecting people's fears in the juridical field, while radically changing both the ways they represent themselves and the objectives of justice itself, in order to account for their activities and request social legitimation.

The link between the perception of crime and the Prosecutor Office's internal proceedings is not really new. The perception of crime influences internal proceedings with the adoption of different ways of dealing with different types of *notitiae criminis*.

The two main ways in which this phenomenon features are, first, the constitution of magistrates' team groups for crimes that are considered particularly urgent or difficult to combat in a specific time and context, and second, the different formal or informal procedures following the attribution of a *notitia criminis* to one specialized group rather than another or to none at all (Blengino, 2007, p. 153ss).

The practice of creating specialized groups within the Prosecutor's office goes back to the 1970s. The spread of the working group method aimed to assign the most strategic and human resources to criminal emergencies, both at the national level, by coordinating between different Public Prosecutor's Offices, and to local judiciary offices.

The terrorism emergency of the 1970s and 1980s led to the creation of specialized groups and a network to combat this phenomenon. Later, in the 1990s, the Mafia and organized crime were the priorities of the prosecution, with greater investment in Prosecutor's offices in Southern Italy, where prosecutors assigned to anti-Mafia pools represented almost half the workforce (Blengino, 2007; Sarzotti, 2007). From the 1990s onwards, the social and economic changes in Italy and the increase in migration led to migration-related urban unrest and street crime becoming a priority, especially in large cities in Northern Italy (Blengino, 2011; Quassoli and Colombo, 2016).

Today, judicial organization is determined by the new input of public perception of crime and citizens' opinions of justice that influence the choices of criminal justice actors. The crisis of the judicial ritual is accompanied by the emergence of the "spectacle trial" and "justice show" (Garapon, 2012) consumed and broadcast through television and newspapers. Building efficiency of justice introduced feedback on customer satisfaction of justice services, meaning that citizens are considered users of a service (Blengino, 2011).

Being the only person charged with media relations, the leadership style of the Chief Prosecutor becomes crucial. Prosecutors who adopt a legalistic approach to judicial action show substantial disinterest in forming relationships with the media system. In contrast, holding interviews and issuing public statements involving citizens on issues of criminal justice and crime alarm seems to be a real media strategy for Prosecutors with a charismatic leadership style (Sarzotti, 2007). The media channel is sometimes used to raise public awareness of the impact of specific regulatory measures on the judicial system. In these cases, the media circuit can serve as a tool for Prosecutors to request and verify the consent of operators in the legal and public field with respect to their organizational strategies. This is done through public disclosure of documents relating to organizational issues on criminal justice problems on the Prosecutor's office websites, with Prosecutors participating in public meetings, conferences, television and newspaper interviews (Blengino, 2011).

The new centrality of the citizen in judicial policies (Garland 2001; Garapon, 2012) requires that the justice system face up to statistical data revealing very low confidence in criminal justice in Italy (Piana, 2016). This lack of confidence in Italian justice is linked mainly to its slowness. With increasing calls for justice and criminal reports and shrinking resources, the criminal system maintains a high rate of criminal trials lapsing under the statute of limitations before they even get to trial, up to 39.9 per cent in some districts. Ministry of Justice data shows the highest incidence of lapses for corporate crimes and crimes against the public administration (Piana, 2016). Then, while reorganizing the criminal justice in a "reactive" way, the managerial logic introduces the idea of "criminal response" turning the classic idea of judicial action into the perspective of "problem solving" (Garapon, 2012, p. 35), in which prosecution becomes a key point between calls for justice, people's fears and efficient justice. Pre-trial investigations – in which the prosecutor decides whether to request the initiation of the criminal trial or not – become crucial in the secondary criminalization process (Hester and Eglin, 1992). In fact, using quick and standardized procedures to prosecute crimes that are considered easy to solve and which are particularly frightening for citizens can represent a useful strategy for Prosecutors to improve performance (Garland, 2001; Garapon, 2012).

We can see the importance given to citizens' concerns and fears in the Turin Public Prosecutor's Office's creation of a team in the late 90s to protect citizens from immigrant nuisances and urban unrest. The reason for the creation of this group – to prevent urban deviance and street crime from going unpunished – was the Chief Prosecutor's desire to listen and respond to the protests of residents' committees (Borgna and Maddalena, 2003; Blengino, 2007). In the meantime, the group's creation also allowed the Public Prosecutor's Office to clear its backlog and speed up criminal action procedures to the local court (Sarzotti, 2007).

Over time, almost all Public Prosecutor's Offices in major Italian cities (including Turin, Milan, Rome, Naples and Palermo) have created special "offices for the definition of simple affairs", "filter offices" for the serial disposal of criminal reports considered simple to rule on or not serious, in order to promote the immediate outcome of the proceedings and achieve economies of scale. These filter offices are mainly composed of administrative and police workers and implement simplified procedures and predetermined investigative protocols with no evaluation by a magistrate. These offices may be crucial in the selectivity of the process of criminalization because a Prosecutor's flagging of a crime as "normal" or "typical" is based both on prejudices and the labelling of citizens' claims and fears that confirm people's beliefs. Furthermore, simple and typical crimes are flagged in very different ways across the country (Zanier, 2011; Blengino and Torrente, 2013; Piana, 2016). For example, the Turin Prosecutor's Office has been considering crimes against urban security to be simple crimes, while the Milan office considers crimes such as evasion, counterfeiting, driving offences and immigration as the jurisdiction of the justice of the peace. Again, considering one crime to be a simple affair or not depends on the Prosecutor's ideas and evaluations concerning criminality in the local context in which he acts: for example, in some Prosecutor's Offices in Southern Italy, theft and drug misdemeanours are not considered urban security offences, but actions committed by the lower levels of hierarchic criminal organizations. For this reason they are assigned to the "organized crime" specialized groups (Blengino, 2007).

It should be emphasized that the permeability between the Prosecutor's organizational strategies and crime perception makes the judicial organization subject to constant changes, both synchronic and diachronic.

The office's organization is never stable. Any changes to its variables can lead to significant changes to its configuration and therefore to justice policies. A change in the strategic apex (Mintzberg, 1979) is one of the most important changes. We can see that in the Turin Public Prosecutor's Office. The rotation since 1998 of three Chief Prosecutors united by the same efficient local legal culture has led to a progressive definition of an efficiency-oriented organization that takes great care to listen to citizens' concerns regarding urban unrest (Blengino, 2011). In recent years, however, political unrest and protests against the construction of the high-speed rail line (TAV) on the Italian–French border, plus this infrastructure's political and institutional importance, has led to gradually shift the way to consider expressions of dissent towards the context of terrorism, leading the Prosecutor's controversial decision to institute criminal proceedings against certain members of the "NO TAV" Committee on charges of terrorism. The last change in the strategic apex and the current global spread of concern about terrorism led to a recent office reorganization abolishing the Urban Safety section altogether. Migrant deviance is no longer considered an urban unrest problem, but is associated with the risk of global terrorism. This fear leads to place it among crimes to be investigated for their alleged dangerous connection to terrorist organizations.

At the synchronic level, it should be noted that Prosecutors' organizational choices have to be approved by the National Board of Judiciary. When they receive particular appreciation, they tend to be shared nationwide in order to create virtuous models of sharing of best practices and coordination between offices. This is what is happened with the organization model created by the Turin Public Prosecutor's Office when it created and subsequently disseminated "filter offices" to deal with "simple affairs", and is also what happened with the creation of coordination between various Public Prosecutor's Offices to counter terrorism and organized crime.

An interesting and peculiar example is the attempt – once again by a Turin prosecutor – to share a common working method among Public Prosecutor's Offices to fight "occupational safety crimes" (Blengino and Torrente, 2013, 2016).

This specific field of action leads us again to observe the weight exerted in criminal proceedings by social variables and actors. This element can be clearly understood if we compare two very important criminal investigations involving deaths and diseases caused by two Italian steel companies: Eternit in Casale Monferrato and Ilva in Taranto, the jurisdiction of the Prosecutors of Turin (in Northern Italy) and Taranto (in the South), respectively.

In both cases, thousands of deaths have been reported to have been caused by pollution produced by these plants. In the Eternit case, the Prosecutor of Turin's strong personality and charisma led him to play a crucial role in bringing the emergence of this peculiar safety-at-work crime to the attention of the criminal justice system and public opinion, and then in obtaining the harshest sentence ever pronounced in Europe against a manager for occupational "accidents" (Blengino and Torrente, 2013, 2016). These results were accompanied and obtained through the definition of scientific investigation strategies, and above all thanks to the massive participation and involvement of victims' committees and the local media.

The local juridical field in which the Prosecutor of Taranto prosecuted the director of the Ilva plant appears to be completely different. Indeed, aside from strictly legal aspects, these two judicial cases have some crucial differences. First, this factory, accused of being the leading cause of pollution in southern Italy, employs over 12,000 people in a region with high unemployment. This caused a great deal of attention and conflict among several actors in the field, with the consequences of the factory shutdown ordered by the Prosecutor provoking strong reaction from the local population, labour unions and institutions. In response, the Italian government approved a specific law to reopen the factory, which the Prosecutor immediately appealed as unconstitutional. Residents were also called to vote in a citizens' referendum to express their disagreement with the factory shutdown. Even the European Commission put the Italian Government on formal notice in 2013 for Ilva's failure to respect EU health and environmental directives. Prosecution against managers and local governors was initiated in 2015. From this perspective, a comparison of the cases highlights the role played by the representation of the victim in the criminalization process (Garland, 2001; Simon, 2007). Significantly, the Ilva investigations did not receive the support of the local population. Despite them being the most probable victims of health damage, the process of victimization was not developed in this case.

Reflections here should be open on people's perception of being victims, as well as on variables determining their over-representation or underestimation of being victims of crimes (Palidda, 2016). In fact, the irrationality of citizens' fears today risks playing the most significant role in leading criminalization processes. Faced with the emergence of new populisms and xenophobic instances, the permeability of the judicial action to citizens' claims puts today's Prosecutors at a crossroads to be guarantors of respect of the fundamental principles of criminal law or to become cooperators in realizing the assumptions of the theory of the criminal law of the enemy.[21]

Notes

1 For a discussion of the development of the European legal paradigm of modernity, the European codification process, and the characterizing relationships between legal power, judiciary power and government power see, among others, Grossi, 2010.

2 Furthermore, according to Kelsen's theory, the legal science proclaims both the ethical indifference and the political neutrality of the law, aiming exclusively to understand the law according to its essence and analysing its structure (Kelsen, [1934] 1970).

3 Argumenting the legal positivism theory, the concept of rule of recognition is used by L.H. Hart (2012) to underline the role of jurisprudence respect to the law into the legal system.

4 Art. 125 Italian Constitution.

5 Art. 112 Italian Constitution.

6 Art. 358 Processual Criminal Code.

7 Italian criminal trials were reformed in depth in 1989, replacing the inquisitorial processual model with the cross-examination system. For an in-depth discussion of this hybrid function of the Prosecutor in Italy, see Guarnieri and Pederzoli, 2002. Regarding the two different ideas of the function of the criminal trial itself emerging in the *common law* and *civil law* models, see especially Damaska, 1991.

8 Art. 111 of the Italian Constitution, reformed by Constitutional Law no. 2 of 23 November 1999. The constitutional reform was followed by Law no. 89 of 4 March 2001 introducing compensation for the excessive delay in trials.

9 As in most continental European legal systems, the Italian judiciary appears as a professional bureaucracy (Guarnieri and Pederzoli, 2002; Piana, 2010; Guarnieri, 2011). The concept of professional bureaucracy refers to organizations in which the line is composed of highly professional workers and the staff is principally composed of administrative employees. It points up the peculiarity of the distribution of roles that distinguishes it from other kinds of organizational structure (Mintzberg, 1979).

10 Referring to the famous distinction between *law in the books and law in action* by Roscoe Pound (910, p. 12ss).

11 It favours negotiation between the prosecution and the defence and a reduction in the charges against the accused (Sudnow, 1965).

12 This expression was created in the 70s to indicate the role assumed by the initiatives taken by some left-wing cultural and political groups within the Italian judiciary in favour of realism in the normative interpretation of the place of traditional exegetical practice. That use of the law played a revolutionary and reformatting role in Italian law (Barcellona, 1973).

13 Art. 1 Legislative Decree no. 106/2006.

14 An essential description of the functioning of criminal justice in Italy is necessary. In Italy, access to both functions of judges and prosecutors takes place following a unique public competition, after which they are assigned to a court or a public prosecutor office. Under certain conditions, a change in career from judge to prosecutor, or vice versa, is allowed. Prosecutors are responsible for receiving private or police complaints and evaluating them to decide whether to prosecute. A Chief Prosecutor governs each Public Prosecutor Office and a number of prosecutors depending on the size of the local district. Prosecutors perform their investigative functions with the help of a staff composed of secretaries and judicial police. The judicial police working with the magistrate follow his directives, helping him in carrying out the investigations. These are personnel detached from local police forces.

15 The case is the one of the Public Prosecutor offices in Turin and in Bari. The first is in the North of Italy, while the second is in the Southern Italy. Their organizations were empirically explored by Claudio Sarzotti, Cecilia Blengino and Giovanni Torrente (Sarzotti, 2007).

16 The concept of *local legal culture* Cotterrell (1997) constitutes a proposal to develop the local dimension of the notion of legal culture. Friedman uses the notion of legal *culture* when he refers to all the "*ideas, values, expectations and attitudes towards law and legal institutions which some public or some part of the public holds*" (Friedman, 1975, p. 34). In this area, he distinguishes between the internal legal culture and the external one. While the latter involves common people's ideas about the law, he considers the internal legal culture as an "*especially important kind of group of legal culture*", one of "*legal professionals – the values, ideologies and principles of lawyers, judges and others working within the magic circle of the legal system*" (Friedman, 1975, p. ivi).

17 This idea arises from Pierre Bourdieu (1986) who considers the juridical field as a space characterized by interactions, balances of power, and even tensions that constantly determine its transformation.

18 The reference is in particular to the constructionist perspective that proposes to conceive "social problems" as the claims-making activities of individuals or groups regarding social conditions they consider unjust, immoral or harmful and that should be addressed. This perspective highlights the process of interaction that produces social problems as social facts in society (Spector and Kitsuse, 2001).

19 Aimed at reducing overcrowding in Italian prisons, the pardon law (Law no. 241 of 31 July 2006) was behind several Prosecutors' decisions not to continue investigations of crimes for which they expected the eventual sentence to not exceed three years (Blengino, 2011).

20 This phenomenon has been particularly significant relating to drug use and illegal migration.

21 We are referring to Jakobs' (1985) theory. For example, in summer 2018, the Prosecutor of Catania accused some NGOs active in the rescue of migrants in the sea between Libia and Italy.

References

Barcellona, P. (1973) *L'uso alternativo del diritto: ortodossia giuridica e pratica politica* (Bari: Laterza).

Barzelay, M. (2001) *The New Public Management. Improving Research and Policy Dialogue* (Berkeley, CA: University of California Press).

Blengino, C. (2007) "Esercizio dell'Aazione Penale e Processi Organizzativi: la Selezione del Crimine come Output della Procura" – in Sarzotti, C. (ed.) *Processi di selezione del crimine. Procure della Repubblica e organizzazione giudiziaria* (Milano: Giuffrè), pp. 117–226.

Blengino, C. (2011) *Percorsi di Giustizia. Efficienza del Sistema Penale e Implementazione delle Politiche Criminali* (Torino: L'Harmattan Italia).
Blengino, C. and G. Torrente (2013), "Nuovo Management Pubblico e Crimini di Impresa: il Caso della Procura di Torino" *Studi sulla questione criminale* 1: 77–95.
Blengino, C. and G. Torrente (2016) "The Choices of the Court Respect Which Crimes to Pursue" – in Palidda, S. (ed.) *Governance of Security and Ignored Insecurities in Contemporary Europe* (London: Routledge), pp. 139–148.
Blumberg, A.S. (1967) "The Practice of Law as Confidence Game: Organizational Cooptation of a Profession" *Law and Society Review* 1: 15–39.
Bona, C. and A. Rumiati (2013) *Psicologia Cognitiva per il Diritto: Ricordare, Pensare, Decidere nell' Esperienza Forense* (Bologna: Il Mulino).
Borgna, P. and M. Maddalena (2003) *Il Giudice e i suoi Limiti* (Roma–Bari: Laterza).
Bourdieu, P. (1986) "La Force du Droit. Eléments pour une Sociologie du Champ Juridique" *Actes de la recherche en Sciences Sociales*, 64: 3–19.
Catellani, P. (1992) *Il Giudice Esperto: Psicologia Cognitiva e Ragionamento Giudiziario* (Bologna: Il Mulino).
Cotterrell, R. (1997) "The Concept of Legal Culture" – in Nelken, D. (ed.) *Comparing Legal Cultures* (Abingdon: Routledge), pp. 13–31.
Cottino, A. and M. Fischer (1995) "Perché la Disuguaglianza di Fronte alla Legge?" – in Cottino, A. and C. Sarzotti (eds) *Diritto uguaglianza e giustizia penale* (Torino: L'Harmattan Italia), pp. 113–142.
Crozier M. (2009) *The Bureaucratic Phenomenon* (New Brunswick and London, Transaction Publishers).
Crozier, M. and E. Friedberg (1997) *L'Acteur et le Système: les Contraintes de l'Action Collective* (Paris: Editions du Seuil).
Damaska, M. (1991) *The Faces of Justice and State Authority* (New Haven, CT: Yale University Press).
Ehrlich, E. [1913] (1976) *Fondamenti della Sociologia del Diritto* (Milano: Giuffrè).
Eisenstein, J. and H. Jacob (1991) *Felony Justice: An Organizational Analysis of Criminal Court* (Lanham, MA: University Press of America).
Esser, J. (1983) *Precomprensione e Scelta del Metodo nel Processo di Individuazione del Diritto: Fondamenti di Razionalità nella Prassi Decisionale del Giudice* (Napoli: Edizioni Scientifiche Italiane).
Fabri, M. (1997) "Discrezionalità e modalità di azione del pubblico ministero nel procedimento penale" *Polis*, XI: 171–192.
Friedberg, E. (1996) *Power and Rules: The Organizational Dynamics of Collective Action* (London: Ashgate Publishing).
Friedman, L.W. (1975) *The Legal System: A Social Science Perspective* (New York: Russell Sage Foundation).
Garapon, A. (2012), *Lo stato minimo. Il neoliberalismo e la giustizia.* Milano: Cortina (orig. 2010. La raison du moindre Etat. Le neoliberalisme et la justice. Paris: Odile Jacob).
Garland, D. (2001) *The Culture of Control: Crime and Social Order in Contemporary Society* (Chicago, IL: University of Chicago Press).
Guarnieri, C. (2011) *La Giustizia in Italia* (Bologna: Il Mulino).
Guarnieri, C. and P. Pederzoli (2002) *La Magistratura nelle Democrazie Contemporanee* (Laterza: Roma-Bari).
Giglioli, P., S. Cavicchioli and G. Fele (1997) *Rituali di Degradazione: Anatomia del Processo Cusani* (Bologna: Il Mulino).

Grossi, P. (2010) *A History of European Law* (Chichester UK: Wiley – Blackwell).
Hart, L.H. (2012) *The Concept of Law* 3rd edn (Oxford: Oxford University Press).
Hester, S. and P. Eglin (1992) *A Sociology of Crime* (London and New York: Routledge).
Hruschka, J. (2009) *La Costituzione del Caso Giuridico: Il Rapporto tra Accertamento Fattuale e Applicazione Giuridica* (Bologna: Il Mulino).
Jakobs, G. (1985) "Kriminalisierung im Vorfeld einer Rechtsgutsverletzung" *Zeitschrift für die gesamte Strafrechtswissenschaft* 97: 751–785.
Kelsen, H. [1934] (1970) *Pure Theory of Law* (Berkley, CA: University of California Press).
Kotter, J.P. (1995) *Leading Change* (Boston, MA: Harvard Business Publishing).
Llewellyn, K. (1930) "A Realistic Jurisprudence. The Next Step" *Columbia Law Revew* 30: 455–456.
Mintzberg, H. (1979) *The Structuring of Organizations* (Upper Saddle River, NJ: Prentice Hall).
Montana, R. (2009) "Pubblico ministero e pratiche di selezione del crimine: Cultura giuridica e rappresentazioni di senso comune: perché si può ancora sperare" *Antigone. Quadrimestrale di critica del sistema penale e penitenziario* 2–3: 274–298.
Mosconi, G. and D. Padovan (eds) (2005) *La Fabbrica dei Delinquenti: Processo Penale e Meccanismi Sociali di Costruzione del Condannato* (Torino: L'Harmattan Italia).
Nelken, D. and M.L. Zanier (2006) "Tra norme e prassi: durata del processo penale e strategie degli operatori del diritto" *Sociologia del Diritto* 1: 146–166.
Palidda, S. (ed.) (2016) *Governance of Security and Ignored Insecurities in Contemporary Europe* (London: Routledge).
Piana, D. (2010) *Magistrati* (Roma: Carocci).
Piana, D. (2016) *Uguale per tutti? Giustizia e Cittadini in Italia* (Bologna: Il Mulino).
Pizzorno, A. (1998) *Il Potere dei Giudici: Stato Democratico e Controllo della Virtù* (Roma-Bari: Laterza).
Pollner, M. (2010) *Mundane Reason: Reality in Everyday and Sociological Discourse* (Cambridge: Cambridge University Press).
Quassoli, F. (1999) "Immigrazione Uguale Criminalità. Rappresentazioni di Senso Comune e Pratiche Organizzative degli Operatori del Diritto" *Rassegna Italiana di Sociologia* 1: 43–75.
Quassoli F. and M. Colombo (2016) "The Governance of Urban Security, Ignored Insecurities and the Securitization of Urban Space (Milan's Case Study)" – in Palidda ,S. (ed.) *Governance of Security and Ignored Insecurities in Contemporary Europe* (London: Routledge), pp. 123–138.
Sarzotti, C. (1995) "Uguaglianza e modelli di processo penale" – in Cottino, A. and C. Sarzotti (eds) *Uguaglianza e giustiziapenale* (Torino: L'Harmattan Italia), pp. 113–141.
Sarzotti C. (2004) "La cultura giuridica dei procuratori generali nelle relazioni inaugurali degli anni giudiziari" – in Balloni, A., G. Mosconi and F. Prina (eds) *Cultura Giuridica e Attori della Giustizia Penal* (Milano: Franco Angeli), pp. 229–254.
Sarzotti, C. (2007) *Processi di Selezione del Crimine: Procure della Repubblica e Organizzazione Giudiziaria* (Milano: Giuffrè).
Simon, J. (2007) *Governing through Crime: How the War on Crime Transformed American Democracy and Created a Culture of Fear* (Oxford: Oxford University Press).
Sudnow, D.N. (1965) "Normal Crimes: Sociological Features of the Penal Code in a Public Defender Office" *Social Problems* 12(3): 255–276.

Spector, M. and J. Kitsuse (2001) *Constructing Social Problems* (London: Transaction Publishers).

Zanier, M.L. (2011) "The Legality Principle within the Italian Criminal Justice System: Normative Principles and Practical Adaptations" – in *Beyond the Statute Law: The "Grey" Government of Criminal Justice Systems* (Macerata: EUM), pp. 95–124.

3 Deferred Prosecution Agreements

Negotiating Punishment Before Conviction?

Simon Bronitt

> "Let the jury consider their verdict", the King said, for about the twentieth time that day.
> "No, no!" said the Queen. "Sentence first – verdict afterwards."
> "Stuff and nonsense!" said Alice loudly. "The idea of having the sentence first!"
> "Hold your tongue!" said the Queen, turning purple.
> "I won't!" said Alice.
> "Off with her head!" the Queen shouted at the top of her voice. Nobody moved.
> (Lewis Carroll, *Alice in Wonderland* (Project Gutenberg Edition, 1865), Ch XII)

Introduction

Over the past decade, the pros and cons of Deferred Prosecution Agreement (DPA) schemes have been much debated within academic, regulatory and policy circles.[1] The prevailing consensus in Australia, which mirrors the position in the United States and United Kingdom, is that DPA schemes provide a valuable, cost-effective regulatory tool for prosecutors and regulatory agencies dealing with serious corporate crime.[2] The principal benefit, brought into sharp focus by the regulatory aftermath of the Global Financial Crisis (GFC) in 2007–2008, is that the DPA schemes avoid, or at least mitigate against, serious collateral harms caused to national and global markets flowing from prosecution action taken (or even threatened) against multinational corporations.[3] While the DPA provides a regulatory response to multinational corporations that are considered "Too Big to Fail" and "Too Big to Jail", it raises objections that corporate impunity (albeit conditionally granted under the terms of the DPA) undermines the rule of law, and ultimately may be ineffective in preventing or changing corporate misbehaviour.[4]

The aim of this chapter is not to rehearse arguments "for" and "against" DPA schemes, a debate that has been exhaustively examined in academic writings, government policy papers and parliamentary submissions.[5] Rather, this chapter has a different focus, namely to examine how DPA schemes support or subvert conviction-based paradigms of criminal justice, and how instruments like the DPA are changing the role of prosecution agencies within the system. Subverting the central place of the criminal trial and punishment is hardly novel: there exist many legal measures with coercive effects, framed in terms of incapacitation and prevention, that do not depend upon either proof of guilt or conviction, but which nevertheless have punitive, coercive and purported deterrent effects. The DPA joins a crowded field of innovative regulatory tools: civil penalties, enforceable undertakings, as well as non-conviction freezing and confiscation orders are now available to combat with a wide range of criminality, both individual and corporate. Part I examines how the DPA, though novel in form, is part of a much longer trajectory of hybrid justice, one which melds a range of purposes and functions, deterrent, punitive, incapacitative, preventive, restorative and restitutionary. Accepting that legal hybrids have been normalised in many modern legal systems, Part II explores how negotiating justice using new hybrids, such as DPAs, poses new challenges for those prosecutors and regulators dealing with corporate crime and misconduct.[6]

Part I – Negotiating DPAs: Bargaining in the Shadow of the Criminal Law?

For the last five years, there has been extensive consultation over whether Australia should adopt a DPA scheme, with the debate focused on whether our scheme should follow the US administrative model or the UK judicial model.[7] A Bill, currently before the Australian Parliament, has been referred to the Senate Legal and Constitutional Affairs Legislation Committee for consideration, with the final report due on 20 April 2018.[8] The economic rationale underlying the proposed DPA scheme is related to a broader policy, which is encouraging corporations to self-report criminal conduct, which from the corporate perspective offers greater certainty in outcomes compared with resolution by litigation, civil and/or criminal.[9]

Under the proposed DPA scheme, corporations suspected of certain serious criminal offences may be invited by the Commonwealth Director of Public Prosecutions (CDPP) to negotiate and enter into an agreement to suspend criminal proceedings upon compliance with certain conditions. Diverging from the US administrative model, which is entirely governed by agency guidelines and policy statements, the Australian model adopts a statutory model, following the approach in the *Crime and Courts Act 2013* (UK). But unlike the UK model, the Australian model would not be subject to independent judicial oversight. Due to concerns relating to the potential breach of separation of powers, which is enshrined in Chapter III of the Australian Constitution, the decision to enter into negotiations, as well as the approval of the final agreement, cannot be vested in a judge or court that exercises federal power. As several expert submissions have noted, the constitutional objection to judicial involvement in the DPA schemes may be overcome by vesting the powers in a retired judge or member of the Administrative Appeal Tribunal.[10] The current Bill under consideration by the Commonwealth Parliament vests this power in an "approving officer", who is defined as an appropriately experienced former judicial officer of a federal, State or Territory court.

Since the UK scheme was introduced in 2013,[11] four DPAs have been approved, though only details of three are publicly available.[12] These include:

- The $33 million (US$) settlement between Standard Bank PLC and the Serious Fraud Office (SFO) in 2015. The indictment alleged that Standard Bank had failed to prevent bribery engaged in by a former sister company that had made a $6 million payment intended to induce members of the Tanzanian Government to favour their proposal for a private placement.[13]
- The £497.25 million settlement between Rolls-Royce and the SFO in 2017. The DPA relates to conduct spanning three decades, including "12 counts of conspiracy to corrupt, false accounting and failure to prevent bribery" occurring across seven jurisdictions.[14]
- The £235 million settlement between Tesco PLC and the SFO in 2017. The DPA relates to allegations of false accounting (with Tesco Stores Ltd, a subsidiary of the retailer, having overstated its profits by £326 million).[15]

Under the UK scheme, the judicial officer must be satisfied that the DPA serves the "interests of justice", and that its terms are "fair, reasonable and proportionate".[16] DPA terms typically require corporations to make payment of a pecuniary penalty, cooperate with investigating authorities and reimburse their investigation costs, engage in remedial action, provide compensation for adversely affected persons, facilitate confiscation of illicit profits or proceeds of crime, and enforcement, as well as submit to governance and organisational reform.[17] The Australian list of proposed crimes covered by the DPA scheme is narrow: foreign bribery, false accounting, dealing with proceeds of crime, money laundering and dishonest conduct, as well as sanctions offences.[18]

Some DPA terms manifest a punitive or more precisely *quasi*-punitive quality,[19] while others serve more preventive, restitutionary or restorative functions. DPAs, like sentencing, serve a range of aims, though unlike modern sentencing legislation these aims are not expressly articulated in the legislation. This deficiency has not been rectified in the proposed Australian Bill, notwithstanding calls for a more coherent policy and philosophy based on preventive and restorative justice.[20] By maintaining the central focus on the DPA's punitive function, following the UK model, the Bill wrongly focuses attention upon whether an agreement is "fair, reasonable and proportionate". Rather than apply this set of limiting principles, which underscore sentencing law and human right derogations (to minimise adverse impacts upon individual rights), the better approach is to focus on whether there are reasonable grounds to believe that the DPA is likely to serve the "public interest" by *effectively* preventing corporate harm and providing compensation.[21] In relation to proportionality, the issue is not whether severity of the pecuniary penalty is proportionate – that is, perfectly correlates or matches the degree of harm and/or culpability of the offender. The Bill's requirement that the approving officer be satisfied that DPA serves the "interests of justice", which simply copies formula in the UK model, is inadvisable, since it comes perilously close to trenching upon Chapter III's constitutional prohibition on vesting judicial roles and powers in administrative functionaries.[22]

Although not contingent upon any formal judicial determination of guilt, the DPA is negotiated in the "shadow of the criminal law". The process that leads to the DPA is administrative rather than judicial in nature. That said, the DPA has many trappings of adversarial justice including the following:

- appointing an independent and experienced "judicious" person (a serving or retired judge) who presides over the process, applies relevant statutory criteria, and ultimately approves and adjudicates upon corporate compliance with the terms of the DPA;
- making formal admissions (relating to facts, if not guilt) linked to specified offences;
- imposing financial or pecuniary "penalties" equivalent to the fines that would apply following conviction, as well as "restorative" options such as providing a public apology and victim compensation.[23]

An analogy may be drawn with the professional rugby players fronting disciplinary "charges" before the "Judiciary" Committees for "Code" violations. The players, who are legally represented, view the hearing as a judicial process. They make pleas, offer defences and submit to penalties when found guilty. Due process must be observed and judgments delivered publicly. But like the DPA process, no court has been constituted to determine whether the "offender" is guilty or not, and the "penalties" imposed are strictly civil in nature, authorised by the relevant sporting codes of conduct or incorporated through contracts of employment used in professional sport.[24] In a similar way, the "legal" process and "punitive" consequences of the DPA, from an external shareholder and market perspective, appears *prima facie* to have the finality of criminal punishment, no different from usual (post-conviction) sentencing outcomes. Since the fines or penalties applied to corporations potentially run into the billions, the settlement of an imminent or ongoing criminal investigation, with attendant media publicity, has an immediate positive effect on the corporation's share price and market confidence.[25] Of course, the conventional sequence of prosecution, conviction and punishment remains a fall-back for regulators, triggered in cases where the corporation fails to adhere to, or breaches, the terms of the DPA.

"Sentence first – verdict afterwards", the Queen of Hearts petulantly demanded in Lewis Carroll's *Alice in Wonderland*, provoking stunned silence from her court, and vigorous objections from Alice! DPAs manifest similar "process inversion", with some trappings of adversarial justice with quasi-punitive and coercive qualities. In the next Part, we examine the legal risks for regulatory agencies engaged in bargaining in the shadow of the law – whether criminal, civil or hybrid – and how policy-makers, prosecutors and regulators, if such measures are to be successful over the long term, must give greater attention to upholding due process, fairness and public confidence in the administration of justice.

Part II – Negotiating DPAs: Unjust Bargaining at the Boundaries of the Criminal and Civil Law?

Justice should neither be bought nor sold.[26] But legal outcomes are often negotiated between the parties. In the resolution of both civil and criminal proceedings, negotiation between the parties is ubiquitous – it defines the scope of the legal dispute, the mode of trial, and the issues of evidence and law that will be contested (or not). Though negotiation is forensically pervasive, when it comes to the *final* judicial determination of legal liability, in either the form of an award of civil damages or imposition of sentence, the law strives to maintain a sharp line between the civil and criminal processes. The Australian High Court has recently examined this question, in two decisions, outlining the respective roles and duties of prosecutors, regulators and courts in "striking just bargains". These decisions in 2014 and 2015 clarified that these roles and duties vary according to whether the proceedings relate to the imposition of criminal, as opposed to civil, penalties.

The daily reality of bargaining between prosecution and defence lawyers is empirically well known,[27] although there are significant differences in how "plea bargaining" takes place between common law jurisdictions. US-style "plea bargaining" that involves a judge "sealing the deal" struck between the prosecution and defence – relating to charge, guilty plea and penalty – is not practised in other common law jurisdictions such as Australia.[28] Indeed, the majority of the High Court in *Barbaro v The Queen; Zirilli v The Queen* reiterated the orthodox attitude to plea bargaining as follows:

> First, it is for the prosecution, alone, to decide what charges are to be preferred against an accused person. Secondly, it is for the accused person, alone, to decide whether to plead guilty to the charges preferred. That decision cannot be made with any foreknowledge of what sentence will be imposed. Neither the prosecution nor the offender's advisers can do anything more than proffer an opinion as to what might reasonably be expected to happen. Thirdly, and of most immediate importance in these applications, it is for the sentencing judge, alone, to decide what sentence will be imposed.[29]

While as a matter of law, the judge in Australia must not be involved plea negotiations, there is extensive scope for charge negotiation between the prosecution and defence. There is much greater transparency and accountability in Australia since the introduction in the 1990s of charge negotiation guidelines. While the difference between various models appears stark, in practice, there is still considerable room for negotiation, since the choice of charges (a matter exclusively for the DPP) has a significant impact on the penalty range, and thus punishment severity, available to the court.[30] For corporations that are under criminal investigation there is a similar scope for negotiation: in relation to foreign bribery and corporate fraud cases, deferred prosecution and settlement agreements are often presented to the public as "major wins", headlining million or even billion dollar penalties. But examined closely, the DPAs or settlements with corporations in the US and UK often relate to lesser charges such as "false accounting"[31] or "failure to prevent foreign bribery".[32] In the Australian context, in 2016 a new false accounting offence was inserted into the *Criminal Code* (Cth); in relation to the latter, a Bill now before Parliament proposes to enact a new offence, modelled on the *Bribery Act 2010* (UK), that criminalises "failing to prevent bribery of a foreign public official".[33] Enacting new ancillary offences provides prosecutors and regulators with an expanded range of legal "bargaining chips" in relation to which legal deals over charge, plea and punishment can be struck.

While the High Court jealously guarded judicial independence in the sentencing process, rejecting judicial involvement in pre-trial sentence indications and prosecutors presenting "done deals" over pleas and penalties for judicial approval, the Court adopted a very different approach to negotiations and agreements reached in relation to civil penalties.

"Civil penalty" is not a legal oxymoron. The past two decades in Australia have witnessed, as in other jurisdictions, a policy shift away from using criminal prosecution to deal with corporate illegality in favour of civil and administrative remedies. Rather than invoke criminal prosecution, the national corporate watchdog, the Australian Security and Investment Commission (ASIC), applies a range of civil measures including pecuniary penalties and enforceable undertakings to deal with violations of corporate law, such as breach of directors' duties.[34] Civil measures are not confined to breaches of corporations law, but extend to other fields such as anti-money laundering laws, as revealed in a number of recent cases involving iconic national business and banking institutions.[35] Australia has an extensive system of civil and administrative penalties operating alongside, or as an alternative to, criminal prosecution across a range of regulatory spheres including consumer and trade practices, corporations and industrial relations law.[36]

The differences between criminal, civil and administrative penalties relate to judicial involvement in the respective processes; while criminal and civil penalties are imposed by a court, administrative penalties are imposed at the discretion of the regulator in accordance with the aims and powers under the enabling legislation. Both civil and administrative penalties, while not contingent upon criminal conviction, nevertheless have significant financial and regulatory consequences.[37]

In *Commonwealth of Australia v Director, Fair Work Building Industry Inspectorate* (2015) 258 CLR 482, the High Court considered whether or not the principles in *Barbaro*, discussed above, apply to legal proceedings used to determine civil penalties. Noting that the imposition of civil penalties lacked the moral stigma of criminal conviction and punishment,[38] the High Court unanimously held that the legal protections that ordinarily applied to criminal trials did not apply to civil penalty proceedings. Moreover, the Court held that regulators in civil penalty proceedings, though statutory office holders, were acting as civil litigants and not prosecutors. Regulators were not bound by the same duties as prosecutors, thus leaving scope for the parties to settle disputes by agreement as to appropriate penalties. In these cases, the role of the court is only to be persuaded that the agreement reached is appropriate, within the permissible range in all the circumstances.[39]

The two spheres of justice – civil and criminal – should remain separate, at least in relation to how criminal and civil penalties are negotiated and imposed.[40] The approach of the High Court in the two decisions considered above, diverges from the international human rights jurisprudence on the right to a fair trial, which focuses on the "substance rather than form" of the legal proceeding in order to determine which fairness guarantees ought to apply.[41] In general terms, the more coercive or punitive a particular legal process, the greater attention must be given to fairness and due process considerations. DPAs granted under the proposed Australian model, in common with other administrative measures, such as enforceable undertakings, are rarely subject to further judicial review. Where such review has occurred in relation to civil penalties or other similarly coercive measures, the courts have sought an exactness of proof far in excess of the statutorily prescribed civil standard based on the "balance of probabilities".[42] Applying this variable hybrid standard of proof in civil penalty proceedings, though creating uncertainty and more challenge for regulators, has the virtue of consistency with contemporary international human rights jurisprudence on the fair trial.[43]

It must be noted that the right to a fair trial under the common law in Australia has a narrow ambit.[44] In its current form, the right is unlikely to extend to pre-trial processes and/or proceedings that have an administrative rather than judicial character. That said, it must be recalled that Australia's obligation to respect Article 6 of the ICCPR is placed not only upon the Judiciary, but also upon the Executive and Legislature. There is clearly scope for enhancing the fairness of the DPA process in relation to the administrative guidance and statutory criteria. It is beyond the scope of this chapter to catalogue all potential unfairness arising from current and proposed DPA schemes, though a review of public submissions identifies the following range of potential risks in the Australian context:

- "Double Jeopardy": in cases where a corporation pays its "penalty" under the DPA, but following its breach, is prosecuted, convicted and punished (again) for conduct arising from same facts and offences covered by the DPA.[45]
- "Full Answer and Defence": the making of admissions is a key part of the DPA, though inclusion of non-contradiction clauses in the agreement may seek to prevent the corporation from contesting or excluding earlier admissions of fact. Such contractual clauses, while common in the US, have the potential to cause unfairness at the trial, limiting the right of the defence to challenge the relevance, weight or admissibility of key evidence supporting the prosecution.[46]

- "Abuse of Process": in cases where the DPA includes recovery of investigation costs, which are often substantial, there is a risk that public confidence in the administration of justice may be undermined. Budgetary pressures may place undue pressure upon the investigative agency to "cut a deal" over charges and penalties, which prejudices the integrity of the DPA process and the public officials involved in the negotiations.

DPA schemes may be inevitable in an era of deregulation that is now reeling from a torrent of corporate scandals, in which both regulators and political leaders demand tougher responses against corporate crime. Greg Medcalf, Chair of Australian Securities and Investments Commission in 2017, made public calls to "Lift the Fear, and Suppress the Greed", which is code for implementing harsh penalties, consistently applied, to deter individual white-collar and corporate crime.[47] Even if tougher penalties and zero tolerance are proven to be effective, they cannot be at the expense of fundamental justice. Fairness in hybrid processes may not precisely conform to that found in the traditional criminal justice model. But to preserve legitimacy, and enhance respect for and compliance with the law, DPA schemes, and related guidelines and policies, must pay special consideration to these interests of fairness.

But this may raise an objection, beyond the scope of this chapter, about whether human rights, including the right to a fair trial, can or should be invoked by corporations.[48] Legal persons, like corporations, are not human beings, and, so it logically follows that corporations should not be considered beneficiaries of *human* rights. Of course, they are bound to respect the human rights of other persons, and the past three decades has seen a significant global movement to fix human rights obligations upon corporations as an aspect of corporate social responsibility.[49] Corporations, for now, are not indisputably holders of human rights. Whatever the outcome of this debate, there are strong practical arguments in favour of ensuring that corporations investigated for wrongdoing – whether criminal, civil or administrative – should be treated fairly. After all, corporations are legal entities constituted by *real* people, who are engaged in joint endeavours as directors, workers and shareholders. If procedural justice research teaches anything, treating corporations and the people who constitute these "legal persons" with fairness, will promote higher levels of compliance with the underlying norm, even where the anticipated costs are adverse to the corporate interest (such as substantial penalties imposed under a DPA).[50]

Conclusion

Corporations, it has long been observed, have "no soul to be damned and no body to be kicked".[51] Perhaps as a result of these corporal limitations, the size of pecuniary penalties and consistency of enforcement dominate the political and regulatory agendas of politicians, policy-makers and regulators. DPAs embody a pragmatic truth about the power of money and markets, namely, that conventional criminal justice responses may not work for multinational corporations that have become "Too Big to Fail" and "Too Big to Jail". But the underlying assumption – that substantial mega-penalties are essential for effective deterrence – is contestable. A recent systematic review of available research concluded that, contrary to the claims of most regulators, prosecutors, judges, economists and legal scholars, there is no convincing evidence establishing that legal sanctions have significant deterrent effects on corporations.[52] Yet for judges, general deterrence often continues to loom large in their decisions imposing record-breaking penalties upon corporations.[53] Applying mega-penalties to corporations for regulatory offences invariably lacks the moral opprobrium felt when fraud and dishonesty convictions attach to individual offenders. There is always the risk that the DPA and associated penalties will be viewed by senior corporate executives and shareholders simply as another "cost of doing business".[54]

DPAs stand at the intersection of two paradigms of criminal justice: on the one hand, there is the idea of criminal justice as a system of surveillance, risk management and coercive control; and, on the other hand, there is the idea of criminal justice as a sequential process of investigation, trial and punishment according to due process of law. In relation to the former, the system seeks to exercise control over "suspect" persons, property and organisations (including legal persons such as corporations); while in relation to the latter, the process is directed to the detection of offenders *and* bringing them to justice before the courts to be dealt with according to law. As explored above, the forensic standards often diverge across these two paradigms: standards of proof, disclosure obligations and other fairness guarantees will be adapted to suit, or even ignored by, new hybrid processes. As this chapter explored, the sharpness of the binary between civil and criminal law is increasingly tested by the emergence of legal hybridity.[55] The legislative legitimation of DPAs in the UK, and likely imminent arrival in Australia, can be viewed as yet another dangerous derogation or exception undermining traditional notions of trial-centred justice and due process. An alternative view is that legal hybridity is another mode of "doing justice" that enlists a range of new civil and administrative remedies for the pursuit of criminal justice ends. In relation to DPAs, the longstanding discretion *not* to prosecute in the public interest is strategically re-purposed for corporate offenders. By adapting, extending and codifying the existing discretion that inheres in the office of public prosecutor, the DPA creates new systems of surveillance, risk management and coercive control over corporate criminality, the costs and benefits of which will continue to be debated for years to come.

Notes

1 Since 2015, public submissions have been invited to the Attorney General's Department, as well as various Senate Standing Committees on the introduction of DPA schemes in Australia: Senate Standing Committee on Economics, Parliament of Australia, *An Inquiry into The Measures Governing the Activities of Australian Corporations, Entities, Organisations, Individuals, Government and Related Parties with respect to Foreign Bribery* (2015); Attorney General's Department, *Improving*

Enforcement Options for Serious Corporate Crime: A Proposed Model for a Deferred Prosecution Agreements Scheme in Australia – Public Consultation Paper (March 2016) www.ag.gov.au/Consultations/Pages/Deferred-prosecution-agreements-public-consultation.aspx. The March 2017 public consultation paper is available from www.ag.gov.au/Consultations/Documents/Deferred-prosecution-agreement-scheme/A-proposed-model-for-a-deferred-prosecution-agreement-scheme-in-australia.pdf. See also, Senate Standing Committee on Legal and Constitutional Affairs, Parliament of Australia, *Crimes Legislation Amendment (Combatting Corporate Crime) Bill 2017* www.aph.gov.au/Parliamentary_Business/Committees/Senate/Legal_and_Constitutional_Affairs/CombattingCrime/Submissions.

2 See Explanatory Memorandum, Crimes Legislation Amendment (Combatting Corporate Crime) Bill 2017 (Cth) 4: DPAs will "avoid some of the … financial costs associated with lengthy criminal investigations and trial processes".

3 It is claimed that enforcement action poses the risk of precipitating major corporate failures, though the evidence on this point is debatable: see Federico Mazzacuva, "Justifications and Purposes of Negotiated Justice for Corporate Offenders: Deferred and Non-Prosecution Agreements in the UK and US Systems of Criminal Justice" (2014) 78(3) *Journal of Criminal Law* 249, 250; Peter Spivack and Sujit Raman, "Regulating the 'New Regulators': Current Trends in Deferred Prosecution Agreements" (2008) 45(2) *American Criminal Law Review* 159, 165.

4 Rule of law concerns relating to threats to equality before the law and separation of powers are discussed in Anesha Gnana Kumar, Eda Ince, Tony Chan and Harkiran Kaur, *Criminal v Civil Penalties: The Art of the Deal with Regulators in Australia* (2017).

5 See for example Simon Bronitt, "Regulatory Bargaining In The Shadows of Preventive Justice: Deferred Prosecution Agreements" in Tamara Tulich, Rebecca Ananian-Welsh, Simon Bronitt and Sarah Murray (eds), *Regulating Preventive Justice: Principle, Policy and Paradox* (Routledge, 2017) 211–226; see also Simon Bronitt, "New Paradigms for Regulating Institutional Child Sexual Abuse: Lessons from Corporate Crime and White-Collar Criminals" in Yorick Smaal, Andy Kaladelfos and Mark Finnane, *The Sexual Abuse of Children: Recognition and Redress* (Monash University Press, 2016) 190; Justin O'Brien, "The Sword of Damocles: Deferred Prosecutions and the Search for Accountability" in Justin O'Brien and George Gilligan (eds), *Integrity, Risk and Accountability in Capital Markets: Regulating Culture* (Hart Publishing, 2013) 161; Peter Spivack and Sujit Raman, "Regulating the 'New Regulators': Current Trends in Deferred Prosecution Agreements" (2008) 45(2) *American Criminal Law Review* 159; Michael Bisgrove and Mark Weekes, "Deferred Prosecution Agreements: A Practical Consideration" (2014) 6 *Criminal Law Review* 416. For submissions to the Senate Standing Committee on the introduction of DPA schemes, see Parliament of Australia, *Submissions received by the Committee* (March 2018) www.aph.gov.au/Parliamentary_Business/Committees/Senate/Legal_and_Constitutional_Affairs/CombattingCrime/Submissions.

6 Simon Bronitt and Susan Donkin, "Australian Responses to 9/11: A New World Legal Hybrid?" in Aniceto Masferrer (ed.), *Post 9/11 and the State of Permanent Legal Emergency: Security and Human Rights in Countering Terrorism* (Springer, 2012) 223.

7 The difference between the schemes is reviewed in Simon Bronitt, "Regulatory Bargaining in the Shadows of Preventive Justice: Deferred Prosecution Agreements" in Tamara Tulich, Rebecca Ananian-Welsh, Simon Bronitt and Sarah Murray (eds), *Regulating Preventive Justice: Principle, Policy and Paradox* (Abingdon, Oxon: Routledge, 2017) 211–226, 215ff.

8 See Crimes Legislation Amendment (Combatting Corporate Crime) Bill 2017 (Cth), introduced 6 December 2017.

9 In relation to foreign bribery offences, the AFP and CDPP recently issued detailed guidance applied to corporations which self-report potential breaches of the *Criminal Code* (Cth). Ten (non-exhaustive) factors were identified as relevant to whether prosecuting a self-reporting corporation is in the public interest: *AFP and CDPP Best Practice Guidelines, Self-Reporting of foreign Bribery and Related Offending by Corporations* (7 December 2017) at [15].

10 This solution has been adopted to the issuing of telecommunications interception warrants in Australia, which has been held to be an administrative function: Simon Bronitt and James Stellios, "Regulating Telecommunications Interception and Access in the Twenty-First Century: Technological Evolution or Legal Revolution?" (2006) 24 *Prometheus* 414.

11 *Crime and Courts Act 2013* (UK) c 22, sch 17, part 1, s 1(1).

12 Serious Fraud Office (UK), *Deferred Prosecution Agreements* (2018) www.sfo.gov.uk/publications/guidance-policy-and-protocols/deferred-prosecution-agreements/.

13 Serious Fraud Office (UK), *Case Information: Standard Bank PLC* (10 December 2015) www.sfo.gov.uk/cases/standard-bank-plc/.

14 Serious Fraud Office (UK), *SFO Completes £497.25m Deferred Prosecution Agreement with Rolls-Royce PLC* (News release, 17 January 2017) www.sfo.gov.uk/2017/01/17/sfo-completes-497-25m-deferred-prosecution-agreement-rolls-royce-plc/.

15 Serious Fraud Office, *SFO Agrees Deferred Prosecution Agreement with Tesco* (News Release, 10 April 2017) www.sfo.gov.uk/2017/04/10/sfo-agrees-deferred-prosecution-agreement-with-tesco/.

16 Guidelines under the Act have been issued to assist prosecutors negotiate DPAs: see Serious Fraud Office (UK), *Deferred Prosecution Agreements: New Guidance for Prosecutors* (News Release, 14 February 2014).

17 The list is not exhaustive. See statutory list of conditions that may be included: *Crime and Courts Act 2013* (UK) c 22, sch 17, part 1, s 5(3)(a)–(g). There is a core expectation however that the corporation granted access to a DPA will "to admit to agreed facts, cooperate with any related investigation, pay a financial penalty and implement a compliance program": Commonwealth, *Parliamentary Debates*, Senate, 6 December 2017, 9907 (Michael Keenan).

18 The rationale for limiting DPAs to these offences is that they "are often difficult to detect, investigate and prosecute": Commonwealth, *Parliamentary Debates*, Senate, 6 December 2017, 9907 (Michael Keenan).

19 My preference for the label "quasi-punitive" for DPAs reflects the fact that "pecuniary" penalties paid under a DPA do not follow any judicial finding of guilt (or legal responsibility) in either the criminal or civil jurisdiction.

20 It has been suggested that the DPAs should be framed around preventive and restorative aims, rather than quasi-punitive and retributive aims: see Simon Bronitt, "Regulatory Bargaining In The Shadows of Preventive Justice: Deferred Prosecution Agreements" in Tamara Tulich, Rebecca Ananian-Welsh, Simon Bronitt and Sarah Murray (eds), *Regulating Preventive Justice: Principle, Policy and Paradox* (Abingdon, Oxon: Routledge, 2017), 211–226. The lack of a coherent restorative philosophy underlying DPA schemes has been criticised by John Braithwaite in "Cultures of Redemptive Finance" in Justin O'Brien and George Gilligan (eds), *Integrity, Risk and Accountability in Capital Markets – Regulating Culture* (Hart Publishing, 2013) 282.

21 This point is developed in Simon Bronitt, "Submission to the Attorney-General's Department Inquiry into Improving enforcement options for serious corporate crime: A proposed model for a Deferred Prosecution Agreement (DPA) scheme in Australia" www.ag.gov.au/Consultations/Documents/Proposed-model-for-a-deferred-prosecution-agreement-scheme-in-australia/Bronnit-DPA-submission.PDF.

22 Constitutional concerns arising out of the use of this terminology are discussed in Simon Bronitt and Zoe Brereton, "Submission to the Senate Legal and Constitutional

Affairs Legislation Committee: Crimes Legislation Amendment (Combatting Corporate Crime) Bill 2017, 4.

23 However pecuniary or financial penalties will ordinarily be discounted where there has been prompt self-disclosure and effective cooperation with authorities. This "discount" is reflected in the proposed DPA scheme, which states that the CDPP, in determining the severity of the financial penalty, must consider the degree of cooperation, the severity of penalty that would apply if convicted, and the other proposed terms contained in the DPA: Crimes Legislation Amendment (Combatting Corporate Crime) Bill 2017 (Cth), cl 17C(3).

24 See further, Rule of Law Institute of Australia, *Sport and the Rule of Law in Australia* (2013) www.ruleoflaw.org.au/wp-content/uploads/2013/12/Rule-of-Law.

25 For example, upon announcement of Takata corporation's "settlement" with US regulators, share prices reportedly increased by 17 per cent: "Takata Fined $1Bn in US over Exploding Airbag Scandal" *BBC News* (online) 13 January 2017 www.bbc.com/news/business-38613030.

26 The ideal is commonly traced to clause 40 of the *Magna Carta 1215* (English version) which provides, "To no one will we sell, to no one deny or delay right or justice".

27 Jacqueline Hodgson and Andrew Roberts, "Criminal Process and Prosecution" in Peter Cane and Henry Kritzer (eds), *The Oxford Handbook of Empirical Legal Research* (Oxford University Press, 2010) provides an excellent survey of empirical research on prosecution, and the wide range of legal and non-legal factors that shape decision-making.

28 Pre-trial negotiation between the defence and prosecution is ubiquitous in many common law systems, though the policies, practices and restrictions on the practices vary: see Carol Brook, Bruno Fiannaca, David Harvey, Paul Marcus, Jenny McEwan and Renee Pomerance, "A Comparative Look at Plea Bargaining in Australia, Canada, England, New Zealand, and the United States" (2016) 57 *William and Mary Law Review* 1147.e.

29 (2014) 253 CLR 58, 76 at [47].

30 Charge negotiation, therefore, is in part negotiation over the penalty *range*, if not a binding agreement between the prosecution and defence on a *precise* agreed penalty.

31 Admissions to federal "books and records" offence feature prominently in settlements or DPAs in the US: see Mike Koehler, "Measuring the Impact of Non-Prosecution and Deferred Prosecution Agreements on Foreign Corrupt Practices Act Enforcement" (2015) 49 *University of California Davis Law Review* 497. In 2016, Australia inserted two new false accounting offences into the *Criminal Code* (Cth), ss 490.1(1(b) and 490.2(1)(b). The offences apply to corporations or individuals that intentionally or recklessly "conceal illegitimate payments by making, altering, or destroying accounting records, or by failing to make or alter accounting records that are required by law to be made or altered". The new offences supplement existing legal measures in the *Corporations Act 2001* (Cth) imposing an obligation to keep financial records (s 286), and not to falsify books (s 1307).

32 *Bribery Act 2010* (UK), s 7.

33 Crimes Legislation Amendment (Combatting Corporate Crime) Bill 2017 (Cth), cl 70.5A.

34 See generally Vicky Comino, *Australia's "Company Law Watchdog": ASIC and Corporate Regulation* (Lawbook Co., 2015). For an empirical study revealing the shift towards civil responses see Jasper Hedges, Helen Louise Bird, George Gilligan, Andrew Godwin, and Ian Ramsay, "The Policy and Practice of Enforcement of Directors' Duties by Statutory Agencies in Australia: An Empirical Analysis" (2017) 40(3) *Melbourne University Law Review* 905.

35 In August 2017, the Commonwealth Bank (CBA) was accused of enabling money laundering and terrorism: Concise Statement, *Chief Executive Officer of the Australian Transaction Reports and Analysis Centre* v *Commonwealth Bank of Australia*

(3 August 2017) www.austrac.gov.au/sites/default/files/20170803-concise-statement-cba-s.pdf. The latest accusation against CBA alleges unconscionable dealing in the manipulation of the interbank interest rates: "ASIC Brings Legal Action Against CBA over Alleged 'Unconscionable Conduct'" *SBS News* (online) 30 January 2018, www.sbs.com.au/news/asic-brings-legal-action-against-cba-over-alleged-unconscionable-conduct. A similar allegation in the UK that individual bank officials' manipulation of the LIBOR rate has led to the prosecution of 12 people. See for example *R v Hayes* [2015] EWCA Crim 1944.

36 Civil penalties are not limited to minor regulatory breaches. As the Federal Court in Australia observed in *Chief Executive Officer of Australian Transaction Reports and Analysis Centre v TAB Limited (No 3)* [2017] FCA 1296, breaches by the TAB Limited of the *Anti-Money Laundering and Counter-Terrorism Financing Act 2006* (Cth) (AML/CTF Act), though "dry in nature" and not deliberate, went to the "heart of the operation" of the AML/CTF Act. Imposing a substantial civil penalty, the court gave special weight to "general deterrence", so that it is known that even minor breaches of the Act have very serious consequences for the regulatory agencies: [17].

37 The distinctions are explained in Australian Law Reform Commission, *Principled Regulation: Federal Civil and Administrative Penalties in Australia*, Report No 95 (2002).

38 *Commonwealth of Australia v Director, Fair Work Building Industry Inspectorate* (2015) 258 CLR 482, [17] and [54]-[55].

39 *Commonwealth of Australia v Director, Fair Work Building Industry Inspectorate* (2015) 258 CLR 482, [57] (French CJ, Kiefel, Bell, Nettle and Gordon JJ) and [78] (Gageler J). French CJ, Kiefel, Bell, Nettle and Gordon JJ delivered a joint judgment with which Keane J agreed (and made additional comments on the nature of the difference between civil and criminal proceedings). Gageler J (in a separate concurring judgment) held at [78] that "[s]ubject to its statutory charter, the regulator is permitted to advocate for a litigious outcome which the regulator considers to be in the public interest". For further discussion of the legal issues prior to the High Court ruling see Rebecca Ananian-Welsh and Katie Glover, "Before the High Court: Commonwealth v Director, Fair Work Building Industry Inspectorate: The End of Penalty Agreements in Civil Pecuniary Penalty Schemes?" [2015] 37 *Sydney Law Review* 417.

40 As Keane J conceded at [89]ff., "It must be acknowledged immediately that the distinction between criminal and civil cases does not hold for all purposes".

41 Australia is a party to the International Covenant on Civil and Political Rights (ICCPR). Article 14 ICCPR guarantees the right, in both criminal and civil proceedings, to a "fair and public hearing by a competent, independent and impartial tribunal established by law". The specific fair trial guarantees for criminal proceedings are enumerated in Art 14.3. See further, Simon Bronitt and Bernadette McSherry, *Principles of Criminal Law* (Lawbook Co, 4th edn, 2017) 127 [2.145].

42 Although the legislature may designate a proceeding as a "civil proceeding", the courts in Australia have continued to apply a modified civil standard of proof first applied by the High Court in *Briginshaw v Briginshaw* (1938) 60 CLR 336; see Vicky Comino, "Australia's 'Company Law Watchdog': The Australian Securities and Investments Commission and the Civil Penalties Regime" (2014) 3 *Journal of Business Law* 228, 246.

43 For an excellent article explaining how the modified civil standard of proof hampers ASIC's ability to develop a coherent enforcement strategy based on the principles of responsive regulation and its enforcement pyramid, see Vicky Comino, "Australia's 'Company Law Watchdog': The Australian Securities and Investments Commission and the Civil Penalties Regime" (2014) 3 *Journal of Business Law* 228, 247.

44 The evolution of the common law right to a fair trial is reviewed in Simon Bronitt and Bernadette McSherry, *Principles of Criminal Law* (Lawbook Co, 4th edn, 2017) 111–126.

45 A collateral issue of cross border "double jeopardy" arose in *R v Innospec* Ltd [2010] EW Misc 7 (EWCC). Thomas LJ was highly critical of the plea agreement struck between the SFO and Innospec, that was part of a global settlement in relation to corruption investigations instituted in the US and UK. The judge reiterated that criminal penalties were a matter for the court alone, criticizing the agreement's inclusion of "civil recovery order" which had served to reduce the overall level of fine. The structure of the agreement sought mitigate against double jeopardy, which in the opinion of Thomas LJ, led to a "wholly unsatisfactory" penalty.

46 For example, further enquiries by the corporation may reveal that the prosecution case was based on incriminating "facts" obtained by illegal or improper means, such as entrapment. The conditions of the DPA may operate to prevent effective challenges by the defence to the admissibility of key prosecution evidence: see further Simon Bronitt, "Regulatory Bargaining in the Shadows of Preventive Justice: Deferred Prosecution Agreements" in Tamara Tulich, Rebecca Ananian-Welsh, Simon Bronitt and Sarah Murray (eds), *Regulating Preventive Justice: Principle, Policy and Paradox* (Routledge, 2017) 220.

47 This phrase was coined by former ASIC Chair, Greg Medcraft, while bemoaning the limited penalties available to regulators to promote both general and specific deterrence. A Senate Inquiry assessing the effectiveness of penalties for white collar crime was heavily influenced by Medcraft's view: Senate Economics References Committee, *"Lifting the Fear and Suppressing the Greed": Penalties for White-Collar Crime and Corporate and Financial Misconduct in Australia* (March 2017).

48 Arguments in favour of granting certain human rights to corporations are canvassed in Michael K. Addo, "The Corporation as a Victim of Human Rights Violations" in Michael K. Addo (ed.), *Human Rights Standards and the Responsibility of Transnational Corporations* (Kluwer Law International, 1999) 187–196.

49 For a review of this debate, see Tom Campbell, "The Normative Grounding of Corporate Social Responsibility: A Human Rights Approach" in Doreen McBarnet, Aurora Voiculescu and Tom Campbell (eds), *The New Corporate Accountability: Corporate Social Responsibility and the Law* (Cambridge University Press, 2007) 529; Tom Campbell, "Corporate Social Responsibility: Beyond the Business Case to Human Rights" in Wesley Cragg (ed.), *Business and Human Rights* (Edward Elgar, 2012) 47.

50 Procedural justice researchers, drawing on Tom Tyler's foundational research in psychology, have just begun to turn their attention to the what motivates corporate, as opposed to individual compliance: see Melissa Rorie, Sally Simpson, Mark Cohen, and Michael Vandenbergh, "Examining Procedural Justice and Legitimacy in Corporate Offending and Beyond-Compliance Behavior: The Efficacy of Direct and Indirect Regulatory Interactions" (2018) *Law & Policy*, Accepted Author Manuscript (24 February 2018).

51 The phrase is attributed to the eighteenth-century English judge, Baron Thurlow, cited in Chris Clarkson, "Kicking Corporate Bodies and Damning Their Souls" (1996) 59(4) *Modern Law Review* 557.

52 The systematic review of corporate deterrence research reported that existing studies were low quality, and that the deterrent effects upon corporations were "mixed": Sally S. Simpson, Melissa Rorie, Mariel Alper, Natalie Schell-Busey, *Corporate Crime Deterrence: A Systematic Review* (Campbell Systematic Review, 2014).

53 See *Chief Executive Officer of Australian Transaction Reports and Analysis Centre v TAB Limited (No 3)* [2017] FCA 1296 at [17] per Perram J:

> It seems to me that I should accept the submission of the parties that this contravention [of the *Anti-Money Laundering and Counter Terrorism Financing Act 2006* (Cth)] was not deliberate and arose from a misunderstanding … However, the requirements of general deterrence necessitate the imposition of a substantial penalty so that it is known that even minor breaches of the Act have very serious consequences.

54 See discussion in Justin O'Brien, "The Sword of Damocles: Deferred Prosecutions and the Search for Accountability" in Justin O'Brien and George Gilligan (eds), *Integrity, Risk and Accountability in Capital Markets: Regulating Culture* (Hart Publishing, 2013) 161, 164.

55 This distinction parallels the distinction drawn between pre-crime and post-crime models of criminal justice, Lucia Zedner, "Fixing the Future? The Pre-Emptive Turn in Criminal Justice" in Bernadette McSherry, Alan Norrie and Simon Bronitt (eds), *Regulating Deviance: The Redirection of Criminalisation and the Futures of Criminal Law* (Hart Publishing, 2009) 35. The broad shift in criminal justice systems toward managing and mitigating dangerousness, risk, and now uncertainty, has had a profound impact on the discipline of criminology: see L Zedner, "Pre-Crime and Post-Criminology?" (2007) 11(2) *Theoretical Criminology* 261.

4 The Public Prosecution Service and the Structuring of Sentencing – The Nordic Case of Denmark

Rasmus H. Wandall

Introduction

The tendency to increase formal structuring of criminal sentencing transcends continents. From North America to South Korea, from Uganda and Ethiopia to Norway, from the Netherlands to Russia and China, structuring of criminal sentencing is on the agenda. Considering this wide span and the diversity that accompanies it, it is striking that the comparative discussion of sentencing is essentially limited to the institutional setup in countries with a common law tradition. Discussions are dominated by statutory guidance, judicial self-regulation and commission-based guidelines and institutionally by the judiciary, the legislature, and sentencing commissions and councils.[1] Notwithstanding a number of continental case studies, the discussion's skewedness towards countries with a common law tradition is difficult to miss.[2] It is with good reason that Roberts invites descriptions of other than the traditional numerical gridline structures of the United States, to contribute to comparative discussion of how to structure sentencing.[3]

This chapter contributes an original description of a very different structuring arrangement of sentencing institutionalized through the Danish prosecution service since the 1990s. Denmark is usually characterized as "loosely structured" together with other Nordic sentencing regimes.[4] However, a range of techniques institutionalized through the prosecution service since the 1990s have rendered sentencing decision-making far from "loosely structured". The article advances the wider argument that current comparative discussions on sentencing have to escape their current focus and embrace the diverse institutional frameworks of sentencing and particularly the regulatory role of the prosecution service.

The chapter is organized in five sections. Section two introduces the legal and institutional landscape of sentencing in Denmark. Section three presents three recent techniques of structuring sentencing. Section four discusses the particular role of the prosecution service to these techniques. Section five discusses the consequences for comparative sentencing and draws the necessary conclusions.

Legal Framework of Criminal Sentencing in Denmark

Every year, Danish authorities hand down a little more than 200,000 sentencing decisions.[5] The main sanctions are fines and imprisonment, with fines accounting for more than 170,000 sentences. Immediate imprisonment and alternatives to immediate imprisonment account for less than 20,000 sentences. The sentencing levels are among the mildest in Europe. The average length of sentences to immediate imprisonment is 7 months. For homicide, the average length is 135 months; for rape, 22 months; for simple violence 4 months; and for robbery 15 months.

To guide penal decision-makers in fixing the punishment, a statutory framework provides high upper sentencing limits and leave sentencers with effectively no lower limits.[6] For example, § 244 provides that simple violence shall be sentenced to a fine or imprisonment of no more than three years. The Criminal Code contains only a few statutorily increased minimum sentences. Imprisonment can be suspended with conditions when imprisonment is considered "unnecessary", §§ 56–57. If the suspended prison sentence is considered insufficient, the sentence can be made conditional on performance of 30 to 300 hours of community service, §§ 62–63. To guide within the sentencing limits, the Criminal Code stipulates general narrative criteria to guide the fixing of sentence, §§ 80–82. § 80 states – like the Finnish criminal code – that consistency in sentencing ("ensartethed") is the main objective and that sentencing should reflect both the severity of crime and the personal and social conditions of the offender. §§ 81 and 82 list a number of aggravating and mitigating circumstances for the court to take into consideration when fixing the punishment. Apart from this statutory guidance, the actual fixing of the sanction and the sentence level is left to the judiciary for further guidance.

The judiciary holds a pivotal role in structuring sentencing through court practice.[7] As a main rule, the Supreme Court settles principled questions of sentencing levels and sentencing criteria,[8] while the two high courts through appeal cases develop normal sentencing levels and identify relevant sentencing criteria in a wider spectrum of offence categories. However, because less than 3 per cent of criminal cases make it to these high courts, it is actually more often the district courts themselves that structure sentencing locally and horizontally.[9] A few official case collections exist to facilitate this function, but mostly, this has been done by way of informally sharing unpublished court practice and case collections.[10]

That is how the normative structuring of sentencing in courts looked until the 1990s and how it continues to be described in the Nordic literature.[11] However, since the early 1990s the prosecution service has attained a new and bigger role and new techniques add significantly to the structuring of sentencing. The techniques are:

1 Preparatory works to statutory amendments.
2 Prosecution guidelines.
3 Prosecution driven court practice database.

The central organization for these techniques' authority is neither the judiciary nor the legislative power in isolation. It is the prosecution service that in turn has emerged as a key agency in structuring sentencing.

Technique #1: Preparatory Works to Statutory Amendments

As already witnessed in England and Wales and in several US jurisdictions, a growing political distrust with the judicial sentencing in Denmark in the 1990s set off a period of introducing more than 50 new sentencing amendments over the next decades.[12] The aggregated effect has been to increase the level and control of sentencing. But unlike many other jurisdictions, the solution was not widespread use of statutory minimum sentences, but instead to guide penal decision-makers through preparatory works to statutory amendments of the Criminal Code. In the sometimes fierce policy debate, with demands for increased minimum sentences on the one hand and the judicial resistance against legislative influence on the other, this particular solution could be sold; politically, because it is enforceable, and judicially, because it is softer than statutory law and officially leaves the final discretion with the court.

There is a long tradition of using preparatory works to inform on sentencing matters. It is the traditional method of communicating the purpose and meanings of the statute and its individual paragraphs, and more recently a primary vehicle for secondary regulation. As Therkelsen documents, the number and sizes of preparatory works has exploded since the 1990s.[13] Preparatory works to the Criminal Code are drafted by the Ministry of Justice (MoJ) and the Director of Public Prosecution (DPP) and can be anything from a single page to more than 100 pages. Preparatory works accompany the statutory drafts through the parliamentary processes. The content of the preparatory works is rarely the subject of substantive debate and uses three different methods to guide sentencing.[14]

With the first approach, the preparatory works identify relevant offence characteristics for discriminating sentencing levels within normal sentencing ranges. An early and illustrative example is statutory amendment L 272 (1989), in which the preparatory works instructed different sentencing levels for different categories of ordinary violence – street violence, bar fights, violence within family, random conflict violence. This approach was used three times in the 1980s, seven times between 1990 and 1999, and 16 times between 2000 and 2010 with statutory amendments to the Criminal Code.

The second approach is numerical. It describes both normal sentencing levels for specific offence categories as well as sentencing points of departures in standard cases. For example, in amendment no L 274 (2012) about prohibition of knives, the preparatory works specified: "it is presumed that first-time offences [...] are punished with a fine of DKK 3000 as a point of departure [...] in second time offences the punishment is to be 7 days immediate imprisonment [...]" (sec. 3.2). The technique has been used more than 20 times since 1989, 16 of these between 2000 and 2010.

The third technique is also numerical but different in approach. It uses the preparatory works to guide relative changes of normal sentencing levels based on descriptions of historical court practice. For example, in L 1549 (2010) about professional fencing, the MoJ specified that the amendment seeks to "increase punishment in cases concerning professional fencing with one third compared with the punishment that currently is sentenced by the courts" (sec. 2.3). In the event that the preparatory works include description of historical sentencing practice, it is the Director of Public Prosecutions who produces these. The technique was used twice before 1999, and eight times between 2000 and 2010.

It is correct when Hinkkanen and Lappi-Sepälä frame preparatory works as soft forms of guidance.[15] They are arguably not binding on judicial courts. However, set in a continental European legal tradition, they are important sources of informing the penal decision-maker of a legally coherent sentencing analysis.[16] Even though the Supreme Court on some occasions has overruled the wording in preparatory works, courts consistently follow the guidance in preparatory works in practice.[17]

Technique #2: Prosecution Guidelines

From the mid-1990s the Director of Public Prosecutions (DPP) followed up the guidance in preparatory works with intensifying the administrative regulation of frontline prosecutors. The DPP has issued 142 original guidelines. They are called "Rigsadvokatens Meddelelser" and are referred to as RMs.[18] Some are less than 20 pages and some longer than 200 pages. Only eight were published prior to 1990, 26 prior to 2000; the rest have been published between 2000 and 2018. Most of them have been updated and revised numerous times. Today, the RMs have been collected into one major digital and searchable RM version. The guidelines are legally binding on prosecutors only, but are also more widely accepted as legitimate legal descriptions of the topics they cover. The RMs organize and communicate guidance in statutory rules, preparatory work and in court practice. But more importantly the RMs "translate" these sources into more practical guidance to prosecutors. In doing so, the RMs add significantly in detail and in process.

RMs cover topics from juvenile offenders, handling cases of individual crime categories from A to Z, how to handle specific evidentiary issues and how to manage internal quality assessment mechanisms. Many of the RMs guide sentencing decisions. In the recently introduced generic template for all future offence-specific RMs, sentencing and penal decision-making is systematically dealt with in section five of all RMs. For example, RM on threats and violence against public employees (revised 2017), or RM on driving while intoxicated (revised 2018).

The RMs guide sentencing in several different ways. First of all, they use narrative guidance with frequent references to both mitigating and aggravating circumstance informing sentencing and frequently exemplify normal sentences by reference to court practice. Second, the guidelines provide both minimum and presumptive sentences for offence categories. Examples are found in the RM about threats and violence against public employees. The guidelines set a presumptive minimum sentence of 20 days' immediate imprisonment for threats, a presumptive 30 days' immediate imprisonment for less than "ordinary" violence and 40–60 days for an "ordinary" case of violence (section 5.1.2). RM on illegal possession of weapons contains an elaborate index of different presumptive sentences for different offence categories and for different criminal histories. For example, for illegal possession of a knife in a public place, the guideline prescribes presumptive sentences for first-time offenders of minimum DKK 3000, and seven to 40 days' immediate imprisonment depending on the aggravating circumstances (section 5.5.3).

Despite the frequent reference to Scandinavian narrative guidance as a contrast to US-based numerical gridlines, the Danish prosecution services has set up several mainstream numerical gridline tables in their RMs. The best example is found in RM on drug crimes. For possession for personal use, the RM draws up a 3 × 39 table with presumptive sentences categorized by drug substance, amount in grams and the number of prior drug convictions. For possession with intent to distribute small amounts of particularly dangerous substances, the RM draws up a second table, 8 × 1, organized by the number of potential distributions and prior convictions. Furthermore, for aggravated cases of possession with intent to distribute (Penal Code § 191), the RM draws up a 13 × 1 table with presumptive prison sentences categorized by substance and amount. For example, 1 kg cocaine has a presumptive sentence of "circa 5 years".

Technique # 3: Prosecution Case Databases

Since 2008, the Director of Public Prosecution has managed a dynamic database of court practice. As of January 2018, it contained 2,899 court cases. The database includes cases that illustrate normal sentencing levels, organizes them in categories and subcategories, reviews them through expert editorial groups and makes them available to all practitioners through a web-based search engine. The official aim of the database is to respond to a demand of practitioners for an answer to the question: "what do courts normally do in cases like this?" Though several journals exist that communicate court practice to practitioners, there has been an experienced lack of available relevant court practice.[19]

The database is designed to combine a horizontal and vertical structure of accountability. Horizontally, it includes and makes available court practice from all districts and does not focus solely on appellate court practice. Of the cases in the database, 51 per cent are district court cases. Vertically, five regional editorial groups with expert senior prosecutors review each case prior to publication in the database. Editorial groups exist for property crimes, violent crimes, organized crime, specialized codes (e.g. environmental crimes, and compensation). The primary selection criteria of cases are if the case represents a "normal sentencing level" and if the case contributes to new practice knowledge not already available in the database. Furthermore, the DPP reviews every submission.

To give an example, in 2013, 643 new cases were submitted. Of these 102 (16 per cent) were rejected. Furthermore, including both regional high court cases and all Supreme Court cases, a judicial vertical structure is inserted in the content of the database as well. Finally, the expert review groups refer to five councils, representing five different areas of criminal law and procedure, each of them responsible for the legal and professional knowledge in the prosecution service, and each of them chaired by a senior prosecutor from the DPP.

Contrary to other case collections in Denmark, the database is dynamic. Each year, new cases are added and old cases are deleted. Although the database includes court practice in all offence categories, the DPP has strategically focused on providing guidance through court practice in particular offence categories. These include:

- Drug crimes
- Robbery
- Violence and threats against public employees and people in exposed positions (§§ 119, 121, 247, 2)
- Simple and aggravated violence (§§ 244, 245)
- Fraud
- Breach of trust
- Violation of animal protection law
- Traffic code
- Illegal weapon
- Expulsion to countries within the EC

The database and the search engine organizes the court practice in categories, leaving a great deal of presumptive sentencing guidance for the individual offence categories. For example, fraud (210 decisions) is divided into IT fraud (39 decisions), insurance fraud (25), credit fraud (18), social welfare fraud (18), unemployment benefit fraud (27), commercial fraud (35), other fraud (46). Each of these categories is again divided into different monetary levels. For example, insurance fraud is divided into DKK 0–100.000 (19 decisions), DKK 100.000–500.000 (5 decisions), and above DKK 500.000 (1 decision). Finally, and importantly, each court case is provided with a title and a headline that places it in a systematic offence structure and allows practitioners to quickly compare decisions and sentences. For example: "AM2012.11.05Ø – insurance fraud, attempt, incorrect information to insurance company about theft of clothes and laptop. DKK 21.000. 50 days imprisonment. Suspended. 2 years' probation". Provided with just one, two or sometimes three such headlines, a presumptive sentence is relatively clear. Importantly, for drug cases, the database and search engine provides an actual gridline table that organizes all 925 court cases by substance, amount in grams, and prior convictions.

The search engine integrates the database of court practice with other and existing sources of law and practice, placing it directly in the general legal framework of criminal procedure and sentencing. The search engine makes the court practice available together with other recognized court practice databases, prosecution guidelines (RM), DPP communications (RI) and instructions as well as reports of court practice for selected areas of law and individual reports and white papers (containing the preparatory works for legal amendments).

The Institutional Role of the Public Prosecution Service

The public prosecution service is at the very centre of the dramatic increase in structuring of sentencing. Unlike many other jurisdictions, no new institutions have been invented. Structuring has taken place through existing and well-established central administration institutions.

To make sense of how this institutional setup has the ability to structure sentencing, it is necessary to have in mind the continental European legal tradition that Nordic – and other Germanic – structuring of sentencing is placed in.[20] The regulatory centre for criminal procedure and sentencing is (the ideal of) a coherent legal system founded in statutory law. The public administration, the public prosecution service, as well as the judiciary all play roles in giving systematic meaning to this statutory foundation and to ensure a coherent legal order. The judicial hierarchy rests in a hierarchy of apex courts and also these are the servants of ensuring a coherent legal system with a basis in statutory law. The high level of professionalization of jurists in the public administration, hereunder the prosecution service, and the high level of professionalization of the judiciary is a testament to this function. This legal tradition has major consequences for the regulation of sentencing decision-making. It means that there is not a space for lawlessness but a space for public institutions searching for the legally rational decision-making relying on court practice and legislative intent; it means that there is not a culture of judicial self-regulation but a culture of law-abiding civil servants who interpret statutory law; and it means that prosecutors while accusatorial are civil servants ideally implementing the will of the statutory power and can be expected to do so.[21]

With this legal tradition in mind, I will outline four ways in which the prosecution service institutionalizes the described techniques of structuring sentencing:

- By taking part in the drafting of preparatory works to statutory amendments
- By using its quasi-judicial role to presenting facts and law to the judicial courts
- By controlling knowledge on normal sentencing levels through its hierarchical organizational structure
- By following up on judicial sentencing practice on behalf of the legislature

Taking Part in the Drafting of Preparatory Works to Statutory Amendments

Preparatory works to statutory amendments constitute a primary source for setting the normal sentencing levels. The prosecution service is a key source.

Acting in the capacity of civil servants, the Office of the Director of Public Prosecution (DPP) is expected to provide the drafting process with the necessary descriptions of historical sentencing levels and often also appropriate levels for future sentencing. For some statutory amendments, the Ministry of Justice (MoJ) requests the DPP to prepare the statutory amendment and its preparatory work in its entirety. But more often, the MoJ requests the DPP to report on current sentencing practice combined with an analysis of normal sentencing levels in the offence categories concerned. The DPP goes about this task hierarchically, requesting the regional prosecutors to collect and submit relevant court practice. The consequence of this practice is that whereas statutory amendments in other jurisdictions are based on sentencing descriptions provided by a sentencing council, a commission, or by research divisions or judicial offices, in Denmark they are oftentimes based on the work of the prosecution service. The many collections of court practice that the DPP publishes through its web-based platform is a byproduct of these reports to the drafting of preparatory works.

The Quasi-Judicial Role to Presenting Facts and Law to the Judicial Courts

The prosecution service is also the organization responsible for bringing sentencing information to the court. First, the prosecutor presents the court with a sentencing recommendation, practically setting the upper limit of the concrete sentencing. Second and concurrent with this accusatorial role, the prosecution is expected to present the court with the facts of law of the case – including impartial guidance in the preparatory works and from court practice on normal sentencing levels. In district courts this presentation can be very informal, but ordinarily the presentation must be substantiated by reference to available authoritative sources, most importantly court practice and case collections, or other authoritative source, e.g. preparatory works. In the regional appellate courts the prosecution must substantiate the claim with a more thorough description of sentencing law and before the Supreme Court, claims must be founded on a complete analysis of available court practice, written sources of law – including historical and present preparatory works, as well as court practice from other – Nordic – countries if relevant. It is easy to recognize the original responsibilities of the French procureur in this role. In ordinary district court cases, it often suffices to refer to the prosecution guidelines' reference to normal sentencing levels, accepting their secondary reference to court practice and preparatory works. DPPs' descriptions of court practice are often sufficient to the judiciary. An undeniably significant contributing factor to this expectation is the historically high authority with which analysis of law of the DPP is met. With this quasi-judicial authority, the prosecution authority is able to present information about normal sentencing levels from both preparatory works, its own guidelines, and its court practice data base, to the judicial courts and other penal decision-makers.

Controlling Knowledge on Normal Sentencing Levels through its Hierarchical Organizational Structure

A strongly centralized and hierarchical organization ties together these opposite ends of prosecution roles in structuring sentencing. This includes a DPP, two regional state prosecutors and 12 local prosecutors, the directors of police in Greenland and in the Faroe Islands, and the special prosecutor on economic and international crimes. The Director of Public Prosecution in turn is governed by the Ministry of Justice, with the Minister as the highest-ranking prosecutor. Prosecutors are career civil servants. None are politically appointed or elected, and no measures of community or political accountability exist locally or regionally. Direct instructions as well as general rules are handed down through the organization. It is this hierarchical organization that makes possible the collection and nationwide dissemination of court practice, that makes nationwide development and implementation of written guidance, and of reviewing and controlling practice, possible.[22] The prosecution service is, in effect, the only nationwide organizational structure that has the setup to guide, implement and follow up on sentencing issues for ordinary cases that do not reach the Supreme Court. Before 1990 this organizational structure was relatively undeveloped. There was no managerial setup to organize the prosecution service and there was no capacity within the DPP to issue general guidance to prosecutors. Since the mid-1990s and in particular since the reform of the police and the prosecution service in 2007, the prosecution has developed into the – by far – most significant regulatory authority in the area of criminal procedure and sentencing law and practice.

Auditing Criminal Sentencing

The fourth institutional role that warrants attention is the prosecution service's auditing of judicial courts' sentencing practices. Because of its key position and organizational power to collect and accumulate sentencing information from individual cases countrywide, and because of its authority as an objective public service institution that derives its obligations from a principle of legality, it is also the obvious agency to have responsibility for auditing the sentencing practice of the judiciary. On several occasions the legislative power has conditioned sentencing increases in the preparatory works that the MoJ audits of sentencing practice of the courts yearly. On these occasions the DPP has audited the sentencing practice of the judicial courts and submitted their analysis of whether the courts have implemented the sentencing increases fully or not.

Conclusions

Thus, from drafting statutory amendments and the guidance in preparatory works, to the implementation in actual sentencing practice, the organizational setup and authority to provide objective knowledge on sentencing practice on a national level, and to a practice of following up on the actual implementation of guidance through the preparatory works, the prosecution service performs a central role in the structuring of sentencing.

Comparing Sentencing across Jurisdictions – Conclusions

It is probably correct, when Roberts states that "the question is what is suitable for the individual jurisdictions".[23] The Danish case study brings to the table a case that departs markedly from what is considered suitable in the jurisdictions that dominate current comparative discussions. It cannot be reduced to statutory power, to judicial self-regulation, or to any new organizational setup to bring relevant stakeholders together in regulation of sentencing. Instead, it shows a typical continental example of newer regulatory techniques developed within century-old legal institutional setups, tied together by the central procedural role of the public prosecution service.

Nordic sentencing guidance cannot be described as narrative only and sentencing decision-making cannot be described as loosely structured. But perhaps most importantly, we cannot confine our understanding of sentencing guidance by reference to judiciary and the statutory law, as current comparative discussions of structuring sentencing do.[24] The central administration and the prosecution service plays too big a regulatory role. Not only because an increasing number of decisions are made by the prosecution, but because the prosecution structures the sentencing of the courts.

Current discussions of how to structure sentencing focus on finding solutions that balance the legislature and the judiciary. Sentencing councils and commissions and their respective guidelines – be they numerical or narrative – are advanced as the most promising solutions.[25] These institutions are meant to fill a "lawless" gap. It seems that if we extend the comparative discussion of how to structure sentencing to jurisdictions beyond those of sentencing commissions and guidelines, this gap is not so lawless after all and Nordic countries from the perspective of guideline systems cannot be referred to as "loosely structured". A continental European perspective shows other institutional arrangements and techniques to structure sentencing. The case study of Denmark is a good example to this effect. It shows a number of structuring techniques that vary from any current presentation of commission-based sentencing guidelines or statutory guidance, and it shows how the prosecution service provides the institutional setup that facilitates the structuring, but which is alarmingly absent from current discussions of how to structure sentencing. Finally, it joins Roberts in ascribing significance to the legal culture in which structuring takes place. Thus, the case study shows that the continental European legal traditions provide the structuring of its authority and its effectivity.

The case study gives rise to a number of discussions. First, the distinction between numerical and narrative guidance surely continues to point to a principled distinction in how decision-making is guided.[26] Yet, as a descriptive marker for differences between entire systems of guidance, it is questionable if it continues to be useful. The case of Denmark illustrates how numerical and narrative techniques are mixed and shows that the association between loose structuring and narrative techniques is difficult to uphold. While it is certainly true that Denmark, as Norway and Sweden, use a range of narrative principles and criteria in both statutory law and judicial practice to guide sentencing, it is also true that gridline systems and other categorical systematizations dominate several important offence categories, just as numerical structures are increasingly used to organize narrative structures. The Danish prosecution-run court practice database is a case in hand.

Second, the role of prosecution service is missing from the comparative discussion of structuring sentencing. It is not only in Denmark that the prosecution plays a distinctly more important role in sentencing than the current discussion suggests. In the Netherlands, perhaps the most prominent structuring of sentencing is performed through the prosecution service. In Denmark, Norway and Sweden, the prosecution service provides significant guidance in criminal procedure. In Switzerland, the prosecution service provides relevant guidance, as do prosecution services in German jurisdictions. The point is made clearer when considering the expanding role of prosecutors in penal decision-making in recent decades. In countries of continental European legal tradition, it is normal to see a prosecution service that operates in a quasi-judicial role and thus performs an important role in connection to the judiciary. The tradition of hierarchical order of state institutions operating under statutory law and the prosecution service expected to present cases "objectively" places the prosecution service in an obvious centre for guiding sentencing decision-making, that is by and large ignored from a common law perspective, which focuses on the increased powers that prosecutors get from the introduction of guideline systems. Any widening of a comparative perspective of structuring sentencing to include continental Europe should include the institutional role(s) of the prosecution service.

Of course, this does raise a new set of questions: given that many of the prosecution guidelines are developed within the prosecution service, to whom are they legally and politically accountable? How are the perspectives of interest groups such as victims, offenders, the public, the correctional department and the judiciary, included? And given the judicial quality of independence, does it not constitute a problem that the prosecution develops the guideline that judges should follow and that the actual supervision and control of consistency in sentencing has the prosecution service in a central role? It is also evident that the changing roles of the prosecution service to manage decisions that were previously managed by the courts only gives further nourishment to the prosecution's role as guiding penal decision-making. It becomes increasingly impossible to – even generally – discuss sentencing decision-making or the structuring of sentencing and penal decision-making without allocating serious attention to the role of the prosecution service and its guiding role.

Third, the Nordic case of Denmark illustrates that if we are to sustain a comparative discussion of how to structure sentencing that bears any meaning to the many individual jurisdictions involved, it is necessary to increase the attention to the legal cultures involved. The role of the prosecution service vis-à-vis the courts described in Denmark bears clear traits of continental European legal culture and would make little sense in either England or United States jurisdictions. The authority of secondary regulation in the preparatory works and the inter-organizational collaboration between courts, prosecution service and correctional department assumes a perception of a system that is not seen in either England or the United States. Also, a difference in legal culture that is barely made visible is that between deep-rooted centralized legal institutions informing judicial discretion versus more recent frameworks of sentencing in United States jurisdictions. I hesitate to include England and Wales, because it differs legally in so many ways from the United States in that respect. There is a striking general alignment of the legal principles and criteria that inform sentencing decision-making through three to four generations of practitioners and law professors in Denmark. The professionalization of judges – being part of the hierarchical system enforcing statutory law – is another relevant distinction of legal culture. Danish judges are career judges, often with pasts in the prosecution service, the Ministry of Justice or other parts of the public administration. They are not politically appointed or elected, but professionally appointed by a national judicial board.

This close institutional knitwear makes for anything but "lawlessness" or "looseness", but for an institutional framework of sentencing probably as tight as the tightest sentencing guideline systems invented. But unlike the sentencing guideline, this has built in the necessary flexibility to allow for fluid changes over time and for the necessary concretization of sentencing decision-making. Of course, it lacks the subjection to formalized democratic structures of legal accountability. However, is there not an argument that the legal accountability itself lies with the statutory framework? Without making any claim for which is better, it should be included as part of this discussion that public confidence in courts, in police, and in the legal system in general, by far favours Nordic and North European countries in comparison with England and Wales and United States. The accountability – it seems – is not a direct one between the sentencing regime and the public (as the English) but one between the public and the legal system as a whole. I have not touched upon the question as to whether judges actually follow this guidance – that is, if it works. There is strong indication that they at least follow the guidance in preparatory works.[27]

Notes

1 E.g. N. Hutton and C. Tata (2000) "Sentencing Reform by Self-Regulation: Present and Future Prospects of the Sentencing Information System for Scotland's High Court Justiciary", *Scottish Journal of Criminology* 6: 37–51; J.V. Roberts (2012) "Structured Sentencing: Lessons from England and Wales for Common Law Jurisdictions", *Punishment and Society* 14: 267–288; Roberts (2012a) "Structuring Sentencing in Canada, England and Wales: A Tale of Two Jurisdictions", *Criminal Law Forum* 23: 319–345; Roberts (2013) "Sentencing Guidelines and Judicial Discretion", *British Journal of Criminology* 51: 997–1013; Arie Freiberg and Karen Gelb (eds) (2013)

Penal Populism, Sentencing Councils and Sentencing Policy (London: Routledge); Sarah Krasnostein and Arie Freiberg (2013) "Pursuing Consistency in an Individualistic Sentencing Framework: If You Know Where You're Going, How do You Know When You've Got There?", *Law and Contemporary Problems* 76: 265–288.

2 Examples of continental case studies include Tatjana Hörnle (2013) "Moderate and Non-Arbitrary Sentencing Without Guidelines: The German Experience", *Law and Contemporary Problems* 76: 189–210; Ely Aharonson (2013) "Determinate Sentencing and American Exceptionalism: The Underpinnings and Effects of Cross-National Differences in the Regulation of Sentencing Discretion", *Law and Contemporary Problems* 76: 161–187; Ville Hinkkanen and Tapio Lappi-Seppälä (2011) "Sentencing Theory, Policy, and Research in the Nordic Countries", *Crime and Justice* 40: 349–404; Rasmus H. Wandall (2006) "Equality by Numbers or Words: A Comparative Study of Sentencing Structures in Minnesota and Denmark", *Criminal Law Forum* 17: 1–41; Peter Tak (2001) "Sentencing and Punishment in The Netherlands" in Michael Tonry and Richard Frase (eds) *Sentencing and Sanctions in Western Countries* (New York and Oxford: Oxford University Press).

3 Roberts (n 1).

4 See for example Aharonson (n 2), Antony Duff (2005) "Guidance and Guidelines", *Columbia Law Review* 105: 1162; Roberts (n 1).

5 210.884 decisions in 2016. Source: Danmarks Statistik www.dst.dk/da/Statistik/emner/kriminalitet/domme.aspx (Accessed 28 February 2018).

6 Using Denmark should present itself as an even harder case than Sweden. The sentencing limits are even broader and the principled nature of the guidance in Sweden more pronounced.

7 For a systematic account of the organization, communication, and use of court practice as a tool for structuring sentencing decision-making, see Rasmus H. Wandall (2012) "Styring af straffen med domsdatabaser" (Governing Criminal Sentencing Through Sentencing Information Systems), *Nordisk Tidsskrift for Kriminalvidenskab*: 265–286.

8 For example, in the cases UfR 2010.2548H, UfR 2010.2552 H, UfR 2011.494 H, UfR 2011.498 H, UfR 2011.502 H, and UfR 2011.504 H, the Supreme Court defined the normal sanction in violations of the newly formulated § 192 a and decided that a distinction between possession in private versus in public was irrelevant for sentencing concerns.

9 Compare Hörnle (n 2) about Germany.

10 Wandall (n 7).

11 Hinkkanen and Lappi-Seppälä (n 2). See also Hörnle (n 2) with a description of the significance of professionalization for structural purposes.

12 About the United States of America, see for example Kate Stith and José A. Cabranes (1998) *Fear of Judging. Sentencing Guidelines in the Federal Courts* (Chicago: University of Chicago Press); about England and Wales, see for example Andrew Ashworth "Sentencing Reform Structures" Michael Tonry (ed.) (1992) *Crime and Justice. A Review of Research.* Chicago (Chicago: University of Chicago Press).

13 Christian Therkelsen (2010) *Lovmotivernes strafudmålingsanvisninger* Dissertation (University of Copenhagen).

14 See Therkelsen (n 13).

15 Hinkkanen and Lappi-Seppälä (n 2).

16 Henrik Zahle (2005) *Praktisk Retsfilosofi* 82 (Ejlers' Forlag København); Gorm Toftegaard Nielsen (2001) "Lovgivere og dommere – hvem regulerer hvad", *Lov og Ret* 3: 10–13; Magnus Matningsdal (2010) "Straffutmåling – politiske direktiver og signaler", *Lov og Rett* 6: 323–339; Bent Carlsen (2010) "Forarbejder og strafudmåling", *Nordisk Tidsskrift for Kriminalvidenskab*: 412–428; Rasmus H. Wandall (2013) "Strafudmåling med lovforarbejder", (Criminal Sentencing Guided by Travaux Préparatoires), *Ugeskrift for Retsvæsen*: 308–319.

17 Wandall (n 7).

18 Available at www.anklagemyndigheden.dk/da/viden-og-statistik (Accessed 1 March 2018).

19 Wandall (n 7).

20 About the use of the concept of legal traditions, see Patrick Glenn (2010) *Legal Traditions of the World. Sustainable Diversity in Law* 4th edn (New York and Oxford: Oxford University Press). The more advanced comparative criminal procedure rightfully questions the usefulness of the distinction between common and civil law as a descriptive entity of entire procedural jurisdictions. This is correct also within comparative sentencing law and practice. There are too many typical civil law techniques that are implemented in the United States and there are too many classic common law techniques that are implemented in continental European countries. However, we should be careful not to deny the benefit of the particularity of legal traditions and cultures as relevant frameworks for understanding the particular sentencing regulations and thus as tools for comparing them across borders.

21 Weigend mentions about German prosecutors, that while this may be the ideal, it is not the reality. Thomas Weigend (2012) "Comparative Perspectives on the Role of the Public Prosecutor" in Erik Luna and Marianne L. Wade (eds) *The Prosecutor in Transnational Perspective* (New York and Oxford: Oxford University Press). That is correct, but the more important observation is that there is a self-perception and an expectation from both the judiciary and other branches of the legal system, that prosecutors should adhere to these ideals.

22 So for example, while the appellate courts hold the power to overturn district court sentences, it is the regional prosecutors who in practice control which sentences are appealed and which are not (by a ratio of ten to one compared to defence attorneys).

23 Roberts (n 1).

24 See for example Oren Gazal-Ayal (ed.) (2013) "A Global Perspective on Sentencing Reform", *Law and Contemporary Problems* 76(1).

25 Roberts (n 1).

26 Duff (n 4) and Wandall (n 2).

27 Wandall (n 7).

Part II

The Role of Prosecutors in Investigations

5 The Role of the Finnish Prosecutor in Preliminary Investigations – Efficiency or the End of Impartiality?

Julia Jansson

Introduction

The police–prosecutor relationship in Finland has a rather complicated history. For centuries, the country had a dualistic model in which the prosecution was organised differently in the countryside and in the cities. In the countryside, an official called *länsman* was simultaneously chief of police, prosecutor and distrainer.[1] In contrast, in the so-called "old" cities, prosecution was in the hands of a specialised prosecutor called *stadsfiskal*.[2] The scattered model was dismantled in 1996, with the reorganisation and unification of the Finnish Prosecution Service, finalised the following year.

Since this reform, there has been a complete organisational separation of the prosecution and police services in the whole country. In the current Finnish model, the role of the police is to investigate crime, while the prosecutor is in charge of the indictment and bringing the case to court. However, collaboration between the police and the prosecutor with regards to preliminary investigations has been increasing in the past years.

This seemingly simple model of organisation has by no means been considered the sole possibility for the arrangement of the police–prosecutor relationship. For exactly two centuries a debate on possible organisational models and divisions of labour has persisted. Both the complete separation of the two entities, and adding more powers, or a leading role, over pre-trial investigations for the prosecutor have received supporters.

The present study suggests that there are a variety of historical and practical reasons why the prosecutor does not and, according to some commentators, should not, supervise or lead preliminary investigations. Simultaneously, the role of the prosecutor in pre-trial investigations has been increasing during the past years, and it seems highly possible that in the near future, the prosecutor in Finland will lead preliminary investigations in at least the most serious cases.

The relationship and the division of tasks between prosecutors and the police is subject of ongoing debate around the world, in both inquisitorial as well as accusatorial systems. By describing and analysing the Finnish debate, this chapter will offer another perspective on the topic of best practices with respect to this relationship.

Historical Development of the Prosecution System in Finland

The Finnish police–prosecutor relationship has been in turmoil during the last 200 years.[3] Finland was a part of Sweden until 1809, when, as a result of a Swedish–Russian war, it was annexed to Russia as an autonomous Grand Duchy. The autonomous status of the country meant that it could maintain many of the Swedish influences in its administration while being a part of the Russian empire.[4] One of the particularities that persisted was the administrative difference between Finland's so-called "old cities",[5] smaller towns and rural areas. In addition to other administrative differences, all three had a different system for the prosecution of crime.

The "old cities" had a relatively vast amount of authority in their governance with regards to the state. They had a specialised public prosecutor, the *kaupunginviskaali* or *stadsfiskal* in Swedish.[6] This role was of Swedish origin, where it had existed since the 1600s. The *stadsfiskals* served under the highest prosecutorial authority, the procurator. The procurator was an official with a rather independent status, working under the Finnish Senate. In contrast, the police service in its entirety was controlled by the Governors, representatives of the crown, the Czar of Russia (see e.g. Jussila, 2004). Later, as Finland gained its independence from Russia in 1917, some of its administrative structures underwent changes. The procurator was replaced by the Chancellor of Justice, who was now the highest prosecutorial authority. The *stadsfiskals* now belonged under the newly formed Ministry of Justice, whereas the police service was organised under the Ministry of the Interior.

The first police offices had been established in two "old cities", Helsinki and Turku, during the second decade of the 1800s. This had created a need to balance the duties of the prosecutors and the police. The roles and duties of the police and the prosecutor were not clearly established and the responsibility over pre-trial investigations was unclear. This provoked a lengthy debate over whether this task should fall to the police or the prosecutor. Different arguments raised in this discussion will be presented later in this chapter.

Still as late as 1978, the *stadsfiskals* of Helsinki were given the right to demand the police conduct an investigation or carry out further investigations, or even the whole criminal investigation, if necessary (Decree 181/1978 4§).[7] In reality, however, this never became common practice and the two worked completely separate from one another (Interviews, 2013, Helminen *et al.*, 2012, pp. 166–169). Finally, the amount of opinions supporting the separation of the investigation and prosecution of crime outweighed contrasting views, which still exists in Finland today.

In the rural areas of the country, the system was completely different in comparison to the "old cities". In the countryside, the *nimismies* or *länsman*, was simultaneously chief of police, prosecutor and distrainer.[8] In addition to the preparation of charges and the prosecution itself, the *länsmans* as chiefs of police were in charge of handling the criminal investigation in its entirety. Thus, as the *länsman* system prevailed in the country, the country had a strong tradition of bringing together prosecutorial and investigative powers. In contrast with the *stadsfiskals*, the *länsmans*, together with the entire police service, were organised under the Ministry of the Interior in 1918.

In smaller towns, which did not belong to the category of "old cities" with a great amount of autonomy, but also were not organised under the *länsman* system that prevailed in the rural areas, the situation lay somewhere between these two extremes. They did not have a separate police office, only police officers, and *stadsfiskals* who were in charge of prosecutions.[9] The separation of police and prosecution was not pronounced and it was the role of the *stadsfiskal* to conduct the preliminary investigations in all criminal matters. In some of them, the prosecutor was also in charge of leading the police office until 1904 (Ignatius, 1900, p. 186; Hietaniemi, 1995, p. 37).

Regardless of continuous discussions with regards to reorganising this complicated system, the division between "old cities", smaller towns and rural areas persisted until the 1990s. During the mid-1990s, reforms that had been planned and pushed to the side during the past 100 years, finally came about. A major change in both the way in which the courts and the prosecution service were organised, as well as in the role of the prosecutor in the criminal process took place almost simultaneously.[10] Due to these changes in the legal framework, the requirements for the Prosecution Service and the prosecutors themselves, as well as for their role in the preliminary investigations, were drastically altered (Government bill 82/1995, p. 29).

The first step in this series of reforms was the unification of the first instance court system in the rural areas and the cities. District Courts replaced all courts of first instance in 1996. Second, the reform of the Prosecution Service in 1996–1997, ended the administrative division between "old cities" and rural areas. In the newly organised Prosecution Service, police and prosecution were completely separated in the whole country. This simplified the structure of the Prosecution Service and ended the tradition of having part-time prosecutors in the *länsmans* offices (Kukkonen and Tolvanen, 2011, p. 81; Helminen *et al.*, 2012, p. 161). All local prosecutors were now called District Prosecutors and the Prosecution Service in its entirety was located under the Ministry of Justice (Act 195/1996; Virolainen and Pölönen, 2004, pp. 67, 70). At first, this reform complicated the flow of information in those districts where the role of the *länsman* (chief of police-prosecutor-distrainer) had guaranteed that the police and the prosecutor worked together. It did not, however, make a major difference in the "old cities" where the separation of these tasks had a long history (Interviews, 2013; Pasterstein, 2009, pp. 9–10).

In 1997, the Act on Public Prosecutors defined the tasks of the prosecutors and other details concerning their positions (199/1997). The Office of the Prosecutor General, replacing the Chancellor of Justice as the highest prosecutorial authority, was created in December 1997. This finalised the reform of the Prosecution Service.

Soon after the reform of the Prosecution Service, the criminal process was drastically altered with the creation of the Criminal Procedure Act of 1997

(689/1997). With the coming into force of the Act, the judicial procedure in the first instance courts became oral, immediate and centralised.[11] In practice, this meant a move from an inquisitorial to an accusatorial system. Previously, it had been the duty of the judge to investigate the facts of a case brought into court by, for instance, interviewing the witnesses. As investigations proceeded in court, several sessions were often needed to deal with one matter. The prosecutor only decided upon the charges based on police investigations and presented these findings in court. Otherwise, s/he remained passive (Interviews, 2013).

In some ways, the role of the prosecutors in the criminal process had already gradually grown towards the end of the nineteenth century. The 1889 criminal law reform had already strengthened the role of the prosecutor by dividing crimes into two categories. This division has roughly remained the same until modern days. The first category consists of the crimes that are publicly prosecuted. The second, smaller category contains crimes that are left for the victim of the crime to prosecute. The victim retained the private right to prosecute alongside the public prosecutors. Nonetheless this reform had a major impact on the duties of the prosecutors.[12] Increasingly, the role of the prosecutor became that of guarding the public right of action (Ignatius, 1900, p. 115). The growth in the importance of the role of the prosecutor can be interpreted as a first step towards an accusatorial tradition in courts. However, the courts still had a very important role in the process in comparison to that of the prosecutors.

The role of the prosecutor in preliminary investigations remained essentially the same for over a century. It went through a major transformation only upon the creation of the Criminal Investigation Act of 1997. The same year, the whole criminal process was altered. Unlike under the previous law, the prosecutor could now decide whether an investigation should be conducted at all, and whether an ongoing inquiry should be discontinued or limited, subject to guidelines (Amendment to CIA 692/1997 3:10).

Previously, the police had the duty to finalise a preliminary investigation even when it was known that prosecution would not be pursued (Interviews, 2013). Additionally, before the reform, the *stadsfiskals* only learned about suspected crimes as they received the finalised investigation record and needed to decide upon the charges.[13] Only then could they have a say on the contents of the inquiry, meaning that they could ask the police to complement the investigation. Such a process unnecessarily slowed things down and in some cases the delay caused elements of proof getting lost or destroyed. This is why nowadays it is mandatory for the police to notify the prosecutor when a new criminal investigation is initiated, except in simplest matters (Government bill, 82/1995, p. 29).

Finally, the Criminal Investigation Act that came into force in January 2014 has made it mandatory for the public prosecutor to oversee and guide the investigation in serious or complicated cases.[14] The guiding of the investigation essentially means that the prosecutor can for example advise the investigative authority in what kind of further inquiries are necessitated for bringing the matter to court (CIA 805/2011, 5:2; Helminen *et al.*, 2012, p. 163; Interviews, 2013).

The prosecutor also acts as head investigator in particular cases where a police officer is a suspect of a criminal investigation (CIA 805/2011, 2:2 and 2:4).

Previously the prosecutor could claim lack of time as grounds for non-participation. Now this is no longer possible (Interviews, 2013). Even if the 2014 Act increased the role of the prosecutor, the police remains formally in charge of the investigation (Government bill 82/1995, p. 158; Law Committee Report 9/1997; CIA 805/2011; 2:1, Virolainen and Pölönen, 2004, pp. 43, 63). The police is in charge of practical investigations and of the use of certain coercive measures, including apprehension, arrest, seizure, and search (Helminen *et al.*, 2012, p. 705). The police and the prosecutor work concurrently; while the police investigates the facts, the prosecutor can build the court case. The aim of the Act was to improve the efficiency of the work of both police and prosecutors (Interviews, 2013).

The changes in the Prosecution Service and the criminal process occurred rather late, in comparison to the amount of voices that had been wishing for such reforms since the early years of the twentieth century. The following parts of the study discuss the arguments used by different sides to the lengthy debate.

Support for Increased Collaboration Throughout Times

Recent reforms have in many ways focused on improving the police–prosecution cooperation, especially during the phase of preliminary investigations. Most of these reforms have been initiated based on highly practical needs (Pasterstein, 2009, p. 14).

Since the 1800s, the lack of collaboration between police and prosecutor has been a key concern. Some commentators have since then argued that in addition to improved collaboration, the reforms should aim at making the prosecutor head investigator in preliminary investigations or even the head of the police service. Another recurring idea has been the joining of police and prosecutorial agencies.[15]

During the period studied, a major reason for demands of increased collaboration or structural changes to the organisation of preliminary investigations was the fact that charges were often poorly prepared. Since the 1800s, in the "old cities", it was the duty of the detective bureau of the police to investigate crime. If necessary, in some cases the *stadsfiskal* was required to participate in preliminary investigations. The mutual assistance model did not function smoothly because of quarrels between the agencies: the police often refused to assist the prosecutor in his duties. Regardless, most of the criticism in the nineteenth century with regard to the efficiency of the investigations was aimed at the *stadsfiskals* (Hietaniemi, 1995, p. 38). Many commentators thought that the *stadsfiskal* should have been, as the *länsman* was, the one conducting the investigations and creating the investigation record (Hietaniemi, 1995, pp. 92–93).

The *stadsfiskals* were criticised for avoiding their duties as they did not oversee police investigations. Because the prosecutors in the "old cities" did not play any part in the investigations, they often produced poorly prepared charges. In order to solve this problem, ideas on having prosecutors in charge of the cities' detective bureaus were presented (Ehrström, 1866; see also Hietaniemi, 1995, pp. 22, 38–39). These ideas were never put into practice, but they resurfaced regularly.

In 1928, the Chancellor of Justice reprimanded the prosecutors for not taking part in police investigations, and for being ill-informed about them. For this reason, they were not prepared to prosecute cases in courts, which slowed the whole justice system down (Charpentier, 1928; Hietaniemi, 1995, pp. 93–94). It was the wish of the Chancellor of Justice to give the *stadsfiskals* the possibility to conduct preliminary investigations themselves, or to ask the police to take charge (Code of Conduct 1927, Circular 1928). Only gradually did the investigation of crime become one of the core functions of the police in Finland as it is today (Hietaniemi, 1995, pp. 22–23).

After World War II, the idea that the prosecutor should be in charge of criminal investigations resurfaced. Once again, the merging of prosecutorial and police functions was planned, but never followed up. Gradually, the complete separation of the two functions was considered as the best solution. Simultaneously, the idea of providing more protection to the accused started to emerge (Hietaniemi, 1995, pp. 304–306).

Reforms in the mid-1990s raised new concerns with regard to the collaboration between police and prosecutor in the pre-trial process. Due to the nationwide separation of police and prosecution in 1996 and the establishment of the accusatorial process with the new Criminal Procedure Act (CPA) in 1997, strengthening the role of the prosecutor in preliminary investigations gained more support.

The oral and centralised hearing imposed by the 1997 CPA notably changed the role of the prosecutor in the criminal process. The power to prosecute and the power to judge were now entirely separated. The prosecutor was now responsible for the clarification of the matter in the process and the court could only handle a matter based on the initiative of the prosecutor. Additionally, the presented charge now limited the target of the trial in a binding way. It became the duty of the prosecutor to collect the evidence and present it to the court. This had major repercussions on the preparation of the case by the prosecutor. (Government bill 82/1995, p. 29; Report of the Law Committee 9/1997; Interviews, 2013; Jääskeläinen, 1997, pp. 154–155; Virolainen and Pölönen, 2004, pp. 43, 63; Pihlajamäki, 2009, pp. 267–268).[16]

The new process required in-depth knowledge of court cases and made it important for the prosecutor to closely follow the course of the investigations ("Syyttäjän toimenkuvan kehittäminen", 2001, p. 15; Illman, 2007, p. 18). The prosecutor now has a major role deciding upon the charges and the prosecution, gathering the relevant background information and the evidence and their themes as well as interviewing witnesses (Helminen *et al.*, 2012, p. 160; Kukkonen and Tolvanen, 2011, p. 81). In the new process, the judge cannot use any material the prosecutor has not raised against the defendant (Interviews, 2013).

The new oral hearing also meant that the prosecutor was now sometimes required to react to surprising turns in the case in court. Thus s/he needs to have thorough knowledge of the case starting from the beginning of the investigation. In addition, the prosecutor is the one responsible for the objectivity and integrity of the evidence produced by the investigation ("Syyttäjän toimenkuvan kehittäminen", 2001, pp. 15, 18). As the prosecutor had previously had a very limited role, while the judge had been actively taken part in the process, the roles of the two were almost reversed as a result of the innovations of the mid-1990s.

During the present decade, some voices have again hoped that the prosecutor could become head of the preliminary investigations. They have argued that this would enhance preliminary investigations and the consideration of charges and remove persisting problems with regard to the flow of information (Expert opinion of Professor Dan Frände, 2010; Expert opinions: Finnish Bar Association, not dated; Prosecutor's Office of Finland Proper, 2010; Working Group of the Supreme Court, 2010; Helsinki District Court, 2010; Rovaniemi Court of Appeal, 2010; Interview Frände, 2015; Commentary of expert opinions, 2011).

In the eyes of these commentators, the Finnish system represents a failed compromise. According to them, the collaborative model easily leads to no one taking final responsibility (Expert opinions: Professor Dan Frände 2010; Finnish Bar Association, not dated; Prosecutor's Office of Finland Proper, 2010). The critics hold that the current system provides wide authority, without ultimate responsibility, to the prosecutor, and leaves open questions of final responsibility over the investigation (Expert opinions: Finnish Prosecutors' Association 2010; Prosecutor's Office of Finland Proper, 2010).

It has also been argued that the prosecutors should be in charge of the supervision of investigations, because such a model would facilitate international collaboration. For instance, in the issuing the European Arrest Warrant, the Finnish system is considered problematic. Many countries require a judicial authority as their collaborative partner, and do not accept the police as one (Interviews, 2013; Interview Frände, 2015). It is possible that the Finnish system will face yet another reform if the EU rejects the use of the Finnish police as a collaborative authority in judicial matters (Interview Frände, 2015).

Advantages of Complete Separation

Arguments supporting a clear separation of prosecutorial powers from police work, have been manyfold and concerned with, for instance, political questions and questions of authority. Partly, they have their roots in the history of the Finnish nation.

In the early years of the twentieth century, the separation of primary investigations and prosecution had strong nationalist backing.[17] The police–prosecutor relationship was a piece in a wider political puzzle, and for this reason it was not considered as purely a matter of legal policy. The restless times in Russia in the early 1900s rippled into Finnish politics, as they caused the Czar to tighten his grip on the whole domain. In 1903–1904, the role of the prosecutor in supervising the police was eliminated and the control of the (Russian-minded) Governors over the police service strengthened (Hietaniemi, 1995, p. 41).The prosecutor remained independent, as he only served under the (Finnish) Procurator (Hietaniemi, 1995, p. 61).

The independence of the prosecutors was important to the nationalists, as it served as a guarantee against Russian influence. During this period, when the police were highly influenced by Russian officials, judicial officers were strong proponents of the Rule of Law. Thus, it was in the (nationalist) Finnish interest to bolster their role in any possible way. In this setting, it is understandable why the idea of the prosecutor as head investigator re-emerged during the early twentieth century: if the prosecutor had a leading role in the investigations, he could use his powers to protect the Finnish Rule of Law (Hietaniemi, 1995, p. 72; "Kertomus Helsingin kaupungin kunnallishallinnosta", p. 125).

Regardless of the nationalists' hopes, it became the role of the police to conduct and supervise all criminal investigations. A debate that took place in the mid-1950s portrays well the minimal role played by the *stadsfiskals* in the "old cities". The debate concerned whether the reports of preliminary investigations conducted by the police should first be sent to the prosecutor or to the court. For instance, Helsinki city *stadsfiskal* Segercrantz argued that the legal expert of the police station and the prosecutor would always draw the same conclusions from the reports in their consideration of charges. For this reason, it was not necessary for the prosecutor to see the files before the court did (Gyllenbögel *et al.*, 1957, p. 7; Segercrantz, 1957, pp. 3–5).

In contrast to the "old cities", in the rural areas, the *länsmans* were still acting as chiefs of police and prosecutors. The bill for the new Act on Criminal Investigation (CIA) reintroduced the idea of completely separating police and prosecutors in 1961. The suggested reforms would have been relatively easy to organise in the "old cities", but it would have meant a dramatic reorganising in the countryside (Hietaniemi, 1995, p. 306). Similarly, in a wider proposition package that concerned preliminary investigations drafted in 1973, the separation of police and prosecution officials was considered vital (Lehtola and Pasanen, 1974, pp. 11–14).

Despite these recurring ideas, the complete separation of police and prosecution only took place in the 1990s. One engine for change was the joining of the European Convention on Human Rights (ECHR) of 1990. The ECHR necessitated that all parties have equal rights, and underlined the importance of the rights of the suspect during preliminary investigations. In a 1993 bill, the Government of Finland argued that because prosecutors had a relatively large amount of decision-making powers, especially since, when they were given responsibility in 1994 over summary penal judgements in less serious criminal matters (Act 692/1993), having an independent prosecutor's agency was the best safeguard for legal security. Such a system safeguarded the rights of the suspect as required by the ECHR, as it kept prosecution entirely separate from both the police and the courts. Along the lines of the ECHR, the role of the prosecutor in looking after also the rights of the suspect was underlined (Government bill 24/1994, p. 5; Virolainen and Pölönen, 2004, pp. 86–88).

Another argument supporting the separation of the police and the prosecutor was the question of impartiality (see e.g. Government bill 92/1995; Expert opinion of Professor Juha Lappalainen, 1986; Kukkonen and Tolvanen, 2011, p. 81). Separating those that make decisions on the charges and those conducting criminal investigations has been considered important because one of the main tasks of the prosecutor is to evaluate alternative hypotheses. Should the prosecutor also act as head investigator and be in charge of guaranteeing the efficacy of the investigation, s/he would be in a worse position to objectively evaluate the possible defects in the investigation process (Helminen *et al.*, 2012, p. 160; Kukkonen and Tolvanen, 2011, p. 81). Comparable arguments have been made since the beginning of the twentieth century.

The impartiality argument seems, however, to have vanished during recent years. Instead, emphasis has been on demands for intensified collaboration between the police and the prosecutor (Report of the Law Committee 9/1997). It has been admitted that even if the role of the prosecutor in the investigation is to remain neutral,[18] s/he is still always tied to the case when participating in the preliminary investigation, and his/her decision may be influenced by a desire to justify the outcomes of the investigations. However, this happens regardless of whether s/he is formally leading the investigation or not (Helminen *et al.*, 2012, pp. 160–161).

In addition to the core values of impartiality, legal security, efficiency and clarity, the leading role of the police in preliminary investigation has been supported by the practical issues of resources. This question has been linked with the amount and quality of professional training. In 1996, when the new Prosecution Service was created, the Government bill stated that only the police, as well as the Customs authorities and the Defence Command in some cases, had the necessary expertise for conducting criminal investigations. As a result, the prosecutors could not take responsibility over the investigative process without such a decision impairing the quality of the investigations (Government bill 131/1996, p. 29).

The reform of the criminal process in 1997 had already markedly expanded the workload of prosecutors and altered the contents of their work. This had necessitated a large amount of training and education. Should the prosecutors have, on top of this, acquired a leading role in the investigations, the amount of training needed would have been massive. It seems likely that the perceived lack of resources and thus also of training has in many cases been one of the key reasons as to why the prosecutors lead or supervise investigations in Finland (see e.g. Government bill 222/2010, p. 31; Helminen *et al.*, 2012, p. 161; Kukkonen and Tolvanen, 2011, p. 81; Interview Tolvanen, 2015; Expert opinions: Professor Matti Tolvanen, 2010; Office of the Ombudsman of the Parliament, 2010).

Finally, one explanation for the complete separation of the prosecution from the investigations is a historical one. Some have suggested that an old battle for authority has left its mark on the current division of roles. It has been argued that the role of the police as head investigator is a remnant of the *länsman*-system period. Thus the leading of the investigations is a position of authority the police have not wished to give up (Interview Frände 2015; Expert opinions:

Prosecutor's Office of Finland Proper 2010; Professor Dan Frände, 2010). However, it has to be noted that during that period the *länsman* was, in addition to being the chief of police, also a prosecutor who had a law degree.

Support for the Collaborative Model

The current Finnish model is somewhat a compromise between the two extremes, the complete separation of police and prosecutor and having a strong prosecutor leading the police and criminal investigations. Both the proponents and the opponents of the idea of the prosecutor as the supervisor of investigations, have supported closer collaboration (see e.g. Law Committee report 44/2010), but such that it is based on more detailed rules. For this reason, the new CIA that clarified and increased collaboration in 2014 was welcomed by both.

According to commentators, the law recognised the special skills and knowledge of both the police and the prosecutor. It supports police collaboration with other officials, and serves the goal to bring all the evidence to the main hearing at once (Expert opinions: Northern Karelia Police Department, 2010; Helsinki Police Department, 2010).

The prosecutors have embraced the opportunity to influence the investigations. Because it is the prosecutor who makes the decision to prosecute and brings the case to court, it is useful from his/her perspective to be able to guide the investigation. This role enables her/him to conduct the work in an efficient manner and improves the quality of work (Illman, 2007, p. 8; Interviews 2013; Expert opinion: Prosecutor's Office of Finland Proper 2010; Interview Frände 2015).[19] If the evidence provided by the investigation is not sufficient or suitable for the purposes of the prosecutor, her/his case can be seriously damaged. Additionally, it is a waste of time if the police are requested to reopen a case that has already been concluded for the purposes of further inquiries. The accusatorial system requires that the matter is investigated as completely as possible. When the case is taken to court, nothing can be missing and all evidence must be available (Interviews, 2013). For this reason, efficient collaboration between police and prosecutor can significantly shorten the length of the criminal process, especially in complicated cases (Expert opinions: Prosecutor General's Office, 2010; Prosecutor's Office of Helsinki, 2010; Interviews, 2013).

In volume crime, it is usually considered to be sufficient that the leader of the investigation can contact the prosecutor if needed (Office of the Prosecutor General 2013). The majority of cases are simple and efficiently investigated also without the presence of the prosecutor (Administration Committee report 50/2010; Committee for Constitutional Law report 66/2010; Kukkonen and Tolvanen, 2011, p. 26). Additionally, as today's police are highly educated, officers are well equipped to evaluate legal matters. The investigators of the most complicated cases, typically economic crimes, usually hold law degrees themselves (Expert opinions: National Police Board 2010; Helsinki Police Department, 2010).

Furthermore, Finnish prosecutors already hold relatively wide powers with regard to coercive measures. For instance, Swedish prosecutors who act as head investigators do not typically use any such powers that Finnish prosecutors do not already possess. Additionally, the possible transfer of the supervision of investigations to prosecutors, would not necessarily guarantee the performance of the criminal process or safeguard the rights of the parties (Government bill 222/2010, p. 31; Tolvanen and Kukkonen, 2011, p. 82). Additional to these reasons, the existing good collaboration between Finnish authorities guarantees, according to some, a smooth process as it is (Expert opinion of the Helsinki Police Department, 2010).

Conclusion

This study has presented the history of the discussion on the police–prosecutor relationship in Finland. As described, there are multiple reasons to why the current model has emerged, including competition over authority between the police and prosecutors; questions and concerns that relate to organisation and impartiality; the perceived lack of resources and training as well as the belief that the current model (especially with the coming into force of the new CIA in 2014) is operational as it is.

It has been especially interesting to find persisting ripples of old historical events. One of such relics is the placing of the prosecution and the police services under the authority of different ministries dating from the Russian era, which still complicates collaboration between the two authorities.

Even if the current model of enhanced collaboration is widely supported, having the prosecutor in charge of preliminary investigations is still sometimes considered a relevant option for two reasons. First, it is perceived that this would improve and enhance the criminal process, and second, it would clarify the division of labour between the police and prosecutors.

Based on the findings of this research, it seems possible that the current arrangement could serve as a stepping-stone towards the prosecutors one day formally supervising investigations.[20] For instance, in the government bill that prepared the CIA of 2014, it was stated that it is necessary to engage prosecutors more and more in the investigations so that they can attain more knowledge and experience upon decision-making in preliminary investigations.[21] This could suggest that formal supervision of investigations by prosecutors is still under consideration, as one of the central problems in furthering this goal has been prosecutors' perceived lack of sufficient expertise, training and skills for this role. When the police–prosecutor cooperation is enhanced, prosecutors gain practical knowledge on the conducting of investigations. It remains to be seen whether such a reform, and the resources required to effectively implement it, will eventuate.

Notes

1 The distrainer is the person who in case of unpaid debt, seizes one's property in order to compel the payment of debts.
2 This same official had additional tasks as well, depending on the city.
3 The historical account in this chapter is partly based on my previous work. See Jansson 2016.
4 Finland had a rather autonomous status within the Russia Empire. See in more detail the governance of the Grand Duchy of Finland e.g. Jussila 2004.
5 These were cities founded before 1959. They had a relatively autonomous role and were themselves responsible for some of the duties that belonged to the state in the countryside.
6 Swedish is the other official language of Finland, alongside Finnish. I will be using the Swedish terms in this study, due to reasons of clarity for (English-speaking) readers.
7 This apparently occurred occasionally but was not common. Conducting criminal investigations requires specific knowledge and skills. Without special training, prosecutors did not possess the necessary skills for this. However, the right to conduct the whole of the investigations was sometimes brought out when the police and the prosecutor disagreed on details (Interviews, 2013).
8 The history of the länsman has been thoroughly covered in Ylikangas, 1996.
9 In small cities, even if a formal separation of the *stadsfiskal* and the police existed, the two often collaborated closely (Interview Frände, 2015).
10 See in more detail below.
11 In a typical criminal trial, there is either one or three judges and possibly also a lay jury, depending on the seriousness of the matter. All material is to be presented orally, as opposed to the previous system, where a large part of the trial was conducted on paper.
12 In special cases, also courts could initiate proceedings (Ignatius, 1900, pp. 236–237).
13 In specific types of complicated crimes, such as the most difficult economic and drug related cases, the police and the prosecutor had build a strong collaboration regardless of the general practices (Interviews, 2013).
14 The decision about which cases are those where collaboration is needed, is based on a collaboration agreement between the police and the prosecutor's office (CIA 805/2011 5:3).
15 Most recently this idea has been expressed in these following Expert opinions: Professor Dan Frände 2010, Finnish Bar Association not dated and Prosecutor's Office of Finland Proper 2010. It has to be noted that during the period studied there have been changes in the ways in which the role of the head of the investigation is understood. Some consider the head investigator as a supervisor; the one who makes decisions mostly on the main points of the investigation, for instance the closing of the investigations or the use of coercive measures. Expert opinion of the Finnish Bar Association, not dated.
16 See in more detail about the accusatorial process e.g. Virolainen, 2011 in: Frände *et al.*, 2012, pp. 208–211.
17 Discussed in more detail below.
18 Tolvanen has compared the requirement of neutrality of the prosecutor to the role of a judge (Tolvanen 66).
19 On the other hand, as Professor Matti Tolvanen has noted, it is also logical to keep the heading of the investigations in the hands of a police official, as the first-hand responsibility over the lawfulness of specific investigative measures and also for the investigation to satisfy the aims listed in CIA 1:2 is the police's. The responsibility of the prosecutor is to supervise that the police conducts the investigation in a manner that serves the function of the consideration of charges and the possible trial (Tolvanen 55).

20 For instance, it seems that investigators are increasingly contacting the prosecutor directly, should they need any support in their work. In case this becomes common practice, it would mean that the prosecutor is de facto leading the investigations and the role of head investigator is changed to a formal role. Interview with Professor Dan Frände 9.1.2015.
21 Government bill HE 222/2010 p. 31.

Sources and Bibliography

Legislation

Code of Conduct for the Stadsfiskal 1927 (Kaupunginviskaalin ohjesääntö).
Decree on Stadsfiskals 181/1978 (Asetus kaupunginviskaaleista).
Government bill 14/1985 (Regarding criminal investigations and coercive measures) (Hallituksen esitys eduskunnalle Esitutkintaa ja pakkokeinoja rikosasioissa koskevaksi lainsäädännöksi).
Criminal Investigations Act (CIA) 449/1987 (Esitutkintalaki).
Act on Summary Penal Judgements 692/1993 (Laki rangaistusmääräysmenettelystä).
Government bill 24/1994 (Regarding the stadsfiskals and summary penal procedures) (Hallituksen esitys Eduskunnalle laiksi kihlakunnansyyttäjästä sekä laiksi rangaistusmääräysmenettelystä annetun lain 9 §:n 2 ja 3 momentin kumoamisesta).
Government bill 82/1995 (Regarding the amendment of the criminal procedure in district courts) (Hallituksen esitys Eduskunnalle rikosasioiden oikeudenkäyntimenettelyn uudistamista alioikeuksissa koskevaksi lainsäädännöksi).
Government bill 131/1996 (Regarding the highest prosecutorial authority, the creation of the Office of the Prosecutor General and District Prosecutors) (Hallituksen esitys Eduskunnalle Suomen Hallitusmuodon ylintä syyttäjää koskevien säännösten muuttamisesta sekä laiksi yleisistä syyttäjistä ja eräiksi niihin liittyviksi laeiksi).
Act on District Prosecutors 195/1996 (Laki kihlakunnansyyttäjistä).
Act on Amending the Criminal Investigations Act (Amendment to the CIA) 692/1997 (Laki esitutkintalain muuttamisesta).
Act on Public Prosecutors 199/1997 (Laki yleisistä syyttäjistä).
Criminal Procedure Act (CPA) 689/1997 (Laki oikeudenkäynnistä rikosasioissa).
Government bill 222/2010 (regarding the amending of the CIA and the Coercive Measures Act (CMA), translation JJ) (Hallituksen esitys Eduskunnalle esitutkinta- ja pakkokeinolainsäädännön uudistamiseksi).
Criminal Investigations Act (CIA) 805/2011 (Esitutkintalaki).

Official Documents

"Kertomus Helsingin kaupungin kunnallishallinnosta". Helsingin kaupunki 1909.
Councellor of Justice circular, n:o 305, DN:o 222/30 1928.
Kari Lehtola and Jukka Pasanen, "Lausunnot ns. esitutkintapaketista, yhteenveto" Oikeusministeriön lainsäädäntöosasto 1974.
Expert opinion of Professor Juha Lappalainen to the Law Committee of the Finnish Parliament 9.10.1986 regarding the Government bill 82/1995.
Law Committee Report 9/1997 (Regarding the amending of the criminal procedure act, JJ) (Lakiasiainvaliokunnan mietintö LaVM: Rikosasiain oikeudenkäyntimenettelyn uudistaminen alioikeuksissa).

Administrative Committee Report 50/2010 on the Government Bill 222/2010. (Hallintovaliokunnan lausunto HaVL, Hallituksen esitys esitutkinta- ja pakkokeinolainsäädännön uudistamiseksi).

Committee for Constitutional Law Report 66/2010 on the Government Bill 222/2010. (Perustuslakivaliokunnan mietintö PeVM, Hallituksen esitys esitutkinta- ja pakkokeinolainsäädännön uudistamiseksi).

Expert opinions on the Government bill 222/2010 to the Law Committee of the Finnish Parliament: The Finnish Bar Association not dated, The Prosecutor General's Office 23.11.2010, Professor Dan Frände 10.12.2010, The Finnish Prosecutors' Association 28.11.2010, The Working Group of the Supreme Court 2.12.2010, Prosecutor's Office of Finland Proper 7.12.2010, The Helsinki District Court 8.12.2010, The Rovaniemi Court of Appeal 7.12.2010, The Northern Karelia Police Department 7.12.2010, Helsinki Police Department 8.12.2010, The National Police Board 2010, Professor Olli Mäenpää 9.12.2010, Office of the Ombudsman of the Parliament 9.12.2010.

Law Committee Report 44/2010 on the Government Bill 222/2010. (Lakivaliokunnan mietintö LaVM: Hallituksen esitys esitutkinta- ja pakkokeinolainsäädännön uudistamiseksi).

Commentary of expert opinions of the Ministry of Justice on the Government bill 222/2010 27.1.2011.

Office of the Prosecutor General, "Esitutkintayhteistyötä koskeva ohje" VKSV:n julkaisusarja, Edita Prima, 2013.

Other Primary Sources

Letter from the Chancellor of Justice Axel Charpentier to the Helsinki city council 14.5.1927, N:o 637.

Letter by the organisatory committee of the Court of First Instance in Helsinki, 29.7.1957, 11 pages. Signatories: Walter Gyllenbögel, Armo Keravuori, K.H. Molin, Fredrik Bruun, Kauko Kuisma and U. Kivi-Koskinen.

Nils-Erik Segercrantz (stadsfiskal), letter to the City Council. Not dated, approximately from 1957.

Bibliography

Ehrström, K.G. (1866) "Anmärkningar rörande Finlands rättegångsordning i brottmål" *Juridiska Föreningens i Finland Tidskrift*: 48–79.

Frände, D., E. Havansi, D. Helenius, R. Koulu, J. Lappalainen, H. Lindfors, J. Niemi, J. Rautio and J. Virolainen (2012) *Prosessioikeus* (Helsinki: SanomaPro).

Helminen, K., M. Fredman, J. Kanerva, M. Tolvanen and M. Viitanen (2012) *Esitutkinta ja pakkokeinot* (Helsinki: Talentum).

Hietaniemi, T. (1995) *Totuuden jäljillä. Suomalaisen rikospoliisin taival* (Vantaa: Keskusrikospoliisi).

Ignatius, K. (1900) *Virallisen syyttäjistön kehittyminen, organisatsiooni ja syyteoikeus* (Helsingfors: Weilin & Göös Aktiebolag).

Illman, M. (2007) *Suomen ja Ruotsin syyttäjien toimenkuvia koskeva vertailu* (Helsinki: Valtakunnansyyttäjänviraston julkaisusarja).

Jansson, J. (2014) *Helsingin syyttäjänviraston historia – Kunniatehtävästä tulosvastuuseen* (Helsinki: Edita).

Jansson, J. (2016) "Drawing the Line between the Prosecutor and the Police in Finland – Two Hundred Years of Search for Best Practices" *Tidskrift utgiven av Juridiska föreningen i Finland* 1–2: 112–136.

Jussila, O. (2004) *Suomen suuriruhtinaskunta 1809–1917* (Helsinki: WSOY).

Jääskeläinen, P. (1997) *Syyttäjä tuomarina* (Helsinki: Suomalainen lakimiesyhdistys).

Kukkonen, R. and M. Tolvanen (2011) *Esitutkinta ja pakkokeino-oikeuden perusteet* (Helsinki: Talentum).

Office of the Prosecutor General (2001) "Syyttäjän toimenkuvan kehittäminen". www.vksv.oikeus.fi/material/attachments/valtakunnansyyttajanvirasto/vksvliitetiedostot/julkaisusarja/6INGzPQZL/1_Syyttajan_toimenkuvan_kehittaminen.pdf Retrieved 13 February 2018.

Pasterstein, D. (2009) Poliisin ja syyttäjän yhteistyön kehittyminen Helsingissä, seurantatutkimus (Unpublished Master's thesis, University of Tampere).

Virolainen, J. and Pölönen, P. (2004) *Rikosprosessin osalliset. Rikosprosessioikeus II* (Helsinki: WSOY).

Ylikangas, H. (1996) *Wallesmanni: Kuusi vuosisataa kansan ja esivallan välissä* (Helsinki: Suomen nimismiesyhdistys).

Interviews

Interviews with 24 former and current prosecutors, police officers, attorneys, judges, writservers and officials of the Ministry of Justice conducted in 2013 for my book (Jansson, 2014). The commentators were promised that all their comments would be referred to anonymously. The list of the interviewees consists of the following people: Juha Hakola, 20.11.2013, Tom Ifström, 10.10.2013, Martti Jaatinen, 22.10.2013, Satu Johansson, 21.10.2013, Jukka Järvinen, 16.12.2013, Jorma Kalske, 16.10.2013, Matti Kuusimäki, 23.10.2013, Hannu Kuusisto, 28.10.2013, Liisa Lehtiö, 4.12.2013 (telephone interview), Päivi Lindholm, 21.10.2013, Jussi Nilsson, 19.12.2013, Matti Nissinen, 14.10.2013, Antero Nuotto, 6.11.2013 (telephone interview), Tapio Nyrhilä 5.12.2013, Kari Penttinen 18.10.2013, Markku Pohjanoksa 28.10.2013, Heikki Poukka, 13.11.2013, Petri Rainiala, 20.11.2013, Jarmo Rautakoski 11.10.2013, Ritva Santavuori 5.11.2013, Seppo Seppälä, 16.12.2013, Antti Simola 29.10.2013, Jorma Uski 22.10.2013, Matti Wikström, 29.10.2013, Annika Zilliacus 18.11.2013. Additionally, I have interviewed Dan Frände, Professor of Criminal Law at the University of Helsinki, 9.1.2015 and Matti Tolvanen, Professor of Criminal Law and Criminal Procedure Law at the University of Eastern Finland 8.1.2015 via email.

6 Framing Prosecutor–Police Relations in Europe – A Concept Paper

Philip Stenning and Julia Jansson

> I think it is of the first importance that policemen should be kept strictly to their functions as policemen, as persons to apprehend and have the custody of the prisoners, and not as persons who are to mix themselves up in the conduct of a prosecution, whereby they acquire a bias infinitely stronger than that which, under any circumstances, naturally attach itself to their evidence.
>
> (Sir Alexander Cockburn, Attorney General of England, in his evidence to the Criminal Law Commissioners considering the role of police as prosecutors (1845))

Introduction

Despite Sir Alexander Coburn's protestations, the responsibility for prosecuting almost all criminal cases in England resided with Chief Constables[1] for 140 years after his evidence to the Criminal Law Commissioners in 1845. Meanwhile, in Scotland during those years, there were legally trained prosecutors, called procurator-fiscals, who not only had exclusive responsibility for making prosecutorial decisions and for conducting all prosecutions in court, but also had authority to supervise and direct the police in their criminal investigations (Moody and Tombs, 1982). During this same period, in almost all continental European countries, police had virtually no formal role at all either in decisions whether prosecutions should be launched, or in the actual conduct of those prosecutions that were. As in Scotland, legally trained prosecutors played a key role in performing these prosecutorial functions, but both they and the police (usually specifically dedicated "judicial police") were supervised and directed in the performance of their investigative and prosecutorial responsibilities by investigating magistrates (in France, for instance, called "*juges d'instruction*").

These are but three examples illustrating how the respective roles of police, legally trained prosecutors and magistrates, and the formal relationships between them in the criminal prosecution process, have varied among European jurisdictions. Yet there has been little scholarship that has explained how and why these very different police–prosecutor relationships developed in different jurisdictions, virtually no comparative empirical research on their implications for the efficacy and outcomes of criminal prosecutions, and very little historical scholarship on when and why these relationships changed within individual jurisdictions.

In this chapter, we set out some ideas about how comparative empirical research into the variations in police–prosecutor relationships in European jurisdictions might be structured, and how data about them might be analysed. The purpose and possible benefit of such research, we believe, would be to ascertain whether some forms of this relationship might be more effective than others in achieving the supposed objectives of prosecution processes, and to what extent different forms of the relationship reflect different priorities among competing objectives.

The Relevance of Procedural Contexts

Most European countries have one of two different kinds of legal system – a civil law or "inquisitorial" system (henceforth referred to as civil law jurisdictions), or a common law or "adversarial/accusatorial" system (henceforth referred to as common law jurisdictions). In a few European countries, for example Malta, their foundational legal system has been adapted somewhat to include features of the other system. The great majority of continental European countries, however, are civil law jurisdictions; a relatively small minority of European countries (notably the United Kingdom, the Republic of Ireland, Cyprus, and Gibraltar) are common law jurisdictions.

In all these countries the criminal prosecution process is generally recognised as having four consecutive phases – an investigative phase, a prosecutorial phase, an adjudicative phase,[2] and (in the event of a conviction) a sentencing and corrections phase. In this chapter, we focus on the first and second, pre-trial, investigative and prosecutorial phases. These two phases typically include a number of consecutive elements: a complaint or accusation of the commission of a criminal offence; an official investigation into the complaint or accusation, culminating in a report; a decision as to whether criminal charges will be laid, and if so who will be charged and with what offences; and decisions about various other pre-trial matters such as whether a person who has been charged will be detained or released pending trial and if released, conditions that may be attached, whether some kind of legal aid will be made available to the accused, etc.

The investigative function is essentially forensic (find the facts) and relies mainly on technical expertise and coercive powers, but also requires some legal knowledge/understanding (knowing what facts could be relevant, criteria of admissibility as evidence, etc.). The prosecutorial function (deciding whether to prosecute, whom to prosecute, what charges to pursue, how and in what court to initiate a prosecution, managing witnesses, etc.) involves more normative "public interest" considerations (e.g. what cases to prioritise and why), requires a high level of legal knowledge (knowing what evidence is admissible and is sufficient to found a successful prosecution, how to present the case effectively in court, what witnesses to call etc.), and requires a more balanced review of the available evidence, including evidence that might exculpate the accused (sometimes referred to in common law jurisdictions as the "minister of justice" concept). The extent of *discretion* that is afforded to officials in exercising these functions varies greatly from one jurisdiction to another, and in particular between civil law and common law jurisdictions. In civil law jurisdictions, a "principle of legality", whereby prosecutions must be initiated when minimum evidential requirements are satisfied, has traditionally been applied to these decisions, although the exercise of discretion with respect to these decisions has increasingly been recognised as acceptable in some civil law jurisdictions. In common law jurisdictions, discretion is the accepted norm, one result of which has been that some form of pre-trial "plea bargaining" has increasingly become the norm in these jurisdictions, with a radical impact on the prosecution process.

In every jurisdiction, the responsibility for these various pre-trial decisions is allocated in some way between police, legally qualified prosecutors, and judicial officers such as magistrates. In broad terms, the allocation of responsibilities between these three kinds of officials and the relationships between them, vary significantly between civil law "inquisitorial" jurisdictions and common law "accusatorial/adversarial" jurisdictions. Traditionally, in civil law jurisdictions, supervision and control over both criminal investigations and pre-trial prosecutorial decisions rests ultimately with investigating magistrates, and police and prosecutors are accountable to such magistrates for the performance of their respective roles in the process. By contrast, in most common law jurisdictions, police, prosecutors and magistrates occupy separate and relatively independent positions, and each enjoys considerable autonomy in performing their respective investigative, prosecutorial and adjudicative roles in the criminal prosecution process. This general description of the respective roles and responsibilities in civil law and common law jurisdictions is an oversimplification, however, because the allocation of responsibilities and the relationships between the police prosecutors and magistrates vary not only between civil and common law jurisdictions, but also between different countries within each of these two kinds of jurisdictions (as, for instance, between England and Scotland, and between France and Italy). Thus, in most common law jurisdictions police combine investigative and prosecutorial responsibilities in the overwhelming majority of "less serious" offences, with only the small minority of the "more serious" cases being prosecuted by legally trained independent prosecutors. Only in a few common law jurisdictions (such as the United States, Canada and Scotland) are the majority of all criminal cases prosecuted by independent legally trained prosecutors. Similar variations can be found among civil law jurisdictions. Thus, in a few civil law jurisdictions, magistrates are not involved in supervising and controlling the police or prosecutors in performing their pre-trial investigative and prosecutorial responsibilities. While in France prosecutors are administratively located within the magistracy (and during their careers may switch between prosecutor and magistrate roles) (Hodgson, 2005), in Italy prosecutors enjoy a wide measure of independence, and are not subject to supervision by investigating magistrates (Di Federico, 2005). This allocation of responsibilities between police, prosecutors and magistrates has been the subject of substantial policy and academic debate in many European countries in recent decades (see e.g. Mathias, 2002).

In this chapter, we focus particularly on the allocations of these responsibilities between police and legally qualified prosecutors (henceforth prosecutors), as prescribed in law as well as occurs in practice, the consequent relationships between police and prosecutors in fulfilling these responsibilities, and to what extent there is some judicial oversight of the exercise of them. We consider whether, and to what extent, these allocations are determined by the fundamental nature of the legal system (civil law or common law) of each jurisdiction, and/or other factors, and what rationales have been advanced for these allocations in each system. We also consider how these allocations have changed over time in individual jurisdictions, and the apparent reasons and rationales for such changes. In doing so, we do not report the findings of comparative empirical research (which has not yet been done); we propose a conceptual framework within which to undertake such systematic cross-jurisdictional comparative empirical research.

A Brief Comment on the Extant Literature

There are several published English-language articles and books on police–prosecutor relations. Most discuss the situation in single countries or jurisdictions, most are based on the situation in the USA, and many of these are now quite outdated (see e.g. Feeley and Lazerson, 1983; McIntyre 1975; Buchanan, 1989; Rowe, 2016). By comparison, the literature on police–prosecutor relations in Europe is relatively small. As with the American literature, most of it discusses the relationship in a single jurisdiction (see e.g. McGloin, 2006; White, 2006; Jansson in this book), although some articles compare two or more countries (e.g. Goldstein and Marcus, 1977; Mathias, 2002; Jasch, 2004; Braum, 2012). Analysis is mostly of the formal legal provisions and policies governing this relationship, rather than based on empirical research (Hodgson, 2001 is an exception). One notable exception in this respect is EuroJustice's report on survey research commissioned by the Dutch Board of Prosecutors-general, under the leadership of Professor Peter Tak of Nijmegen University, which includes country reports on the police–prosecutor relationship in 25 EU member states. While this report is very helpful in demonstrating how this relationship varies from one European country to another, it does not include comparative analysis of the implications and effects of these variations, the rationales behind them, or how, when and why they have changed over time. It is this more fine-grained empirical research that we are arguing needs to be done now.

The Importance of Prosecutor–Police Relations in the Prosecution Process

We theorise that the importance of understanding the allocation of responsibilities between police and prosecutor in the criminal prosecution process, and consequent prosecutor–police relations in exercising these responsibilities, is that they reflect, to varying degrees, the extent to which key values associated with prosecution processes are prioritised and upheld. We suggest seven such key values, which are:

a Impartiality (and avoiding "tunnel vision")
b Independence (especially from political control)/separation of powers
c Equity (similar cases treated similarly)
d Efficiency/cost effectiveness
e Expertise/competence (allocation of responsibilities to those best qualified to exercise them)
f Checks and balances ("two heads better than one")
g Effective political/public accountability

The key question that needs to be explored is how different allocations of responsibility between police and prosecutors reflect, and are intended to reflect, in law *and* in practice, the relative importance ascribed to these key values. We propose a three-level analysis in which a value is identified as apparently of high, medium or low priority in these arrangements.

By way of example, we suggest the following indicators of these variables:

Impartiality:	**High**	• complete separation of prosecutor and police functions (prosecutors do not supervise police investigations, and police do not decide whether a prosecution should be initiated)
	Medium	• partial separation of prosecutor and police functions (prosecutors supervise some, but not all police investigations, and police may make prosecutorial decisions in some cases)
	Low	• no clear separation of prosecutor and police functions (investigative and prosecutorial functions are combined in the same agency (e.g. police prosecutors) or prosecutors supervise all police investigations)
Independence:	**High**	• complete separation of prosecutor and police functions • police and prosecutors governed by judiciary/ magistrates, not politicians
	Medium	• partial separation of prosecutor and police functions • police and prosecutors governed by judiciary/ magistrates and politicians
	Low	• no clear separation of prosecutor and police functions • police and prosecutors governed by politicians, not judiciary/magistrates

Equity:	**High**	• police and prosecutors both organised nationally • police and prosecutors governed by principle of legality
	Medium	• police organised locally, prosecutors nationally • police and prosecutors exercise discretion subject to guidelines
	Low	• police and prosecutors both organised locally • police and prosecutors exercise largely unfettered discretion
Efficiency/cost effectiveness:	**High**	• no clear separation of prosecutor and police functions
	Medium	• partial separation of prosecutor and police functions
	Low	• complete separation of prosecutor and police functions
Expertise/ competence:	**High**	• complete separation of prosecutor and police functions
	Medium	• partial separation of prosecutor and police functions
	Low	• no clear separation of prosecutor and police functions
Checks and balances:	**High**	• complete separation of prosecutor and police functions
	Medium	• partial separation of prosecutor and police functions
	Low	• no clear separation of prosecutor and police functions
Political/public accountability:	**High**	• police and prosecutors accountable to politicians
	Medium	• limited accountability to politicians
	Low	• police and prosecutors not accountable to politicians

By "partial separation of prosecutor and police functions" we envisage two kinds of situations: (1) allocation of responsibilities between police and prosecutors varies according to the seriousness of the offence (e.g. police prosecute less serious offences, prosecutors prosecute more serious offences); (2) police are required to consult with prosecutors, but are not subject to direction by them, except in specified types of cases (e.g. before deciding on what charges to lay in high-profile or especially complex cases).

Institutional Characteristics and Key Values

It will be noted that we have posited that the extent to which police and prosecutors are organised nationally or locally reflects the priorities placed on the key values that we have identified; for example, by way of ensuring equity in investigatory and prosecutorial decision-making – that is, whether uniformity and consistency, or local variability, is prioritised. Our supposition is that central organisation favours equity more than local organisation, but that the implications of local organisation may be mediated through the implementation of central policy that is effectively required to be adhered to in local decision-making. Also, "medium" priority for equity may be reflected if either the police, or more significantly prosecutors, are organised nationally, while the other is not (a situation that currently exists, for instance, in England and Wales).

In measuring relevant institutional characteristics, we suggest that the following factors need to be considered:

a **The police**

i How organised

- centrally or locally
- division of functions

a all functions within a single organisational hierarchy
b separation of functions (e.g. general vs. investigative, responsible to different authorities – "judicial police")

ii Administrative location/accountability

- part of the national executive, responsible to a minister
- part of local administration, responsible to a local authority (e.g. Police and Crime Commissioner, mayor, or other local police governing authority)
- a blend of both

iii Functions

- purely investigative
- investigative and prosecutorial
- investigative and prosecutorial in some (usually less serious) cases, but purely investigative in others (usually more serious cases)

iv Independence

- from political direction/control
- from judicial direction/control
- from direction/control by prosecutors
- subject to direction/control/supervision by all or any of (a) politicians, (b) magistrates, (c) prosecutors

b **Prosecutors**

i How organised

- centrally or locally
- single organisation or multiple organisations (some specialised, e.g. the Serious Fraud Office in the UK)

ii Administrative location/accountability

- part of the national executive, responsible to a minister
- part of local administration, responsible to a local authority
- a blend of both
- part of judicial arm of government, responsible to judiciary/magistracy
- some blend of both

iii Functions

- purely prosecutorial
- investigative as well as prosecutorial (undertake investigations themselves or supervise/direct investigations by others, such as police)
- investigative and prosecutorial in some (usually more serious) cases, but purely prosecutorial in others (usually less serious cases)

iv Independence

- from political direction/control
- from judicial direction/control
- from direction/control by more senior prosecutors
- subject to some direction/control/supervision by all or any of (a) politicians, (b) magistrates, (c) more senior prosecutors

c **Magistrates**

Functions

- Purely judicial, with no investigative responsibilities other than issuing warrants etc. for certain investigative functions (arrest and detention, search and seizure, surveillance, wiretapping, etc.)
- Judicial, investigative and prosecutorial responsibilities
- Undertake investigations themselves
- Supervise or control investigations by (a) police and/or (b) prosecutors
- Ultimately responsible, or not, for prosecutorial decisions

Addressing the Allocation of Responsibilities

In order to understand how responsibilities are allocated between these three officials, at a minimum the following questions will need to be addressed:

1. Who decides whether an investigation will be undertaken?
2. Who has control over the process of the investigation, and how it will be undertaken?
3. Does the investigator have to consult with the prosecutor (or investigating magistrate) during the investigation? Or is this at the investigator's discretion?
4. When the investigation is considered by the investigator to be completed, what happens next?
   - Does the investigator decide whether the case will proceed to prosecution, and if so what charges will be laid?
   - Or does the investigator turn the file over to someone else (e.g. an investigating magistrate or a prosecutor)? If so, does the investigator have discretion whether to do so or not, or is the investigator required to in all cases?
5. If there is negotiation over what charges will be laid (e.g. plea bargaining), who is typically responsible for these negotiations, who participates in them, and who has the authority to approve the final agreement?
6. Who ultimately decides whether a prosecution will go ahead or not? If yes, who conducts the prosecution (serves as the prosecutor in court)?
7. Do the answers to these questions vary according to (a) whether it is a serious offence or a not so serious one? and/or (b) where decisions are made (e.g. in a city or in a rural area?).
8. Have the answers to these questions changed is any significant way during the last 30 years? If so, how, and what developments have caused the allocation of responsibilities to change in the way that they have? What rationales have been expressed for these changes?

These questions will need to be used as a guide to interpreting the documentary materials (legislation, policy documents, court rulings, etc.), as well as a basis for interviews with practitioners.

Considering and Understanding Change

As we noted earlier, significant changes in the allocations of responsibilities between police and prosecutors, and in the consequent relations between them, have occurred in many jurisdictions over the years. By way of example, over the last 40 years significant changes in this respect have occurred in England and Wales. Prior to the mid-1980s, both investigative and prosecutorial responsibilities were accorded to the police, under the direction of local Chief Constables, in all but a few of the most serious or high profile cases (in which the national Director of Public Prosecutions or the Attorney General was involved). Chief Constables retained lawyers in private practice to represent them as prosecutors in court. In 1985, however, following the recommendations of a royal commission of inquiry, a new national prosecutorial institution, the Crown Prosecution Service (CPS), modelled on the prosecution service in one of the Canadian provinces, was introduced by the *Prosecution of Offences Act.* Staffed by legally trained prosecutors, the CPS now took over responsibility for prosecutorial, but not investigative, decisions in all cases. Since then, and in light of experience with the new arrangements, prosecutorial responsibility with respect to some less serious offences has been handed back to the (regionally organised) police. Julia Jansson (Chapter 5 in this book) has documented some quite similar developments in the recent history of prosecutions in Finland, and we are aware that similar changes have occurred in other European countries. We should discover, through comparative research, whether there is any discernible general trend in Europe in this respect.

We need to understand the reasons for such changes as these, the rationales invoked to justify them, and the extent to which they reflect changes in the priorities that are accorded to the various key values that we have identified (for instance a higher value is placed on efficiency), or other (e.g. political or economic) factors. Two factors that may be of importance in this respect in Europe, are: (1) the influence of the *European Convention on Human Rights*, and its enforcement through the European Court of Human Rights; and (2) the move towards increasing "harmonisation" of law enforcement and justice in Europe in the face of the increasingly transnational character of certain kinds of crime and the relaxation of border controls (Schengen Agreement). Key developments with respect to the second of these have been the establishment of Europol as a transnational police institution, and recent moves to establish a European Prosecutor.

Conclusion

In this chapter, we have tried to go beyond the extant literature in exploring how we might develop a more fine-grained understanding of how police and prosecutors work with each other in the criminal prosecution process, and how constitutional, legal, institutional, organisational and political factors structure and influence such relationships in practice in European jurisdictions. We have argued that it will be instructive not only to understand these relationships as they are in theory and in practice in different jurisdictions now, but also how and why they have changed over time in so many jurisdictions, and what arguments have been made for these changes. Most specifically, we have argued that these relationships may reflect different ideas about the values and objectives that the police–prosecutor relationship is intended to reflect and achieve, and which, among a number of competing values and objectives in this respect, should be accorded priority. Perhaps, if in-depth research on these matters can be undertaken in multiple jurisdictions in which these priorities appear to differ, we may be able to discern some "best practices" in this relationship that could optimise the achievement of all the potentially competing objectives. This may contribute to the utility of "borrowings" between different legal systems (in particular between inquisitorial and accusatorial models of the criminal prosecution process), which have become increasingly common in the late twentieth and early twenty-first centuries, to improve performance not only in domestic jurisdictions, but also in the emerging international criminal prosecution institutions.

Notes

1 Chief Constables retained private practising lawyers, referred to as prosecuting solicitors, to conduct prosecutions on their behalf in more difficult cases.
2 This phase includes, in some cases, one or more appeals as well as a trial, and in some jurisdictions may also include various kinds of pre-trial processes presided over by judges or magistrates.

Some Relevant Sources for Such Research

Bardens, J. (2014) "Charging Decisions and Police-Led Prosecutions" (London: House of Commons Library) – accessible online at http://researchbriefings.files.parliament.uk/documents/SN06840/SN06840.pdf.

Baumann, T. (2015) "Staatsanwaltschaftliche Ermittlungstätigkeit In Deutschland: Umfang und Struktur der Verfahrenserledigung" (Wiesbaden: Statistisches Bundesamt) – accessible online at www.destatis.de/DE/Publikationen/WirtschaftStatistik/2015/03/StaatsanwaltschaftlicheErmittlungstaetigkeit_032015.pdf?__blob=publicationFile.

Braum, S. (2012) "Prosecutorial Control of Investigations in Europe: A Call for Judicial Oversight" – in Luna, E. and M. Wade (eds) *The Prosecutor in Transnational Perspective* (Oxford: Oxford University Press), pp. 67–81.

Buchanan, J. (1989) "Police-prosecutor Teams: Innovations in Several Jurisdictions" *National Institute of Justice, Research in Action* – reprinted from NIJ Reports, No. 214 (May–June 1989) – accessible online at www.ncjrs.gov/pdffiles1/Digitization/120288NCJRS.pdf.

Council of Europe (2000) *What Public Prosecution in Europe in the 21st Century* (Strasbourg: Council of Europe Publishing).

Damaška, M. (1981) "The Reality of Prosecutorial Discretion: Comments on a German Monograph" *American Journal of Comparative Law* 29: 119–138.

Dervieux, V., M. Benillouche and O. Bachelet (2002) "The French System" – in Delmas-Marty, M. and J. Spencer (eds) *European Criminal Procedures* (Cambridge: Cambridge University Press), Ch. 4, pp. 218–291.

Di Federico, G. (2005) "The Independence and Accountability of the Public Prosecutor – in Search of a Difficult Equilibrium: The Cases of England, France and Italy" *Mediterranean Journal of Human Rights* 9(2): 93–118.

Elsner, B., C. Lewis and J. Zila (2008) "Police Prosecution Service Relationship within Criminal Investigation" *European Journal on Criminal Policy and Research* 24(2): 203–224.

Euro Justice (n.d.) *Country Reports* – accessible online at www.eurojustice.org/sitemap/ (each country report includes a section on "The Relation between the Public Prosecutor and the Police").

European Journal of Crime, Criminal Law and Criminal Justice (2000) *Special Issue: The Future of the Public Prosecutor's Office in the European Union: Proceedings of the Leuven Conference on 25 May 2000* 8(3): 149–318. – Includes articles on Belgium, England and Wales, France, Germany and The Netherlands.

Feeley, M. and M. Lazerson (1983) "Police-Prosecutor Relationships: An Interorganizational Perspective" *Empirical Theories about Courts*: 216–243.

Feeney, F. (1998) *German and American Prosecutions: An Approach to Statistical Comparison* (Washington, DC: U.S. Bureau of Justice Statistics) – accessible online at www.bjs.gov/content/pub/pdf/gap.pdf.

Gilliéron, G. *Public Prosecutors in the United States and Europe: A Comparative Analysis with Special Focus on Switzerland, France and Germany* (Heidelberg/New York/Dordrecht/London: Springer-Verlag).

Goldstein, A. and M. Marcus (1977) "The Myth of Judicial Supervision in Three "Inquisitorial" Systems: France, Italy and Germany" *Yale Law Journal* 87(2): 240–283.

Great Britain, Royal Commission on Criminal Procedure (1981a) *Report* (Sir Cyril Phillips, Chairman) Cmnd 8092 (London: H.M.S.O.) – Chs. 6 and 7 [Reviews main arguments for and against police as prosecutors – recommending police as prosecutors be replaced by an independent Crown Prosecution Service, staffed by lawyers].

Great Britain, Royal Commission on Criminal Procedure (1981b) *The Investigation and Prosecution of Criminal Offences in England and Wales: The Law and Procedure* (London: H.M.S.O.).

Herrmann, J. (1974) "The Rule of Compulsory Prosecution and the Scope of Prosecutorial Discretion in Germany" *University of Chicago Law Review* 41(3): 468–505.

Hodgson, J. (2001) "The Police, the Prosecutor and the Juge D'Instruction: Judicial Supervision in France, Theory and Practice" *British Journal of Criminology* 41(2): 342–361.

Hodgson, J. (2005) *French Criminal Justice: A Comparative Account of the Investigation and Prosecution of Crime in France* (Oxford/Portland, OR: Hart Publishing).

Hodgson, J. (2010) "The French Prosecutor in Question" *Washington & Lee Law Review* 67: 1361–1411.

Jansson, J. (2016) "Drawing the Line between the Prosecutor and Police in Finland – Two Hundred Years of Search for Best Practices" *Tidskrift utgiven av Juridiska föreningen i Finland (JFT)* 1–2: 112–136.

Jasch, M. (2004) "Police and Prosecutions: Vanishing Differences between Practices in England and Germany" *German Law Journal* 5(10): 1207–1216.

Jehle, J-M. (2009) *Criminal Justice in Germany: Facts and Figures* 5th edn (Berlin: Federal Ministry of Justice). Accessible at www.tamilnet.com/img/publish/2011/05/Criminal_Justice_Germany_en.pdf.

Jehle, J. and M. Wade (eds) (2006) *Coping with Overloaded Criminal Justice Systems: The Rise of Prosecutorial Power across Europe* (Berlin: Springer-Verlag).

Kyprianou, D. (2008) "Comparative Analysis of Prosecution Systems (Part 1): Origins, Constitutional Position and Organization of Prosecution Services" *Cyprus and European Law Review* 6: 467–499.

Kyprianou, D. (2008) "Comparative Analysis of Prosecution Systems (Part 11): The Role of Prosecution Services in Investigation and Prosecution Principles and Policies" *Cyprus and European Law Review* 7: 61–90.

Kyprianou, D. (2010) *The Role of the Cyprus Attorney General's Office in Prosecutions: Rhetoric, Ideology and Practice* (Heidelberg/New York/Dordrecht/London: Springer-Verlag).

Langbein, J. (1974) "Controlling Prosecutorial Discretion in Germany" *University of Chicago Law Review* 41(3): 439–467.
Ligeti, K. (ed.) (2013) *Toward a Prosecutor for the European Union, Volume 1: A Comparative Analysis* (Oxford/Portland OR: Hart Publishing) – includes descriptions of the prosecution systems in 20 European countries.
Luna, E. and M. Wade (eds) (2012) *The Prosecutor in Transnational Perspective* (Oxford: Oxford University Press).
Mathias, E. (2002) "The Balance of Power between the Police and the Public Prosecutor" – in Delmas-Marty, M. and J. Spencer (eds) *European Criminal Procedures* (Cambridge: Cambridge University Press), pp. 459–487.
McGloin, J. (2006) "A Historical Consideration of the Police and Prosecution/Courts in Northern Ireland" *International Criminal Justice Review* 16(2): 77–98.
McIntyre, D. (1975) "Impediments to Effective Police-Prosecutor Relationships" *American Criminal Law Review* 13(2): 201–231.
Moody, S. and J. Tombs (1982) *Prosecution in the Public Interest* (New York: Columbia University Press).
Rowe, B. (2016) "Predictors of Texas Police Chiefs' Satisfaction with Police-Prosecutor Relationships" *American Journal of Criminal Justice* 41(4): 663–685.
Schram, G. (1969) "The Obligation to Prosecute in West Germany" *American Journal of Comparative Law* 17(4): 627–632.
Sessar, K. (1979) "Prosecutorial Discretion in Germany" – in McDonald, W. (ed.) *The Prosecutor* (Beverley Hills, CA: Sage Publications), pp. 255–276.
Siegismund, E. (2003) "The Competence of the Police in Investigation Proceedings" – in *Effective Administration of the Police and the Prosecution in Criminal Justice* (Work product of the 120th international senior seminar) (Tokyo: UNAFEI), pp. 35–57 – accessible online at www.unafei.or.jp/english/pdf/RS_No60/No60_09VE_Siegismund1.pdf.
Siegismund, E. (2003) "The Public Prosecution Office in Germany: Legal Status, Functions and Organization" – in *Effective Administration of the Police and the Prosecution in Criminal Justice* (Work product of the 120th international senior seminar) (Tokyo: UNAFEI), pp. 58–74 – accessible online at www.unafei.or.jp/english/pdf/RS_No60/No60_09VE_Siegismund1.pdf.
Tak, P. (2003) *The Dutch Criminal Justice System: Organization and Operation* (Amsterdam: Boom Juridische uitgevers/Justitie) – esp. Chapters 4 and 6.
Terrill, R. (2003) "France" – in Terrill, R., *World Criminal Justice Systems* 5th edn (Cincinnati, OH: Anderson Publishing), Ch. 3 (pp. 210–266).
Ward, J. (2015) "Transforming 'Summary Justice' through Police-led Prosecution and 'Virtual Courts': Is 'Procedural Due Process Being Undermined?" *British Journal of Criminology* 55(2): 341–358.
White, R. (2006) "Investigators and Prosecutors or, Desperately Seeking Scotland: Reformulation of the 'Phillips' Principle" *Modern Law Review* 69(2): 143–182.
Zila, J. (2012) "Prosecutor Powers and Policy Making in Sweden and Other Nordic Countries" – in Luna, E and M. Wade (eds) *The Prosecutor in Transnational Perspective* (Oxford: Oxford University Press), pp. 235–250.

7 Police Prosecution and Access to Justice for People with Disabilities

Penelope Weller[1]

Introduction

Recent inquires in Australia have documented the disproportionate levels of violence and abuse experienced by people with disabilities.[2] At the same time, research has identified disproportionate numbers of people with mental health issues, intellectual disability and cognitive disabilities in the prison system.[3] This chapter evaluates the access to justice debates concerning people with disabilities in the criminal justice system from the perspective of the Convention on the Rights of Persons with Disabilities ("CRPD").[4] The main focus of the paper is the human rights issues associated with the prosecution of people with cognitive impairment involved with low-level offences. The paper argues that the hidden nature of disability limits the efficacy of current prosecution arrangements, pointing to the CRPD as a way forward.

Department of Prosecution Guidelines in Victoria

The prosecutorial arrangements for people with cognitive impairment who commit low-level offences vary across Australian jurisdictions. This chapter examines the prosecutorial discretion of police in Victoria, Australia. In Victoria, the decision to prosecution low-level offences rests with the police.[5] With respect to the exercise of discretion, the key question of "when should the duty of strict enforcement (of the law) give way to other considerations", is approached through structured policy guidelines issued by the Director of Public Prosecutions.[6]

The recently revised "Policy of the Director of Public Prosecutions for Victoria" states that prosecution should only proceed if there is a reasonable prospect of a conviction and a prosecution is required in the public interest.[7] With respect to the question of whether or not there is a reasonable prospect of conviction, factors that the prosecution "should have regard to" include whether or not it is possible that the evidence will be excluded, whether there is a reason to suspect the evidence may have been "concocted" and the reliability of any admissions.[8] "Any other matter relevant to whether a jury or magistrate would find the person guilty" is also relevant.[9] These factors should be actively considered when a person with cognitive impairment comes in contact with the police.

With respect to the question of public interest, offence-related factors include the seriousness of the offence, whether the offence is of considerable public concern, the age of the offence and whether the offence is triable only on indictment. Offender-related factors include culpability, the offender's antecedent and background, the age, physical health, mental health or special infirmity of the offender and whether the offender is willing to cooperate in the investigation or prosecution of others. Victim-related factors include the victim's attitude to prosecution, their entitlement to compensation, their age, physical health, mental or special infirmity.[10] Other factors include community protection, the likely sentence, the prevalence of the offence, the need for deterrence, the need to maintain public confidence, whether the consequence of conviction would be unduly harsh and oppressive, any special circumstances, the age physical health, mental health or special infirmity of any witness, obsolescence, or obscurity of the law, whether prosecution would be counter-productive, the availability of any alternative, the likely length and expense of a trial, whether a sentence has already been imposed and any mitigating or aggravating circumstances.[11] In short the structured discretion is very "loose".

The guidelines state that in cases involving offenders with cognitive impairments "particular attention must be given to whether a prosecution is in the public interest".[12]

> It may not be in the public interest to prosecute such as offence where the offence is not serious, the offender's cognitive impairment reduces their moral culpability, the offender is of no danger to the community and the prosecution is likely to result in an unconditional discharge.[13]

With respect to those who commit offences while detained involuntarily in psychiatric hospitals, regard must be had to:

- whether the offence was committed while the offender was resisting detention. It may not be in the public interest to prosecute a mentally ill person who was detained involuntarily for resisting that detention;
- the person's treatment and medication regime both at the time of the offence and at the time the prosecution is being considered;
- whether a prosecution would be likely to be harmful to the person or medically inappropriate.[14]

These considerations suggest a general policy that supports limited prosecution of individuals with cognitive impairment or mental illness. However, the final paragraph in the relevant section of the policy indicates a preference for prosecution.[15]

Anecdotal evidence suggests that police prosecutors in Victoria are reluctant to withdraw charges without concrete evidence of a direct causal relationship between the disability or mental illness and the criminal behaviour in question. For example, in instances where a person's criminal actions occur during a psychotic episode, it is reported that police prosecutors are reluctant to accept documentation of the person's compulsory admission to a mental health facility as evidence that the person's behaviour was directly affected by acute mental illness.

The DPP guideline on discretion to prosecute must be read in conjunction with the *Crimes (Mental Impairment) Act 1997* (Vic).[16] The Crimes (Mental Impairment) Act replaces the common law defence of insanity with a statutory defence of mental impairment in Victoria.[17]

The Crimes (Mental Impairment) Act defines unfitness as an inability to understand the trial process because the person's mental processes are disordered or impaired.[18]

The key issue with respect to the operation of the Crimes (Mental Impairment) Act in the Magistrates' Court, is that the Magistrates' Court has no power to make orders in relation to people found not guilty because of mental impairment, or jurisdiction to determine fitness to stand trial. In the summary jurisdiction of the Magistrates' Court, the matter must either proceed to committal or the charges must be withdrawn. If an accused establishes a defence of mental impairment ("mental impairment"), the court must discharge the accused.

The Crimes Mental Impairment Act places the prosecutorial decision in the summary jurisdiction as a choice between discharge of the matter on one hand, or escalation to a higher court on the other. This lacunae in the law may encourage inappropriate escalation of some matters to a higher court. Another effect is to encourage police prosecutors to overlook mental impairment because established of impairment may lead to complete discharge.

Cognitive Impairment as a Hidden and Complex Disability

The disincentive to identify cognitive impairment are amplified by the "hidden" nature of disability. Cognitive impairment is commonly undetected, confused with personality traits or interpreted as mental illness or aggression.[19] Many people with cognitive impairment experience poor memory and concentration, have a reduced ability to plan and problem solve and exhibit inflexible thinking.[20] Many experience emotional instability, irritability and impulsivity that may sometimes lead to inappropriate behaviour.[21]

Cognitive impairment goes unnoticed because it is deeply entwined with the disadvantage experienced by many people with disabilities. Forty-five per cent of people with disabilities live in poverty or near poverty.[22] Many experience loss of employment, identity, social relationships, networks and financial security leading to dislocation and homelessness.[23] Women and girls with disability experience violence and abuse at significantly higher rates than others, more frequently, for longer, in more ways and by more perpetrators.[24] They are more likely to have developed cognitive impairment as a result of physical abuse.[25]

The systemic disadvantages experienced by people with cognitive impairment increase the likelihood of contact with the criminal justice system. Social disadvantage, poor housing or homelessness make people with cognitive disabilities vulnerable to contact with police.[26] They are more likely to be arrested, questioned and detained for minor public order offences compared with others.[27] They are also vulnerable to manipulation and exploitation by other offenders, and more likely to have their motivations misconstrued by police.[28]

The Prison Population

Recent research in New South Wales shows that 77 per cent of the adult prison population have mental health conditions, 49 per cent have brain injuries, and 8 per cent have intellectual disabilities.[29] Similar figures are reported in Victoria.[30]

Disadvantage and disability are also the primary characteristics of indigenous prisoners. In the last census in 2016, Aboriginal and Torres Strait Islander people were 2.8 per cent of Australia's total population (ABS, 2016). In June 2017 they constituted 28 per cent of the total Australian prison population (ABS, 2017). Aboriginal and Torres Strait Islanders experience higher rates of disability than the general population, and are also overrepresented in prison populations, Aboriginal and Torres Strait Islanders being 15 times more likely than other Australians to be imprisoned.[31] Jim Ogloff and colleagues note that the rate of severe cognitive impairment amongst the Aboriginal and Torres Strait Islander prison inmates is likely to be disproportionality high.[32]

With respect to women, 87 per cent of women in prison in Australia have experienced abuse of some kind,[33] with 64 per cent of women in a Victorian prison having a history of physical or sexual abuse.[34] The experience of physical abuse was twice as high for women with drug or alcohol abuse problems, in whom drug overdose is identified as a direct cause of impairment.[35]

People who come in to the prison system are more likely to have repeat contact with it. People with cognitive impairment are also more likely to remain "caught up" in the criminal justice system. People with cognitive impairment are less likely to seek and receive appropriate legal help, less likely to access appropriate support services, more likely to receive custodial sentences, and more likely to be placed in custody following breaches of community correction orders.[36]

In Victoria the general recidivism rate is 44.1 per cent,[37] while over half young prisoners aged 18 to 24 return to prison within two years.[38] Holland, Persson, McClelland and Berends report a 73 per cent recidivism rate for people with intellectual disabilities, compared to 52 per cent for the general prison population (2007). The combined effect of memory and behavioural deficits means they are less able to deal with the supervision demands placed on them by the courts, resulting in violations of parole and probation orders.[39] High recidivism rates demand consideration of the context of disadvantage into which prisoners are released. In a current study with people with cognitive impairment with experience in the criminal justice system in Victoria,[40] researchers found that people experienced intimidation, stress, misunderstanding and confusion at all stages of the criminal justice process including arrest and interview by police, court attendance and obtaining legal representation, sentencing, incarceration and release back into the community, and undertaking parole and Community Correction Orders. These observations suggest that people with cognitive impairment are vulnerable in multiple and complex ways.

Response to Vulnerable People

The concern with "vulnerable" people in the criminal justice system is of long standing. Particular attention was drawn to the experience of Aboriginal and Torres Strait Islander people in the courts in the 1970s. For example in *R v Anunga* (1976) the court articulated a protocol, referred to as the Anunga rules, for interviewing indigenous Australians.[41] In *Ebatarinja v Deland* (1998) the court was concerned with the effect of hearing impairment on those involved in the criminal justice process.[42] A subsequent inquiry by the Senate Community Affairs References Committee found that *Ebatarinja v Deland* noted that "undiagnosed hearing impairment ... could ... render that conviction unsafe".[43] Hearing loss frequently underpins poor or limited understanding of English amongst indigenous communities, amplifying the prevalence of acquiescence in criminal proceedings.[44] The principal focus for change at this time was on improved police training to encourage the use of interpreters[45] and improve police responses to "vulnerable" people.[46]

In the 1980s, the focus included intellectual disability, persons with developmental disabilities, children and young people, persons from non-English speaking backgrounds and "other persons".[47] The overarching concern in this period was the communication deficit. It was recognised that people who speak a language other than English, those with cognitive impairment, those who are young and whose education has been interrupted may have difficulty communicating in formal and stressful situations, and may struggle to understand the complex or unusual questioning that police may regard as crucial to police interviews.[48]

More recently, researchers have considered cognitive disability and mental illness. Ochoa and Rome noted that people with cognitive disability are vulnerable in police interactions because they are "typically passive, placid, and, important for police to note, highly suggestible".[49] They may have difficulties remembering information, be unable to focus or control behaviour and be unable to recognise and respond to social cues. Unusual responses may be misinterpreted by police.[50] Travis observed that police officers appeared to be insufficiently aware of the needs of mentally ill suspects, especially with respect to the need to caution during a police interview.[51] Godfredson, Thomas, Ogloff and Luebbers report that police awareness with respect to mentally ill offenders has improved but further training is required.[52]

Interview Friends

Beyond the standard call for improved police training, a key response has been legislative reforms and practices that provide support for vulnerable people who come in contact with police. Common statutory mechanisms include positive requirements to engage interpreters, to ensure the presence of a legal representative (especially for Aboriginal and Torres Strait Islanders) and to ensure the presence of a support person. In the ACT and Commonwealth laws, provision is made for an "interview friend".[53] The legislation in New South Wales and Queensland refers to people who provide support. In Victoria the scheme of independent third persons (ITP) is recognised in the police standing orders. While "police training" in "disability awareness" is in place in some jurisdictions there is little evidence that it is appropriately targeted or effective.

The exact role of "support persons" in Australia is ill-defined and under-theorised. In Victoria, where volunteer Independent Third Parties (ITP) support people with "impaired mental state or capacity" when they are questioned by police,[54] the Office of the Public Advocate has called for an expansion of the ITO role, arguing that ITPs should be present for longer and should encompass referral to social support agencies.[55] Internationally, the support role is more developed. For example, Swedish law provides for the judicial appointment of "personligt ombud" (PO) to assist a person to make legal decisions.[56] The PO functions as a legal mentor and is often referred to as an "assistant" or "advocate". These are trained social workers or lawyers who are able to "argue effectively for the client's rights in front of various authorities or in court", as required.[57] The PO scheme is both a social service and a legal structure, and provides for a range of support relationships for people with disabilities and other disadvantaged people. The scheme has been identified by the High Commission of Human Rights as an approach that is compatible with states' party obligations under the CRPD (2007, ch. 6; see also Herr, 2003, p. 432).[58]

The Effect of the CRPD

The CRPD demands a re-evaluation of the way law, policy administration and practice recognises and supports the human rights of people with disabilities.[59] The quality of the changes required by the CRPD are illustrated by the CRPD's key concepts: the social model of disability, social participation, non-discrimination and access to justice.

The social model of disability refers to the idea that "disability" is a product of social exclusion and marginalisation (rather than an inherent characteristic of a person).[60] With respect to social participation, the CRPD construes social and legal "exclusion in all aspects of life" as the basis of discrimination against people with disability. The refiguring of discrimination as exclusion recognised that anti-discrimination legislation in domestic jurisdictions has not addressed the structural barriers that confront people with disabilities.[61] Moreover, discrimination in the CRPD is measured against the rights enjoyed by "others" – that is, the rights enjoyed by non-disabled members of society.[62]

Discrimination in the CRPD also encompasses "denial of reasonable accommodation". The reasonable accommodation mechanism provides a framework for the adjustment of systems or mechanism that create barriers for people with disabilities. Eilionóir Flynn describes reasonable accommodation as "the obligation to modify existing structures, systems or processes to accommodate the particular requirements of an individual with disability" (2015, p. 54).[63] Discussing reasonable accommodation in the context of access to legal services generally, Flynn suggests that reasonable accommodation obligations may include provision of information to people with disabilities in a range of different formats, such as electronic formats, Braille, sign language or easy to read documents;[64] and the establishment of disability specific legal clinics or centres. Such obligations are directly relevant to the access to justice debate in Australia. Reasonable accommodation obligations will also be engaged when a person requires support to exercise their legal capacity.[65]

CRPD General Comment 1 by the Committee on the Rights of Persons with Disabilities provides an authoritative interpretation of article 12. The committee states that "[d]enial of legal capacity must not be based on personal traits such as gender, race, or disability, or have the purpose or effect of treating the person differently".[66] While individuals may have different cognitive capabilities, a "person's lack of mental capacity must never be the basis for a denial of legal capacity".[67] Tests or hurdles in the law that rely on a determination of mental capacity therefore offend the principles of direct and indirect discrimination because they distinguish on the basis of disability, and have a disproportionate impact on people with cognitive impairment.[68] Article 12 denotes a radical revision of "special measures" in the law that are based on rationales of protection.

What Should Be in Place?

The Australian Human Rights Commission (2014) inquiry into disability in the criminal justice system noted the absence of systems to book independent accredited communication support workers; limited access to legal representation; ignorance about human rights; a lack of appropriate adjustments; multiple instances in which people with disabilities, particularly people with intellectual disabilities and psychosocial disabilities, were interviewed without appropriate support persons; and multiple instances in which other supports were not provided.[69] The AHRC report recommended the development of an Australia Disability Justice Strategy, setting out the guiding principles that should underpin it, rather than the "stopgap" measures noted above.

A recent report the Victorian Ombudsman recommended that the deficits in the justice process in Victoria be addressed by a whole of government approach, justice reinvestment and expansion of problem-solving courts.[70] Reaching beyond this narrow assessment, the CRPD calls for a radical revision of law and policy concerning people with disabilities in the justice system. In particular it prompts us to think beyond the systems approach to "universal design".[71] A universal-design approach would require a full analysis of the way police and prosecution work may be appropriately altered to accommodate disability.

Conclusion

Contrary to the myths that surround our understanding of criminality, people who come into contact with the criminal justice system are likely to be both victims and offenders and people with disabilities. There are likely to be multiply disadvantaged and marginalised in complex and intersecting ways. Drawing on the language used by Martha Fineman (2008), in the criminal justice system, "vulnerability" is the norm, not the exception.[72] This chapter urges a revitalisation of the access to justice debate from a CRPD perspective. To do so is challenging. To do otherwise, condemns the most vulnerable people with disabilities to entrenched disadvantage.

Notes

1 Professor and Director of Juris Doctor Program, Graduate School of Business and Law, RMIT University, Melbourne.
2 Victorian Equal Opportunity and Human Rights Commission (VEOHRC), "Beyond Doubt, The Experiences of People with Disabilities Reporting Crime" (VEOHRC, Carlton, Australia 2014), Australian Human Rights Commission (AHRC), "Equal Before the Law, Towards Disability Justice Strategies" (AHRC, Canberra, Australia 2014), Victorian Government Productivity Commission (VGPC), "Access to Justice Arrangements" (VGPC Inquiry Report No 72 Canberra, Australia 2014), Australian Law Reform Commission, "Equality, Capacity and Disability in Commonwealth Laws, Final Report" (ALRC Report 124, Sydney, Australia 2014) and a recent Senate Inquiry, Parliament of Australia Senate Community Affairs References Committee, "Violence, Abuse and Neglect Against People with Disability in Institutional and Residential Settings, including the Gender and Age Related Dimensions, and the Particular Situation of Aboriginal and Torres Strait Islander People with Disability, and Culturally and Linguistically Diverse People with Disability" (Parliament of Australia Canberra, Australia 2015).
3 Loic Wacquant, *Prisons of Poverty* (Minneapolis: University of Minnesota Press, 2009); Chris Cunneen, Eileen Baldry, David Brown, Melanie Schwartz, Alex Steel and Mark Brown, *Penal Culture and Hyperincarceration: The Revival of the Prison* (Ashgate, Surrey UK, 2013).
4 Convention on the Rights of Persons with Disabilities (CRPD) (adopted 13 December 2006, entered into Force 3 May 2008) 2515 UNTS 3. Australia has signed and ratified the CRPD and optional protocol.
5 Simon Bronitt and Philip Stenning, "Understanding Discretion in Modern Policing" (2011) 35 *Criminal Law Journal* 319–332.
6 Director of Public Prosecutions Victoria, "Policy of the Director of Public Prosecutions for Victoria" (Director of Public Prosecutions Victoria, Melbourne, Australia) www.opp.vic.gov.au accessed 11 January 2018.
7 Ibid., 1[3].
8 Ibid.,1[4].
9 Ibid.
10 Ibid., 2[6].
11 Ibid., 2–3[6].
12 Ibid., 3[8].
13 Ibid., 3[8].
14 Ibid., 3–4[8].
15 Ibid., 4[9].

16 Director of Public Prosecutions Victoria, "Director's Policy: Crimes (Mental Impairment) and Unfitness to be Tried" (Director of Public Prosecutions Victoria, Melbourne, Australia 2015) www.opp.vic.gov.au accessed 3 January 2018.
17 *Crimes (Mental Impairment) Act 1997* (Vic) ("CMIA 1997"), s 1(b).
18 CMIA 1997, s 6.
19 Nicola Fortune and Xingyan Wen, "The Definition, Incidence and Prevalence of Acquired Brain Injury in Australia" (no DIS 15, Australian Institute of Health and Welfare, Canberra, Australia 1999).
20 Louise O'Rance, "Disability in Australia: Acquired Brain Injury" (Bulletin 55, CAT no AUS96, Australian Institute of Health and Welfare, Canberra, Australia 2007).
21 Ibid.
22 PwC, *Disability Expectations: Investing in a Better Life, A Stronger Australia, Achieving Better Outcomes for People with a Disability and their Families* (PwC 2011) www.pwc.com.au/industry/government/assets/disability-in-australia.pdf accessed 3 January 2018, 11.
23 Eileen Baldry, Leanne Dowse, Phillip Snoyman, Melissa Clarence and Ian Webster, "A Critical Perspective on Mental Health Disorders and Cognitive Disability in the Criminal Justice System" in Chris Cunneen and Michael Salter (eds), *Proceedings of the Second Australian and New Zealand Criminology Conference, 19–20 June 2008, Sydney, Australia* (The Crime & Justice Research Network, University of New South Wales, Sydney, Australia 2009), 30–45.
24 Carolyn Frohmader, "Submission to the Australian Government Consultation Paper: Family Violence – Improving Legal Frameworks" (Women With Disabilities Australia, Rosny Park, Australia 2010), 6.
25 Victorian Government Department of Human Services (DHS), "Acquired Brain Injury and Mental Illness: Issues Paper" (DHS Melbourne, Australia 2004); Martin Jackson, Glen Hardy, Peter Persson and Shasta Holland, "Acquired Brain Injury in the Victorian Prison System" (Corrections research paper series, no 04, Victorian Government Department of Justice, Melbourne, Australia 2011), 9.
26 Parliament of Victoria Family and Community Development Committee, "Inquiry into Supported Accommodations for Victorians with a Disability and/or Mental Illness" (Parliamentary paper no 240, Parliament of Victoria, Victoria, Australia 2009).
27 Victorian Government Department of Justice (DOJ), "Beyond Bars: Alternatives to Custody" (People with an Intellectual Disability and the Criminal Justice System: Fact Sheet 10 DOJ Melbourne, Australia 2007).
28 Leanne Dowse, Melissa Clarence, Eileen Baldry, Julian Trofimovs and Sharleen James, "People with Mental Health Disorders and Cognitive Disabilities in the Criminal Justice System: The Impact of Acquired Brain Injury" (University of New South Wales Report prepared for Brain Injury Association of NSW and Brain Injury Australia, Sydney, Australia 2011), 10.
29 Ruth McCausland, Eileen Baldry, Sarah Johnson and Anna Cohen, People with Mental Health Disorders and Cognitive Impairment in the Criminal Justice System: Cost-benefit Analysis of Early Support and Diversion (University of New South Wales and PwC, Sydney, Australia 2013).
30 Martin Jackson *et al.*, "Acquired Brain Injury" (n 25). Forty-two per cent of men and 33 per cent of women in the prison population have acquired brain injury, compared to 2.2 per cent of the population. See also Victorian Ombudsman, "Investigation" (n 36), 88.
31 AHRC, "Equal Before the Law" (n 2), 12, 13.
32 See also: James R.P. Ogloff, Jenny Patterson, Margaret Cutajar, Karen Adams, Stuart Thomas and Chris Halacas, "Koori Prisoner Mental Health and Cognitive Function Study" (Report prepared for the Department of Justice, Victoria. Melbourne, Australia: Centre for Forensic Behavioural Science, Monash University &

Victorian Institute of Forensic Mental Health & Victorian Aboriginal Community Controlled Health Organisation, 2013) www.corrections.vic.gov.au/ accessed 3 January 2018.

33 Holly Johnson, "Drugs and Crime: A Study of Incarcerated Female Offenders" (Research and Public Policy Series Paper no 63, Australian Institute of Criminology, Canberra, Australia 2004), xiv.

34 See generally: Angela H. Kim, S. Allen, M. Asbridge, J. Petgrave and S. Brochu "Traumatic Brain Injury and Early Life Experiences Among Men and Women in a Prison Population" (2014) 20(4) *Journal of Correctional Healthcare* 271–279.

35 Ibid.

36 Victorian Ombudsman, "Investigation into the Rehabilitation and Reintegration of Prisoners in Victoria, Discussion Paper" (Victorian Ombudsman Melbourne, Australia 2014), 24.

37 Victorian Ombudsman, "Investigation" (n 36), 3.

38 Ibid., 3.

39 Ibid.

40 Jess Richter, Anna Howard, Brigid Henley, Rob Hulls, Penelope Weller, Stan Winford, RMIT University, Jesuit Social Services and the Centre for Innovative Justice.

41 *R v Anunga* (1976) 11 ALR 412 at 412. See also: Martine B. Powell, "Practical Guidelines for Conducting Investigative Interviews with Aboriginal People" (2000) 12 *Current Issues in Criminal Justice* 181–197 for a discussion of a five-stage protocol for interviews that is "interviewee centred" and allows the interviewee to determine the vocabulary and content as much as possible, pp. 181–197.

42 *Ebatarinja v Deland* (1998) 194 CLR 444.

43 Parliament of Australia Senate Community Affairs Reference Committee, "Hear Us: Inquiry into Hearing Health in Australia" (Commonwealth of Australia, Canberra, Australia 2010), 121, 142.

44 Kimberley Interpreting Service, *Indigenous Language Interpreting Services: Discussion Paper* (2004), 3 cited by Lorana Bartels, *Police Interviews with Vulnerable Adult Suspects* (Canberra, Australian Institute of Criminology, Research in Practice Report no 21, July 2011).

45 Michael M Cooke, "Caught in the Middle: Indigenous Interpreters and Customary Law" in Law Reform Commission of Western Australia (LRCWA), *Aboriginal Customary Laws, Project 94, Background Papers* (Perth, Australia 2006); Committee on the Rights of Persons with Disabilities (CRPD), *General Comment No 1 Article 12: Equal Recognition Before the Law* (2014) UN Doc CRPD/C/GC/; Diana Eades, *Sociolinguistics and the Legal Process* (Multilingual Matters, Bristol 2010); Diana Eades, *Aboriginal English in the Courts: A Handbook* (Queensland Department of Justice and Attorney-General, Brisbane 2000).

46 See, e.g. Kevin Smith and Steve Tilney, *Vulnerable Adult and Child Witnesses* (Oxford: Oxford University Press, 2007) cited in Lorana Bartels, "Police Interviews with Vulnerable Adult Suspects" (Research in Practice Report no 21, Australian Institute of Criminology, Canberra, Australia 2011).

47 Tasmanian Law Reform Institute (TLRI), "Consolidation of Arrest Laws in Tasmania" (TLRI Issues Paper No 10, TLRI Hobart, Australia 2006), 32 cited in Lorana Bartels, *Police Interviews with Vulnerable Adult Suspects* (Research in Practice Report no 21 Australian Institute of Criminology, Canberra, Australia 2011).

48 David Dixon and Gail Travis, *Interrogating Images: Audio-visually Recorded Police Questioning of Suspects* (Sydney, Australia: Institute of Criminology Press, 2007).

49 Theresa A. Ochoa and Jessie Rome, "Considerations for Arrests and Interrogations of Suspects with Hearing, Cognitive and Behavioral Disorders" (2009) 9(5) *Law Enforcement Executive Forum Journal* 125–136, 133.

50 Ibid., 134.

51 Dixon and Travis, *Interrogating Images* (n 48).

52 Joel W. Godfredson, S.D.M. Thomas, J.R.P. Ogloff and S. Luebbers, "Police Perceptions of Their Encounters with Individuals Experiencing Mental Illness: A Victorian Survey" (2011) 44(2) *Australian & New Zealand Journal of Criminology*, 180–195.

53 *Crimes (Forensic Procedures) Act 2000* (ACT), s 4(1).

54 Office of the Public Advocate (OPA), *Breaking the Cycle, Using Advocacy-Based Referrals to Assist People with Disabilities in the Criminal Justice System* (Carlton, OPA, 2012), 28.

55 Ibid.

56 Leslie Salzman, "Guardianship for Persons with Mental Illness – A Legal and Appropriate Alternative?" (2011) 4 *St Louis University Journal of Health Law & Policy* 279.

57 Inclusion Europe, "Choices: A Platform on Supported Decision Making, "Swedish Personal Ombudsman Service (PO) for People with Mental Health Problems" (2014) www.right-to-decide.eu/2014/08/swedish-personal-ombudsman-service-po-for-people-with-mental-health-problems/ accessed 3 January 2018.

58 United Nations Office of the High Commission of Human Rights, "From Exclusion to Equality: Realizing the Rights of Persons with Disabilities, Handbook for Parliamentarians on the Convention on the Rights of Persons with Disabilities and its Optional Protocol" (No 14 2007) UN Doc HR/PUB/07/6, ch 6. See also: Stanley S. Herr, "Self-Determination, Autonomy, and Alternatives to Guardianship" in Stanley S. Herr, Lawrence O. Gostin and Harold Hongju Koh (eds), *The Human Rights of Persons with Intellectual Disabilities, Different but Equal* (Oxford University Press, Oxford, UK 2003) 429–452, 432.

59 Philip French, *Disabled Justice: The Barriers to Justice for Persons with Disability in Queensland* (Disability Studies and Research Institute for Queensland Advocacy Incorporated, Brisbane, Australia 2007), 3.

60 Tom Shakespeare, "The Social Model of Disability", in Leonard Davis (ed.), *The Disability Studies Reader* (4th edn, Routledge, New York 2013), 214–221.

61 Samuel R. Bagenstos, "The Future of Disability Law" (2004) 114(1) *Yale Law Journal* 1–83 www.yalelawjournal.org/ accessed 3 January 2018, 548.

62 Robert Sampson, "The Community" in James Q. Wilson and Joan Petersilia (eds), *Crime and Public Policy* (Oxford University Press, Oxford, UK 2011).

63 Eilionóir Flynn, *Disabled Justice? Access to Justice and the UN Convention on the Rights of Persons with Disabilities* (Surrey: Ashgate, 2015).

64 Ibid., 57.

65 Ibid., 60.

66 CRPD *General Comment No 1* (n 45) para 9.

67 Ibid., paras 13, 14.

68 Ibid., para 9.

69 AHRC, "Equal Before the Law" (n 2), 19.

70 Victorian Ombudsman, "Investigation into the Rehabilitation" (n 36), 153.

71 CRPD, art 2.

72 Martha Albertson Fineman, "The Vulnerable Subject: Anchoring Equality in the Human Condition" (2008) 20(1) *Yale Journal of Law & Feminism* http://digital commons.law.yale.edu/yjlf/vol. 20/iss1/2 accessed 3 January 2018.

Bibliography

Australian Bureau of Statistics (ABS) (2016) "Census of Population and Housing – 2016 Census Counts – Aboriginal and Torres Strait Islander People" (No 2075.0, ABS Canberra, Australia) www.abs.gov.au/ accessed 3 January 2018).

Australian Bureau of Statistics (ABS) (2017) "Corrective Services, Australia, June Quarter 2017" (No 4512.0, ABS Canberra, Australia). www.abs.gov.au/ accessed 3 January 2018.
Australian Human Rights Commission (AHRC) (2014) "Equal Before the Law, Towards Disability Justice Strategies" (AHRC, Canberra, Australia).
Australian Law Reform Commission (2014) "Equality, Capacity and Disability in Commonwealth Laws, Final Report" (ALRC Report 124 Sydney, Australia).
Bagenstos, S.R. (2004) "The Future of Disability Law" *Yale Law Journal* 114(2): 1–83 www.yalelawjournal.org/ accessed 3 January 2018.
Baldry, E., L. Dowse, P. Snoyman, M. Clarence and I. Webster (2009) "A Critical Perspective on Mental Health Disorders and Cognitive Disability in the Criminal Justice System" – in Cunneen, Chris and Michael Salter (eds), *Proceedings of the Second Australian and New Zealand Criminology Conference, 19–20 June 2008, Sydney, Australia* (The Crime & Justice Research Network, University of New South Wales, Sydney, Australia).
Bartels, L. (2011) "Police Interviews with Vulnerable Adult Suspects" (Research in Practice Report no 21 Australian Institute of Criminology, Canberra, Australia).
Bronitt, S. and P. Stenning (2011) "Understanding Discretion in Modern Policing" *Criminal Law Journal* 35: 319–332.
Colantonio, A., H. Kim, S. Allen, M. Asbridge, J. Petgrave and S. Brochu (2014) "Traumatic Brain Injury and Early Life Experiences Among Men and Women in a Prison Population" *Journal of Correctional Healthcare* 20(4): 271–279.
Committee on the Rights of Persons with Disabilities (2014) *General Comment No 1 Article 12: Equal Recognition Before the Law*. UN Doc CRPD/C/GC/.
Cooke, M.M. (2006) "Caught in the Middle: Indigenous Interpreters and Customary Law" – in Law Reform Commission of Western Australia (LRCWA), *Aboriginal Customary Laws, Project 94, Background Papers* (Perth, Australia).
Cunneen, C., E. Baldry, D. Brown, M. Schwartz, A. Steel and M. Brown (2013) *Penal Culture and Hyperincarceration: The Revival of the Prison* (Surrey: Ashgate).
Director of Public Prosecutions Victoria (2014) "Director's Policy: Prosecutorial Discretion" (Director of Public Prosecutions Victoria, Melbourne, Australia) www.opp.vic.gov.au accessed 3 January 2018.
Director of Public Prosecutions Victoria (2015) "Director's Policy: Crimes (Mental Impairment) and Unfitness to be Tried" (Director of Public Prosecutions Victoria, Melbourne, Australia) www.opp.vic.gov.au accessed 3 January 2018.
Dixon, D. and G. Travis (2007) *Interrogating Images: Audio-Visually Recorded Police Questioning of Suspects* (Sydney, Australia: Institute of Criminology Press).
Dowse, L., M. Clarence, E. Baldry, J. Trofimovs and S. James (2011) "People with Mental Health Disorders and Cognitive Disabilities in the Criminal Justice System: The Impact of Acquired Brain Injury" (University of New South Wales Report prepared for Brain Injury Association of NSW and Brain Injury Australia, Sydney, Australia).
Eades, D. (2000) *Aboriginal English in the Courts: A Handbook* (Queensland Department of Justice and Attorney-General, Brisbane, Australia).
Eades, D. (2010) *Sociolinguistics and the Legal Process* (Bristol: Multilingual Matters).
Ebatarinja v Deland (1998) 194 CLR 444.
Fineman, M.A. (2008) "The Vulnerable Subject: Anchoring Equality in the Human Condition" *Yale Journal of Law & Feminism* 20(1) http://digitalcommons.law.yale.edu/yjlf/vol. 20/iss1/2 accessed 3 January 2018.

Flowers, N., J. Lord and A.S. deFranco (2012) *Human Rights YES! Action and Advocacy on the Rights of Persons with Disabilities* (Human Rights Education Series Topic Book 6, 2nd edn University of Minnesota Human Rights Research Center, Minneapolis).

Flynn, E. (2015) *Disabled Justice? Access to Justice and the UN Convention on the Rights of Persons with Disabilities* (Surrey: Ashgate).

Flynn, E. and A. Arstein-Kerslake (2014a) "The Support Model of Legal Capacity: Fact Fiction or Fantasy?" *Berkeley Journal of International Law* 32: 124–143.

Flynn, E. and A. Arstein-Kerslake (2014b) "Legislating Personhood: Realising the Right to Support in Exercising Legal Capacity" *International Journal of Law in Context* 10: 81–104.

Fortune, N. and X. Wen (1999) "The Definition, Incidence and Prevalence of Acquired Brain Injury in Australia" (no DIS 15, Australian Institute of Health and Welfare, Canberra, Australia).

Fredman, S. (2011) *Discrimination Law* 2nd edn (Oxford: Oxford University Press).

French, P. (2007) *Disabled Justice: The Barriers to Justice for Persons with Disability in Queensland* (Disability Studies and Research Institute for Queensland Advocacy Incorporated, Brisbane, Australia).

Frohmader, C. (2010) "Submission to the Australian Government Consultation Paper: Family Violence – Improving Legal Frameworks" (Women With Disabilities Australia, Rosny Park, Australia).

Godfredson, J.W., S.D.M. Thomas, J.R.P. Ogloff and S. Luebbers (2011) "Police Perceptions of their Encounters with Individuals Experiencing Mental Illness: A Victorian Survey" *Australian & New Zealand Journal of Criminology* 44(2): 180–195.

Herr, S.S. (2003) "Self-Determination, Autonomy, and Alternatives to Guardianship" – in Herr, Stanley S., Lawrence O. Gostin and Harold Hongju Koh (eds), *The Human Rights of Persons with Intellectual Disabilities, Different but Equal* (Oxford: Oxford University Press).

Holland, S., P. Persson, M. McClelland and R. Berends (2007) "Intellectual Disability in the Victorian Prison System: Characteristics of Prisoners with an Intellectual Disability Released from Prison 2003–2006" (Corrections Research Paper Series, Paper No 02 Victorian Department of Justice, Melbourne, Australia).

Inclusion Europe (2014) "Choices: A Platform on Supported Decision Making, 'Swedish Personal Ombudsman Service (PO) for People with Mental Health Problems' ", www.right-to-decide.eu/2014/08/swedish-personal-ombudsman-service-po-for-people-with-mental-health-problems/ accessed 3 January 2018.

Jackson, M., G. Hardy, P. Persson and S. Holland (2011) "Acquired Brain Injury in the Victorian Prison System" (Corrections research paper series, no 04, Victorian Government Department of Justice, Melbourne, Australia).

Johnson, H. (2004) "Drugs and Crime: A Study of Incarcerated Female Offenders" (Research and Public Policy Series Paper no 63, Australian Institute of Criminology, Canberra, Australia).

Kanter, A.S. (2009) "The United Nations Convention on the Rights of Persons with Disabilities and its Implications for the Rights of Elderly People under International Law" *Georgia State University Law Review* 25(3): 527–573.

Kimberley Interpreting Service (2004) *Indigenous Language Interpreting Services: Discussion Paper* (Kimberley Interpreting Service, Broome, Australia) www.kimberley interpreting.org.au/index.html accessed 3 January 2018.

Kumari Campbell, F. (2005) "Legislating Disability: Negative Ontologies and the Government of Legal Identities" – in Tremain, S. (ed.), *Foucault and the Government of Disability* (Ann Arbor, MI: University of Michigan Press).

Lawson, A. (2008) *Disability and Equality Law in Britain: The Role of Reasonable Adjustment* (Oxford: Hart).

Lord, J.E. (2013) "Screened Out of Existence: the Convention on the Rights of Persons with Disabilities and Selective Screening Policies" *International Journal of Disability Community and Rehabilitation* 12(2). www.ijdcr.ca/VOL12_02/articles/lord.shtml accessed 3 January 2018.

McCausland, R.E. Baldry, S. Johnson and A. Cohen (2013) People with Mental Health Disorders and Cognitive Impairment in the Criminal Justice System: Cost-benefit Analysis of Early Support and Diversion (University of New South Wales and PwC, Sydney, Australia).

McSherry, B. (2012) "Legal Capacity under the Convention on the Rights of Persons with Disabilities" *Journal of Law and Medicine* 20: 22–27.

Ochoa, T.A. and J. Rome (2009) "Considerations for Arrests and Interrogations of Suspects with Hearing, Cognitive and Behavioral Disorders" *Law Enforcement Executive Forum Journal* 9(5): 125–136.

Office of the Public Advocate (OPA) (2012) *Breaking the Cycle, Using Advocacy-based Referrals to Assist People with Disabilities in the Criminal Justice System* (Carlton, Australia: OPA).

Ogloff, J.R.P., J. Patterson, M. Cutajar, K. Adams, S. Thomas and C. Halacas (2013) "Koori Prisoner Mental Health and Cognitive Function Study" (Report prepared for the Department of Justice, Victoria). Melbourne, Australia: Centre for Forensic Behavioural Science, Monash University & Victorian Institute of Forensic Mental Health & Victorian Aboriginal Community Controlled Health Organisation) www.corrections.vic.gov.au/ accessed 3 January 2018.

O'Rance, L. (2007) "Disability in Australia: Acquired Brain Injury" (Bulletin 55, CAT no AUS96, Australian Institute of Health and Welfare, Canberra, Australia).

Parliament of Australia Senate Community Affairs Reference Committee (2010) "Hear Us: Inquiry into Hearing Health in Australia" (Commonwealth of Australia, Canberra, Australia).

Parliament of Australia Senate Community Affairs References Committee (2015) "Violence, Abuse and Neglect Against People with Disability in Institutional and Residential Settings, including the Gender and Age Related Dimensions, and the Particular Situation of Aboriginal and Torres Strait Islander People with Disability, and Culturally and Linguistically Diverse People with Disability" (Parliament of Australia Canberra, Australia).

Parliament of Australia Senate Select Committee on Regional and Remote Indigenous Communities (2010) "Indigenous Australians, Incarceration and the Criminal Justice System, Final Report 2010" (Parliament of Australia, Canberra, Australia).

Parliament of Victoria Family and Community Development Committee (2009) "Inquiry into Supported Accommodations for Victorians with a Disability and/or Mental Illness" (Parliamentary paper no 240, Parliament of Victoria, Victoria, Australia).

Perlin, M. (2011) *International Human Rights and Mental Disability Law, When the Silenced Are Heard* (Oxford: Oxford University Press).

Powell, M.B. (2000) "Practical Guidelines for Conducting Investigative Interviews with Aboriginal People" *Current Issues in Criminal Justice* 12: 181–197.

PwC (2011) *Disability Expectations: Investing in a Better Life, a Stronger Australia, Achieving Better Outcomes for People with a Disability and their Families* www.pwc.com.au/industry/government/assets/disability-in-australia.pdf accessed 3 January 2018.

R v Anunga (1976) 11 ALR 412.

Rushworth, R. (2011) *Out of Sight, Out of Mind: People with Acquired Brain Injury and the Criminal Justice System* (Brain Injury Australia Policy Paper prepared for the Australian Government Department of Families, Housing, Community Services and Indigenous Affairs, Ryde, Australia).

Salzman, L. (2011) "Guardianship for Persons with Mental Illness – A Legal and Appropriate Alternative?" *St Louis University Journal of Health Law & Policy* 4: 279–330.

Sampson, R.J. (2011) "The Community" – in Wilson, James Q. and Joan Petersilia (eds), *Crime and Public Policy* (Oxford, UK: Oxford University Press).

Shakespeare, T. (2013) "The Social Model of Disability" – in Davis, L. (ed.), *The Disability Studies Reader* 4th edn (New York: Routledge).

Shakespeare, T. (2013) "Nasty, Brutish, and Short? On the Predicament of Disability and Embodiment" – in Bickenbach, J.E.F. Felder and B. Schmitz (eds), *Disability and the Good Human Life* (Cambridge: Cambridge University Press).

Smith, K. and S. Tilney (2007) *Vulnerable Adult and Child Witnesses* (Oxford: Oxford University Press).

Stein, M.A., J.E. Lord and D.W. Tolchin (2012) "Equal Access to Health Care under the UN Disability Rights Convention" – in Rhodes, R.M. Battin and A. Silvers (eds), *Medicine and Social Justice: Essays on the Distribution of Health Care* 2nd edn (Oxford: Oxford University Press).

Tasmanian Law Reform Institute (TLRI) (2006) "Consolidation of Arrest Laws in Tasmania" (TLRI Issues Paper No 10, TLRI Hobart, Australia).

United Nations High Commissioner for Human Rights (2009) "Thematic Study by the Office of the High Commissioner for Human Rights on Enhancing Awareness and Understanding of the Convention on the Rights of Persons with Disabilities" UN Doc A/HRC/10/48.

United Nations Office of the High Commission of Human Rights (2007) "From Exclusion to Equality: Realizing the Rights of Persons with Disabilities, Handbook for Parliamentarians on the Convention on the Rights of Persons with Disabilities and its Optional Protocol" (No 14) UN Doc HR/PUB/07/6.

Victorian Equal Opportunity and Human Rights Commission (VEOHRC) (2014) "Beyond Doubt, the Experiences of People with Disabilities Reporting Crime" (VEOHRC, Carlton, Australia).

Victorian Government Department of Human Services (DHS) (2004) "Acquired Brain Injury and Mental Illness: Issues Paper" (DHS Melbourne, Australia).

Victorian Government Department of Justice (DOJ) (2007) "Beyond Bars: Alternatives to Custody" (People with an Intellectual Disability and the Criminal Justice System: Fact Sheet 10 DOJ Melbourne, Australia).

Victorian Government Productivity Commission (VGPC) (2014) "Access to Justice Arrangements" (VGPC Inquiry Report No 72 Canberra, Australia).

Victorian Law Reform Commission (VLRC) (2007) "Review of the Bail Act: Final Report" (VLRC Melbourne, Australia).

Victorian Law Reform Commission (VLRC) (2014) "Review of the Crimes (Mental Impairment and Unfitness to be Tried) Act 1997 Report" (VLRC Melbourne, Australia).

Victorian Ombudsman (2014) "Investigation into the Rehabilitation and Reintegration of Prisoners in Victoria, Discussion Paper" (Victorian Ombudsman Melbourne, Australia).

Wacquant, L. (2009) *Prisons of Poverty* (Minneapolis, MI: University of Minnesota Press).

Weller, P. (2010) "Right to Health – The Convention on the Rights of Persons with Disabilities" *The Alternative Law Journal* 35(2): 66–71.

Weller, P. (2013a) *New Law and Ethics in Mental Health Advance Directives: the Convention On The Rights Of Persons With Disabilities and the Right to Choose* (Sussex: Routledge).

Weller, P. (2013b) "Towards a Genealogy of Coercive Care" – in Freckelton, I. and B. McSherry (eds), *Coercive Care: Rights Law and Policy* (Oxon: Routledge).

Weller, P. (2014) "Reconsidering Legal Capacity: Radical Critiques, Governmentality and Dividing Practices" *Griffith Law Review* 23: 498–518.

Weller, P. (2008) "Supported Decision Making and the Achievement of Non-Discrimination: The Promise and Paradox of the Disabilities Convention" *Law in Context, International Trends in Mental Health Laws* 26(2): 85–110.

8 Roles of Lawyers and Investigators in Investigations of International Crimes

Melanie O'Brien

Introduction

International criminal courts and tribunals (ICCTs) have unique structures differing from domestic courts. No one structure applies to all ICCTs, with some being wholly international (e.g. the International Criminal Court [ICC]), and others hybrid forms (e.g. the Special Court for Sierra Leone [SCSL]).[1] Some are UN bodies (e.g. the International Criminal Tribunal for the Former Yugoslavia [ICTY]), others independent entities (e.g. the ICC), and yet others embedded in the domestic legal system of the host country (e.g. Extraordinary Chambers in the Courts of Cambodia [ECCC]).[2] These differences result in variations in the role of the prosecutor at an international level, at times substantially contrasting to roles at domestic level.

ICCTs employ personnel from around the globe (Romano, 2012, pp. 244–246). Personnel education, training and experience are gained from a multitude of legal systems, where education and training differs and roles for both lawyers and police vary. Police and lawyers generally have very distinct roles in a domestic context. The title of "prosecutor" (or a local equivalent title) is applied to many lawyers; and for the most part, police investigate and lawyers prosecute crimes. Yet in the practice of ICCTs, lawyers and investigators often have overlapping roles, and there is technically only one "Prosecutor" (with the exception of the ECCC, which has co-Prosecutors) and one or two Deputy Prosecutors by title. International courts do not have their own police force, but instead have "investigators". Lawyers hold titles such as "legal officer" (research lawyers) or "legal counsel" (lawyers in practice).

This chapter assesses the varying and at times overlapping roles of investigators and lawyers, considering their relationship to one another and their roles in investigations, including interviewing suspects as a case study activity that effectively demonstrates how the role of the prosecutor varies from domestic to international systems. A brief overview of the domestic roles of police and the prosecutor is offered. A comparison of the backgrounds of the investigators and the lawyers is provided, and then assessment of how these differences matter with regards to interviewing suspects. The analysis demonstrates how the role of lawyers as prosecutors in an international context evolves from the experience at domestic level.[3]

Methodology

Principal research for this project was conducted through qualitative analysis of interviews undertaken with current and former staff of ICCTs.[4] Participants were current or former staff of the ICTY, the International Criminal Tribunal for Rwanda (ICTR), the SCSL, the Special Tribunal for Lebanon (STL), the ECCC, and the ICC. Some participants had worked for multiple tribunals and courts. Participants held roles in the courts and tribunals of investigator, lawyer (of various levels including Prosecutor) or legal officer (legal advisory). The participant countries of origin were Australia, the USA, Italy, Sri Lanka, Bulgaria, the UK and Germany. This provided for an assortment of participants from common law, civil law and mixed common-civil law backgrounds. However, the majority of participants were from common law backgrounds.[5] This is due to the availability of interviewees in Australia to the author, as well as the number of personnel working in ICCTs from countries such as the USA and Australia (Townsend, 2012).[6] Participants were classified as "investigators" (previously worked as police only, working/ed as investigator at international level, N=8), "lawyer" (previously worked as lawyer only, working/ed as lawyer at international level, N=6), "police and lawyer" (initially worked as police but then changed to lawyer, working/ed as lawyer at international level, N=2), "lawyer and police" (initially worked as a lawyer but then changed to police, working/worked as investigator at international level, N=1) and "legal advisory" (lawyer but working/ed in legal advisory capacity, N=2).[7] A total of 19 participants were interviewed, in The Hague, Sydney, Lyon and Phnom Penh.

The interviews consisted of two sections. The first delved into participants' backgrounds: education, work experience, professional training in interview techniques, and experiences interviewing suspects at domestic and international levels. The second part of the interview assessed the participants' use of specific interview techniques. This chapter draws from the data from the first part of the interviews, focusing on the background and experience of lawyers and investigators at the ICCTs. Previous publications by this author have discussed the findings from the second part of the interviews (O'Brien, 2012; O'Brien and Kebbell, 2014).

This chapter also analyses the roles of prosecutor and police/investigators through primary sources (statutes of ICCTs; rule of procedure and evidence of ICCTs; and decisions of ICCTs); and draws from scholarly assessment of the role of the prosecutor and police/investigators at both domestic and international stages. While there is a great deal of literature on the process at the ICC of initiating an investigation and discussion on the Rome Statute's provisions related to investigations, there is a limited amount of scholarly literature on the practicalities of the investigation process (Keegan, 1997; Bergsmo and Wiley, 2008; Van Tuyl, 2008; Groome, 2011; Fujiwara and Parmentier, 2012; War Crimes Research Office, 2012).

Domestic Role of Police and Prosecutors

This section provides a brief overview of the role of the police and the prosecutor in national jurisdictions. It focuses on the two Western legal traditions: the adversarial or common law systems, and the inquisitorial or civil law systems. Other legal systems such as the Chinese sui generis system and the Islamic legal system are not considered, as the international criminal court regimes are based on the two main Western legal traditions (Merryman and Perez-Perdomo, 2007, p. 4).[8] This section aims only to provide a brief overview of the differences, focusing on the main concepts relevant to this chapter, but readers should note variances exist between states within common law and civil law systems (Ambos, 2000).

Specific tasks and jurisdiction of police in common law and civil law systems are addressed below, but it is pertinent to point out the overall function of police is "a broad mandate to prevent, detect and control crime and disorder" (Grieve, Harfield and MacVean, 2007, p. 20). In order to carry out this function, police are permitted to, inter alia, use force, arrest suspects, investigate crime, interview witnesses and suspects, conduct patrols, carry weapons, disperse people, seize evidence and even provide disaster relief (Bowling and Sheptycki, 2012, pp. 33–34). On a daily basis, police have a "peace-keeping" role, with a proactive outlook, in which they "preserve order" (or police disorder) through activities such as policing public events and problematic geographical zones (Grieve, Harfield and MacVean, 2007, pp. 21, 65–68).

Adversarial/Common Law Systems

> In the criminal justice system, the people are represented by two separate yet equally important groups: the police, who investigate crime; and the district attorneys, who prosecute the offenders.

This well-known opening narration from the popular TV show *Law & Order* provides a succinct summary of the roles of police and lawyers in many common law systems, each of which for the most part functions independently of each other and falls under the authority of different executive branches (e.g. Ministry of Justice, Attorney-General's Department or Minister for Policing) (Ambos, 2000, p. 91). There are exceptions to this separation of authority, such as in the United States at federal level, where the FBI and prosecutors both fall under the remit of the Department of Justice (The United States Department of Justice n.d.). In common law systems, crime investigation is undertaken by the police (Ambos, 2000, p. 104). The police interview witnesses and suspects and collect evidence in a crime investigation, subsequently providing the evidence to the public prosecutor for the prosecutor to take forward to court (Gilliéron, 2014, pp. 73–75), where their role "is to lay before a jury what the Crown considers to be credible evidence relevant to what is alleged to be a crime".[9] Prosecutors can be involved in the direction of police investigations, and have discretion whether or not to proceed with a case; there is no obligation to prosecute (the principle of opportunity) (Ambos, 2000, pp. 95, 98–99). These roles are distinct yet mutually dependent and cooperative.

Inquisitorial/Civil Law Systems

The position of the prosecutor in civil law systems can differ. They can either be situated in the judiciary (under the supervision of the court) (Merryman and Perez-Perdomo, 2007, p. 105; Ambos, 2000, p. 93) or in the executive (such as under the remit of the Attorney General) (Gilliéron, 2014, pp. 313–314; Ambos 2000, pp. 93–94). Some civil law systems provide prosecutors with discretion to prosecute (e.g. France, the principle of opportunity or expediency), but others mandate prosecution if "there is good reason to suspect that an offense has been committed" (e.g. Germany and Switzerland, the principle of procedural legality) (Ambos, 2000, pp. 97, 99–100; Gilliéron, 2014, p. 315). In some jurisdictions, an examining judge or magistrate (*juge d'instruction*) has investigative power, although this is a less common option (Gilliéron, 2014, pp. 319–320).[10] The role of the prosecutor and the *juge d'instruction* is to determine the truth, and thus, they hold a neutral role. Evidence in a criminal investigation is kept in a dossier centrally controlled by the *juge d'instruction* rather than by the police or prosecutor.

Police in civil law systems are functionally subordinate to the prosecutor. Police conduct investigation of crime, but an investigation is usually instigated by the prosecutor and is supervised by the prosecutor (Gilliéron, 2014, pp. 183–188, 266–267, 291–293). In some circumstances, the police investigation is supervised by the *juge d'instruction.*[11] However, in practice, often the police investigate first and inform the prosecutor at a later stage of the investigation (with the exception of serious matters, which are immediately referred to the prosecutor) (Gilliéron, 2014, pp. 184–187, 267, 292–293). Powers of the police may vary depending on the nature of the investigation and crime (Gilliéron, 2014, p. 292). Prosecutors may also conduct their own investigations, either after at least a preliminary investigation has been run by police or independently and to the exclusion of the police (Gilliéron, 2014, pp. 188, 266, 293).

Backgrounds of Lawyers and Investigators in International Criminal Courts and Tribunals

Given the separate roles of police and lawyers, education and training is different. In the past, police have generally had professional training at a police academy and then on-the-job training, although more recently, in addition to this training, police are undertaking university study (such as in criminology, criminal justice, leadership or law). Lawyers start instead with university study (a law degree) and then undertake professional practice experience and qualifications. At the international level, some lawyers have undertaken post-graduate study such as a Masters in International Law.[12] Police are trained in, inter alia, investigation, interviewing, physical fitness, use of firearms, use of vehicles, operational safety and report writing. Lawyers are trained in different law subject-areas (both compulsory and elective), the functions of the legal system and of law, advocacy and litigation skills, client liaison skills, legal document drafting and more. Thus it is evident that a police officer and a lawyer undertake a position at an international criminal court or tribunal from very different starting points with regard to their education, training and experience.

Role of Lawyers and Investigators in International Criminal Courts and Tribunals

Interestingly, in the initial phase of the ICC, most investigators were human rights lawyers.[13] Subsequently, more police officers were employed as investigators. At the ICC, the Investigation Division falls under the authority of the Office of the Prosecutor (OTP). The ICC states that "the Investigation Division is in charge of providing investigative expertise and support, coordinating field deployment of staff and security plans and protection policies, and providing crime analysis and analysis of information and evidence" (International Criminal Court, n.d.).[14] Also within the OTP, "the Prosecution Division prepares the litigation strategies and conducts prosecutions, including through written and oral submissions to the judges" (International Criminal Court, n.d.).[15] The judiciary is a separate organ of the ICC, and judges do not have investigatory powers (International Criminal Court, n.d.). Investigation teams are joint teams; consisting of lawyers from the OTP's Prosecution Division, investigators from the Investigation Division, and cooperation advisors from the Jurisdiction, Complementarity and Cooperation Division (JCCD) (Townsend, 2012, pp. 291–293).[16]

The role of the prosecutor is in line with that of the prosecutor in a common law system, where the prosecutor presents the case against the accused.[17] However, the ICC Prosecutor must,

> [i]n order to establish the truth, extend the investigation to cover all facts and evidence relevant to an assessment of whether there is criminal responsibility under [the Rome] Statute, and, in doing so, investigate incriminating and exonerating circumstances equally.[18]

In addition, the Prosecutor is also obligated to disclose

> evidence in the prosecutor's possession or control which he or she believes shows or tends to show the innocence of the accused, or to mitigate the guilt of the accused, or which affect the credibility of prosecution evidence.[19]

That said, in trial, the Prosecutor is entrusted with prosecuting perpetrators in an adversarial manner and not as a neutral party.[20]

Thus, the ICC's design is a hybrid of common law and civil law structures: investigators are under the remit of the OTP; investigations are for the most part carried out by investigators but at times lawyers are involved; the OTP must investigate exculpatory as well as incriminating evidence; and the judicial and prosecutorial structure of trials is overall adversarial.

Prosecutorial obligation to investigate and disclose exculpatory evidence does not exist in the ICTY, ICTR or the SCSL (Boas *et al.*, 2011, p. 227). However, the role and power of the prosecutor at the ICC, ICTY, ICTR and SCSL with regard to investigations are similar: conducting on-site investigations, collecting and examining evidence, and interviewing witnesses, victims and suspects (Boas *et al.*, 2011, p. 226). In terms of prosecutorial discretion, at these courts and tribunals, it is the prosecutor who decides whether or not to undertake an investigation and to go forward with prosecution. The ICC functions differ from the other tribunals, though, in that there are multiple trigger mechanisms for an investigation: *proprio motu* from the Prosecutor, a Security Council referral, or a state referral.[21] Different rules of investigatory discretion apply to each trigger. A decision not to investigate in the case of a state or Security Council referral can be challenged in the Pre-Trial Chamber (PTC), although even if the PTC suggests the Prosecutor reconsider her decision, it ultimately remains the discretion of the Prosecutor to not investigate (Boas *et al.*, 2011, p. 183).[22] The Prosecutor's verdict not to investigate for a *proprio motu* investigation is not subject to appeal before the PTC (Boas *et al.*, 2011, p. 183),[23] although authorisation to investigate must be granted by the PTC (Boas *et al.*, 2011, p. 184).[24]

At the ICTY and ICTR it is the prosecutor who undertakes investigations, and these investigations are carried out by both investigators and lawyers. The charging is also effected by the prosecutor and not subject to any form of authorisation or appeal to the judiciary (Boas *et al.*, 2011, p. 224). That said, as with the ICC, the role of investigators and lawyers in investigations is still closer to the common law system, where investigators carry out investigatory work and lawyers undertake trial preparation and prosecution. Investigators are however, as in the ICC, under the authority of the Prosecutor (Boas *et al.*, 2011, p. 224).

One participant who had worked as a police officer and a lawyer in a common law country and then as a lawyer in multiple international courts confirmed that working in an international court was a different process to the domestic setting.[25] For a common law lawyer, this is particularly so in the ECCC, whose structure contrasts markedly with that of the above-discussed courts and tribunals. The ECCC is for the most part an inquisitorial court (although there are common law elements introduced, such as witness questioning and the public nature of the trial).[26] Judges play a significant role in the ECCC, which contrasts with their separate role in a common law court system. ECCC judges are investigative judges,[27] meaning that investigators – or rather, judicial police, as they are termed at the ECCC – work not for the prosecutor, but for the judges. Judges are impartial and investigation must include both incriminating and exculpatory evidence.[28] Initial investigations are carried out by the Co-Prosecutors, who subsequently submit an Introductory Submission to the Judges, who investigate the facts in the Introductory Submission (and any Supplementary Submission, if submitted) (Extraordinary Chambers in the Courts of Cambodia n.d.).[29] In the initial investigation, the judicial police are permitted to work under instruction of the Co-Prosecutor, but once the investigation is passed to the Co-Investigating Judges, the judicial police remain under judicial authority.[30]

Charging of suspects is carried out by the judges and not the prosecutor. ECCC lawyers have no contact with witnesses before they testify, and it is the judges who decide which witnesses to call.[31] In this sense, the ECCC system provides prosecutors with less control (although, one participant remarked, not less work), and follows the *juge d'instruction* model of the civil law system. Thus it is a very different structure in which investigators and lawyers from common law and most civil law systems find themselves working.

One participant noted the biggest challenge for common law lawyers in the ECCC civil law system is the questioning style.[32] Leading or suggestive questions are not permitted in the ECCC. Another significant challenge is the complicated nature of the process for disclosure of information. Documentation and other evidence is the property of judges. Consequently, lawyers must file a request to the judge for disclosure of information to the defendant; a process that is very time-consuming.[33] This results in a much slower pace of the trial than other ad hoc tribunals such as the ICTY.[34]

For investigators of international crimes, their role is very different to that of a police officer. The powers and functions mentioned above (under Domestic Role of the Police and Prosecutors) do not all apply to international investigators. Investigators do not have the power to carry weapons, use force, arrest suspects, conduct patrols or provide disaster relief. This is a significant variation from the role of domestic police, and highlights the nomenclature of "investigator" rather than police. International investigators are tasked *only* with investigating crime and not any of the supplementary tasks engaged in by domestic police such as keeping peace or preserving order.

While granting investigators the power to arrest suspects would seem in keeping with the role of ICCTs, this has never been an option for any international courts and tribunals. Instead, powers of arrest are retained by states and thus carried out by police within their jurisdictional territory. This is in keeping with the nature of cooperation of ICCTs, and their status not as "supreme" courts but stand-alone courts with limited jurisdiction. However, this limitation has proven to be a severe impediment to functionality of international courts and tribunals, where reliance on states to arrest and surrender suspects means many suspects have taken years (even decades) to detain, or remain at large.[35]

An international investigator's powers do not remain consistent. The ambit of investigator powers is reliant on agreement with the host state (location of investigation). These agreements mean that tasks international investigators are able to undertake remain at the discretion of local authorities. This deference to state sovereignty results in diversity of actions that investigators can actually implement themselves: in some countries operations are carried out in full by investigators, whereas in others the host countries requires investigations (including interviews – see below) to be performed by local police. Lack of cooperation from states can result in investigatory challenges, such as difficulty in obtaining evidence or accessing witnesses (Keegan, 1997, pp. 122–123).[36]

Suspect Interviewing

Interviewing of suspects, witnesses and victims is a critical part of the collection of evidence for forensic purposes. Interviews are vital because witness, victim and suspect testimony is the main form of evidence presented at international trials. Investigations take place after the crimes have been committed, at times many years, and the testimony of people who perpetrated, witnessed or experienced the atrocities can provide the context and details of the crimes, especially where documentation or images may not exist. Proving international crimes is a complex task that requires not only proving that a specific crime was committed and by whom it was committed (as is needed in a domestic case), but also the context in which the crime was committed (e.g. armed conflict) and the status of the person who committed the crime (e.g. military commander). This subsection concentrates on the roles of lawyers and investigators in suspect interviewing as a case study investigation activity.

Interviewing a suspect of international crimes contrasts with interviewing a suspect of domestic crimes. In general, suspects – perpetrators – of international crimes are eager to talk. At a domestic level, a suspect will talk initially when they are arrested, because they want to extract themselves from their current situation, but once they have a lawyer, they no longer participate.[37] This does not happen in the international context, where international suspects usually have an agenda, for example a desire to ascertain what kind of and how much information on them the international court has, or a desire to sell themselves and their story/message (particularly so with politicians).[38] However, this does not mean that perpetrators of international crimes are disposed to *confess*, particularly at the leadership level, where perpetrators are consciously engaged in criminal enterprise – shaping the course of the atrocities and instructing others to carry out the crimes.[39] Rather, perpetrators seek to justify their conduct, placing it in the context of armed conflict (where "bad things happen") or as a valid course of action in order to protect their interests (whether they are national, territorial or otherwise); or minimise their own role in the crimes (O'Brien, 2012; Combs, 2002; Combs, 2006).[40] In addition, a suspect's willingness to talk may depend on the situation on the ground in their state; that is: are they at risk if they provide testimony (e.g. Kenya) or do they want to show a new regime that they cooperated with the ICC (e.g. Libya)?[41]

Even without a confession, a perpetrator's disposition to being interviewed signifies the importance of personnel being able to undertake these interviews. The crucial nature of interviews to the evidentiary and forensic process of international trials means that effective interview technique by court personnel is essential. Hence we must ask: who carries out interviews of suspects, does this mean a departure from their experience in their previous domestic role, and is this variation in role problematic in terms of experience to be applied to suspect interviews?

In the majority of ICCTS, interviews are not only carried out by investigators, but also by lawyers.[42] All lawyers interviewed in the survey had conducted suspect interviews as part of investigations. As an example, a suspect interview for the ICC is carried out by at least one investigator and a lawyer (as well as technical support staff such as a sound recorder, interpreter where required, etc.). However, there are times when the interview is not carried out by ICC personnel, but rather by local police. This is dependent on cooperation agreements, as the ICC must continually work with state authorities and cannot operate outside the parameters of host state permissions.[43] For example, in Egypt and Tunisia, the ICC is permitted to operate freely as it needs, while some Middle Eastern states require their own prosecutors to be present.[44] Investigations cannot be carried out without state consent; a limiting factor that has contributed to an inability to investigate in the Darfur region (Wouters, Verhoeven and Demeyere, 2008, p. 285).[45]

Former police survey participants were all trained in some form of investigative interview techniques. Investigators surveyed were trained in aspects such as body language, use of different question types (e.g. open, closed), and building rapport (Collins, Lincoln and Frank, 2002; Öhrn, 2009). In common law countries such as the UK, Australia and Canada, the trend is cognitive interviewing, and some form of the PEACE interview structure: planning and preparation; engage and explain; account clarification and challenge; closure; evaluation (Kebbell and Wagstaff, 1999; Milne and Powell, 2010; Dando *et al.*, 2010). In the USA, the Reid Technique is preferred (Adcock, 2011; Eastwood, 2011). Thus, we can see that there is a certain similarity in training of police at domestic level, but also differences. It is also not necessarily the case that these techniques are effective when applied in different cultures (O'Brien, 2012; O'Brien and Kebbell, 2014).

One survey participant lawyer from the USA was trained in the Reid Technique, an interview technique used by police.[46] However, in general, lawyers have not been trained in interview techniques, either at university or as vocational training. This means that many lawyers are not able to apply specialised techniques or experience when undertaking interviews of suspects of international crimes. In-court questioning is different from interviewing; both have different goals and a different context (including different rules that apply to types of questions permitted). Interviewing is a much more comprehensive style of questioning, with a broad goal of eliciting as much information as possible – a fact-finding activity. In contrast, in-court questioning is more restricted, used to reveal particular facts that are already known to the questioner. Lawyers who interview suspects at the international level, having not previously done so, are able to avail themselves of their training and skills in cross-examination to apply in suspect interviews.[47] Cross-examination questioning is similar to the open-ended style questioning useful for some elements of suspect interviewing (usually the first phase, before interview questions become more focused).[48] These open-ended questions are used to set up certain aspects of a suspect's story from which they can later draw upon to challenge the suspect on the details and facts. Yet, despite this knowledge of cross-examination techniques that can be applied, there is a need for particular specialised techniques to be practised by those conducting suspect interviews. This highlights a need for specialised training for legal professionals joining ICCTs in order for them to be able to undertake the interviewing element of their prosecutorial role.

Conclusion

The roles of the prosecutor and of police in domestic legal systems vary between and within common law and civil law jurisdictions. In common law systems, police investigate and prosecutors prosecute, although their relationship is interdependent. In civil law systems, investigations are led by prosecutors or examining judges and may or may not involve the police.

At ICCTs, these roles and relationships differ from domestic situations and from each other. No single international criminal court or tribunal has an investigatory structure that echoes any domestic setting. Of course the arrangement of ICCTs is influenced by domestic systems, but in being international, these courts and tribunals borrow from both civil and common law schemes. Thus, the roles of the prosecutor and of the investigator at international level offer lawyers and investigators a different working experience from their domestic practice, in particular during investigation. This is the case even if, for example, a common law lawyer is working in a predominantly common law-influenced international court structure (or likewise for civil law).

For police, their role as investigator has stark differences to that of domestic police duties. Internationally, an investigator has no powers of arrest, and is reliant on local authorities for investigatory jurisdiction, which fluctuates depending on the host state. The position of investigators in the international criminal legal system is derived from civil law, where investigators are not independent but are under the authority of either the prosecutor or an investigating judge.

Prosecutors in ICCTs also engage with investigations in a manner similar to that of civil law systems: prosecutors direct the investigators, and lawyers participate in investigations – particularly interviews. A notable exception to this is at the ECCC, where prosecutors only undertake initial investigations, and the principal investigations are effectuated by judges, who supervise the Judicial Police. This change of role for prosecutors to direct involvement in investigations, in particular for common law lawyers, is significant. Interviewing suspects of international crimes is an essential part of evidence-gathering in international crime investigations, with forensic testimony the most important form of evidence given. Thus it is crucial that ICCTs ensure that personnel employed are trained in interview techniques, with the acknowledgement and practice that different techniques may be needed for different tasks, to establish uniformity of capability and furnish all staff with the expertise to conduct interviews and thus execute their role as investigator or prosecutor.

Notes

1 For discussion of some of the difficulties in marrying the different global systems into ICCTs, see Carter and Pocar (2013).
2 For structures of the different courts, see Romano *et al.* (2004); Schabas (2006); Schabas (2007).
3 This chapter does not include a discussion of the specific role of "The Prosecutor" in ICCTs, which has been covered elsewhere; see e.g. Reydams *et al.* (2012); Stenning (2014).
4 Research was conducted over several years, when the author was a Research Fellow at the Centre of Excellence in Policing and Security, Griffith University; and in the author's current role as a Postdoctoral Research Fellow at the University of Queensland TC Beirne School of Law. The author would like to thank participants for their time and providing insight into their experiences.
5 This, however, echoes the staffing structures at the international court; see Romano's (2012, p. 239) breakdown of the SCSL staff in 2012, noting that all Office of the Prosecutor staff were from common law countries.
6 For example, the investigation section of the ICTY was established by an Australian police detective. Bob Reid (Chief of Operations, ICTY), was a NSW police detective and has been working at the ICTY since 1994, holding the positions of Investigations Team Leader, Investigations Commander, Deputy Chief of Investigations and Deputy Chief of Prosecutions. He was the lead investigator in the first ICTY trial of Duško Tadić. Romano (2012, p. 239) notes 12 of 16 posts at the SCSL were filled by US nationals.
7 In this chapter, participants are referred to solely as "lawyer" or "investigator" in order to avoid any potential identification of survey participants.
8 On the specific role of the prosecutor and the police in investigations in China, see Ambos (2000). On the Islamic legal framework, see generally Fouladvand (2014, pp. 1039–1046).
9 *Boucher v The Queen* [1955] SCR 16, Rand J (Supreme Court of Canada).
10 The *juge d'instruction* has been abolished in Germany, Italy and most Latin American states (Merryman and Perez-Perdomo, 2007, p. 130).
11 In France, "[e]xamining magistrates supervise the work of the judicial police in investigation of serious offenses (*délits graves*), whereas public prosecutors supervise their work in investigations of manifest offenses (*flagrant délit*) and preliminary investigations (*enquête préliminaire*)" (Gilliéron, 2014, p. 292).
12 Five lawyer participants had post-graduate degrees (from both common law and civil law countries).
13 Interview with ICC lawyer, The Hague (November 2011).
14 International Criminal Court, "Regulations of the Office of the Prosecutor" (23 April 2009) ICC-BD/05-01-09, reg 8 ("OTP Regulations").
15 Ibid., reg 9.
16 Ibid., regs 32, 35.
17 However, the ICC Prosecutor is also obligated to disclose "evidence in the prosecutor's possession or control which he or she believes shows or tends to show the innocence of the accused, or to mitigate the guilt of the accused, or which affect the credibility of prosecution evidence"; Rome Statute of the International Criminal Court (adopted 12 July 1998, entered into force 1 July 2002) 2187 UNTS 90, art 67(2) ("Rome Statute").
18 Ibid., art 54(1)(a).
19 Ibid., art 67(2).
20 For discussion of the *Lubanga* trial and its relationship to the issue of exculpatory evidence and the role of the Prosecutor in this regard, see eg De Vos (2011); *Prosecutor v Lubanga* (Decision on the Consequences of Non-Disclosure of Exculpatory

Materials Covered by Article 54(3)(e) Agreements and the Application to Stay the Prosecution of the Accused, Together With Certain Other Issues Raised at the Status Conference on 10 June 2008) Trial Chamber I, Case No ICC-01/04-01-06/1401, 13 June 2008; *Prosecutor v Lubanga* (Decision on the Prosecution's Urgent Request for Variation of the Time-Limit to Disclose the Identity of Intermediary 143 or Alternatively to Stay Proceedings Pending Further Consultations with the VWU) Trial Chamber I, Case No ICC-01/04-01/06-2517 Red, 8 July 2010.

21 Rome Statute arts 13, 14, 15.

22 Ibid., art 53(3)(a).

23 Ibid., art 15(6).

24 Ibid., art 15(3).

25 Interview with ECCC lawyer, Phnom Penh (November 2015).

26 Ibid.

27 "Law on the Establishment of the Extraordinary Chambers in the Courts of Cambodia for the Prosecution of Crimes Committed during the period of Democratic Kampuchea, with inclusion of amendments as promulgated on 27 October 2004" (NS/RKM/1004/006) ("ECCC Law"); investigative power is allocated in art 23.

28 Extraordinary Chambers in the Courts of Cambodia, "Internal Rules (Rev. 9)" (as revised 16 January 2015), r 55(5) ("ECCC Internal Rules").

29 ECCC Law art 23.

30 ECCC Internal Rules r15.

31 Interview with ECCC lawyer, Phnom Penh (November 2015).

32 Ibid.

33 Ibid.

34 This is also due to the civil law–common law mix of process. In civil law, a judge relies on a case file and few or no witnesses are called. At the ECCC, the case file is used but witnesses are also called. Consequences are a slower trial, but a thorough investigation (ibid.).

35 For example, Ratko Mladić was indicted by the ICTY in 1995 but not arrested and surrendered until 2011; the ICC arrest warrant for Sudanese President Omar Al Bashir was issued in 2009 but he remains at large, despite having visited state parties to the Rome Statute.

36 There were particular challenges in investigating suspects in Libya (Kersten, 2015). Safety and security of investigators, particularly in conflict and immediate post-conflict situations, can also be a significant barrier to investigation capabilities.

37 Interview with ICC lawyer, The Hague (November 2011).

38 Ibid.

39 Interviews with ICC lawyers, The Hague (November 2011). Another ICC lawyer stated that lower level perpetrators are more comfortable admitting crimes, although this still may be limited to crimes committed "around them"; Interview with ICC lawyer, The Hague (November 2011).

40 Multiple interviewees had interviewed suspects who sought to justify their conduct. This is also evident in the testimonies (and media statements) of defendants throughout the trials of ICCTs. One exception was Rwanda, where there was a strong indoctrination about "coming clean" as part of reconciliation (although this did not necessarily equate to remorse); Interview with STL Lawyer, The Hague (November 2011).

41 Interview with ICC lawyer, The Hague, November 2011.

42 Exceptions: the early structure of the ICTY (changed in 2001), and the SCSL, where a "functional separation model" was applied, distinctly separating investigators and analysts from the prosecutors (Fujiwara and Parmentier, 2012, pp. 589–594; Van Tuyl, 2008).

43 Interview with ICC lawyer, The Hague, November 2011. Rome Statute pt 9 sets out the rules of International Cooperation and Judicial Assistance; there are individual

cooperation and assistance agreements with states; and states each enact their own laws on ICC cooperation.
44 Interview with ICC lawyer, The Hague (November 2011).
45 With regard to Darfur, ongoing conflict was also an obstacle to investigation (Fouladvand 2014, pp. 1058–1059).
46 Interview with ICTY lawyer, The Hague (November 2011).
47 Interview with ICC lawyer, The Hague (November 2011).
48 Interestingly, in contrast, civil law lawyers required training in courtroom examination; interview with ICTY lawyer, The Hague (November 2011).

Bibliography

Adcock, J.M. (2011) "Is the Reid Technique Really the Problem?" *IIRG Bulletin* 3(1) 6–8.

Ambos, K. (2000) "The Status, Role and Accountability of the Prosecutor of the International Criminal Court: A Comparative Overview on the Basis of 44 National Reports" *European Journal of Crime, Criminal Law and Criminal Justice*, 8(2): 89–118.

Bergsmo, M. and W.H. Wiley (2008) "Human Rights Professionals and the Criminal Investigation and Prosecution of Core International Crimes" – in Skåre, S., I. Burkey and H. Mørk (eds) *Manual on Human Rights Monitoring. An Introduction for Human Rights Field Officers* 3rd edn (Oslo, NORDEM).

Boas, G., J.L. Bischoff, N.L. Reid and B.D. Taylor III (2011) *International Criminal Law Practitioner Library: International Criminal Procedure* The International Criminal Law Practitioner vol. 3 (Cambridge: Cambridge University Press).

Bowling, B. and J. Sheptycki (2012) *Global Policing* (London: Sage).

Carter, L. and F. Pocar (eds) (2013) *International Criminal Procedure: The Interface of Civil Law and Common Law Legal Systems* (Cheltenham: Edward Elgar Publishing).

Collins, R., R. Lincoln and M.G. Frank (2002) "The Effect of Rapport in Forensic Interviewing" *Psychiatry, Psychology and Law* 9(1): 69–78.

Combs, N.A. (2002) "Copping a Plea to Genocide: The Plea Bargaining of International Crimes" *University of Pennsylvania Law Review* 151: 1–157.

Combs, N.A. (2006) "Procuring Guilty Pleas for International Crimes: The Limited Influence of Sentence Discounts" *Vanderbilt Law Review* 59: 69–151.

Dando, C.J., R. Wilcock, C. Behnkle and R. Milne (2010) "Modifying the Cognitive Interview: Countenancing Forensic Application by Enhancing Practicability" *Psychology, Crime & Law* 17(6): 491–511.

De Vos, C.M. (2011) "Prosecutor v Lubanga 'Someone Who Comes between One Person and Another': Lubanga, Local Cooperation and the Right to a Fair Trial" *Melbourne Journal of International Law* 12(1): 217–136.

Eastwood, J. (2011) "Is the Reid Technique Really the Solution? A Reply to Adcock" *IIRG Bulletin* 3(1): 9–13.

Extraordinary Chambers in the Courts of Cambodia (n.d.) *Office of Co-Investigating Judges* [website] www.eccc.gov.kh/en/organs/office-co-investigating-judges.

Fouladvand, S. (2014) "Complementarity and Cultural Sensitivity: Decision-Making by the International Criminal Court Prosecutor in the Darfur Situation" *International Criminal Law Review* 14(6): 1028–1066.

Fujiwara, H. and S. Parmentier (2012) "Investigations" – in Reydams, L., J. Wouters and C. Ryngaert (eds) *International Prosecutors* (Oxford: Oxford University Press), p. 572.

Gilliéron, G. (2014) *Public Prosecutors in the United States and Europe: A Comparative Analysis with Special Focus on Switzerland, France, and Germany* (Switzerland: Springer).

Grieve, J., C. Harfield, and A. MacVean (2007) *Policing* (London: Sage).

Groome, D. (2011) *The Handbook of Human Rights Investigation: A Comprehensive Guide to the Investigation and Documentation of Violent Human Rights Abuses* 2nd edn (Scotts Valley, CA: Createspace).

International Criminal Court (n.d.) *Judicial Divisions* [website] www.icc-cpi.int/about/judicial-divisions.

International Criminal Court (n.d.) *Office of the Prosecutor* [website] www.icc-cpi.int/about/otp.

Kebbell, M.R. and G.F. Wagstaff (1999) "The Effectiveness of the Cognitive Interview" – in Canter D., and L. Alison (eds) *Interviewing and Deception* (Aldershot: Ashgate-Dartmouth), pp. 23–40.

Keegan, M.J. (1997) "The Preparation of Cases for the ICTY" *Transnational Law & Contemporary Problems* 7: 119–127.

Kersten, M. (2015) "Justice after the War: The ICC and Post-Gaddafi Libya" – in Fisher K.J., and R. Stewart (eds) *Transitional Justice and the Arab Spring* (Abingdon: Routledge), p. 188.

Merryman, J.H. and R. Perez-Perdomo (2007) *The Civil Law Tradition: An Introduction to the Legal Systems of Europe and Latin America* (Stanford, CA: Stanford University Press).

Milne, B. and M. Powell (2010) "Investigative Interviewing" – in Brown J.M., and E.A. Campbell (eds) *The Cambridge Handbook of Forensic Psychology* (Cambridge: Cambridge University Press), pp. 208–214.

O'Brien, M. (2012) "Guilt Admissions and Interview Techniques in International Criminal Courts and Tribunals" *CEPS Briefing Paper* 12: 6.

O'Brien, M. and M. Kebbell (2014) "Interview Techniques in International Criminal Courts and Tribunals" – in Bull, R. (ed.) *Investigative Interviewing* (New York: Springer), p. 91.

Öhrn, H.J. (2009) "Results and Rapport: A Police Interviewer's Dilemma" *IIIRG Bulletin* 1(1): 15–20.

Reydams, L., J. Wouters, and C. Ryngaert (eds) (2012) *International Prosecutors* (Oxford: Oxford University Press).

Romano, C. (2012) "The Judges and Prosecutors of Internationalized Criminal Courts and Tribunals" – in Romano, C., A. Nollkaemper and J.K. Kleffner (eds) *Internationalized Criminal Courts: Sierra Leone, East Timor, Kosovo, and Cambodia* (Oxford: Oxford University Press), p. 235.

Romano, C., A. Nollkaemper, and J.K. Kleffner (eds) (2004) *Internationalized Criminal Courts and Tribunals: Sierra Leone, East Timor, Kosovo, and Cambodia* (Oxford: Oxford University Press).

Schabas, W.A. (2006) *The UN International Criminal Tribunals: The Former Yugoslavia, Rwanda and Sierra Leone* (Cambridge: Cambridge University Press).

Schabas, W.A. (2007) *An Introduction to the International Criminal Court* 3rd edn (Cambridge: Cambridge University Press).

Stenning, P. (2014) "The Politics of Prosecution: The Role of the Prosecutor of the International Criminal Court" – in de Lint, W., M. Marmo and N. Chazal (eds) *Criminal Justice in International Society* (New York and London: Routledge), pp. 86–116.

The United States Department of Justice (n.d.) *Organizational Chart* [website] www.justice.gov/agencies/chart.

Townsend, G. (2012) "Structure and Management" – in Reydams, L., J. Wouters and C. Ryngaert (eds) *International Prosecutors* (Oxford: Oxford University Press), p. 171.

Van Tuyl, P. (2008) *Effective, Efficient, and Fair? An Inquiry into the Investigative Practices of the Office of the Prosecutor at the Special Court for Sierra Leone* (Berkeley, CA: War Crimes Studies Center University of California Berkeley).

War Crimes Research Office (2012) *Investigative Management, Strategies, and Techniques of the Interntional Criminal Court's Office of the Prosecutor* (Washington, DC: American University Washington College of Law).

Wouters, J., S. Verhoeven and B. Demeyere (2008) "The International Criminal Court's Office of the Prosecutor: Navigating between Independence and Accountability?" *International Criminal Law Review* 8(1): 273–317.

Part III

The Nature and Extent of Prosecutorial Discretion

9 The Riddle of Prosecutorial Discretion

Victoria Colvin

Introduction

The Sphinx is drowsy,
The wings are furled;
Her ear is heavy,
She broods on the world.
"Who'll tell me my secret,
The ages have kept? ..."[1]
("The Sphinx",
Ralph Waldo Emerson)

Decisions whether to proceed with criminal prosecutions invariably attract controversy. Prosecutors' power is greatest in exercising their discretion in determining which allegations of crime will proceed through the court process; in a process governed by the rule of law few would argue that there should not be accountability for such power. Yet in common law systems, there has been no consensus as to what form prosecutorial accountability should take and how it is to be structured. What is the decision that is being scrutinized? Like Emerson's Sphinx, prosecutorial discretion is often seen as mysterious and impenetrable.

This is not without reason. The decision to prosecute sits at the nexus of a myriad of interests. The decision is an integral part of the criminal justice system, which is by its nature a highly adversarial process. It lies within the legal sphere, and requires highly specialized legal knowledge to make. At the same time, it also requires an assessment of the public interest, a matter of broad public concern. Because of this, while a decision to prosecute has an immediate effect in relation to the individual, the decision may also have an impact on broad long-term societal interests. This means that questions of morality, wrongfulness and societal consensus may affect the decision, and may be affected by it. These unique sets of factors therefore pose a challenge to understanding prosecutorial discretion and the controversies that inevitably surround it.

This chapter begins by discussing the public interest test in the exercise of the discretion to prosecute. It then examines how discretion has been dealt with in the scholarly literature. It considers aspects of the decision that make it inherently susceptible to disputes: the diverse purposes that underlie the criminal law; conflicts regarding the appropriate role of individual interests in public prosecutorial decision-making; and the nature of prosecution as an enforcement decision. It will be argued that the decision to prosecute must be seen as situated at a nexus of competing considerations, no one of which is determinative.

The Public Interest Test

Public prosecutors in common law systems employ a two-step test to determine whether an allegation of criminal misconduct should proceed to court. In the first step, called the evidentiary test, the strength of the case is assessed to determine if there is a sufficient probability of conviction at trial. Even if the case meets the evidentiary test, the prosecutor must still consider if the public interest requires a prosecution.

The public interest test is deeply engrained in the role of the common law prosecutor. In 1951, Sir Hartley Shawcross QC, Attorney General for England and Wales, told the House of Commons:

> It has never been the rule in this country – I hope it never will be – that suspected criminal offences must automatically be the subject of prosecution. Indeed, the very first regulations under which the Director of Public Prosecutions worked provided that he should ... prosecute, amongst other cases: "wherever it appears that the offence or the circumstances of its commission is or are of such a character that a prosecution in respect thereof is required in the public interest". That is still the dominant consideration.[2]

Matters where the public interest test determines whether the case proceeds are not infrequent. Although quantitative studies on prosecutorial decision-making are rare, in 1994, Crisp and Moxon examined 1,286 files terminated by the Crown Prosecution Service, and found that in 24 per cent of non-motoring cases and 35 per cent of motoring cases decisions not to proceed were made on public interest grounds.[3]

This discretion, although broad, is not unconstrained. As Dworkin has observed, "Discretion, like the hole in a doughnut, does not exist except as an area left open by a surrounding belt of restriction" (Dworkin, 1978, p. 31). Many public prosecution services in common law systems have formulated lists of factors that may be relevant to the decision to prosecute. Generally, the factors can be grouped into those that focus on the seriousness of the offence, those that focus on the anticipated results of the prosecution and those that focus on the prosecution process itself.[4] The policies confirm the breadth of that discretion. For example, the Code for Crown Prosecution Service for England and Wales states that:

> The questions identified are not exhaustive, and not all the questions may be relevant in every case. The weight to be attached to each of the questions,

> and the factors identified, will also vary according to the facts and merits of each case ... It is quite possible that one public interest factor alone may outweigh a number of other factors which tend in the opposite direction.[5]

This discretion to determine whether prosecution is in the public interest leaves significant scope for the prosecutor in weighing factors (Ashworth, 1987; Sanders, 1988).

Morality, Social Consensus and "Wrongfulness"

The need for prosecutors to make determinations of the "seriousness" of an alleged offence or the harm done to victims requires prosecutors to make significant decisions that cannot be determined solely from the face of the law. Length of available penalty and other statutory indications of seriousness of the offence do not in themselves explain how the gravity of criminal allegations are assessed. Rogers has argued that the concept of seriousness of an offence is of limited assistance in deciding whether to prosecute, and that the prosecutor should instead focus on identifying a need for punishment as the ultimate consequence of a criminal proceeding (Rogers, 2006, pp. 783–787). This approach would have the welcome effect of improving transparency and possibly reflection in decision-making, but leaves open the question of how the prosecutor determines the need for punishment.

There is an extensive history of scholarly debate on the role of religion, morality and social consensus, and how these concepts relate to the law. This debate has most commonly been framed in regard to the substantive criminal law: the question of whether certain acts should be crimes. But it is also relevant to the question of the discretion to prosecute: what matters should enter the court system.

Historically, a distinction was drawn between acts that were inherently wrong, called *mala in se*, and acts that were wrong because they were prohibited by law, called *mala prohibitum* (Wolfe, 1981). As Blackstone said:

> An act is said to be mala in se ... when it is inherently and essentially evil, that is, immoral in its nature and injurious in its consequence, without any regard to the fact of its being noticed or punished by the law of the state.[6]

The distinction between the two categories was traditionally grounded in religious ideas, and the relevance of the concepts to the modern criminal law has been questioned, as it is difficult to apply to modern offences (Gray, 1995; Davis, 2006). But the distinction had practical consequences, and demonstrates the relevance of ideas about the nature of wrongful conduct to enforcement.

Prior to the passage of the English *Bill of Rights*,[7] when the sovereign had the power to dispense with laws, offences which were *mala in se* were considered beyond the power of the sovereign to dispense with ("The Distinction between 'Mala Prohibita' and 'Mala in se' ", 1930: 77). For an offence that is *mala prohibitum*, where wrong flows from prohibition by the state, the idea that the state may elect to forgo enforcement is not conceptually problematic. By contrast, conceiving of an offence as *mala in se*, wrong independent of state prohibition or enforcement of the law, makes a decision by the state to forgo the potential for criminal sanctions more questionable.

Concepts of morality and social consensus regarding contentious issues, particularly homosexuality, were the catalyst for the Hart–Devlin debate of the 1960s. Devlin argued that society had a right to protect itself, and therefore to criminalize conduct on which there was a broad social consensus of undesirability even if no actual harm could be attributed to the conduct in question. Hart challenged this conception of the relationship between morality, criminal law and social consensus. He suggested that there was no reason that social consensus at a particular time should be granted priority in determining criminalization. The Hart–Devlin debate has been followed by a rich scholarship on the role of morality in law (see, e.g. Fuller, 1964; Blom-Cooper and Drewry, 1976; Kirby, 1983; Lyons, 1993; Dworkin, 1994; and Kramer, 2004).

Although the relationship of concepts of morality to law may be a matter of dispute, this does not mean that concepts of morality may not influence decision-making and criticisms of decisions at the individual level. Concepts of morality may be decisive. As Greenawalt has noted, the discretion to prosecute may act to nullify the law in individual cases where law and morality conflict (Greenawalt, 1987, pp. 348–356). Individual concepts of morality may bear on a prosecutor's assessment of that person's culpability, and therefore the need to prosecute his or her conduct. Greenawalt uses the example of an individual who assaulted a man who had sexual intercourse with that individual's underage sister. But this involves some assessment by the prosecutor of the social utility of those beliefs.

Decisions to prosecute may impact on the enforcement of the criminal law in areas where there is a lack of social consensus or changing social views. This can be seen in relation to issues surrounding the criminalization of abortion, homosexual acts, domestic violence and impaired driving. Shifting social values may be reflected in decisions to prosecute either before or independently of any change in the substantive criminal law. In terms of the impact of the law in society, these enforcement decisions, and the habitus they reflect, may be as significant as or more so than the substantive criminal law on the books.

Discretion and the Criminal Law

As Galligan has noted, the exercise of discretion is affected by the subject matter of the decision that is made. Each area of discretion has unique characteristics (Galligan, 1986, p. 3). The discretion to prosecute and how it is viewed is inextricably linked to the criminal law. But the criminal law, the manner with which it is enforced and the principles that underlie it are the subject of controversy. Aspects of the nature of criminal law lead to adversity, not only in process, but at the level of ideas.

The discretionary nature of the decision to prosecute is often stated, but what is less often grappled with is the question of what that means for how the decision is structured and how the prosecutor is held accountable. Simply put, if a decision is "discretionary", what does that imply?

Beginning with Dicey (1915), discretionary powers have long been criticized for the potential for arbitrary decision-making. Over time, as large numbers of decisions are made by different officials, the outcome of inconsistent results becomes likely or even inevitable.[8] Although the criminal law is highly precise, discretion introduces an element of potential unpredictability, which is at odds with the codified nature of the criminal law. But the nature of this "unpredictable" element of discretion is not well understood.

A simple definition of discretion is the power to make a choice where the result is not dictated, but is rather left up to the decision maker. Craig defines discretion as a situation "where there is power to make choices between courses of action or where, even though the end is specified, a choice exists as to how that end should be reached" (Craig, 2012, p. 533). Similarly, as the High Court of Australia has stated:

> In general terms, discretion refers to a decision-making process in which "no one [consideration] and no combination of [considerations] is necessarily determinative of the result". Rather, the decision-maker is allowed some latitude as to the choice of the decision to be made.[9]

Galligan has noted that in common usage discretion connotes autonomy. He suggests that "[t]o have discretion is, then in its broadest sense, to have a sphere of autonomy within which one's decisions are in some degree a matter of personal judgement and assessment" (Galligan, 1986, p. 8). However, Galligan and other scholars have expanded on this basic or "core" view of discretion. More nuanced understandings of discretion have emphasized the role of setting the standards that govern the decision-making process as a key element of discretionary decision-making.

Davis has said: "A public officer has discretion whenever the effective limits on his power leave him free to make a choice among possible courses or action or inaction" (Davis, 1971). As Bronnit and Stenning have noted, although this is a widely cited definition of discretion, this broad definition "does not distinguish between acceptable and unacceptable bases for discretion", and they note that Davis himself went on to clarify how discretion was constrained by guidelines and standards (Bronnit and Stenning, 2011).

Dworkin describes three concepts of discretion, two weak and one strong. Under the first form of weak discretion, the decision maker has a power of judgement, but the standards that must be applied are prescribed. He describes the second form of weak discretion as final decision-making authority. This second form of weak discretion has been criticized as not describing true discretion (Galligan, 1986, p. 14), and will not be utilized in this discussion.

Finally, strong discretion involves the decision makers having their own power to set standards (Dworkin, 1978, pp. 31–32).

Although the decision itself, in the sense of choosing an outcome, is unquestionably an important part of discretion, it is only a part of the process of exercising discretion. Dworkin's concept of strong discretion is valuable because the power to set standards may ultimately be more significant to outcomes than the power of choice itself, as the standards may determine or strongly influence the outcome.

Galligan has also conceived of the power to set standards as integral to the exercise of discretion, going so far as suggesting that there is no true discretion without the power to establish standards. He describes the term discretion as meaning in its "stronger and more central sense as an express grant of power conferred on officials where determination of the standards according to which power is to be exercised is left largely to them" (Galligan, 1986, p. 1). Galligan goes on to note:

> Discretionary power is often characterized in terms of the authority to choose amongst alternative courses of action … This is true but oversimplified if the above claims regarding the requirements of rational decision-making are accepted: on the assumption that one's choices must be reasoned, discretion consists not in the authority to choose amongst different actions, but to choose amongst different courses of action *for good reason.* The course of action cannot be separated from the reasons, and therefore the standards on which it is based. [Emphasis in original.]
>
> (Galligan, 1986, p. 7)

Galligan's more expansive concept of discretion, being more than just a power to decide, but also potentially including a power to set standards (Galligan, 1986, pp. 8–12), is conceptually similar to Dworkin's "strong" discretion.

Dworkin's concept of strong discretion, and Galligan's idea of discretion as inherently containing a standard-setting power, provide a broader concept of discretion, both in the scope of the power and potentially in the time frame over which the discretionary decision-making process operates and the entities who may be considered to have a part in the making of the decision. Standards may be set long before an individual decision is made, and they may be chosen or influenced by persons other than the primary decision maker. This suggests that discretion is not limited to a single point in time or a single person as the decision maker. When discretion is taken as including standards it becomes broader, as standards may be set organizationally, or a single decision maker may adopt standards that apply to multiple decisions that he or she may make.

Other scholars have broadened the concept of discretion in a different direction, as involving not only the entities with decision-making and standard-setting powers, but also as encompassing the process and the participation of interested parties.

Cartier has argued that rather than an exercise of power, discretion should be conceived of as a dialogue between decision-maker and affected person (Cartier, 2004, 2005 and 2009; see also Sossin, 1993; Handler, 1986). While the former concept focuses on discretion as a top-down exercise of power, the latter considers it in the context of submissions made and considered. The exercise of discretion involves the development of principles, which may guide the decision.

Cartier's concept of discretion as dialogue was developed in the context of obligations of procedural fairness, including hearings where the parties are able to present their arguments to decision makers, and often with reasons for the decision being provided.[10] This can be contrasted with the circumstances surrounding the prosecutorial charging decision. In addition, the decision to prosecute does not always involve consultation in the form of procedural fairness/ natural justice, due to the nature of the decision reflecting the bringing or continuation of criminal charges. With the exception of policies requiring consultation with victims or police, what consultations may occur are often informal and occur at the discretion of the prosecutor. If representations are made to the decision maker, they are usually informal and ad hoc, and reasons may not be provided.

The concepts of strong or standard-setting discretion and of discretion as dialogue are valuable in that they broaden the concept of what discretion is beyond the traditional focus on the decision maker and the decision as a point in time. However, there are limitations on the utility of these concepts, particularly of discretion as dialogue, when applied to the decision to prosecute. In the case of the decision in the criminal justice system, dialogue by itself is insufficient to account for the highly controversial and adversarial nature of proceedings and the wide diversity of affected interests, some of which are inherently antagonistic.

This broader concept of discretion as a process occurring over time has implications for the role of accountability mechanisms in understanding how accountability mechanisms may be employed by interested parties seeking to question or reverse decisions. Accountability can be considered a third "dimension" to discretion, as the exercise of discretionary decision-making power may be evaluated, and in some cases nullified, in a variety of spheres that function under different rules than the original prosecutorial agency. The addition of accountability mechanisms to the concept of discretion further broadens the process, as a single discretionary decision may move through multiple "fields" as mechanisms of accountability are employed.

The scholarship has therefore conceptually broadened discretion in two dimensions: weak (simply a decision-making power) versus strong (standard setting), as well as top-down (discretion as an exercise of power) versus collaborative (discretion as a process involving the decision maker and interested parties). At the same time, however, three other elements are critical: the factor of purpose, the role of interested parties and the implications of the nature of the discretion as an enforcement decision.

Challenges in Framing the Discretion to Prosecute

Purpose and the Substantive Criminal Law

Recognizing purpose as a fundamental guiding factor helps to clarify some of the controversies that may surround prosecutorial decision-making. The discretionary power of the prosecutor is linked to the nature of the criminal law. The prosecutor is charged with determining when the process of enforcing the criminal law against an individual should be set in motion. But the purpose underlying the criminal law itself is in dispute, leading to inevitable controversies about the question of what factors should influence the decision whether to prosecute in the public interest.

The purpose underlying the grant of discretionary power has been recognized as a key element guiding decision makers. In *Roncarelli v Duplessi*, a seminal Canadian case on discretion that has been followed in other common law jurisdictions, it was found that discretionary power must be exercised in accordance with the purpose for which it was granted, even where the grant of authority has no restrictions on its face. Rand J said:

> In public regulation of this sort there is no such thing as absolute and untrammelled "discretion", that is that action can be taken on any ground or for any reason that can be suggested to the mind of the administrator; no legislative Act can, without express language, be taken to contemplate an unlimited arbitrary power exercisable for any purpose, however capricious or irrelevant, regardless of the nature or purpose of the statute. Fraud and corruption in the Commission may not be mentioned in such statutes but they are always implied as exceptions. "Discretion" necessarily implies good faith in discharging public duty; there is always a perspective within which a statute is intended to operate; and any clear departure from its lines or objects is just as objectionable as fraud or corruption.[11]

Scholars, too, have emphasized the importance of purpose. Nonet and Selznick have identified purpose as integral to what they call responsive law (Nonet and Selznick, 1978; see also Nonet, 1980):

> A responsive institution retains a grasp on what is essential to its integrity while taking account of new forces in its environment. To do so, it builds upon the ways integrity and openness sustain each other even as they conflict. *It perceives social pressures as sources of knowledge and opportunities for self-correction.* To assume that posture, an institution requires the guidance of purpose. Purposes set standards for criticizing established practice, thereby opening ways to chance. [Emphasis in original.]
>
> (Nonet and Selznick, 1978, p. 77)

Social pressures as a source of guidance, however, raise questions of how the prosecutor is to assess issues of morality and social consensus. Although these issues are not irrelevant, equating them to purpose in the criminal law context may oversimplify the issue.

Galligan has questioned Nonet and Selznick's use of purpose on the grounds that purpose may not be sufficiently objectively ascertainable in a manner that will attract consensus for it to be used as a guiding factor when discretion is evaluated (Galligan, 1986, pp. 100–104). This concern about whether purpose can be determined with sufficient certainty is particularly germane to the question of whether an underlying purpose to the criminal law can be determined with sufficient certainty to guide prosecutorial decision-making.

In the English system the criminal law evolved as common law offences that were subsequently codified into statute (Colvin and McKechnie, 2012: [1.10]). As a result of this history, there is no single agreed statement of the purposes of the criminal law. Efforts to describe the purposes of the criminal law have identified diverse and broadly stated purposes. Some scholars have adopted the American Law Institute's *Model Penal Code*'s statement of the purposes of the criminal law (Card, Cross and Jones, 2006, p. 3; Ormerod, 2011, p. 4). The Code lists the following purposes:

a To forbid and prevent conduct that unjustifiably and inexcusably inflicts or threatens substantial harm to individual or public interests
b To subject to public control persons whose conduct indicates that they are disposed to commit crimes.
c To safeguard conduct that is without fault from condemnation as criminal
d To give warning of the nature of conduct declared to be an offence
e To differentiate on reasonable grounds between serious and minor offences.[12]

The purposes underlying the criminal law were also commented on in the report of the Wolfenden Committee on Homosexual Offences and Prostitution.[13] The committee described the purpose of the criminal law as being:

> to preserve public order and decency, to protect the citizen from what is offensive or injurious, and to provide sufficient safeguards against exploitation and corruption of others, particularly those who are especially vulnerable.

Even this relatively simple formulation could be divided into multiple purposes.

Thus, Walker, for example, identifies 13 distinguishable forms of purpose underlying the criminal law, ranging from the "protection of the human person … against intentional violence, cruelty or unwelcome sexual approaches" to the "prevention of acts which, even if the participants are adult and willing, are regarded as 'unnatural' " (Walker, 1972: 41).

The decision whether to prosecute is a form of discretion that is particularly vulnerable to theoretical disputes. The purpose underlying the legislative grant of discretionary power is a key guiding element to how those powers should be exercised. Without clear guidance by purpose, the proper exercise of the discretion to prosecute is susceptible to dispute.

The Role of the Individual

The decision to prosecute may have significant personal consequences for affected individuals. These include not only the accused and the identified victim of the alleged offence, but also witnesses and potential future victims of crime. A question interlinked with the question of the purpose the criminal law is to serve is that of how prosecutors are expected to weigh the interests of these individuals and how they are to be balanced against each other, and against broader societal interests.

The public prosecutor represents the state, and broadly speaking, the public interest. Their role carries with it the expectation of neutrality and dispassionate application of the law.[14] The decision to prosecute involves collectively held interests, such as the interest of society that allegations be resolved and wrongdoers receive appropriate consequences. However, when making the decision to prosecute, the interests of individuals are undeniably affected, and are part of the public interest in how the decision is made.

This tension is most apparent when the interests of victims are considered. Victims are not a monolithic category: they may support or oppose a prosecution for a wide variety of reasons. Their interests must also be assessed against not only those of society, but also against other affected individuals: the potential accused's interest in not facing unwarranted proceedings, witnesses who may suffer stress or personal safety issues, and even future victims of the same accused if the prosecution does not proceed. However, with the victim's rights movement, the view that the victim is a legal stranger to the proceedings has been increasingly questioned (Garawke, 1994; Ashworth, 2000). Currently, the role of the victim is in flux, and there is no conclusive answer to the question of how the prosecutor should relate to the victim of a reported crime at the pre-trial stage, when there has been no court ruling on the merits of the case.

Historically, as prosecution moved into the hands of public officials in the nineteenth century, the role of the victim in the proceedings diminished (Garawke, 1994, p. 597). Prior to the institution of the office of the public prosecutors, victims of crime and other private citizens were significant agents responsible for bringing prosecutions, although they were subject to controls such as the tort of malicious prosecution as well as a system of inducements, such as Tyburn tickets (Kirchengast, 2006; Hay 1983). The Attorney General, the closest historical precursor to the public prosecutor, acted for the Crown rather than individual victims, but prosecuted few cases (Edwards, 1964). When modern police forces were created in the early nineteenth century they soon became de facto prosecutors in England. However, their relationship with victims was not a source of significant debate.

The victims' rights movement has brought this question into sharp focus. Although the movement focuses on many areas of the treatment of victims by the criminal justice system, including communications with victims and their treatment in court, the role of the victim in decisions to prosecute has been under-examined. The question of whether and to what extent the interests of victims should have a role in these decisions and, if so, what this role should be, is linked to the question of the purpose of the criminal law.

It has been noted that victims have an ambiguous status in the criminal justice system (Edwards, 2004). Rhetoric may say they are at the "heart" of the criminal justice system, but this idea is in practice misleading (Fenwick, 1995; Hall, 2010). At present the law is clear that the Crown is the prosecuting party. However, there is a question about what weight the prosecutor should give the wishes of victims in making the decision to prosecute. How the interests of victims are to be treated in the public interest portion of the decision raises questions of the purpose of the criminal law and how competing interests are to be weighed.

Flatman and Bagaric note this issue of balance, observing that consultation with victims may give rise to the perception that they have too much influence on decisions whether to commence or continue prosecutions in light of their role in the criminal justice system. They argue, however, that the prosecutor's duty of fairness, well established in connection with the accused, should be extended to the victim on the basis that they also have important interests at stake in the criminal process (Flatman and Bagaric, 2001, p. 250). They suggest that this duty can be met by the prosecutor giving weight to the victim's views and interests where appropriate, particularly where there is sufficient evidence to proceed and the question is whether prosecution is in the public interest. Fairness, in this concept, rests on what the victim has at stake in the criminal process.

If a criminal matter can be considered a conflict, then the role of the victim in the proceedings comes into sharper focus. Christie conceives of conflicts as potentially valuable property for several reasons, including their potential for norm-clarification and debate on what the law should be (Christie, 1977). He argues that conflicts should be seen as belonging primarily to the direct participants: in the criminal system, to the accused and the victim. However, his suggestions for reform focused on the sentencing process. He rejects the idea of reform of the guilt-determining part of the process, and does not consider the question of the charging part of the system. Although Christie's criticisms are not directed at the charging stage, they have application to an analysis of how charging is conceived of. In particular, the idea of ownership in a conflict, and the idea that victims have a stake in the criminal process, lies at the heart of many of the criticisms levied at the criminal justice system by the victims' rights movement.

The Limits of the Role of the Prosecutor

A further challenge to how prosecutorial discretion is conceived of is the nature of the decision as a gatekeeping decision rather than an adjudicative one. A decision to prosecute is in effect a decision to enforce the law. Although the decision does not in itself result in legal sanctions, it opens the door to the sanctions of conviction and sentencing. A decision not to prosecute denies access to the criminal justice system.

A prosecutor cannot adopt a blanket policy of non-prosecution of certain offences as such a policy would be at risk of being found to be an unconstitutional dispensation or suspension of the law.[15] Nor can police or prosecutors adopt policies that amount to blanket policies of declining to enforce the law, as this is a breach of their duties.[16] However, when a large number of such decisions not to prosecute are made, and there are no decisions to prosecute, the practical result may be indistinguishable from non-enforcement.

Even falling short of this, enforcement decisions may affect the practical impact of the criminal law. As Nigel Walker has noted, the stigma of offences will vary widely. Decisions regarding enforcement may contribute to how offences are viewed in society: Walker gives the example of how traffic tickets are enforced, usually administratively and sometimes even by post, as an example of how offences may become "astigmatised" (Walker, 1980, pp. 143–163). Prosecutorial discretion deals with enforcement of the criminal law, not the criminal law itself, but enforcement decisions impact on the substantive law.

However, the need for predictability and certainty in the criminal law may influence how that discretion is structured. Arbitrary and unpredictable enforcement could be seen as incompatible with the structured framework of the criminal law. Prosecutorial policies that provide transparency to the process of enforcement could also be seen as an extension of the move to certainty in the reach of the criminal law that motivated its statutory codification. However, a prosecutorial policy that suggests that some crimes might be prosecuted less frequently than others, even if the crimes carry equal penalties and seem on the terms of the statute to be equally serious, introduces a level of uncertainty to the criminal process.

Conclusion

The decision to prosecute sits at the nexus of both individual concerns and broad societal debate. It occurs over time, involving multiple stakeholders, but does not occur in the context of a formal hearing. The prosecutor's decisions may be influenced by concepts of morality, which may or may not reflect societal views in controversial areas. What emphasis is given to the interests of individuals and how the role of the victim is conceptualized may also affect the outcome.

Questions of legitimate public and personal interest may be at stake in decisions to prosecute. It is not sufficient to say that the decision to prosecute on behalf of the public is entrusted to an impartial and dispassionate prosecutor: even if such a thing were possible, the issues and interests at stake in decisions to prosecute are not easily reduced down to a problem that can be solved in a "dispassionate" manner. Nor is it enough to say that a public prosecutor must be "accountable" for how their powers are exercised. Particularly in regard to decisions not to prosecute, structuring mechanisms of accountability is not a simple matter. When accountability is viewed as a component of the discretionary process, the need for caution becomes clear. What interests are represented and advanced, how vulnerable parties are protected and how disputes are resolved become critical.

This chapter has examined a number of issues that shape and underlie debates about individual charging decisions. Ultimately, it is argued that the decision to prosecute is sui generis, situated as it is in the enforcement of the criminal law, affecting individual interests, serving a gatekeeping rather than adjudicative function, and drawing on questions of morality, social consensus and harm. None of these factors is individually determinative of how the discretion is exercised, and any efforts to understand how the discretion operates and to structure accountability mechanisms must take all into account. The riddle of how to understand prosecutorial discretion resists simple answer. It can only be addressed by embracing its complexities.

Notes

1 Ralph Waldo Emerson, "The Sphinx" in Emerson's Prose and Poetry, ed. by Joel Porte and Saundra Morris (Norton & Co, 2001), 1–6.
2 UK, H.C. Debates, vol. 483, col. 681, (29 January 1951).
3 Debbie Crisp and David Moxon, Case Screening by the Crown Prosecution Service: How and Why Cases Are Terminated (HM Stationary Office, 1994).
4 See, i.e., Crown Prosecution Service, The Code for Crown Prosecutors, 7th edn, s. 4.12(a).
5 CPS, The Code for Crown Prosecutors, ibid., s. 4.10–4.11.
6 William Blackstone, Commentaries on the Laws of England (15th edn, 1809).
7 *Bill of Rights 1689*, 1 Will. & Mary, sess. 2, c. 2 (UK).
8 See *R v TV*, [1992] 1 SCC 749 at 760, citing *R v. Poirier*, Man. Prov. Ct, 7 June 1989, unreported, 11–12.
9 *Coal and Allied Operations Pty Ltd v Australian Industrial Relationship Commission* (2000) 203 CLR 194, 204, quoting from *Jago v District Court (NSW)* (1989) 168 CLR 23, 76 per Gaudron J. *Coal and Allied Operations Pty Ltd v Australian Industrial Relationship Commission* (2000) 203 CLR 194, 204.
10 It should be noted that in some jurisdictions, prosecutors are required to give a hearing to potential accused and/or victims before making a decision whether to prosecute: see, e.g. Constitution of the Republic of South Africa Act of 1996, s. 179(5)(d).
11 *Roncarelli v Duplessis*, [1959] SCR 121, 140.
12 American Law Institute, *Model Penal Code* (1961).
13 Wolfenden committee on Homosexual Offences and Prostitution (1957) Cmnd 247.
14 *Boucher v R* (1954) 110 CCC 263 at 270, Rand J.
15 *Bill of Rights 1689*, 1 Will. & Mary, sess. 2, c. 2 (UK); *R v Catagas* (1977), 81 DLR (3d) 396 (Man CA).
16 *R (Blackburn) v Commissioner of Police of the Metropolis* [1968] 2 QB 118.

References

Ashworth, A. (1987) "The 'Public Interest' Element in Prosecutions" *Criminal Law Review* 595.

Ashworth, A. (2000) "Victims' Rights, Defendants' Rights and Criminal Procedure" – in Crawford A., and J. Goodey (eds) *Integrating a Victim Perspective Within Criminal Justice* (London: Dartmouth Publishing).

Blom-Cooper, L. QC and G. Drewry (1976) *Law and Morality* (London: Duckworth).
Bronnit, S. and P. Stenning (2011) "Understanding Discretion in Modern Policing" *Criminal Law Journal* 35: 319.
Card, Cross and Jones (2006) *Criminal Law* 17th edn (Oxford: Oxford University Press).
Cartier, G. (2004) "Reconceiving Discretion: From Discretion as Power to Discretion as Dialogue" (SJD thesis, University of Toronto).
Cartier, G. (2005) "Administrative Discretion as Dialogue: A Response to John Willis" *University of Toronto Law Journal* 55(3): 629.
Cartier, G. (2009) "Administrative Discretion and the Spirit of Legality: From Theory to Practice" *Canadian Journal of Law and Society* 24(3): 313.
Christie, N. (1977) "Conflicts as Property" *The British Journal of Criminology* 17: 1.
Colvin, E. and Justice J. McKechnie (2012) *Criminal Law in Queensland and Western Australia* 6th edn (London: Butterworths).
Craig, P. (2012) *Administrative Law* 7th edn (London: Sweet & Maxwell), p. 533.
Davis, K. (1971) *Discretionary Justice: A Preliminary Inquiry* (Baton Rouge, LA: Louisiana State University Press).
Davis, M.S. (2006) "Crimes *Mala in Se*: An Equity-Based Definition" *Criminal Justice Policy Review* 17(3): 270.
Dicey, A.V. (1975) *Introduction to the Study of the Law of the Constitution* (1915. Reprint, London: Macmillan).
Dworkin, G. (ed.) (1994) *Morality, Harm, and the Law* (Boulder, CA: Westview Press).
Dworkin, R. (1978) *Taking Rights Seriously* (Cambridge, MA: Harvard University Press).
Edwards, I. (2004) "An Ambiguous Participant: The Crime Victim and Criminal Justice Decision-Making" *British Journal of Criminology* 44: 967.
Edwards, J. Ll. J. (1964) *Law Officers of the Crown* (London: Sweet & Maxwell).
Fenwick, H. (1995) "Rights of Victims in the Criminal Justice System: Rhetoric or Reality?" *Criminal Law Review* 843.
Flatman G. and M. Bagaric (2001) "The Victim and the Prosecutor: The Relevance of Victims in Prosecution Decision-Making" *Deakin Law Review* 6: 238.
Fuller, L.L. (1964) *The Morality of Law* (New Haven, CT: Yale University Press).
Galligan, D. (1986) *Discretionary Powers* (Wooten-under-Edge: Clarendon Press).
Garawke, S. (1994) "The Role of the Victim during Criminal Court Proceedings" (1994) *University of New South Wales Law Journal* 17(2): 595.
Gray, R.L. (1995) "Eliminating the (Absurd) Distinction between Malum in Se and Malum Prohibitum Crimes" *Washington University Law Quarterly* 73: 1369.
Greenawalt, K. (1987) *Conflicts of Law and Morality* (Oxford: Oxford University Press).
Hall, M. (2010) "The Relationship between Victims and Prosecutors: Defending Victims' Rights?" *Criminal Law Review* 31.
Handler, J. (1986) *The Conditions of Discretion* (New York: Russell Sage Foundation).
Hay, D. (1983) "Controlling the English Prosecutor" *Osgood Hall Law Journal* 21: 165.
Justice Kirby, M.D. (1983) "Morality and Law: Old Debate, New Problems" The Tenth Walter Murdoch Lecture Delivered at Murdoch University on 13 September 1983.
Kirchengast, T. (2006) *The Victim in Criminal Law and Justice* (Basingstoke: Palgrave Macmillan).
Kramer, M.H. (2004) *Where Law and Morality Meet* (Oxford: Oxford University Press).
Lyons, D. (1993) *Moral Aspects of Legal Theory* (Cambridge: Cambridge University Press).
Nonet, P. (1980) "The Legitimation of Purposive Decisions" *California Law Review* 68(2): 263.

Nonet, P. and P. Selznick (1978) *Law and Society in Transition: Toward Responsive Law* (Piscataway, NJ: Transaction Publishers).
Ormerod, D. (2011) *Smith and Hogan Criminal Law* 13th edn (Oxford: Oxford University Press).
Rogers, J. (2006) "Restructuring the Exercise of Prosecutorial Discretion in England" *Oxford Journal of Legal Studies* 26(4): 775.
Sanders, A. (1988) "Incorporating the 'Public Interest' in the Decision to Prosecute" – in Hall Williams, J.E. (ed.) *Role of the Prosecutor* (Aldershot: Avebury).
Sossin, L. (1993) "The Politics of Discretion: Toward a Critical Theory of Public Administration" *Canadian Public Administration* 36(3): 364.
Walker, N. (1972) *Sentencing in a Rational Society* (London: Pelican Books).
Walker, N. (1980) *Punishment, Danger, and Stigma: The Morality of Criminal Justice* (New York: Barnes & Noble Books).
"The Distinction between 'Mala Prohibita' and 'Mala in se' in Criminal Law" (1930) *Columbia Law Review* 30(1): 74.
Travis Wolfe, N. (1981) "Mala in se: A Disappearing Doctrine?" *Criminology* 19: 131.

10 Prosecuting Domestic Violence Cases

Listening to Victims

Heather Douglas[1]

Introduction

Increasingly criminal offences committed in the context of domestic violence present a special case for prosecutors in Western countries. Historically, violence in the home was shielded from criminal justice intervention. Both the practice of "rule of thumb", that permitted a man to beat his wife with a rod as long as its circumference was no larger than a man's thumb, and the immunity against prosecution for rape in marriage survived for many years (Lemon, 2001, p. 2; ALRC/NSWLRC, 2010, p. 1121). Views about the role of the criminal law in response to physical and sexual violence perpetrated on a victim by a current or former intimate partner (domestic violence) have changed significantly over the past 50 years. Now, domestic violence is clearly recognised in law, policy and law reform reports as a criminal offence that should be prosecuted in the interests of victim safety and perpetrator accountability (State of Victoria, 2016; ALRC/NSWLRC, 2010, 561; Department of Justice, 2016). Despite changes in public perception and in legal responses, including the recognition of domestic violence in legislation and the removal of the marriage immunity for charges of rape, there are difficulties associated with prosecuting domestic violence cases and it is reported that domestic violence continues to be under-prosecuted (ALRC/NSWLRC, 2010, pp. 353–354). In response to these social changes, and to the difficulties inherent in prosecuting domestic violence cases, prosecution policies in Australia, and in other countries, have identified the need for special approaches to be taken in prosecuting these types of cases.

The approach of prosecution decision-making guidelines and policies to offences committed in the context of domestic violence has received relatively little attention in Australian research (Holder, 2001, p. 14). This is in contrast, for example, to the experience of the United States of America (USA). When the *Violence Against Women Act* was introduced in the United States in 1994 it included the promotion of a strong criminal justice approach to domestic and family violence. It supported so-called "no-drop" policies that mandated prosecution where there is sufficient evidence regardless of the victim's view. These policies created profound change (Stark, 2007, pp. 37–39) with prosecutors in some USA jurisdictions placing extreme pressure on women to testify against their violent partners; on some occasions arresting and incarcerating them in order to gain their cooperation (Goodmark, 2014, p 2). Debate about the utility of no-drop policies in the context of prosecuting crime in domestic violence cases in the USA endures (Coker, 2001; Gruber, 2012; cf. Hanna, 1996), although the effect of these policies remains under-researched (Worral, Ross and McCord, 2006, p. 472). In Australia there has been a heightened interest in domestic and family violence and the role of the criminal justice response to it. Australia's *National Plan to Reduce Violence Against Women and their Children* (Council of Australian Governments, 2011, p. 27), a recent Royal Commission (State of Victoria, 2016, p. 10) and a Special Taskforce into domestic violence (Qld Special Taskforce, 2015, pp. 14, 41) all identify concerns about prosecutorial decision-making in this context but stop short of supporting the introduction of USA-type no-drop policies.

This chapter begins by reviewing the role of the criminal law in responding to domestic violence. It then considers the reasons that have been put forward to explain the under-prosecution of domestic violence offending before turning to explore the approach taken in guidelines for prosecution prepared by Public Prosecutions Offices throughout Australia. The main reason identified for the under-prosecution of domestic violence offences in Australia is the victim's lack of cooperation, and prosecutorial guidelines have attempted to address this concern in a range of ways. The chapter concludes with a consideration of the preferred way to approach this issue and argues that, while there may be some cases where prosecutions should proceed in the absence of the victim's support, victims should neither be mandated to take part nor prosecuted for retraction or obstructing the course of justice except in exceptional circumstances and where there is some malicious purpose able to be determined.

Criminal Justice Responses and Perpetrator Responsibility

Generally, domestic violence is understood as a pattern of behaviour involving a perpetrator's exercise of coercive control over the victim (Stark, 2007). Overwhelmingly, the victims of domestic violence are the former or current female intimate partners of a male perpetrator (Qld Special Taskforce, 2015, p. 15). The definitions of domestic violence vary between Australian jurisdictions and while not all behaviours that are defined as domestic violence are criminal, many are (Burton, 2003, p. 301). Obvious examples include assault, criminal damage and stalking.

The role of the criminal law as a response to domestic violence has been a key area of discussion in debates about justice responses. Dobash identifies that the criminal justice system plays two "vitally" important roles in the domestic violence sphere (2002, pp. 315–316; Burton, 2003, pp. 301, 313). The first is "symbolic" – that the justice system as a social institution sets the limits of acceptable behaviour and criminalisation may convey that the activity is taken seriously by government. The second role is "real" in that the effects of the prosecution and sentencing are experienced by both perpetrators and victims of domestic violence. However, Coker has identified some concerns associated with crime control strategies as a response to domestic violence. She argues that a focus on crime control deflects attention and resources away from other strategies, that a focus on strengthening the crime control model results in greater state control of women – particularly marginalised women – and that the criminal justice response cannot provide the safety women need (Coker, 2001, p. 805). In particular, she opposes any form of mandatory prosecution approach for these reasons but also notes a further consequence that where prosecution processes are mandatory women lose an opportunity to "leverage" agreements from the batterer in exchange for withdrawing the prosecution (Coker, 2001, p. 805).

There is no clear evidence that a criminal response to domestic violence is effective in deterring violence or increasing safety. In his review of literature about the effect of prosecution of domestic violence-related charges, Garner observed there were confusing messages from the research suggesting variously: that prosecution has no effect on repeat offending; that increased prosecution in specialised courts increased reoffending; that no-drop prosecution policies increase reoffending but, the initiation of charges reduces offending (Garner, 2005, p. 570). Despite these uncertainties, the *Australian National Plan to Reduce Violence Against Women and their Children* aims to "promote responses from criminal justice agencies" (Council of Australian Governments, 2011, p. 26). A number of Australian states have also identified the aim of improving the criminal justice response to domestic violence in key policy documents. For example, with the underlying goal of ensuring perpetrator accountability, the New South Wales government's plan to tackle domestic violence has five priority elements including "a strengthened criminal justice system response" (NSW Government, 2014, p. 30; also Qld Special Taskforce, 2015, pp. 41, 14). Notably members of the community tend to view domestic violence as criminal behaviour. Webster and colleagues (2014, p. 89) surveyed over 17,000 people and found that 96 per cent of respondents believed that domestic violence was a criminal offence. Yet, it is reported that domestic violence continues to be under-prosecuted (ALRC/NSWLRC, 2010, pp. 353–354). Given the public and institutional support for criminal prosecution it is important to ask: why then are domestic violence offences under-prosecuted?

Explaining Under-Prosecution

One of the reasons for low rates of prosecution has been argued to be the lack of offences that appropriately capture the behaviours that often characterise domestic violence. For example, financial abuse or emotional abuse are usually not covered by existing offences (Douglas, 2015). However, the claim of under-prosecution relates to many of the offences already found in criminal statutes, not just to those behaviours that are not encapsulated in existing crimes. While considerations relating to practical constraints and organisational pressures are doubtlessly influential in decisions to prosecute (Romain and Freiburger, 2013,

p. 290), two of the reasons identified for low prosecution rates in domestic violence cases are that victims don't cooperate and, relatedly, that police or prosecution services decide not to prosecute (ALRC/NSWLRC, 2010, p. 563; Qld Special Taskforce, 2015, p. 14), in spite of the availability of sufficient evidence.

In many domestic violence cases the victim's testimony will be essential to a successful prosecution. In this context victims are often particularly vulnerable and their circumstances are usually complex. Victims of domestic violence are regularly pressured or threatened, or may be encouraged by the accused as part of the ongoing and controlling dynamics of domestic violence, to withdraw their complaint or give false evidence. This has been recognised by the judiciary. In a recent case a perpetrator of domestic violence was successfully prosecuted for assault and property damage but also for "doing an act to influence a witness" (*Crimes Act 1900* (NSW) s 323(a)). The perpetrator unsuccessfully appealed against sentence and the New South Wales Court of Criminal Appeal recognised: "It is within the common experience of courts that many charges of domestic violence cannot be prosecuted because the defendant manages to persuade the complainant, including by threatening violence, not to give evidence against him".[2]

There are many underlying reasons that may explain the victim's fears. For example she may fear that giving evidence will exacerbate the violence (Hirschel and Hutchison, 2001, p. 56). Victims may fear deportation as a result of uncertain immigration status and this may cause some victims to withdraw their support for prosecution (Taylor and Putt, 2007). Victims may want the relationship to continue or to resume (Groves and Thomas, 2014, p. 92) for a range of reasons including loyalty, love and affection (*Lusted v MRB* [2013]: [68]), financial need, concern for the children's welfare (Holder, 2001, p. 9) and wider family pressures (Buel, 1999, p. 19). Finally victims may fear the process of giving evidence, or being cross-examined or believe the sentence will be insufficient (Douglas, 2018).

A number of suggestions have been put forward, and procedural and legal reforms made, to address some of these issues. Changes include requiring screens or CCTV to be used in court while victims give evidence so they are shielded from the perpetrator's view, and better case management to ensure victims are not required to attend court more than necessary (Australasian Institute of Judicial Administration, 2018, [5.3]). While such changes may improve the court experience, they do not address many of the fears and personal reasons victims may have for not wanting to testify. Madden-Dempsey identifies four types of cases where prospective victim-witnesses may become a challenge for prosecutors: the victim requests dismissal of the charge; the victim's testimony contradicts the prosecution's case; the victim fails to testify; and the victim publicly requests dismissal while at the same time covertly advises prosecutors she wants the case to proceed (Madden-Dempsey, 2009, p. 17; see also Groves and Thomas, 2013, p. 93). Improved knowledge and understanding about the reasons underlying the reluctance of a victim to testify has implications for the approach of prosecutors.

Police or Prosecution Services Decide Not to Prosecute

Throughout Australia, police powers in response to domestic violence are very broad. Police can apply for protection orders, arrest perpetrators and initiate prosecution. It has been suggested that police interventions are oriented towards safety, and this might explain their focus on obtaining protection orders, an option not generally available to police in the USA (Hageman-White and others, 2015, p. 61). USA research has identified that there is a strong connection between the police response to domestic violence call-outs and later decisions to commence a prosecution, especially in non-fatal cases and less serious criminal matters (Worral, Ross and McCord, 2006, p. 479). In many cases police working in the Australian context may approach a domestic violence call out as a "civil" situation and investigate the need for a protection order, rather than identifying the situation as, also, a potential crime scene. This approach may result in a failure to collect evidence for possible use in a later prosecution (Crime and Misconduct Commission, 2005, p. 48). In her study of police practices in the United Kingdom in the late 1990s, Hoyle identified that the policing culture was focused on the civil protection order system and she found that this was one of the factors operating as an impediment to prosecution of domestic violence crimes (Hoyle, 1998, p. 101; Cretney and Davis, 1996, p. 166). Similar conclusions have been reached in Australian research. In its recent consideration of domestic violence, the Queensland Special Taskforce identified the police focus on the civil protection order system and concluded that increased criminal prosecution of perpetrators was an important goal (Qld Special Taskforce, 2015, pp. 14, 318).

It is police decision-making at the early stage of intervention that will often be pivotal in relation to whether a prosecution takes place. Police decisions to initiate criminal charges (and thus carry out appropriate investigations) occur in the shadow of prosecutorial guidelines and the evidence available to support a prosecution. For example, research has found that one of the most important factors influencing a decision not to proceed with criminal charges was the victim's desire to *not* have the perpetrator charged (Crime and Misconduct Commission, 2005, pp. 45, 48). One study found that a significant number of police hold the view that many victims drop charges (Crime and Misconduct Commission, 2005, pp. 35, 49, 79) and in other reviews police have frequently referred to "the reluctance or hostility of victims as witnesses" as the reason prosecutions do not go ahead (Qld Special Taskforce, 2015, p. 318; Dawson and Dinovitzer, 2001, p. 619). Similarly in her study of police practices, Hoyle identified that police were frequently of the view that a successful prosecution relied on the victim's willingness to give evidence at a subsequent trial and she also concluded that this factor operated as an impediment to prosecution (Hoyle, 1998, p. 101; Cretney and Davis, 1996, p. 166). Notably, the approach of police to victims when attending call-outs to domestic violence incidents may also have implications for the behaviour of victims reporting incidents of domestic violence (Hickman and Simpson, 2003) and potentially this influence might extend to a victim's decision to cooperate with prosecution authorities later in the process.

A recent review of complaints about police handling of domestic violence matters in New South Wales identified failure to investigate (19 per cent); prosecution issues, for example a failure prepare a proper brief of evidence (9 per cent), and failure to arrest/lay appropriate charges (6 per cent), as three of the most common complaints (NSW Ombudsman, 2011, p. 24). In Queensland, a recent taskforce on domestic violence identified similar concerns and recommended that the Police Service "develops and implements a strategy for increasing criminal prosecution of perpetrators of domestic and family violence through enhanced investigative and evidence-gathering methodologies" (Qld Special Taskforce, 2015, pp. 41, 14). Similarly the Victorian Royal Commission into Domestic Violence recommended greater emphasis on police investigation processes, noting the need for greater police support in relation to investigation and that detectives should be embedded in police family violence teams (State of Victoria, 2016, p. 100). Some USA jurisdictions have encouraged training in "evidence-based policing and the adoption of specific evidence gathering techniques" (Ellison, 2002, p. 840), which focus on investigating the crime with the assumption that the victim will not participate. Strategies include separate interviews with the victim and alleged perpetrator on arrival, interviews with children and neighbours, special techniques used for questioning the alleged perpetrator, photographing the victim and scene and collecting evidence such as weapons and bloodied clothing and recording details of medical interventions (Ellison, 2002, p. 841).

Research into factors affecting prosecutorial decision-making specifically about domestic violence cases is contradictory (Worral, Ross and McCord, 2006, pp. 477–478). O'Neal, Tellis and Spohn (2015, p. 1238; Ulmer, 2012, p. 25) describe prosecutors as the "gatekeepers" of the criminal justice system, and yet they note the largest gap in knowledge about case processing is in understanding prosecutorial discretion in intimate partner crime, specifically sexual assault. In their study, Worral, Ross and McCord (2006) concluded, among other things, that arrest and serious injury to the victim were associated with prosecutors' charging decisions around domestic violence assaults. Research conducted by Spohn and Holleran (2001) suggests that prosecutors are more likely to prosecute when the offence is serious, when the victim has clearly suffered "real" harm, and when the evidence against the suspect is strong. However, the prosecution drivers that Spohn and Holleran identify might be seen as an awkward fit with domestic violence offending. Notions of serious offending are often associated with traditional crimes such as physical assault. Sometimes criminal offending in cases involving domestic violence such as threats, stalking and minor damage to property may not be perceived as serious if they are understood outside of the coercive and controlling context in which they occur (Stark, 2007, ch 7). There has long been a concern that criminal offences committed in the context of domestic violence may be deemed trivial by police, and they have been criticised for many years for disregarding the severity of domestic violence on the basis that it is "domestic" (Qld Special Taskforce, 2015, p. 3). Furthermore, the harm resulting from domestic violence may be difficult to quantify in the absence of specialist psychological and psychiatric evidence and it is often not manifested in a physical injury. Finally, as identified earlier, the key evidence for the prosecution may be the testimony of a reluctant or uncooperative victim or one who may be perceived as lacking credibility. In their research about intimate partner sexual assault O'Neal, Tellis and Spohn (2015, p. 1240) suggest that because the likelihood of conviction is uncertain, prosecutors develop "'perceptual shorthand' that incorporates stereotypes of real crimes and credible victims". Their study found that prosecutions of intimate partner sexual assault were less likely if prosecutors doubted the victim's credibility, where additional domestic violence factors such as assault were not present, or where the victim was uncooperative in the prosecution, often even when other evidence including police photographs of injuries was available. They suggested that common misconceptions arise that intimate partner sexual assault is often a "trivial domestic squabble", which may be addressed with counselling (O'Neal, Tellis and Spohn, 2015, p. 1253).

Domestic Violence: Prosecutorial Guidelines in Australia

In most of Australia's six States and two Territories, Directors of Public Prosecutions have developed specialist guidelines and policies in relation to prosecutions of offences involving domestic and family violence. Queensland stands out. While the Queensland Police Operational Procedures Manual states that police "should hold users of violence responsible and accountable for their behaviour by commencing related criminal charges where appropriate" (Queensland Police, 2017, [9.3]), Queensland's prosecutorial guidelines do not identify any special treatment for decision-making about the prosecution of domestic violence related offences (DPP Qld, 2016).

Policies in other Australian jurisdictions vary slightly, however one of the common assumptions underlying them is that victims of domestic violence are vulnerable, that retraction or lack of cooperation in prosecution is common, and that victim's decisions to withdraw support for prosecution must be scrutinised. Thus, the distinctive feature of the policies is their focus on providing information that helps to explain some of the behaviours of victims of domestic violence and also how to manage and respond to uncooperative victims. How the various policies respond to this issue reflects either a "carrot" or "stick" approach or sometimes both.

While the South Australian prosecution guidelines do not include any specific policies about the prosecution of domestic violence cases, the South Australian Office of the Director of Public Prosecutions supports a witness assistance programme that provides information to victims involved in the prosecution of domestic violence-related offending. Under a heading "withdrawing charges", the information identifies that it is common for victims of domestic and family violence to change their minds about proceeding with charges. It explains that victims who wish to withdraw charges will be required to meet with a solicitor, investigating officer and witness assistance officer to discuss the decision and "learn about the process surrounding the decision to proceed or not" (DPP SA, n.d.). This discussion seeks to provide information about the process and the supports available to victims and considers the history of violence and risks to children, among other topics. The explicit aim of this approach is to include victims in the decision-making around prosecution and it might be perceived as a "carrot" approach that has been developed on the basis that a well-informed and supported victim will be more likely to cooperate in a prosecution. However, the requirement to meet with three justice professionals may be intimidating and overwhelming and may in fact be experienced as pressure and coercion.

New South Wales prosecutorial guidelines state that in cases involving domestic violence offences any request by the victim that proceedings be discontinued should be carefully considered in accordance with the specific protocol for reviewing Domestic Violence offences (DPP NSW, 2007, p. 19). Predictably, the guidelines note that it is not uncommon for victims to request a discontinuance of prosecution and they outline a range of reasons for why this might occur (DPP NSW, 2007, appendix E). The specific protocol identifies a number of checks and balances designed to ensure that there is a clear understanding of the basis on which the victim wishes to discontinue the prosecution. If the reason seems to be fear or coercion the officer in command must be notified. The protocol then lists a range of specific issues to be considered in cases where a victim wishes to discontinue. These include matters such as relationship history, police call-out history, and the effect on children. Prosecutions can only be discontinued after consultation with certain service providers. Notably, in a number of cases NSW victims have faced criminal prosecution when they have recanted allegations of abuse (Robinson, 2013; Begley, 2015).

The Victorian Office of Public Prosecutions has developed a specific Family Violence Policy, which outlines relevant definitions and includes a section dealing with a victim who retracts their complaint (DPP Vic, 2011, [6]). The policy focuses attention on considerations about vulnerable witnesses and how they may be best supported to give evidence. However, it also specifically identifies that a complainant may make a statement inconsistent with her or his original statement and in such circumstances charging the victim may take place but only with the instructions from the Director of Public Prosecutions or Chief Crown Prosecutor (DPP, 2011, [6]). While this offence is available in other jurisdictions, a specific practice in domestic violence cases is highlighted in the Victorian guidelines. Victoria Police in its code of practice for the investigation of family violence notes that "often [domestic violence] is criminal behaviour" (Victoria Police, 2017, [1.2]). One of the aims of the Victoria Police code of practice is to "hold perpetrators of family violence accountable for their behaviours by laying criminal charges where appropriate … and by increasing successful prosecutions" (Victoria Police, 2017, [1.2]). The Victoria Police code of practice tries to strike a balance between focusing on victim risk and safety and perpetrator accountability. It sets out certain compulsory police actions that should be based on risk assessment (Victoria Police, 2017, [3]) and directs that police should investigate all family violence incidents that come to police attention and collect background material. It identifies the need for police to speak to all parties in private (Victoria Police, 2017, [2.3.1]). Victim vulnerability and support is emphasised, suggesting a collaborative approach between victims, police and prosecution.

The four remaining jurisdictions clearly emphasise the possibility of proceeding with a criminal prosecution of a domestic violence offence in the absence of the victim's cooperation in certain circumstances. Western Australian prosecutorial guidelines identify that the principles of dealing with general criminal prosecutions may sometimes conflict with the principles to be applied in prosecuting domestic violence offences. The guidelines note: "although the attitude of the victim of the alleged offence to a prosecution remains an important factor, it is not to be regarded as decisive" and that if there is available evidence "irrespective of the wishes or presence of the victim" that provides a reasonable prospect of conviction then the matter should go to hearing unless there are exceptional circumstances (DPP WA, 2005, pp. 42–43). Notably, the policy specifically states that the victim's wishes are not an exceptional circumstance. Although no Australian jurisdictions have a mandatory prosecution or "no-drop" approach, Northern Territory (DPP NT, 2016, [21]) Tasmania (Department of Justice, 2016, p. 8), and the Australian Capital Territory (ACT) (Cusson and Lyneham, 2012, p. 109) purport to have a pro-arrest and pro-prosecution approach to matters involving domestic violence. The Northern Territory guidelines have the strongest language in relation to this issue. They note "suitable prosecutions may proceed without the evidence of an unwilling victim" and prosecutors should determine whether there is a circumstantial case based on evidence from witnesses other than the victim (DPP NT, 2016: [21]). In the ACT, the decisions to charge and arrest remain at the officer's discretion but they "should not be influenced by the wishes of the victim" (Cussen and Lyneham, 2012, pp. 8–9). Relatedly, Tasmanian government policy states that: "prosecutors would decline victim's requests to withdraw charges where sufficient evidence exists to proceed and would refer victims to other support services" (Department of Justice and Industrial Relations, 2003, p. 54 and appendix 5.1).

The Tasmanian Safe at Home reforms were introduced in 2004 and presented a response to domestic violence built on the core premise that domestic violence is a crime. A review of the policy, ten years after it was introduced, determined that the pro-arrest, pro-prosecution policies were seen by many as great strengths of the approach in Tasmania (Department of Justice, 2014, p. 9). However it has been suggested that the approach has had both positive and negative results. Positive results have included that the victim does not have to take the lead in proceedings as the State has taken on that responsibility; support services are available to victims; and magistrates have the prospect of rehabilitating offenders (Department of Justice, 2014, p. 13). On the negative side, it was reported that some victims simply wanted the violence to stop and to maintain the family unit; some victims feared the arrest of the partner and consequent retaliation;

victims may be reluctant to call the police and worry that their matter will be reported to the police without their consent; unnecessary removal of children and prosecution of breaches committed by the victim but originally incited by the perpetrator (Department of Justice, 2014, p. 14).

Victim Autonomy

So-called "no-drop" or "mandatory" prosecution policies that require prosecutors to pursue a case where there is sufficient evidence regardless of the victim's wishes to dismiss charges have often been advocated by those working with victims of domestic violence (Houston, 2014). Arguments in support of such policies claim that they will ensure greater perpetrator accountability for crimes involving domestic violence. They are also justified on the basis that the responsibility for the decision to prosecute should not be left with victims of domestic violence who often fear their violent partner's response, frequently with good reason, and regularly face extreme pressure and coercive tactics from the alleged offender to have the charges dismissed or reduced (Goodmark, 2004, p. 17). Further, it is suggested that if the decision is taken out of the hands of victims, they will no longer bear the responsibility for the subsequent punishment of the offender. While such approaches may increase the prosecution of domestic violence-related crimes (Smith and Davis, 2001), there are some unintended consequences and potentially significant costs involved.

Many researchers have identified that domestic violence results in controlling and limiting the freedom of the victim (e.g. Stark, 2007, p. 12), and coercive prosecution policies may be experienced by victims as an extension of this control and limitation on freedom. One study involving interviews with victim-advocates noted the irony inherent in "no-drop" policies, observing that while such policies are targeted at preventing victims being coerced *not* to testify by their abusers, the effect is that victims are coerced into testifying by the State (Nichols, 2014, p. 2135). Goodmark has considered the effect of coercive prosecution policies on abused women and their ability to act autonomously. She identifies that while it is argued that the coercive nature of battering creates a context that precludes battered women from exercising their free will, women who have been battered are still capable of exercising some form of autonomy or agency, even though the choices that they make are shaped by the context of the abusive relationship (Goodmark, 2009, p. 25). Others have identified the problematic assumption that all women within coercively controlling relationships are so subject to the will of their partners that they are unable to exercise the ability to choose suggesting a kind of "reduced capacity" (Hall, 2009, p. 269). Goodmark argues that restoring power to women who have been battered should be a priority in crafting domestic violence law and policy (2009, p. 29) and coercive policies sit uneasily with this aim. Elsewhere she has expressed concern that advocates for battered women should not replace one form of control with another, they should not "tell battered women what to do and how she should do it" (Goodmark, 2004, p. 30; Coker, 2001, p. 807).

On a more practical level coercive prosecution may have negative effects on women's safety. One of the main aims of coercive prosecution practices is to deter future criminal offending through prosecution, and thus ultimately ensure greater protection of victims from future violence. However, Cerulli and her colleagues (2014, p. 556) suggest that "it is the legal leverage, indicated by a victim's contact with the prosecutor and strengthened by her wish to proceed, that protects future safety". Similarly, O'Connor (1999, p. 944) identifies the decision whether to assist in a prosecution as a moment where the victim could "take control in a relationship in which she previously was powerless" but that where a policy mandates engagement with prosecutorial services she may ironically "be driven to side with her battering partner, further entrenching her in the abusive relationship". In her study of mandatory arrest laws and "no-drop" policies, Smith interviewed battered women and found that while many supported coercive prosecutorial interventions, some reported that they may be less likely to report future domestic violence to the police prosecution services if their views, preferences and opinions are ignored (Smith, 2000, p. 1386).

Conclusion

The criminal justice response to domestic violence is now considered a significant part of the overall response to domestic violence. While improving the rates of criminal prosecution of domestic violence is important from both a symbolic and real perspective (Dobash, 2003) the theoretical concerns and practical costs associated with coercive policies are convincing (Gruber, 2012, p. 584). Other ways have been identified that may help to address the under-prosecution concern. At the outset, an assumption by first responders (usually police) that victims will retract or ultimately be uncooperative is unhelpful as it is likely to influence police decision-making around evidence collection. When police have collected evidence appropriately and in a timely way, a more convincing brief will be able to be developed. Confronted with a well-prepared brief, victims may be more willing to participate, as they may not feel completely responsible for the prosecution of the perpetrator.

There is also an important role for prosecutors in facilitating victim engagement with the prosecution process. As Australian prosecution guidelines and approaches have developed over recent years to respond to the public policy emphasis on criminal prosecution of domestic violence crimes, to date, they have largely avoided the sidelining of victims from the decision-making process. While there have been some prosecutions of complainants who have retracted their statements, this is relatively rare compared to the USA experience. Studies have found that victims of domestic violence value consistency, information, support and time to think through their options (Holder and Mayo, 2003, p. 20). When these values are applied, victims of domestic violence are more likely to support the prosecution and feel satisfied with the experience (Holder and Mayo, 2003, p. 20). Research suggests that a supported decision-making approach in the context of prosecuting domestic violence is the preferred one. Along with equipping prosecutors with a better understanding about the dynamics of domestic violence and relatedly the reasons for why a victim may recant, supported decision-making is largely the approach adopted in Australian prosecution guidelines.

Notes

1 I would like to express my thanks to Ms. Jessica Downing-Ide for her research assistance in the preparation of this chapter.

2 *R v Evans* [2017] NSWCCA 281 [46] (Adamson, J., Hoeben, C.J. and Davies, J. agreeing).

References

Australian Law Reform Commission and New South Wales Law Reform Commission (2010) "Family Violence: A National Legal Response" (Report, Australian Law Reform Commission and New South Wales Law Reform Commission) ("ALRC/NSWLRC").

Australasian Institute of Judicial Administration (2018) "National Domestic and Family Violence Bench Book" (Australasian Institute of Judicial Administration).

Begley, P. (2015) "Domestic Violence Complainant Charged with Contempt" *Sydney Morning Herald* (20 December 2015).

Buel, S. (1999) "Fifty Obstacles to Leaving, *aka*, Why Abuse Victims Stay" *Colorado Lawyer* 28(10): 19.

Burton, M. (2003) "Criminalising Breaches of Civil Orders from Protection from Domestic Violence" Crim LR 301.

Cerulli, C., C.L. Kothari, M.E. Dichter and K.V. Rhodes (2014) "Victim Participation in Intimate Partner Violence Prosecution: Implications for Safety" *Violence Against Women* 20(5): 539.

Coker, D. (2001) "Crime Control and Feminist Law Reform in Domestic Violence Law: A Critical Review" *Buffalo Criminal Law Review* 4: 801.

Council of Australian Governments (2011) "National Plan to Reduce Violence Against Women and their Children 2010–2022" (Report, Australian Government, Department of Social Services).

Cretney, A. and G. Davis (1996) "Prosecuting 'Domestic' Assault" Crim LR 162.

Crime and Misconduct Commission Queensland (2005) *Policing Domestic Violence in Queensland* (Report, Crime and Misconduct Commission Queensland) ("Crime and Misconduct Commission").

Cussen, T. and M. Lyneham (2012) "ACT Family Violence Intervention Program" (Technical and Background Paper No. 52, Australian Institute of Criminology).

Dawson, M. and R. Dinovitzer (2001) "Victim Cooperation and the Prosecution of Domestic Violence in a Specialized Court" *Justice Quarterly* 18(3): 593.

Department of Justice Tasmania (2016) "Strengthening Our Legal Responses" (Report, Department of Justice Tasmania) ("Department of Justice").

Department of Justice and Industrial Relations Tasmania (2003) "Safe at Home: A Criminal Justice Framework for Responding to Family Violence in Tasmania" (Options Paper, Department of Justice and Industrial Relations) ("Department of Justice and Industrial Relations").

Director of Public Prosecutions Northern Territory (2016) "Director's Guidelines" (Office of the Director of Public Prosecutions Northern Territory) ("DPP NT").
Dobash, R.E. (2002–2003) "Domestic Violence: Arrest, Prosecution, and Reducing Violence" *Criminology and Public Policy* 2: 313.
Douglas, H. (2015) "Do We Need a Specific Domestic Violence Offence?" *Melbourne University Law Review* 39(2): 434.
Douglas, H. (2018) "Legal Systems Abuse and Coercive Control' *Criminology & Criminal Justice* 18(1): 84
Ellison, L. (2002) "Prosecuting Domestic Violence without Victim Participation" *MLR* 65: 834.
Garner, J. (2005) "What Does 'The Prosecution' of Domestic Violence Mean?" *Criminology and Public Policy* 4: 567.
Goodmark, L. (2004) "Law is the Answer: Do We Know for Sure?" *St Louis University Public Law Review* 23: 7.
Goodmark, L. (2009) "Autonomy Feminism: An Anti-Essentialist Critique of Mandatory Interventions in Domestic Violence Cases" *Florida State University Law Review* 37: 1.
Goodmark, L. (2014) "Stalled at 20: VAWA, the Criminal Justice System, and the Possibilities of Restorative Justice" *CUNY Law Review* 18(1): 48.
Groves, N. and T. Thomas (2014) *Domestic Violence and Criminal Justice* (London: Routledge).
Gruber, A. (2012) "A 'Neo-Feminist' Assessment of Rape and Domestic Violence Law Reform" *Journal of Gender Race and Justice* 15(3): 583.
Hageman-White, C., C. Humphreys, L.M. Tutty and K. Diemer (2015) "Overview of Current Policies on Arrest, Prosecution, and Protection by the Police and the Justice System as Responses to Domestic Violence" – in Johnson, H.B. Fisher and V. Jaquier *Critical Issues on Violence Against Women: International Perspectives and Promising Strategies* (London: Routledge), p. 47.
Hall, M. (2009) "Prosecuting Domestic Violence: New Solutions to Old Problems" *International Review of Victimology* 15: 255.
Hanna, C. (1996) "No Right to Choose: Mandated Victim Participation in Domestic Violence Prosecutions" *Harvard Law Review* 109(8): 1849.
Hickman, L.J. and S.S. Simpson (2003) "Fair Treatment or Preferred Outcome? The Impact of Police Behaviour on Victim Reports of Domestic Violence Incidents" *Law and Society Review* 27(3): 607.
Hirschel, D. and I. Hutchison (2001) "The Relative Effects of Offense, Offender and Victim Variables on the Decision to Prosecute Domestic Violence Cases" *Violence Against Women* 7(1): 46.
Holder, R. (2001) "Domestic and Family Violence: Criminal Justice Interventions" (Issues Paper No. 3, Australian Domestic and Family Violence Clearinghouse).
Holder, R. and N. Mayo (2003) "What Do Women Want? Prosecuting Family Violence in the ACT" *Current Issues in Criminal Justice* 15(1): 5.
Houston, C. (2014) "How Feminist Theory Became (Criminal) Law: Tracing the Path to Mandatory Criminal Intervention in Domestic Violence Cases" *Michigan Journal of Gender and Law* 21(2): 217.
Hoyle, C. (1998) *Negotiating Domestic Violence: Police, Criminal Justice and Victims* (Oxford: Clarendon Press).
Lemon, N. (2001) *Domestic Violence Law* (St Paul, MN: West Group).
Madden-Dempsey, M. (2009) *Prosecuting Domestic Violence: A Philosophical Analysis* (Oxford: Oxford University Press).

Nichols, A. (2014) "No-Drop Prosecution in Domestic Violence Cases: Survivor-Defined and Social Change Approaches to Victim Advocacy" *Journal of Interpersonal Violence* 29(11): 2014–2042.

New South Wales Government (2014) "It Stops Here: Standing Together to End Domestic and Family Violence in NSW" (Report, New South Wales Government).

NSW Ombudsman (2011) "Audit of NSW Police Force Handling of Domestic and Family Violence Complaints" (Special Report to Parliament, NSW Ombudsman).

O'Connor, C. (1999) "Domestic Violence No Contact Orders and the Autonomy Rights of Victims" *Boston College Law Review* 40: 937.

O'Neal, E., K. Tellis and C. Spohn (2015) "Prosecuting Intimate Partner Sexual Assault: Legal and Extra-Legal Factors That Influence Charging Decisions" *Violence Against Women* 21(10): 1237.

Office of the Director of Public Prosecutions New South Wales (2007) "Prosecution Guidelines" (Office of the Director of Public Prosecutions New South Wales) ("DPP NSW").

Office of the Director of Public Prosecutions Northern Territory (2011) "Guidelines of the Director of Public Prosecutions" (Office of the Director of Public Prosecutions Northern Territory) ("DPP NT").

Office of the Director of Public Prosecutions Queensland (2016) "Director's Guidelines" (Office of the Director of Public Prosecutions Queensland) ("DPP Qld").

Office of the Director of Public Prosecutions South Australia (n.d.) "Domestic and Family Violence Prosecutions" (Office of the Director of Public Prosecutions South Australia) ("DPP SA").

Office of the Director of Public Prosecutions for Western Australia (2005) "Statement of Prosecution Policy and Guidelines" (Office of the Director of Public Prosecutions for Western Australia) ("DPP WA").

Office of Public Prosecutions Victoria (2011) "Director's Policy: Family Violence" (Office of Public Prosecutions Victoria, revised 2015) ("DPP Vic").

Queensland Police (2017) *Operational Procedures Manual* (Queensland Police).

Robinson, N. (2013) "No Change for Domestic Violence Policy" *The Australian* (10 May).

Romain, D. and T. Freiburger (2013) "Prosecutorial Discretion for Domestic Violence Cases: An Examination of the Effects of Offender Race, Ethnicity, Gender and Age" *Criminal Justice Studies: A Critical Journal of Crime, Law and Society* 26(3): 289.

Smith, A. (2000) "It's My Decision, Isn't It? A Research Note on Battered Women's Perceptions of Mandatory Intervention Laws" *Violence Against Women* 6(12): 1384.

Smith, B. and R. Davis (2001) "An Evaluation of Efforts to Implement No-Drop Policies: Two Central Values in Conflict" (Report, National Institute of Justice, US Department of Justice).

Special Taskforce on Domestic and Family Violence in Queensland (2015) "Not Now, Not Ever: Putting an End to Domestic and Family Violence in Queensland (Report, Special Taskforce on Domestic and Family Violence in Queensland) ("Qld Special Taskforce").

Spohn, C. and D. Holleran (2001) "Prosecuting Sexual Assault: A Comparison of Charging Decisions in Sexual Assault Involving Strangers, Acquaintances and Intimate Partners" *Justice Quarterly* 18: 651.

Stark, S. (2007) *Coercive Control: How Men Entrap Women in Personal Life* (Oxford: Oxford University Press).

State of Victoria (2014–2016) "Royal Commission in Family Violence: Summary and Recommendations" (Parliamentary Paper No. 132, State of Victoria).

Taylor, N. and J. Putt (2007) "Adult Sexual Violence in Indigenous and Culturally and Linguistically Diverse Communities in Australia" (Trends and Issues in Crime and Criminal Justice No. 345, Australian Institute of Criminology).
Ulmer, J. (2012) "Recent Developments and New Directions in Sentencing Research" (2012) *Justice Quarterly* 29: 1.
Victoria Police (2017) "Code of Practice for the Investigation of Family Violence" (Victoria Police, 3rd edn), p. 1.
Webster, K., P. Pennay, R. Bricknall and A, Ward. (2014) "Australians' Attitudes to Violence against Women: Full Technical Report, Findings from the 2013 National Community Attitudes towards Violence Against Women Survey (NCAS)" (Report, Victorian Health Promotion Foundation).
Worral, J., J. Ross and E. McCord (2006) "Modeling Prosecutors' Charging Decisions' (2006) *Crime and Delinquency* 52(3): 472.

Cases

Lusted v MRB [2013] TASMC 9 (19 February 2013).
R v Evans [2017] NSWCCA 281.

Legislation

Crimes Act 1900 (NSW).
Violence Against Women Act 1994.

11 Prosecutorial Discretion about Special Measure Use in Australian Cases of Child Sexual Abuse

Jane Goodman-Delahunty, Natalie Martschuk, Martine Powell and Nina Westera

Introduction

Interest in the influence of prosecutorial discretion has increased internationally in recent years, although empirical studies remain scarce. A Prosecutorial Reform Index developed for the American Bar Association Rule of Law Initiative included discretionary functions among 28 factors that provide "an empirical basis for examining the status and role of prosecutors and the environment in which they work in transitioning states throughout the globe" (American Bar Association, 2018a). In particular, the guidance recommended that decisions to discontinue proceedings be justified in writing and recorded in the prosecutors' files (American Bar Association, 2018b). In Australia, prosecution guidelines encourage or require consultation between the prosecutor, the complainant and the police regarding significant case decisions, and many encourage or require prosecutors to give reasons to people who have a legitimate interest in their discretionary decisions, particularly decisions not to prosecute (Royal Commission into Institutional Responses to Child Sexual Abuse, 2017, Parts III-VI, p. 280).

Special Measures in Cases of Child Sexual Abuse

In cases of child sexual abuse (CSA), the acquittal rate at trial is notably higher than that for other crimes (Zhou, 2010). To improve the experience of CSA complainants, whether adults or children at the time of trial, and the quality of the evidence they provide, special measures for the giving of evidence by vulnerable complainants were legislatively implemented in all Australian jurisdictions. For instance, a complainant may give evidence via closed circuit television (CCTV) or audio-visual link from a room away from the courtroom, or a pre-recorded videotaped investigative interview of the complainant by police may be used in lieu of direct evidence from the complainant at trial to spare the complainant the burden of repeatedly answering similar questions about the abusive events. Eligibility for the use of special measures varies somewhat by state (Royal Commission into Institutional Responses to Child Sexual Abuse, 2017, Parts VII–X, pp. 20–26).

The potential link between the use of special measures and case outcomes was underscored by the New South Wales Parliament when amending special measures legislation: "The option for a complainant to give evidence by closed-circuit television [...] may mean the difference between proceeding to trial and having to withdraw a prosecution because the complainant is not prepared to give evidence" (NSW Parliamentary Debates, 2004). The present study contributes to the body of empirical research on prosecutorial discretion and attrition in CSA cases (Mac Murray, 1988) by examining records placed in prosecutors' files about the use of special measures in CSA cases in three Australian jurisdictions, and the relationship between those considerations and decisions to discontinue proceedings.

Studies of Prosecutorial Discretion and Uses of Special Measures

Law reform processes require a retrospective evaluation of the actual impact of special measures (Jaffe, Crooks and Wolfe, 2003; Righarts and Henaghan, 2010). Early studies of the use of available special measures for vulnerable witnesses disclosed a gap between the law and prosecutorial practices. For instance, interviews with 63 Australian child complainants, 39 caregivers and 28 legal professionals revealed that despite special measures legislation, not one child witness participant in Queensland had given evidence via CCTV at committal or trial, and 43 per cent of children in New South Wales were denied CCTV at trial against their wishes (Eastwood, 2003). Where CCTV use was discretionary, prosecutors discouraged its use to secure a conviction (Eastwood and Patton, 2002, p. 120).

A mixed method evaluation of 17 trials assessing uses of special measures as part of a child sexual assault specialist jurisdiction pilot in New South Wales included 57 stakeholder interviews (Cashmore and Trimboli, 2005). Three issues pertinent to the present study were identified. First, lawyers expressed the view that good child witnesses were more effective in person in court than via CCTV (p. 38). Second, lawyers noted that credibility assessments of complainants in pre-recorded interviews were impaired by distances from the camera or the camera angle because their facial expressions were not visible (p. 36). Third, although complainants preferred not to discuss their abuse allegations with multiple solicitors and crown prosecutors in the course of the legal proceedings, continuity of prosecutors was often lacking (p. 42). A recent series of interviews with 43 prosecutors, defence counsel, judges and Witness Assistance Service (WAS) staff revealed ongoing concern that the assessment of the credibility of complainants in CSA cases was impaired by the presentation of pre-recorded or CCTV evidence in comparison with in-person testimony in court (Royal Commission into Institutional Reponses to Child Sexual Abuse, 2017, Parts VII–X, p. 28).

Studies reliant on interviews with stakeholders in the criminal justice process have been criticised for their unrepresentative convenience samples (Cossins, 2006), and anecdotal reports from self-selected interviewees (Robinson, 2014). One method that overcomes these research limitations is a manual file review of a sample of all relevant cases within a specified time period. Reviews of prosecution files are an effective way to objectively evaluate the extent to which legislative provisions for special measures are applied in practice (Charles, 2012). This method was adopted in the present study.

Aims of the Present Study

This study examined contemporary practices in CSA cases to present the complainant's evidence by reviewing prosecutorial considerations regarding uses of special measures with vulnerable complainants in three Australian jurisdictions. The purpose of this study was to examine (a) the extent of prosecutorial support for and use of special measures; (b) reasons for their use or non-use; and (c) their impact on case outcomes and decisions to discontinue a case.

Method

The Study Sample

Purposive sampling, which entails selecting files on the basis of criteria that best align with the research aims, is the standard method used for file selection in reviews of prosecutors' files (Burton, Evans and Sanders, 2006), and was employed to gather prosecutors' files from three Australian jurisdictions: New South Wales (NSW), Victoria (VIC) and Western Australia (WA). Approval to conduct the study was obtained from the relevant University Human Research Ethics Committees.

Due to the sensitive nature of the files, the Royal Commission into Institutional Responses to Child Sexual Abuse issued notices and summonses for the files. To obtain a representative sample of 60 contemporary prosecutors' files, the summonses requested the production in each jurisdiction of: (a) the ten most recent files involving CSA offences where the alleged abuse occurred before 2010 and the trial was conducted after 2010; (b) the ten most recent files that involved CSA offences where both the alleged abuse and trial occurred after 2010. Responsive files were produced for review at the respective Offices of the Directors of Public Prosecution (ODPP).

The final study sample consisted of 59 case files containing CSA allegations by a total of 83 complainants (NSW: 25; VIC: 26; WA: 32). Most complainants were female (83.1 per cent) and under the age of 18 years (60.2 per cent) at the time of trial. Several cases had proceeded to trial more than once; 12 per cent of the cases in the sample never proceeded to trial. Before coding was completed on one file, it was removed by NSW ODPP when the verdict was appealed.

File Contents

The files ranged in size from approximately 500 to 15,000 pages. The cases involved between 1 and 4 complainants (1 complainant: 42 cases; 2 complainants: 13 cases; 3 or more complainants: 4 cases), and a maximum of 3 defendants.

Most files contained police briefs (81.0 per cent), partial or full trial transcripts (75.9 per cent), copies of court file documents (69 per cent), and materials produced under subpoena (58.6 per cent). Other evidential material included transcripts (and video recordings) of police interviews of the complainants and defendants; school records, medical and/or psychiatric records of the complainants; criminal records of the complainants and/or defendants; photographs and transcripts of phone conversations between complainants and defendants. Additional documents on file were copies of emails, correspondence and handwritten notes.

Research Procedures

Researchers trained in law and psychology inspected the documents in each case file and gave priority to records of telephonic or in-person conferences with or about the complainant, and records of contact between the complainant and other criminal justice practitioners (e.g. police, witness support officers, and expert witnesses). Core excerpts reflecting consideration of the use of special measures were recorded verbatim. The focus of this chapter is the results of qualitative analyses of those excerpts.

Quantitative Coding

A coding protocol was developed based on a preliminary review of a random subset of five ODPP files. Categorical variables analysed for this study were Consistency of assigned counsel (0=no change; 1=1–2 changes; 2=3–4 changes; 3=5+ changes); Prosecutor conference with complainant (0=no; 1=yes); Consideration of special measures (0=no; 1=yes); Type of special measure used at trial (1=CCTV from a remote room at court; 2=CCTV away from court; 3=pre-recorded police investigative interview; 4=pre-recorded pre-trial hearing; 6=in-person); Complainant gender (1=male; 2=female); Case disposition (0=discontinued, 1=guilty plea; 2=jury trial; 3=bench trial); and Verdict (0=not guilty; 1=guilty; 2=guilty of some charges, acquittal on others).

To assess inter-rater reliability, a random sample of 20 per cent of the files was dual-coded (two contemporary and two historical cases in each jurisdiction). Krippendorff's alpha was used to calculate the inter-rater reliability of the categorical variables. Inter-rater reliability ranged between $\alpha=.59$ and $\alpha=.91$ (agreement rate: .73–.94) for the categorical variables. The intra-class correlation applied to continuous variables ranged from .91 to 1.0. Problematic variables were redefined before coding proceeded. Discrepancies were discussed among the coders until agreement was achieved.

Qualitative Thematic Analysis

To discern trends or patterns in the reasoning underlying the use of special measures in practice, in-depth, systematic qualitative analyses were conducted of text excerpts extracted from prosecutors' file entries that made explicit reference to considerations of these measures. Where cases involved multiple complainants, these excerpts were compiled separately for each complainant. Records about special measure use that were devoid of any accompanying explanation (e.g. a record that merely reflected that the complainant testified at trial via CCTV, without further details) were excluded from the thematic analysis as they offered no insight into prosecutors' reasoning.

The thematic analysis conformed to the six guidelines for best practice in thematic analysis using an inductive approach (Braun and Clarke, 2006). First, the researchers immersed themselves in the contents via repeated reading. Second, the researchers paid attention to each sentence and phrase in the file excerpts to code notable features and repeated content. Third, the coded excerpts were collated and sorted into overarching themes. Fourth, the excerpts were re-read to ensure internal consistency within each theme, and that the themes represented the data set as a whole. Amendments to the themes were made where necessary to clarify their meaning. Fifth, themes were defined and named to identify the essence of each theme and the overall narrative they related. Sixth, illustrative examples were selected to capture the essence of each theme.

The prevalence of each theme was computed by complainant, and by jurisdiction. These frequencies provided insight into the salience of the themes.

Results and Discussion

Consistency of Assigned Counsel

The files were screened for changes in lead prosecutors because consistency of assigned counsel promotes better rapport with complainants and greater insights into their capacity to give their best evidence with or without special measures. In only 23.6 per cent of cases was there no change in the lead prosecutor. More than half of the cases experienced 1–2 changes in lead counsel (54.5 per cent) while prosecutors were reassigned more frequently in one fifth of the cases (3–4 changes: 12.7 per cent; 5 or more: 9.1 per cent). Most consistency in assigned prosecutors was evident in Western Australia (no change: 40.0 per cent), whereas in Victoria (no change: 21.1 per cent) and New South Wales (no change: 6.3 per cent), stability of assigned prosecutors was rare, as shown in Figure 11.1. Three or more changes in lead counsel during the prosecution process was the norm for 42.1 per cent of complainants in Victoria. Differences between the states were significant, χ^2 (4, 54)=12.93, p=.012, Phi=.485. The number of changes per case in prosecutors was unrelated to the number of complainants (r=–.139, p=.313). Information on the number of prosecutors briefed to appear in court was available in 74.6 per cent of the case files, showing similar trends. On average, 2.27 advocates were briefed (range 0–5; *Mdn*=2). This varied by state. In WA, there was more consistency in prosecutors briefed for trial (M=1.70) than in NSW (M=2.50) and VIC (M=2.83).

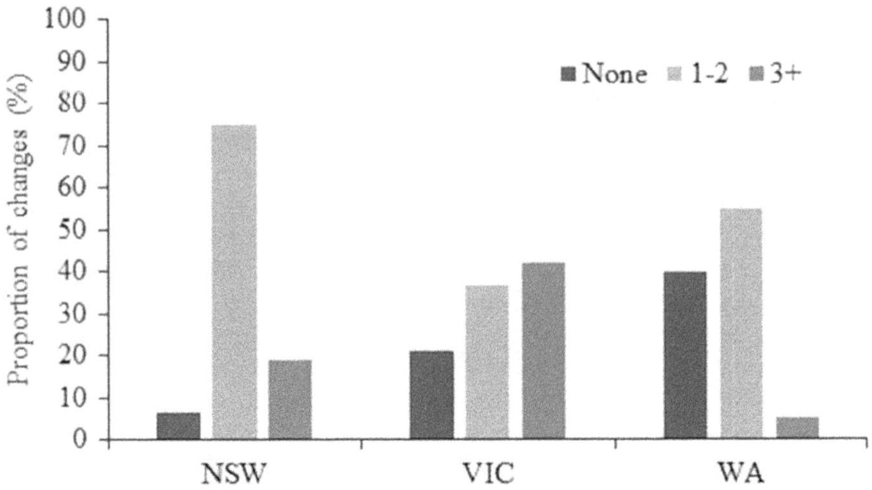

Figure 11.1 Changes in Lead Prosecutor by State (percentage).

Use of Special Measures

Documented consideration of special measures was available for all complainants in Western Australia (n=32), where a form was used specifically to capture complainant preferences. Records to this effect were located for all but one complainant in Victoria (n=25), and were absent from the files of four complainants in New South Wales. These considerations were routine in Western Australia, and in all cases with child complainants in Victoria. Overall, special measures were considered for 92 per cent of complainants (n=76), for most child complainants (93.3 per cent) and the majority of adult complainants (84.2 per cent), as shown in Figure 11.2.

Reasons for Use or Non-Use of Special Measures

Records reflecting the consideration of special measures were coded and for a total of 72 complainants were amenable to thematic analysis. Results revealed four distinct themes encompassing the reasoning underlying prosecutors' decisions on uses of special measures: (a) legislative compliance; (b) the complainant's psychological and social needs; (c) reliance on WAS staff and other criminal justice professionals; and (d) the logistics of special measure use. These themes are discussed in turn. Illustrative quotations from documents in the case files are identified parenthetically by a four-digit case number assigned by the researchers, the method(s) used to present the complainants' evidence at trial, and the case outcome.

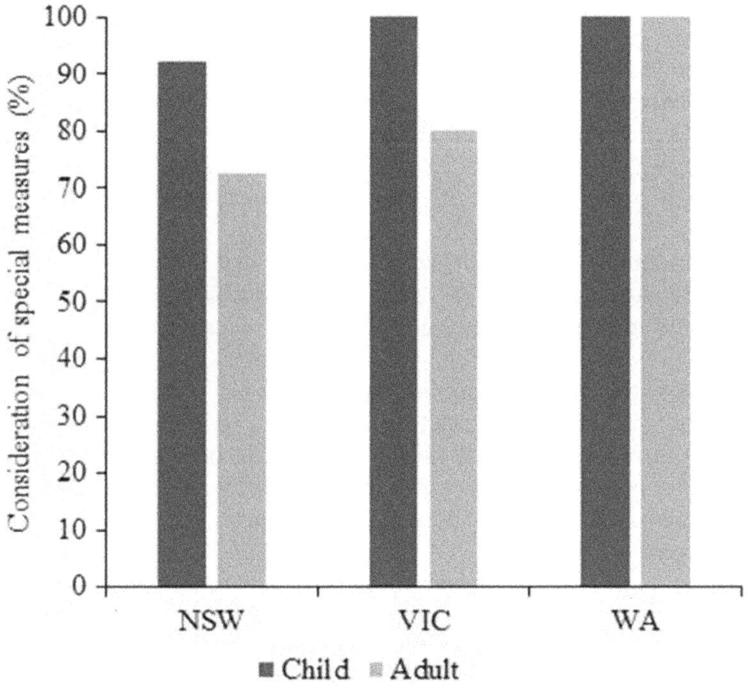

Figure 11.2 Consideration of Special Measures for Child and Adult Complainants by State (percentage).

a Legislative Compliance

The duty to comply with legislation on special measures was mentioned for just over two-thirds of the complainants (69.4 per cent). References to legislative compliance were unrelated to the case outcome (no mention: 57.1 per cent convictions; mentioned: 55.3 per cent convictions). This theme was often depicted in formal notices to the court about how complainants would give evidence and in documented bookings of facilities for special measures. In Western Australia, complainants submitted an application to the District Court stating their preferred option to give evidence and copies of these documents were maintained in the prosecutors' case files.

Many prosecutors specified the factors that rendered a complainant eligible to give evidence via special measures under the enabling legislation. One prosecutor documented the use of special measures as "obvious" (3020, police interview, CCTV, conviction), while others noted complainants' "automatic" status as special witnesses or affected children (3017, police interview, CCTV, acquittal).

Complainants over the age of 18 years at the time of trial were not always deemed eligible for special measures. For example, the qualification of one complainant as a special witness was queried by a WAS practitioner after he sought to give evidence via CCTV. The prosecutor responded:

> Yes – any complainant in a sexual offence case, (aside from indecent abuse, which is a relatively minor charge) is automatically entitled to it, regardless of age, gender, relationship to the accused, or how long ago the alleged offences occurred.
>
> (3001.1, CCTV, conviction)

In Victoria, a presumption of eligibility was made in a joint trial in which both complainants were under the age of 18 years when the accused was charged. A referral to WAS and court closure was requested (2006, police interview, CCTV, conviction).

One prosecutor noted that the legislation required all incest cases to be conducted "in camera", that the complainant was entitled to be accompanied by a support person, and requested CCTV evidence (1206; in person, conviction). Conversely, another prosecutor documented that a complainant's preference to give evidence in person conflicted with the legislation enabling CCTV evidence (3003, in person, conviction).

In some cases, records implied that special measures were implemented without consulting complainants. In certain cases, confusion or disagreement between members of the prosecution team about compliance with the legislation was documented. In one instance, the supervising prosecutor applied to use a pre-recorded police interview for a nine-year-old complainant, but the lead prosecutor assigned to the case did not favour this option. Ultimately, the supervisor insisted that this measure was preferable because of the complainant's young age and the risk of re-traumatisation if a second interview to secure evidence-in-chief were conducted (3012, police interview, CCTV, conviction).

b Addressing the Complainant's Needs

The dominant theme documented by prosecutors in considering special measures was the needs of the complainant, psychological and social. This theme emerged for 72.6 per cent of the complainants. Almost two-thirds of the records within this category centred on the complainants' preferred mode for giving evidence, their psychological wellbeing and social circumstances. Notably, cases in which the prosecutors considered the complainants' particular needs were more likely to result in a conviction (66.0 per cent) (27.8 per cent; χ^2 (1, 68)=6.37, p=.012, Cramer's V=.340).

Further analyses of file records addressing the needs of the complainant yielded seven distinct subthemes: (i) the complainant's preference for giving evidence; (ii) tension between the prosecutor and the complainant's caregivers; (iii) the complainant's mental health; (iv) the complainant's temperament; (v) the complainant's desire to be isolated from the accused; (vi) benefits to the complainant of using special measures; and (vii) the complainant's credibility at trial. The extent to which each subtheme was mentioned is displayed in Table 11.1. Examples of each subtheme are provided next.

I COMPLAINANT'S PREFERRED METHOD OF GIVING EVIDENCE

The complainant's preferred method of giving evidence was the most prevalent factor documented in addressing complainants' needs, but the extent to which prosecutors took this information into account varied. In many cases, complainants and/or their parents or guardians were consulted about the presentation of their evidence at trial. When asked for their preferences, complainants were often unsure which special measure best suited their needs. Records of their uncertainty revealed gaps in communication and guidance about special measures. When some complainants opted to give evidence at trial in person, provisions were nonetheless made for CCTV facilities in the event that the complainants changed their minds. One WAS officer advised the prosecutor to accommodate changing preferences:

> Both girls are undecided about using CCTV or not, but we encouraged them to put that down on their paperwork, saying that they could alter it later if they chose to.
>
> (3011, CCTV, acquittal)

Records in the files showed that complainants changed their preferences in both directions: at times, those initially choosing to give evidence via a special measure switched to in-person evidence at trial, and at other times the opposite was true. For instance, in an historical case, arrangements were made for a complainant aged 35 years to give evidence against a family member via CCTV. The complainant lived in a rural area where the court had no CCTV facility, so the trial was moved to the city. Ultimately, the complainant testified at trial in person (1207, partial convictions).

Table 11.1 Proportion of Subthemes Related to the Complainant's Needs (percentage)

Subthemes Related to the Complainant's Needs	*Per cent*	*Number of Mentions*
Complainant preference	65.3	47
Complainant mental health	40.3	29
Complainant temperament	16.7	12
Tension between the prosecutor and caregiver	13.9	10
Complainant desire to be isolated from the accused	12.5	9
Benefits to complainant of special measures	9.7	7
Complainant credibility at trial	9.7	7

Note
N=72 complainants.

II TENSION BETWEEN THE PROSECUTION AND THE COMPLAINANTS' CAREGIVERS

In many cases involving child complainants, the complainant's parents and other caregivers were active decision makers regarding special measure use. Caregivers were usually protective, seeking to shield complainants from the stress of criminal proceedings. In a case that involved two complainants, emails from their mother and aunt indicated their concern that the remote witness room was unfamiliar and in close proximity to the trial court (unlike the WAS offices where they had previously been taken): "It is of serious concern to me because they are far away and not in the same building" (3019, CCTV, conviction).

Some complainants' caregivers obstructed the rapport established between the prosecutor and complainants. One prosecutor noted that the complainant's mother dominated and belittled the complainant, and tried to speak for him although he was perfectly capable of speaking for himself (2008, in person, acquittal). In another case, email correspondence from a prosecutor to a WAS officer advised that it was "highly desirable for the complainant to give evidence again". In reply, the officer cautioned that the complainant's mother might discourage her from giving evidence and emphasised the need to talk directly to the complainant as the trial date approached (2009, in person, partial conviction). In these cases, ascertaining the complainants' preference was more challenging for prosecutors and WAS staff. For example, one complainant's guardian had a drinking problem and refused to consult the complainant on grounds that the complainant did not want to proceed with the trial or speak about the abusive events. Ultimately, the WAS officer contacted the complainant directly (3021, CCTV, acquittal).

In cases of intrafamilial or parental abuse, the caregivers' support of complainants was often influenced by complex family dynamics. For example, caregivers were often protective of the accused, blamed the complainant and were reluctant to report issues to police.

III COMPLAINANT'S MENTAL HEALTH

In approximately one-quarter of the cases, mental health issues of the complainants were perceived to affect both their capacity to give reliable evidence and the prosecution of these cases. The fragility of some complainants was readily apparent in records referring to them as "suicidal" (1205.2, in person, conviction); "mentally distressed" (2003, CCTV, acquittal); or suffering from "depression and anxiety" (2004, discontinued). One social worker from the WAS stated: "It would be preferable if counsel could attend [a pre-committal WAS conference] because this complainant is quite anxious – as most sex complainants are with giving evidence" (2010.1, pre-recorded interview, CCTV, discontinued).

Delays in trial dates were generally viewed as unhelpful. For example, a social worker's notes reflected that one complainant, who had voiced feelings of shame and difficulty in expressing emotion as a result of the abuse she had experienced, was struggling with low self-esteem and a sense of dislocation from her family unit. Although she had previously demonstrated suicidal ideation, she did not have current thoughts of self-harm or suicide, thus the social worker urged the prosecutor to avoid delay in scheduling the trial (3019.1, CCTV, conviction).

The use of special measures was not adequate to safeguard the wellbeing or secure the evidence of all complainants. One trial was postponed three times because of the complainant's precarious mental health. Correspondence from the investigating police officer alerted the prosecutor that giving evidence would be very traumatic for the complainant, and that it was doubtful she would be able to answer questions as required. The complainant's psychologist confirmed that the complainant suffered from more than typical anxiety and discomfort associated with giving evidence about this type of matter:

> The court process will no doubt trigger extreme anxiety, and when anxious, [complainant's] ability to access language, recall facts, and sequence events could become severely impaired. When feeling threatened [complainant] can become aggressive or cry uncontrollably.

The WAS officer recommended that the prosecutor withdraw the case on grounds that she would "not make it through cross-examination" and the stress of a trial would re-traumatise her and jeopardise her physical and psychological health. Nonetheless, the matter proceeded to trial on the prosecution's fourth attempt (1101, police interview, CCTV, acquittal). During the trial, the complainant fled, and was chased down the street by the prosecutor. Another complainant engaged in self-harm as a coping strategy. She chose to give evidence in person at trial, which damaged her credibility (3011.3, discontinued).

IV COMPLAINANT'S TEMPERAMENT

Attention to the complainant's temperament was documented in 16.7 per cent of the cases to ensure that special measure use was compatible with the complainant's individual needs. For instance, one prosecutor recorded that the complainant was willing to attend court, but preferred not to have much contact with the prosecution (3009, CCTV, conviction.). Further examples illustrated how different prosecutors took the individual sentiments and disposition of complainants into account: "Shy young woman who is supportive of the prosecution and understands the difficulties that these matters face" (1203, CCTV, conviction); "Better to build rapport now and have the complainant as comfortable as she can be before giving evidence next week" (2010.1 police interview, CCTV, conviction).

V COMPLAINANT'S PREFERENCE TO BE ISOLATED FROM THE ACCUSED

Records in prosecutors' files revealed that, for some complainants, proximity to the accused compounded the negative experience of giving evidence. This was illustrated by a verbatim record of a conversation between a prosecutor and a complainant who had been sexually abused by her stepfather on numerous occasions:

> PROSECUTOR: How do you feel about going to court?
> COMPLAINANT: I don't really want to go with [accused] being there, because I don't really want to see [accused] again.
> PROSECUTOR: Can you cope with talking about it?
> COMPLAINANT: I think I can cope with it, but I may be upset. I want for him not to be near me, and to not see him.
>
> (1108, CCTV, conviction)

Similarly, at a pre-trial conference with the prosecutor, one complainant asked whether the accused would be able to see her on the screen, and was concerned that he might find her later on (2018, police interview, CCTV, partial conviction). The prosecutor responded that this was "highly unlikely". In another case, the prosecutor was unable to meet the concerns of a ten-year-old complainant who wanted her face covered when giving pre-recorded evidence so that the accused could not see her. The prosecutor added:

> Unfortunately there is nothing we can do to stop the accused from seeing [Complainant 2's] face. He is entitled to be in the courtroom during his trial and obviously we want the judge and jury to see her face as she gives evidence.
>
> (3019.2, CCTV, conviction)

These cases demonstrated that the complainants' preferences were not fully addressed by available arrangements for physical separation from the accused.

VI BENEFITS TO THE COMPLAINANT OF SPECIAL MEASURES

Consensus was expressed by criminal justice practitioners that special measures supported the complainants' wellbeing by alleviating stressors associated with court attendance. This view was particularly prominent where pre-trial hearings were routinely used. For instance, a prosecutor explained that the complainant's presence was not required at trial because the complainant's evidence-in-chief, cross-examination and re-examination would all be presented to the court in the form of a pre-recorded police interview and video-recorded pre-trial hearing (3014, police interview, CCTV, conviction). This view was documented in several cases:

> Ideally, I would like the complainant's evidence to be pre-recorded prior to the trial, as that is most likely to be less stressful for her.
>
> (3017, police interview, CCTV, acquittal)

> It has been my experience that children who are given this opportunity perform better when giving evidence as a result of reduced wait times and minimisation of court attendance, which ultimately assists in the reduction of fatigue, distraction and feelings of anxiety for young children.
>
> (3019.2, CCTV, conviction)

At times, the special measures were counter-productive. For example, in some instances, repeated questioning before the trial traumatised and frustrated complainants making them reluctant to provide further evidence (3004, police interview, CCTV, discontinued).

VII THE COMPLAINANT'S CREDIBILITY AT TRIAL

In a small proportion of cases, perceptions of the complainants' credibility at trial influenced consideration of special measures. Some prosecutors who perceived that a complainant's demeanour or behaviour might damage the case used special measures deliberately to obviate the complainant's appearance before a jury. In one case in which a complaint gave evidence in person at trial, the jury acquitted. In a second trial on this matter, the prosecutor arranged for the complainant to give evidence via CCTV, and secured a conviction. This strategy was more evident when complainants were perceived as overly emotional or volatile. For instance, one complainant over 18 years of age with a mental impairment wanted to give evidence in person so he could give the accused a "verbal spray". He was advised that it was preferable to use the Remote Witness Facility (2014, CCTV, conviction). In another case, the prosecutor's consideration centred on the risk that the complainant would be unpredictable in the witness box if he gave evidence before a jury (2008, in person, acquittal).

One prosecutor's conference notes about the complainant indicated that on CCTV recordings she appeared confident and well-spoken and thus her credibility would be enhanced by giving evidence in person (1108, CCTV, conviction). This implied that the use of special measures before trial offered prosecutors a strategic opportunity to evaluate a complainant's capacity to give evidence in person at trial, even if this was not the preference of the witness. Where pre-trial questioning via alternate measures generated inconsistencies in the complainants' accounts, these were construed to reduce the complainants' credibility, resulting in discontinuance of the case or of certain charges.

c Reliance on Witness Assistance Support Staff and Other Criminal Justice Professionals

Records reflecting prosecution reliance on WAS staff and other criminal justice professionals to implement special measures were found for one half of the complainants (51.4 per cent). This theme referred to the critical liaison between complainants, caregivers, prosecutors and other criminal justice practitioners on the use of special measures in a particular case. Witness support staff typically accompanied complainants to legal proceedings from the commencement of a case to the final stages of the criminal justice process. Prosecutors relied on witness support staff to provide continuity by maintaining contact with complainants, securing complainants' support for the prosecution, and calming their negative emotions. The presence or absence of this theme was not associated with verdict. Two subthemes within this category were distinguished: (i) the central role of witness support officers; and (ii) the interaction between criminal justice professionals prior to the implementation of special measures.

I THE ROLE OF WITNESS ASSISTANCE SUPPORT STAFF

WAS officers supported complainants and their caregivers, enabling prosecutors to focus on legal aspects of the case. For instance, a pre-trial review memorandum disclosed that although the ODPP had never contacted either complainant, the WAS maintained regular contact with them and their families (3011, CCTV, acquittal). Correspondence from support officers often specified how the complainant would give evidence. In one case, the WAS initiated consideration of special measures via email to the prosecutor: "[Complainant] advised that she is not sure whether she'll give evidence in court or in the Remote Witness Facility" (2009, in person, partial conviction).

Support officers were often responsible for familiarising complainants with the court or remote witness facilities. In a case with three complainants, a WAS officer explained CCTV, and showed the complainants the courtroom (1101, police interviews, CCTV, acquittal). In another state, the support officers prepared the complainant for court, liaised with his father, and facilitated the presence of an interpreter at trial (1105, police interview, CCTV, acquittal). The extent to which support officers influenced the complainant's choice of methods to give evidence was unclear.

II INTERACTION BETWEEN CRIMINAL JUSTICE PROFESSIONALS

Prosecutors, at times, commenced consultations with complainants by correcting misinformation. In one case, police records documented the preference of a complainant aged 19 years, with severe anxiety, to testify via videolink about events that took place two years earlier. When the police officer advised her that if the rape charges proceeded, she was required to give evidence in person, she was "upset and angry". The prosecutor had to rectify this misinformation in numerous conferences before the trial (2005, CCTV, acquittal).

In another case, the complainant's mother was informed by a police officer that after the complainant gave her first statement, her evidence in the case was complete. Conversely, the prosecutor explained that the complainant still needed to pre-record her evidence-in-chief and would be required to appear for cross-examination by the defence at a pre-trial hearing (3017, police interview, CCTV, acquittal). Consideration of special measures by police officers appeared driven primarily by the complainant's age.

Records of contact between prosecution and defence counsel showed that defence counsel supported the proposed use of special measures and did not perceive them as detrimental to the accused. For instance, defence counsel communicated to the prosecution that there would be no issues if the complainants gave evidence via CCTV (1106, CCTV, acquittal). In another state, an email from a defence solicitor suggested that videolink was common, and the solicitor went on to state: "[I have] never seen any negative difference, from a defence point of view, in evidence, because of CCTV" (3005, police interview, CCTV, acquittal). However, defence support for special measures was by no means ubiquitous. Responding to late objections and challenges to their scheduled use required prosecutors' attention.

Logistics in Using Special Measures

Prosecutors attended to the logistics involved in using special measures. This theme arose for approximately one-third of complainants (30.6 per cent, n=22). At times, the prosecutor personally advised the complainant of her right to give evidence via remote facilities, and introduced her to the CCTV room (2005, CCTV, acquittal).

CCTV technology appeared to benefit complainants who lived in rural or remote areas. In WA, for example, a prosecutor applied for the complainant and two witnesses to give evidence by videolink from their hometown in a rural area to spare them the anxiety and logistical difficulties associated with travel (3021, CCTV, acquittal). By comparison, giving evidence across international jurisdictions was not favoured, ostensibly because trial preparation was more challenging. In a case in which the complainant was living overseas, the prosecutor advised the complainant's caregiver:

> [Complainant] could give evidence by videolink from [overseas]. The advantage of the complainant and yourself coming back for the pre-recording is that the complainant would get to speak with the prosecutor in person, and develop some rapport. It would be easier to show her the interview she did with police shortly before she will give evidence; she would be in the same time zone, and any documents could be easily shown to her as she would be in the court building.
>
> (3017, pre-recorded video, CCTV from overseas, acquittal)

Access to CCTV facilities became a driver of trial schedules, and overbooked CCTV facilities increased complainants' waiting time to testify. In one case, defence counsel and the complainant's family had to arrange their schedules around the availability of CCTV for two-day use (3020, police interview, CCTV, conviction). In another case, the prosecutor documented difficulties in booking a room with WAS for the pre-trial argument preceding the special hearing (2013, police interview, CCTV, discontinued). A solicitor from the Specialist Sex Offences Unit recommended that to avoid leaving the complainant "sitting around", the sequence in which witnesses gave evidence might have to be reshuffled (2013 police interview, CCTV; 2 hung juries, bench trial acquittal). After a problem arose in recording one complainant's evidence-in-chief, the complainant had to be re-questioned by the Crown in another courtroom on the second day of the trial to record that portion of the evidence-in-chief (1204, CCTV, outcome unknown).

In another case, the prosecutor initially argued that CCTV was infeasible for a psychologically impaired complainant due to the extensive evidence on which the complainant was required to comment (1101, CCTV, police interview, acquittal). A total of four separate pre-recorded police interviews were conducted with the complainant, generating a large volume of material that might potentially be referred to at trial. As a result, the expectation was that the complainant would give evidence for approximately one and a half to two days. This prosecutors' judgment may have been correct, because ultimately, the complainant testified via CCTV, and the accused was acquitted.

The cost of the audio-visual link was one factor influencing prosecutors' considerations of special measures. A memorandum from one prosecutor disclosed that the cost of videolink for one or two hours far exceeded the cost of flying a witness interstate, including accommodation and local transfers (2010, CCTV, partial conviction).

Special Measures and Discontinued Cases

The prosecution was discontinued in the cases of ten complainants (12 per cent) in the study sample. In three instances, discontinuance was unrelated to the use of special measures because the defendant entered a guilty plea or passed away. Documents on file for the seven remaining complainants revealed that discontinuance was due to their heightened vulnerability in combination with either inadequate social support (n=5) or inconsistencies in their evidence generated by the use of special measures that were deemed to negatively affect their credibility (n=5).

The vulnerability of the complainants whose cases were discontinued was exacerbated by either their own fragile mental or physical health (n=3), intellectual disability (n=2), young age (n=1) or circumstantial factors, such as family dynamics in cases of intrafamilial abuse (n=3), and caregivers with mental (n=2) or physical impairments (n=1). These findings replicated those of Mac Murray (1988, p. 19) three decades ago in a qualitative study of prosecutorial discretion and attrition in CSA cases in Massachusetts, USA. While the presence of these factors increased the potential benefit of special measures to these particularly vulnerable complainants, neither WAS staff nor the prosecutors provided the intensive and ongoing support needed by these complainants to give their best evidence.

No record of any consideration of special measures was located in the files of three complainants whose cases were discontinued. Two of those complainants had intellectual impairments. Although legislation on special measures presumes CCTV use with complainants who have intellectual disabilities (Royal Commission into Institutional Responses to Child Sexual Abuse, 2017, Parts III-IV, p. 282), the presence of an intellectual disability was perceived as a barrier precluding evidence sufficient to secure a conviction.

Inconsistencies that emerged in the complainants' evidence were rated as a major issue in 7.8 per cent of the cases, leading to a decision to discontinue the prosecution before trial in cases of five complainants. For example, after reviewing conflicting accounts by a complainant of one aspect of the abusive events, the prosecutor concluded that "[t]he complainant's credibility [was] irreparably damaged and we cannot say that there are reasonable prospects of conviction" (3011.3). These inconsistencies emerged in accounts given under repeated questioning by police interviewers or prosecutors on multiple different occasions ($n=4$) or under cross-examination ($n=1$). The particular vulnerability of these complainants was a likely contributing factor to the inconsistencies. In two cases, file notes confirmed discussions with the complainants of what prosecutors regarded as serious consequences of these disparities in their evidence.

Conclusion

This study revealed more widespread confidence in special measures than was observed in earlier studies, with general consensus that special measures support a vulnerable complainant's wellbeing and ability to give reliable evidence. The majority of prosecutors' files showed that special measures were considered in preparing cases for trial. Primary consideration was given to the complainant's needs, including the complainant's preference to use special measures, the complainant's mental health, desire to be isolated from the accused, and the complainant's credibility. As in the case of adult sexual assault (Lievore, 2004), assessments of a complainant's credibility were important in the exercise of discretion by prosecutors to use special measures and to discontinue cases, but these were integrated with the use of special measures.

Overall, the findings of this study established that the gap between the legislation on special measures and their use in practice was narrowed. Adult complainants were more likely than children to be perceived as ineligible for special measures. Prosecutors relied on WAS staff to liaise with complainants, provide emotional support, and accompany complainants to relevant legal proceedings. In future cases, more continuity in prosecution team staffing is desirable to improve the consultation process and decision making. An important outcome of the study was the finding that consideration of special measures did not compromise the conviction rate.

Acknowledgements

This chapter was based on research funded by a grant to Martine Powell, Jane Goodman-Delahunty and Nina Westera from the Australian Royal Commission into Institutional Responses to Child Sexual Abuse. We are grateful to Alexandra Lonergan, Melissa Martin, and Ida Nguyen for coding assistance, and to Alexandra Lonergan for thematic analysis.

References

American Bar Association (2018a) *Rule of Law*. Retrieved from www.americanbar.org/advocacy/rule_of_law.html.

American Bar Association (2018b) *Prosecutorial Reform Index: Factors*. Retrieved from www.americanbar.org/advocacy/rule_of_law/publications/assessments/pri/pri_factors.html.

Braun, V. and V. Clarke (2006) "Using Thematic Analysis in Psychology" *Qualitative Research in Psychology* 3: 77–101.

Burton, M., R. Evans and A. Sanders (2006) *Are Special Measures for Vulnerable and Intimidated Witnesses Working? Evidence from the Criminal Justice Agencies* (London: Home Office).

Cashmore, J. and L. Trimboli (2005) *An Evaluation of the NSW Child Sexual Assault Specialist Jurisdiction Pilot* (Sydney, Australia: New South Wales Bureau of Crime Statistics and Research).

Charles, C. (2012) *Special Measures for Vulnerable and Intimidated Witnesses: Research Exploring the Decisions and Actions Taken by Prosecutors in a Sample of CPS Case Files.* (London: Crown Prosecution Service).

Cossins, A. (2006) "Prosecuting Child Sexual Assault Cases: Are Vulnerable Witness Protections Enough?" *Current Issues in Criminal Justice* 18(2): 299–317.

Eastwood, C. (2003) "The Experiences of Child Complainants of Sexual Abuse in the Criminal Justice System" *Trends & Issues in Crime and Criminal Justice* 250: 1–6. (Canberra, Australia: Australian Institute of Criminology).

Eastwood, C. and W. Patton (2002) *The Experiences of Child Complainants of Sexual Abuse in the Criminal Justice System* Report to the Australian Institute of Criminology (Canberra, Australia: Australian Institute of Criminology) www.aic.gov.au/crc/reports/eastwood.html.

Jaffe, P.G., C.V. Crooks and D.A. Wolfe (2003) "Legal and Policy Responses to Children Exposed to Domestic Violence: The Need to Evaluate Intended and Unintended Consequences" *Clinical Child and Family Psychology Review* 6: 205–213.

Lievore, D. (2004) "Victim Credibility in Adult Sexual Assault Cases" *Trends and Issues in Crime and Criminal Justice* No 288 (Canberra: Australian Institute of Criminology).

Mac Murray, B.K. (1988) "Prosecutorial Decision Making and Case Attrition for Child Sexual Abuse: A Qualitative Approach to Case Rejection Decisions" *The Prison Journal* 68: 11–24.

NSW Parliamentary Debates (2004) *Legislative Council 24 June 2004* p. 1 (John Della Bosca).

Robinson, O.C. (2014) "Sampling in Interview-based Qualitative Research: A Theoretical and Practical Guide" *Qualitative Research in Psychology* 11: 25–41.

Royal Commission into Institutional Responses to Child Sexual Abuse (2017) *Criminal Justice Report, Parts III-VI, Parts VII-X and Appendices* (Sydney, Australia: Author).
Righarts, S. and M. Henaghan (2010) "Public Perceptions of the New Zealand Court System: An Empirical Approach to Law Reform" *Otago Law Review* 12: 329–344.
Zhou, J. (2010) "Challenges in Prosecuting Child Sexual Assault in New South Wales" *Criminal Law Journal* 34: 306–322.

12 Community Prosecution Code Enforcement in Dallas, Texas

Effects on Serious Crime

John L. Worrall, Andrew P. Wheeler and Justine Medrano

Disorder and blight present vexing problems for law enforcement officials the world over. Such conditions may inspire fear, prompt people to become withdrawn, signal an area that is worth avoiding, and thereby encourage deviance and criminality. Police have responded with alternatives to traditional reactive patrol, namely with the implementation of "broken windows" (Wilson and Kelling, 1982) and problem-solving initiatives (Goldstein, 1990). Scores of creative strategies have been explored; many, research suggests (Braga *et al.*, 2015), have yielded modest public safety improvements. These initiatives have primarily been confined to policing. Only recently have other criminal justice officials, and particularly prosecutors, begun exploring the possible crime prevention benefits of targeting low-level signs of disorder and decline.

Historically, American prosecutors adopted a "felony case processor" model (Coles, 2008) rooted in a Progressive Era attempt to professionalize the criminal justice system. They were viewed as responsible solely for deciding who should be prosecuted and brought to trial. This perspective was echoed in the 1967 President's Commission on Law Enforcement and the Administration of Justice, which promoted a view that prosecutors were merely responsible for deciding whether alleged offenders should be charged and tried in court. During the 1960s and 1970s, however, a crisis of legitimacy in policing encouraged a focus on crime prevention and problem-solving (Kelling and Moore, 1988). Prosecutors soon came to realize, as the police had, that traditional case-processing strategies were inadequate. A new prosecutorial paradigm was necessary.

Starting in the 1980s, prosecution in America began to move from a reactive case-processing approach to what has been called a "strategic" model (Worrall, 2008). Enterprising officials in Manhattan, New York; Portland, Oregon; Kings County, New York; and Montgomery County, Maryland, began implementing new community-focused initiatives, following on the heels of similar developments in policing. They realized that failure to attend to underlying conditions and precursors of crime would result in the same offenders repeatedly passing through their offices. In Portland, prosecutors were deployed into neighbourhoods to target quality-of-life problems (Boland, 1998). Other offices reorganized themselves such that prosecutors were assigned cases in specific geographic areas, which was intended to ensure familiarity with the issues and persons involved in their cases (Goldkamp, Irons-Guynn and Weiland, 2002). Since then prosecutors have continued to adopt new and innovative techniques to prevent and control crime (Nugent and Rainville, 2001). Collectively, these efforts have been labelled "community prosecution" (Nugent, 2004).

At the risk of simplification, community prosecution brings prosecutors together with other criminal justice officials, government workers, service-providers and community members to identify quality-of-life problems (e.g. graffiti, prostitution, aggressive panhandling, disorder) and develop solutions to address community concerns. Many such solutions put formal prosecution on the "back burner", sometimes seeking to avoid it altogether (Coles, 2000). As initially envisioned, community prosecution consisted of six operational elements: a mix of proactive (e.g. anticipatory actions directed towards root causes of crime) and reactive (e.g. prosecuting offenders identified by police) strategies; clearly defined target areas, emphasis on problem-solving, public safety, and quality-of-life issues; stakeholder partnerships; use of varied enforcement mechanisms (e.g. arrest, forfeiture, code enforcement, litigation, prosecution); and long-term strategizing. Recently, community prosecution has been conceptualized in more concise terms:

> (1) partnerships with a variety of government agencies and community-based groups, (2) use of varied enforcement methods, including problem-solving techniques to address crime and public safety issues, and (3) community involvement.
>
> (Nugent-Borakove and Fanflik, 2008)

Despite community prosecution's growing popularity, few studies have evaluated its effects on crime (see: www.courtinnovation.org for an overview of available research). Fewer still have employed rigorous research designs aimed at detecting improvements *over time*. To address this shortcoming, our study presents the first place-based evaluation of a community prosecution strategy, particularly with respect to effects over time on serious offending. The research setting is the city of Dallas, Texas. We explore whether the work of city attorney/code enforcement teams in specific locations throughout the city (called Proactive Focus Areas, or PFAs) are associated with reductions in serious crime. Admittedly, community prosecution can exist in a variety of forms, many without a specific "enforcement" component. Nevertheless, the Dallas approach fits the community prosecution model with its focus on targeting minor problems in order to improve neighbourhood conditions and reduce serious crime.

Legal Authority for Code Enforcement

All US laws are hierarchical, with federal law at the highest level, local ordinances at the bottom, and state and county equivalents somewhere in between. Federal laws must be observed in every state. If state law contradicts federal law, federal law supersedes. Likewise, a state's law must be observed within its boundaries; local and county contradictions must be resolved in favour of the state. Finally, ordinances are county and/or city laws; they cannot conflict with either state or federal law. Ordinances are the purview of code enforcement officials.

Thinking specifically of *crime*, a federal crime is the violation of a law passed by the US Congress. With rare exceptions, federal crimes contain an interstate component or are otherwise of national interest. They are prosecuted by US Attorneys in federal district courts. Most criminal law in the US actually exists at the state level. State criminal codes penalize conduct ranging from murder and rape to petty theft and littering. State crimes, incidentally, are *enforced* at the county level. General jurisdiction courts at the county level hear criminal cases involving violations of state law; district attorneys, who are county employees (with the elected District Attorney being the chief prosecutor), prosecute offenders in superior court. At the lowest level of the criminal offence hierarchy are code violations. Municipal and county codes (also called charters and ordinances) facilitate the administration of government at the local level. They are expressly authorized by state law, otherwise state law would occupy the bottom of the American legal hierarchy.

Violations of state and federal laws are enforced by duly authorized peace officers (e.g. Federal Bureau of Investigation Special Agents at the federal law, local police officers at the municipal level). In contrast, code violations are typically enforced by state-certified code officers from city departments of code compliance or their equivalents. Code officers are not authorized to carry weapons and do not possess arrest authority; they generally enforce code compliance with a continuum of responses ranging from notification of violation to "administrative citation". The former affords the recipient an opportunity to correct the problem without additional action; the latter is akin to a parking ticket/citation. Continued violations may result in additional citations, appearance before a governing body (e.g. building commission), and/or the imposition of a property lien. Code officers identify violations through a mixture of complaints from third parties or proactive observations.

It is not uncommon for a municipal or county code (or codes) to name hundreds of conceivable violations. Most, though, fall into the following categories: building, zoning and public nuisance. Examples include improper outdoor storage, parking violations (e.g. yard parking), unkempt lawns, building disrepair/dangerous structures, inoperable vehicles, damaged fences, substandard housing, trash accumulation, stagnant water/swimming pools, improper signage, unauthorized business activities, excessive animals, unpermitted construction, too many residents on a property, dead/diseased vegetation, excessive noise and view obstruction. Code violations are assumed to threaten community health, compromise residents' quality of life and even reduce property values. Code *enforcement*'s mission is to mitigate against such eventualities.

Code Enforcement as Community Prosecution

Community prosecution emphasizes problem-solving, partnership and community engagement (Wolf, 2013). It need not focus on low-level offences, but most of the popular and replicated initiatives have. As Wolf observed: "When community prosecution first emerged in the early 1990s, many programs targeted low-level crime almost exclusively" (Wolf, 2010). With rare exceptions, this pattern has continued. A perusal of recent community prosecution initiatives (see: www.courtinnovation.org) reveals a focus on problems such as homelessness, truancy, shoplifting, graffiti, public drunkenness and other quality-of-life issues.

Code enforcement, like community prosecution, is also focused on low-level offending. Indeed, code enforcement's *raison d'être* is to foster clean, healthy and safe communities, free from disorder and blight. This makes code enforcement a natural partner in any community-based criminal justice initiative. Interestingly, though, code enforcement has been largely ignored in the criminal justice literature. Only a handful of authors have even mentioned it!

In *Making the Second Ghetto: Race and Housing in Chicago, 1940–1960*, Arnold Hirsch (1983) argued that lax enforcement of housing codes played a significant role in neighbourhood deterioration, though his argument was not formally tested. Daley and Meislin (1988) drew similar conclusions in New York City, namely that inadequate code enforcement led to problems in the city's housing stock. Sampson's discussion of the intersection between housing policies and crime presents the issue cogently:

> As we know, neighborhood deterioration has important negative consequences for crime. Neighborhood conditions provide readily observable evidence of the extent of local decline. Visual signs of physical deterioration and social disorganization ... include junks and trash, boarded up housing, and stripped or abandoned cars ... Hence, while city code enforcement may seem to be a policy arena far removed from crime, the evidence suggests otherwise – *lax enforcement of municipal codes leads to neighborhood deterioration, which in turn encourages crime.* [Emphasis added.]
>
> (Sampson, 1989)

In Dallas, Texas, the research setting for this project, code enforcement officials are paired with city attorneys to engage in crime prevention. "Community prosecution code enforcement" is the term we use to describe this unique partnership. We discuss the operational approach in a dedicated section later, but for now it bears mentioning that the Dallas team approach fits almost perfectly with the definition of community prosecution. It is a partnership designed for the purpose of solving low-level problems that threaten community standards and quality-of-life. We now discuss the initiative's theoretical underpinnings, then we delve further into the details of the research setting and the Dallas approach to community prosecution.

Theoretical and Empirical Foundations

Until the 1970s, the primary purpose of policing in America was deterrence (Nagin, 2013). Research soon revealed, however, that law enforcement's obsession with crime detection and offender apprehension failed to yield dividends. The famous Kansas City Preventive Patrol study (Kelling *et al.*, 1974) found that preventive patrol was largely ineffective. Similarly, rapid response did little to reduce crime or the fear thereof (Spelman and Brown, 1984). Reflecting on those studies, David Bayley bluntly observed that "[t]he police do not prevent crime" (Bayley, 1994, p. 3). A perception that "nothing works" began to permeate policing scholarship. Reformers soon proposed community-based strategies (e.g. Trojanowicz and Bucqueroux, 1990; Greene and Mastrofski, 1988). At around the same time, Wilson and Kelling's widely heralded "broken windows" theory was proposed (Wilson and Kelling, 1982). In their view, police should target low-level problems to prevent the spread of serious crime.

Broken windows theory did not discount the role of deterrence, however, nor did it devalue community engagement; it simply turned attention to other mechanisms behind the crime problem. Indeed, recent evaluations of focused policing strategies suggest that the police can capably deter crime (Weisburd and Eck, 2004; Telep and Weisburd, 2012). Likewise, community policing strategies launched in the 1980s operated in tandem with law enforcement initiatives premised on broken windows theory.

Broken windows theory calls for a police focus on disorder. Interestingly, the theory was presented in the *Atlantic Monthly*, a popular magazine, not in a scholarly outlet. As such, certain conceptual details were lacking (Weisburd *et al.*, 2015). For example, Wilson and Kelling failed to articulate a clear set of hypotheses specifying *how* disorder could lead to serious crime. Even despite this limitation, broken windows theory was elevated to the level of dogma in criminal justice theory and practice. To this day, the theory underlies a variety of law enforcement initiatives, despite an overall lack of reputable studies testing its formulations (Braga *et al.*, 2015).

Importantly, Wilson and Kelling (1982) did not claim that disorder leads *directly* to serious crime – though many have interpreted broken windows theory that way. For example, Sampson and Raudenbush (1999) explored the relationship between disorder and serious crime after controlling for "collective efficacy", or social cohesion/mutual trust among neighbours and a willingness to work together on behalf of the neighbourhood common good (Sampson *et al.*, 1997). After doing so, they found little to no association between disorder and crime. This prompted others, including Kelling, to argue that broken windows theory never posited a direct relationship between disorder and crime (e.g. Gault and Silver, 2008; Bratton and Kelling, 2006; Hinkle and Weisburd, 2008). Rather, the theory proposed an *indirect* pathway between disorder and crime through increased fear and reduced informal social controls. Any complete test of broken windows theory must then test whether police-driven efforts to reduce disorder reduce residents' fear, then increase informal social control, and finally reduce crime. Only one study appears to have incorporated all four dimensions – with a randomized controlled trial (Weisburd *et al.*, 2011).

A number of policing strategies besides those strictly premised on broken windows (such as "order maintenance", "zero-tolerance", and "problem-solving") also draw connections between disorder and serious crime (Braga *et al.*, 2015). Indeed, almost any policing approach that attempts to produce order and reduce crime through cooperation, partnership and engagement with community members does not ignore disorder (Cordner, 1998; Eck and Maguire, 2006). Disorder and crime are therefore connected, just in a complex and continually developing manner.

Theoretical nuances aside, a number of studies point to a clear connection between disorder and crime. Taking stock of this literature, Braga and his colleagues conducted a systematic review and meta-analysis of 30 randomized experimental and quasi-experimental tests of disorder-based policing, concluding that "... these strategies yielded consistent crime reduction effects across a variety of violent, property, drug, and disorder outcome measure" (Braga *et al.*, 2015, p. 580). Moreover, "[t]hese findings provide support for police paying attention to social and physical disorder when seeking to reduce more serious crimes in neighborhoods" (Braga *et al.*, 2015, pp. 580–581). They recommend that police departments should continue to target disorder. Presumably, then, any organized effort to target disorder should lead to reductions in serious crime. Code enforcement seems a natural fit. In other words, code violations are the low-level signs of disorder that may lead to serious offending.

Intervention and Research Setting

In Dallas, the City Attorney's Office is the chief prosecutor for Class C misdemeanours. Class C misdemeanours are criminal offences for which the penalty is a fine of not more than $500. Examples include disorderly conduct, illegal dumping, public intoxication, graffiti, littering, illegal land use and maintaining a substandard structure. The City Attorney's Office also possesses authority to use civil remedies to enforce housing standards, zoning requirements and a host of other city ordinances. These conditions afford the City of Dallas a unique opportunity to engage in community prosecution.

During the intervention period, 11 city attorneys were paired with 11 state-certified code officers, also Dallas employees (6 other prosecutors served as community prosecutors involved in other activities). They worked in pairs in 22 Proactive Focus Areas (PFAs) to identify substandard commercial and residential properties that, in their view, negatively affect the surrounding community. Their place-based focus sought to positively affect the health, safety and welfare of the citizens of Dallas by seeking the voluntary or court-ordered abatement of code violations at various residential and commercial properties.

Each team member learned about properties from neighbours, business owners, patrol officers and city inspectors, and also from their own frequent travels through their assigned geographic areas. When problem properties were identified, team members would often conduct extensive research related to the property's ownership, land use type and permit history. This up-front research allowed the attorneys and inspectors to understand the underlying issues that led to the physical decline or mismanagement of the property. These could include a tangled or clouded title; unpaid taxes or liens, bankruptcy, foreclosure, or other litigation involving the property; renters/squatters engaging in criminal activity; or long-term illegal land use, among other complexities. Team members would locate the owners and meet with them on offending properties so the owners could develop a full awareness of the problems associated with their properties.

In instances when another department (e.g. Dallas Fire and Rescue, Stormwater, Building Inspection, or Parking Enforcement) or agency (e.g. Texas Alcoholic Beverage Commission, Texas Department of Licensing and Regulation, Texas Comptroller's Office, and Texas Commission on Environmental Quality) regulates the use of a particular property, the community prosecution team would invite agency representatives to be present at any meetings with the owner for inspections of the property.

In many cases, the teams were able to work with property owners to develop plans for voluntary abatement of code violations and/or criminal activity occurring at targeted properties. When those initiatives failed, the team members would use escalating forms of enforcement in instances where there were immediate health or safety hazards – or when the owner was not willing to voluntarily abate all issues. Escalating enforcement could include civil or criminal citations, referral of the property for tax or lien collection efforts, or civil lawsuits, among other strategies.

In sum, the Dallas approach was based on the idea that prosecutors, working closely with code enforcement officers, could be more effective than traditional law enforcement-oriented approaches to the crime problem. Prosecutors have more legal "leverage" and, as such, are in a unique position to mobilize property owners and officials both inside *and* outside of traditional law enforcement organizations. Finally, prosecutors and code enforcement officers may be better poised to focus on specific types of disorder that are at the root of neighbourhood decline, perhaps more so than police.

Methods

Dallas is home to approximately 1.3 million people, making it the ninth largest city in the United States (1 July 2014 Census estimates). It is also the largest urban centre of the fourth most populous metropolitan area in the country, the Dallas Fort Worth (DFW) Metroplex, which has a population of over seven million. The city covers an area of 385.8 miles. Interestingly, three smaller cities are located entirely within the Dallas city limits. Cockrell Hill, on the southwest side of the city, is home to approximately 4,500 people. Highland Park and University Park, both affluent enclaves, are located in the north central part of the city. They are home to over 30,000 people.

Our study covers the years 2012–2015. The Dallas community prosecution code enforcement teams commenced their efforts in the latter part of 2012. Teams continue to this day to work throughout the city, but this study focuses on 22 PFAs that started/stopped at various points throughout the four-year period for which data were obtained. Some were still active at the end of 2015; others had ceased operations. A benefit of having PFA activities start and/or stop at various points between 2012 and 2015 is that the periods during which community prosecutors were inactive in these areas serve as "controls".

Figure 12.1 depicts the spatial locations of the PFAs over the study period as white spaces with dotted perimeter lines.[1] The PFAs tended to be smaller, with an average area of one-half of a square mile and population of 5,000.[2] The largest PFA (called the Northwest PFA) was approximately one by two miles in size. The smallest, called "Five Points", was one-half mile by three-quarters of a mile in size. Figure 12.1 also shows that the PFAs were spread throughout Dallas. In only one case were they immediately adjacent to one another (see: Whitehurst and Forest Audelia located in the northeast section of the city). Both were separated, however, by a major highway.[3]

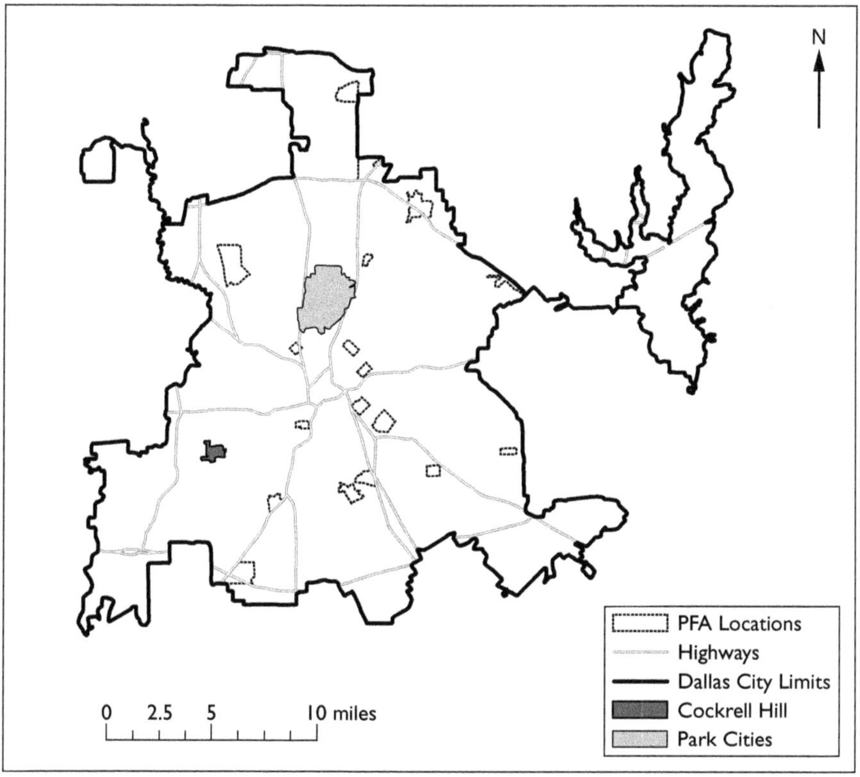

Figure 12.1 Spatial Location of PFAs within the City of Dallas.

Several of the PFAs changed shape over the study period, most often by expanding their borders. These locations were concatenated for our study, and the *greater* region was used as the area over the entire four-year period. Thus a total of 22 PFAs were collapsed into 19 unique areas. The measures used in this study (code enforcement actions, offence reports and arrests) were geocoded to the address level and assigned to particular PFAs if they were inside the polygons that defined their respective PFAs. The geocoding for the code enforcement and police data was completed by the Dallas Department of Code Compliance and the Dallas Police Department, respectively. Arrests were assigned to PFAs based on the location of initial police incidents.

It is important to note that the PFAs were not standardized geographically. Their boundaries were decided upon by prosecutors who had worked in and were familiar with the areas. There was no concerted effort, for example, to ensure equal numbers of commercial and residential properties in each PFA. As mentioned, each PFA was somewhat comparable in size (about a half square mile on average), but the uneven sizes of each PFA may have had implications for the analyses reported below.

Outcome and Explanatory Measures

The outcome measure used in this study was total Part I and Part II crime complaints (both officer- and citizen-initiated crime reports), which we call Total Crime. These data were obtained via the Dallas Police Department and included *all* penal code crime incidents, regardless of seriousness.

We also included arrests associated with those incidents as a control variable in our statistical models. It should be underscored that arrests were linked to specific crime incidents, thus facilitating separation of the PFA teams' efforts from police activity already occurring in the areas. These variables were aggregated to counts per month, from January 2012 through December 2015. This resulted in a total of 48 months, for a total of 912 observations (i.e. 19×48) in our panel dataset. Code enforcement data were obtained from the Dallas Department of Code Compliance and covered a wide variety of complaints. Summary statistics (for PFA/years) appear in Table 12.1.

Table 12.2 shows the frequency of the code enforcement complaints that occurred over 1,000 times over the four year period *within* the PFA locations (with remaining violations assigned to the "Other" category). Several of the code enforcement complaints were not used in our analyses, however, because they

Table 12.1 Summary Statistics

Variable	*Obs.*	*Mean*	*Std. Dev.*	*Min.*	*Max.*
Total Crime	912	98.59	86.77	5	428
Arrests	912	8.77	9.57	0	53
Total Code Violations	912	69.67	88.36	0	759

Table 12.2 Code Violation Type Frequencies

Code Violation Type	*Frequency*
High Weeds	9,768
Litter	11,877
Mow	10,673
Substandard Structure	4,947
Signs – Public Right of Way	2,305
Graffiti Abatement Request	2,009
Obstruction Alley/Sidewalk/Street	1,632
Graffiti Private Property – Residential/Commercial	1,568
Heavy Clean Request	1,519
Illegal Dumping	1,459
A/C Inoperable Apts	1,172
Bulky Trash Violations	1,150
Other	14,129
Total	64,208

were not part of the PFA initiative. These constituted only a small number of violations.[4] All code enforcement incidents were aggregated to monthly counts within each time period, just as they were for police incidents. As seen in Table 12.2, code enforcement encompasses a wide variety of complaints. The "Other" category encompassed over 20 per cent of the total and included a wide variety of minor nuisance complaints.

The final measure used in the study denoted the presence/absence of the PFA intervention. The majority of the PFAs (13) were under the intervention from March 2012 through the end of the time period (December 2015). Four of the other PFAs had an intervention period beginning in October 2014 and ending December 2015. The remaining two areas operated from September 2013 to December 2015 and October 2014 to September 2015. The intervention variable was coded with a one during months in which community prosecutions were active within the PFAs, zero otherwise.

Estimation Technique

Ordinary least squares regression is not equipped to deal with repeated observations on the same units of analysis. As such, we estimated a series of fixed effects regression models using the – xtreg – command in Stata. Our fixed effects model, in matrix notation, looks like this:

$$y_{i,t} = \alpha_i + \beta x_{i,t} + \varepsilon_{i,t}$$

The dependent variable "$y_{i,t}$" refers to total crime in unit i at time t. Separate intercepts for each unit are denoted by "α_i". "$\beta x_{i,t}$" represents the regression coefficients for each unit/time. We included various combinations of predictors in our models, as reported below. Finally, "$\varepsilon_{i,t}$" is the error term.

Results

Regression results appear in Table 12.3. We began by estimating three contemporaneous (i.e. same period) regressions of total crime on various predictors. Model 1 reports the effects on total crime of the same-period intervention variables. Model 2 adds arrests, again to control for other law enforcement activities in the PFA at the time. Finally, Model 3 interacts the intervention variable with total code enforcement violations. This goes further than examining just the effect on crime of the presence/absence of the intervention; it is akin to a measure of dosage. While the interaction variable was not significant, the intervention variable showed a robust and inverse association with total crime. In other words, the presence of the intervention in any unit/time combination was associated with less crime. The arrest variable was not significant, which is to be expected.

The last three columns of Table 12.3 report the results of regression models in which the predictors were lagged one period. Arguably these models offer a better depiction of reality than contemporaneous models because there is likely a delay between the intervention and crime reductions; it takes time for expected crime reduction benefits to manifest. According to models 4, 5 and 6, the intervention variable was once again significant and in the expected direction. The PFA team activities were associated with subsequent reductions in total Part I and Part II crimes in the areas where they engaged in code enforcement activities. Also, the arrest variable was significant in model 6, which is to be expected (delay between arrest and crime reduction benefits thereby obtained). All told, the results reported in Table 12.3 suggest that the community prosecution/code enforcement teams' efforts were significantly associated with reductions in total crime in the PFAs. Displacement or diffusion may have occurred, but the analysis did not explore those.

Table 12.3 Fixed Effects Regression Results

	Contemporaneous Effect			*Lagged Effect*		
	1	*2*	*3*	*4*	*5*	*6*
Intervention	–8.04**	–8.82**	–8.61**	–9.42**	–7.79**	–7.06*
	(2.40)	(2.46)	(2.89)	(2.42)	(2.47)	(2.90)
Arrests	–	0.24	0.20	–	–0.51**	–0.55**
	–	(0.17)	(0.17)	–	(0.17)	(0.17)
Code Total	–	–	0.06**	–	–	0.06**
	–	–	(0.02)	–	–	(0.02)
Intervention*	–	–	–0.00	–	–	–0.01
Code Total	–	–	(0.02)	–	–	(0.02)
F Test That All u_i=0	690.72*	331.7**	333.56**	678.64	348.23**	351.16**

Notes
* = significant at 5%; ** = significant at 1%.

Discussion and Conclusion

Sampson (1989) found that neighbourhood deterioration has important negative consequences for crime. This has prompted a wide range of problem-solving initiatives, such as proactive policing and community prosecution. Our study focused on community prosecution, and particularly code enforcement activities involving teams of city attorneys and code enforcement officers in Dallas, Texas. Teams engaged in a number of activities, most notably code enforcement actions aimed at reducing disorder and blight in several proactive focus areas throughout the city.

The study covered the years of 2012–2015; the Dallas community prosecution code enforcement teams began their efforts in the latter part of 2012. Teams are still operating presently throughout the city; however, we focused on 22 PFAs that started/stopped at various points throughout the four-year period for which data were obtained.

PFAs were spatially identified and tracked using official data, then collapsed into 19 unique areas. Areas were geocoded and arrests were assigned to PFAS based on the location of initial police incidents. Our analysis showed that the community prosecution/code enforcement initiative was associated with reductions in Part I and Part II crime. Both contemporaneous and lagged effects were observed. We also included a measure of "dosage" (i.e. the number of code enforcement activities), but it was not significant. In essence, the presence of the intervention in any unit/time combination was associated with reductions in crime. The mere presence of the teams in PFAs, it seems, paid dividends; the *amount* of activity each team engaged in was not particularly consequential.

Limitations

Ours was the first place-based assessment of the effectiveness of community prosecution and code enforcement on Part I and Part II crimes. Although results suggest crime declined in the targeted PFAs, it must be noted that this study was conducted in just one city. As such, results are not generalizable to other jurisdictions. Moreover, not all cities that implement community prosecution pair up with a city code enforcement officer to prevent and control crime. In other words, we make no claim that community prosecution/code enforcement is the best approach to community prosecution – or even community prosecution at all.

Dallas has been one of the longest operating community prosecuting cities, since 2001. Our evaluation, however, commenced in 2012; a narrow timeframe was thus examined. We cannot speak to the efficacy of other community prosecution programmes that predated 2012 or are in operation currently.

Another limitation of our study is the lack of control areas. Ideally, data on problematic areas similar to PFAs (i.e. those with code enforcement problems, crime problems, a good deal of high-density housing, etc.) but in which no community prosecution activities took place could have been collected. These areas, then, could be compared to the PFAs. At the same time, though, our approach to analysis was not completely bereft of controls. Instead of control *areas*, we were able to include control *times*. In other words, the periods before and after PFA activity (i.e. those coded with a zero in our statistical models) helped achieve a measure of control. It is not uncommon in panel models to compare the intervention period to the pre-intervention period.

Another possible concern is that crime nationwide was trending downward during approximately the same timeframe for which we collected data. While this may be true on the whole, it was not the case in Dallas. The official violent crime rate per 100,000 people in Dallas was 675 in 2012, 664 in 2013 and 665 in 2014 (2015 data were not available as of this writing). The property crime rate was 4,374 in 2012, 4,165 in 2013 and 3,589 in 2014. Save for the apparent drop in property crime between 2013 and 2014, the rates were mostly static.

Despite these issues, our study suggests that proactive community collaboration among city attorneys, code enforcement officers, police departments and community residents may reduce crime and improve neighbourhood safety. Additionally, the Dallas community prosecution/code enforcement approach may serve as a model to other jurisdictions that have similar populations and neighbourhood problems.

Conclusion

Community prosecution emphasizes problem-solving, partnership and community engagement through a collaborative approach to prevent and control crime by having prosecutors and the community partner together to identify and address neighbourhood issues, and develop solutions collectively. Although community prosecution has been popular and implemented worldwide, few evaluations of its efficacy exist. Even fewer studies have employed rigorous research designs in order to detect longitudinal effects on crime. Our study presents the first place-based evaluation of community prosecution, with a focus on the possible effects over time on serious offending in Dallas, Texas. Results suggest that city attorney/code enforcement teams, by seeking the voluntary or court-ordered abatement of code violations and criminal activity at residential and commercial properties, may have been able to improve quality of life in targeted areas. Such a holistic and collaborative approach, which involves frequenting neighbourhoods and interacting with stakeholders, not just engaging in enforcement, could well be emulated in other jurisdictions, and perhaps internationally.

Notes

1 The other GIS layers used in Figure 12.1 were obtained publicly from either http://gis.dallascityhall.com/homepage/shapezip.htm or www.dallasopendata.com/.

2 Population averages were calculated by taking the proportional areal allocation between reporting areas (a Dallas PD construct) and PFAs. Reporting areas are often smaller than PFAs. Population information was taken from the 2010 census.

3 The Park Cities are shaded in light grey with dots. Cockrell Hill is shaded in dark grey. The large odd-looking formation connected to the eastern part of the city is Lake Ray Hubbard, including the park areas immediately adjacent to it. Another annexed lake, North Lake, also sits connected in the northwest part of the city. The two lake areas have no residential population.

4 The complaints not included are ten carryout bag violations, zero rain device/freeze gauge violations, 83 shopping cart decal violations, 92 STEP decal violations, 93 STEP licence violations, 98 Water conservation violations, 99 water conservation violations and zero wood vendor violations, for a total of 475 incidents.

References

Bayley, D. (1994) *Police for the Future* (New York: Oxford University Press).

Boland, B. (1998) "Community Prosecution: Portland's Experience" – in Karp, D.R. (ed.) *Community Justice: An Emerging Field* (Lanham, MD: Rowman & Littlefield).

Braga, A.A, B.C. Welsh and C. Schnell (2015) "Can Policing Disorder Reduce Crime? A Systematic Review and Meta-analysis" *Journal of Research in Crime and Delinquency* 52: 567–588.

Bratton, W.J. and G.L. Kelling (2006) "There Are No Cracks in the Broken Windows" *National Review Online*, 28 February.

Coles, C.M. (2000) *Community Prosecution, Problem-Solving, and Public Accountability: The Evolving Strategy of the American Prosecutor* (Working Paper No. 00-02-04) (Cambridge, MA: Harvard University, John F. Kennedy School of Government).

Coles, C.M. (2008) "Evolving Strategies in 20th-Century American Prosecution" – in Worrall, J.L. and M.E. Nugent-Borakove (eds) *The Changing Role of the American Prosecutor* (Albany, NY: SUNY Press).

Cordner, G. (1998) "Problem-Oriented Policing vs. Zero Tolerance" – in Shelly, T. and A. Grant (eds) *Problem-Oriented Policing: Crime-Specific Problems, Critical Issues, and Making POP Work* (Washington, DC: Police Executive Research Forum).

Daley, S. and R. Meislin (1988) "New York City, the Landlord: A Decade of Housing Decay" *New York Times* 8 February.

Eck, J. and E. Maguire (2006) "Have Changes in Policing Reduced Violent Crime? An Assessment of the Evidence" – in Blumstein, A. and J. Wallman (eds) *The Crime Drop in America* 2nd edn (New York: Cambridge University Press).

Gault, M. and E. Silver (2008) "Spuriousness or Mediation? Broken Windows According to Sampson and Raudenbush (1999)" *Journal of Criminal Justice* 36: 240–243.

Goldkamp, J.C. Irons-Guynn and D. Weiland (2002) *Community Prosecution Strategies: Measuring Impact* (Philadelphia, PA: Crime and Justice Research Institute).

Goldstein, H. (1990) *Problem-Oriented Policing* (New York: McGraw-Hill).

Greene, J.R. and S.D. Mastrofski (1988) *Community Policing: Rhetoric or Reality* (New York: Praeger).

Hinkle, J.C. and D. Weisburd (2008) "The Irony of Broken Windows Policing: A Micro-place Study of the Relationship between Disorder, Focused Police Crackdowns and Fear of Crime" *Journal of Criminal Justice* 36: 503–512.

Hirsch, A. (1983) *Making the Second Ghetto: Race and Housing in Chicago, 1940–1960* (Chicago, IL: University of Chicago Press).

Kelling, G.L. and M.H. Moore (1988) "The Evolving Strategy of Policing" – in *Perspectives on Policing* (Cambridge, MA: National Institute of Justice and Program in

Criminal Justice Policy and Management, John F. Kennedy School of Government, Harvard University).

Kelling, G.L., T. Pate, D. Dieckman and C.E. Brown (1974) *The Kansas City Preventive Patrol Experiment: A Summary Report* (Washington, DC: Police Foundation).

Nagin, D. (2013) "Deterrence in the Twenty-first Century" *Crime and Justice: A Review of Research* 42: 199–263.

Nugent, M.E. (2004) *What Does it Mean to Practice Community Prosecution? Organizational, Functional, and Philosophical Changes* (Alexandria, VA: American Prosecutors Research Institute).

Nugent, M.E. and G. Rainville (2001) "The State of Community Prosecution: Results of a National Survey" *The Prosecutor* 35: 26–28, 30–33.

Nugent-Borakove, M.E. and P.L. Fanflik (2008) "Community Prosecution: Rhetoric or Reality" – in Worrall, J.L. and M.E. Nugent-Borakove (eds) *The Changing Role of the American Prosecutor* (Albany, NY: SUNY Press).

Sampson, R.J. (1989) "The Impact of Housing Policies on Community Social Disorganization and Crime" *Bulletin of the New York Academy of Medicine* 66: 526–533.

Sampson, R.J. and S. Raudenbush (1999) "Systematic Social Observation of Public Spaces: A New Look at Disorder in Urban Neighborhoods" *American Journal of Sociology* 105: 603–651.

Sampson, R.J., S.W. Raudenbush and F. Earls (1997) "Neighborhoods and Violent Crime: A Multilevel Study of Collective Efficacy" *Science* 277: 918–924.

Spelman, W. and D.K. Brown (1984) *Calling the Police: Citizen Reporting of Serious Crime* (Washington, DC: US Department of Justice).

Telep, C.E. and C. Weisburd (2012) "What Is Known about the Effectiveness of Police Practices in Reducing Crime and Disorder?" *Police Quarterly* 15: 331–357.

Trojanowicz, R. and B. Bucqueroux (1990) *Community Policing: A Contemporary Perspective* (Cincinnati, OH: Anderson).

Weisburd, D. and J.E. Eck (2004) "What Can Police Do to Reduce Crime, Disorder, and Fear?" *The Annals of the American Academy of Political and Social Science* 593: 42.

Weisburd, D., J.C. Hinkle, A.A. Braga and A. Wooditch (2015) "Understanding the Mechanisms Underlying Broken Windows Policing: The Need for Evaluation Evidence" *Journal of Research in Crime and Delinquency* 52: 589–608.

Weisburd, D., C. Hinkle, C. Famega and J. Ready (2011) "The Possible 'Backfire' Effects of Hot Spots Policing: An Experimental Assessment of Impacts on Legitimacy, Fear and Collective Efficacy" *Journal of Experimental Criminology* 7: 297–320.

Wilson, J.Q. and G.L. Kelling (1982) "Broken Windows: The Police and Neighborhood Safety" *Atlantic Monthly* 249: 29–38.

Wolf, R.V. (2010) *Community Prosecution and Serious Crime: A Guide for Prosecutors* (New York: Center for Court Innovation).

Wolf, R.V. (2013) "Community Prosecution" –in Peak, K.J. (ed.) *Encyclopedia of Community Policing and Problem Solving* (Thousand Oaks, CA: Sage).

Worrall, J.L. (2008) "Prosecution in America: A Historical and Comparative Account" – in Worrall, J.L. and M.E. Nugent-Borakove (eds) *The Changing Role of the American Prosecutor* (Albany, NY: SUNY Press).

Part IV

Prosecutors, Politics and Accountability

13 Prosecution and Politics in Germany

The Struggle for Independence

Michael Jasch

Growing Pressure on Prosecutors: Recent Examples from Germany

Being a public prosecutor has become a difficult job in recent years. Once the public and the media become interested in a particular criminal case, the prosecutor's decision is analysed in detail and criticised harshly by one side or the other – regardless of whether he charges the suspect or he decides to drop the case. Long before he reaches a decision on the case, the investigative steps of police and the Prosecution Service will be watched thoroughly by the public, political parties and special interest groups.

Sometimes, investigating in specific directions might even cost a prosecutor his or her job. In August 2015, this happened to Germany's highest-ranking prosecutor, Harald Range. The head of the National Prosecution Service started preliminary proceedings against two internet bloggers who had reported on the surveillance of the internet, conducted by the German Office for the Protection of the Constitution, a secret service agency responsible for protecting the internal security of the country. The Office regarded these critical weblog reports as potential treason and thus reported the alleged offence. They reported this also hoping to trace the internal information leak through the course of subsequent investigations. Thus, the Prosecution Service started investigations against the internet activists.[1] The investigation very quickly resulted in a massive public outcry, claiming that the prosecution was neglecting the constitutional rights of freedom of speech and freedom of the press. Mr. Range complained about the Ministry's attempts to end the investigation and called this an "unacceptable interference in the independence of justice".[2] The Minister, however, denied allegations that he had tried to influence the decision of the prosecution service. After a few weeks of public turmoil, the Minister of Justice ordered the proceedings to be stopped and sent Harald Range immediately into retirement.

The political dimension of conflicts between prosecutors can be illustrated by the case of Gregor Gysi, a very popular left-wing politician in Germany who grew up in the former GDR. For years, his political opponents claimed that he had collaborated with the East German secret police, and that he had been lying in court about this fact after reunification. The pre-trial process turned into a legal scandal during legal proceedings in Hamburg: the investigating prosecutor concluded that there was not sufficient evidence against Gysi and decided to drop the case. The city of Hamburg's Chief Prosecutor, however, ordered him to bring the case to court. But the prosecutor in charge objected formally to this directive and the dispute became public.[3] Finally, more than two years after the investigation had begun, Hamburg's Ministry of Justice settled the conflict between the prosecutors and decided not to charge the politician. In the end, observers got the impression that the political orientation of those involved might have influenced the way the case had been handled. These cases are, of course, not typical of the everyday workload of prosecutors, yet they illustrate how politicians, the political discourse and public opinion may greatly influence the work of prosecutors in Germany.

The Role of the Prosecution Service in Germany

Unlike in common law jurisdictions, the prosecution service in Germany is the most important criminal justice institution during pre-trial proceedings, and quite possibly for the entire criminal case. It is the "head of the pre-trial investigation", concerned with two major duties: first, to lead criminal investigations and to supervise police work (§§ 160, 161 StPO). Second, when the investigations are completed, to decide whether or not to bring the case to court (§ 170 StPO). For a long time, it has been disputed whether the Prosecution Service belongs to the judiciary or rather to the executive power of the state. Today, however, there is a broad consensus among lawyers that the Prosecution Service is a unique authority of the criminal justice system, combining elements of both these powers of the state.[4]

Theoretically, the work of the Prosecution authority is governed by the principle of legality, which compels the prosecutor to conduct investigations in every case of reasonable suspicion of criminal offence. That does not, of course, mean that every offender will be charged in court. During recent decades, the legislator has introduced various possibilities for prosecutors to discontinue criminal proceedings out of court. Especially since the 1980s, the principle of legality has been undermined substantially by provisions based on the principle of opportunity.

In general, the 16 German states are individually responsible for their justice systems. They are, however, bound to the provisions of the national law such as the penal code, the statutory provisions concerning the organisation of courts and prosecution authorities and the criminal procedure law. Thus, there is no such thing as a uniform criminal justice policy in Germany. Within the framework of the national Criminal and Criminal Procedure Code, the details of the application of the law are up to the state government. With regard to the Prosecution Service, the issuing of guidelines on how to deal with minor crimes and criteria for dropping cases at the pre-trial level are important instruments of the Ministry of Justice of the state. Besides the prosecution authorities of the states, there is also the National Prosecution Service. The National Prosecution Service, subordinate to the national Ministry of Justice, is only responsible for the investigation and prosecution of offences affecting the internal and external security of Germany, such as terrorism, espionage, treason and illegal arms trafficking.

At the national as well as at the state level, the Public Prosecution Service is organised as a strictly hierarchical institution. Unlike judges, prosecutors are not independent. According to § 146 *Gerichtsverfassungsgesetz* (Judicator Act) they are obliged to follow orders given by their supervisors within the local authority. The Minister of Justice is located at the top of the hierarchy of every Prosecution Service, entitled to give general guidelines as well as instructions in individual cases to the prosecution authorities of his or her state. Therefore, every single prosecutor may receive directives either from his or her immediate superior (internal directives) or from the Minister of Justice (external directives). Thus, it is obvious that prosecutors are not independent from the executive power and that they are regarded as subordinated civil servants, although they are involved in the administration of justice.

The Public Prosecution Service: The Historical Background

In Germany's criminal justice system, the Public Prosecution Service is a relatively young institution, originally imported from French Law. The very first prosecution authority was established in 1848 in Berlin. However, it was not until 1877 that the Public Prosecution Service was introduced in all the German states by the *Reichsstrafprozessordnung* (Criminal Procedure Code). Its evolution is inherently linked to the rise of democracy and civil society in the wake of the French Revolution. According to contemporary justification, the objective behind the establishment of a Prosecution Service was twofold: first, to separate the investigation of a criminal case from the judging process. Previously, both functions had been allocated to the judge, who received the case directly from the police. And, of course, it became obvious that such a combination of investigative and judicial functions produces serious risks for an unbiased trial against the accused. Second, the investigative powers of the police should be limited and controlled by a new organisation that is exclusively bound to the Rule of the Law. The Prosecution Service was meant to be a tool against arbitrary acts and misuse of power by the police. Section 6 of the Prussian Directive on the Introduction of Jury Courts[5] stated that

> Public Prosecutors must take care that the trial takes place in accordance to the law. They must ensure that no criminal offender avoids punishment as well as that no one who is innocent will be wrongly sentenced.

This quote characterises the role of the Prosecution Service to date: it was – and is today – intended by the law to be the "most objective legal authority in the world".[6] Hence, in the first place, the introduction of the Prosecution Service has to be regarded as a means to: (1) protect the interests of the person accused of a criminal offence and (2) strengthen the authority of the law with regard to criminal proceedings.

From the beginning, the prosecution service was a strongly hierarchical organisation with lawyers who had to comply with the instructions of their superiors, and the head of the prosecution service subordinated to the Ministry of Justice. It might be crucial for the understanding of contemporary problems with regard to the independence of prosecutors to consider the motives behind the creation of the German Prosecution Service in the nineteenth century. Interestingly, research on the reasons for the implementation of the Prosecution Service offers very different interpretations.

For a long time, the general opinion has been that the implementation of a Prosecution authority was merely in the interest of the rule of law and of a liberal and modern justice system. It appeared to be an enormous advancement that the functions of investigation and judgement were separated, and that lawyers – and not police officers – became the heads of the pre-trial process.[7] Thus, the question of independence of the Prosecution Service or individual prosecutors was apparently not an issue at all. At the end of the nineteenth century this independence was not perceived as a problem, simply because prosecutors were part of the justice administration, but not of the Ministry of the Interior that is responsible for the police. This becomes very clear from the work of Eberhard Schmidt, the most prominent legal historian of post-war Germany, who writes: "There was no need to give independence to the Prosecution Service, precisely because it had been subordinated to the Ministry of Justice".[8] According to Schmidt, the Ministry of Justice does not represent the power of the State, but rather its obligation to the law.

From a contemporary point of view, such an interpretation appears to be almost a bit naive. It is hard to imagine that there are Ministers of Justice in modern governments who act without any political interests and bonds, sphinx-like, solely as an executor of the law. And it is also hard to believe that this was the political situation in Germany at the end of the nineteenth century. Thus, today some historians and lawyers take a fundamentally different, rather critical point of view with regard to the motives behind the introduction of the Prosecution Service: they claim that the Prosecution Service was meant to be a powerful instrument of the state from the beginning. From this perspective, it can be seen that the government wanted to have a larger influence on prosecution decisions and the use of appeals. The executive created the new institution in order to control criminal proceedings and to keep an eye on independent and sometimes rebellious judges.[9]

Growing Demands for Independence: What Has Changed?

Since then, the organisational framework for the Prosecution Service as well as for the individual prosecutors has essentially not changed. Today, Germany's Prosecution Service is still a hierarchical organisation of civil servants, and it is still supervised by the Ministry of Justice. However, the demand for a completely independent Prosecution Service has increased in recent years. This raises the question as to the reasons for these new demands for independence.

If it were true, that – as Schmidt puts it – Public Prosecutors and the Ministry of Justice are merely obliged to the law, and if the perception of the Prosecution Service as the "most objective authority of the world" corresponds to the reality, the growing concern about the role of the Prosecution Service would be surprising.

Growing Importance of Pre-Trial Decisions

Since the 1990s, the pre-trial stage of criminal proceedings has become more important than ever before. Germany's criminal justice system is characterised by a comparatively high percentage of cases dealt with outside the court. Diversion strategies began in the 1980s, mainly in the field of juvenile justice, and spread successfully in the criminal justice system through to the end of last century. Step by step, Parliament has introduced a comprehensive system of powers to discontinue criminal proceedings not only for the court, but also for the Prosecution Service.

Today, 52 per cent of all cleared cases suitable for prosecution are resolved outside of court. They are dealt with by the Prosecution Service, either by means of terminating proceedings under certain obligations for the offender (including community work or a fine), or without any conditions because the alleged offence is just a relatively minor crime. A further 26 per cent are terminated with a fine, proposed by the Prosecution Service and confirmed by a judge in a purely written procedure without a trial (*Strafbefehl*). Only 21 per cent of the cleared cases of indictable offences go to court.[10]

The great significance of diverting minor cases from going to court has, of course, increased the importance of the Public Prosecution for the justice system dramatically. And it raises questions as to the separation of powers, which is perceived to be a fundamental principle of a justice system in democratic states. Already in 1980 a German lawyer published his doctoral thesis entitled "The Public Prosecutor – a Judge prior to the Judge?".[11] He argued, that the fundamental principle of a fair trial could be at risk if the Public Prosecution Service amounts to a judicial authority because of its increasing power to terminate a case according to the principle of opportunity either with or without conditions for the suspect.

Nevertheless, the strategy of "decriminalisation by procedural law" has proven to be quite successful from a criminological perspective since it has reduced the number of repeat offenders and possible stigmatisation of criminal offenders. Moreover, the states are not willing to deal with all those cases by means of a – much more expensive – criminal trial. The only meaningful alternative, to my view, would be decriminalising certain deviant behaviour so that these acts would not be defined as a crime that would need a trial.

In addition, out-of-court-agreements between the Prosecution and the defendant concerning the outcome of a trial has increased the importance of the Prosecution Service in the criminal justice system. Such deals, well known in the Anglo-American legal system for decades, have been introduced recently in Germany's criminal procedure law[12] as well. According to the law, deals have to be proposed by the judge and must be negotiated publicly in the courtroom. It was the intention of the legislation to preserve the court as the key player in criminal proceedings. Yet, the legal acknowledgement of such deals has strengthened the position of the prosecution in the pre-trial phase.

Increasing Uncertainty of Criminal Laws

In recent decades, the legal definition of what constitutes a criminal offence has become increasingly wide and uncertain. This applies to the criminal legislation in Germany, and, I am afraid, to other European countries as well. First, more and more frequently it is already a crime "to be dangerous". Traditionally, criminal law penalises human behaviour that harms an individual or collective right. In recent decades, however, criminal law tends to swiftly penalise certain behaviours that put legal rights at risk. We find offences of this kind in the anti-terrorism legislation as well as in the traffic code and environmental laws.

Second, new regulations have been introduced for such infractions as hate crime, criminal laws prosecuting membership in, or any support of, international terrorist groups or organised crime and penal laws against phenomena as different as money laundering, stalking and human trafficking. Criminal law is increasingly used as a political means to resolve all kinds of social problems – an attempt that can never be successful in the long run. Inevitably, penal laws of this kind are often phrased as generally as the social problems they want to address. The more criminal laws become vague and uncertain, the more discretionary powers arise for prosecutors who have to decide whether a certain behaviour falls under the law and – in many cases – whether a prosecution might be in the public interest or not.

Trial by Media

The important role of mass media for all social and political processes has been discussed for decades. Of course, the increasing importance of mass media, including social media networks like Facebook, Twitter etc., also affect the criminal justice system. Prosecutors are often in a conflict between two general principles: on the one hand, the Prosecution Service has to protect the privacy of every suspect, and to ensure that the presumption of innocence will be met through the course of the investigation. On the other hand, the media and the public in general have a legitimate interest in information concerning criminal investigations.[13] This applies to criminal cases that have been of special interest only for a specific local community, and especially to cases involving individuals with a strong public presence, like politicians or celebrities, which have regional or national consequences.

The information that criminal investigations have collected against a particular person could be a very powerful tool in the hands of public prosecutors.[14] In cases of international white-collar crime, the fact that criminal investigations are conducted against the CEO or a senior executive of a large company have a dramatic impact on the stock market and may destroy billions of euro or dollars of market value. Moreover, cooperation between the media and prosecutors may produce a specific dynamic for the course of the trial: once a case has been discussed widely in the media, it will be more difficult for the prosecution to drop proceedings.

If the suspect is a well-known politician, the fact that this person has been arrested or interrogated normally leads to his or her resignation from public office, even though the case might result in an acquittal or a termination of proceedings several months later. In 2012, a single prosecutor even managed to bring down the German head of state, Christian Wulff, simply by accusing him of corruption. The political pressure was so strong that Wulff had to resign when the prosecution charged him. Later, during the trial, it turned out that there was no sufficient evidence at all against him and Wulff was acquitted in the end.

Politics through Courts

Finally, the hierarchical structure allows for the government to use prosecutors as a means for its political interests and to pursue a strategy of "politics through courts". There is, however, a general tendency in Western societies to resolve political problems by means of the criminal law, or to attempt to do so at least. Whenever there is a controversial debate about political decisions or developments, there will be someone who reports an alleged offence to the Prosecution Service. This applies to local problems as well as to global politics. In 1999, German solicitors reported Chancellor Gerhard Schroeder and other members of the government to the Prosecution Service because the German Air Force took part in the war in the former Republic of Yugoslavia. In the US, lawyers tried to prosecute former President George Bush because he had justified the war in Iraq with lies.[15] In Germany, left-wing politicians called for the prosecution of George Bush and the head of the CIA due to the use of torture against suspects in Iraq, Afghanistan and Guantanamo.[16] Included among other detainees was a German citizen who had been wrongfully captured and detained in Guantanamo for months. Just a year ago, when Germany received unprecedented high numbers of refugees in 2015, about 400 citizens from a right-wing political movement charged Chancellor Angela Merkel with treason and smuggling of human beings, arguing she was not authorised to let the refugees in.[17] All these reports of top-ranking politicians have so far been without any success. Up until now, there have not been any successful attempts by the Ministry of Justice to directly influence the prosecution of such high-ranking officials for these actions.

It should also be noted that the decision-making process in everyday cases might be of political relevance as well. Since the majority of cases are dealt with outside court on the basis of the principle of opportunity, government can influence the policies of prosecution services by means of general guidelines, codes of practice and setting of priorities. This becomes obvious concerning the fight against soft drugs such as cannabis: the possession of small amounts of cannabis frequently results in a termination of proceedings. However, the definition of "small amount" differs between five and 15 grams in different states of Germany, whereas some states do not apply fixed criteria at all and leave it to the discretion of the prosecution.

Taking the overall situation into account, critics claim that

> because of its monocratic organisation and the dependence on directions from the government, the Prosecution Service constitutes an instrument of politics. In political issues and cases covered by the media, there are individual directives. In everyday-cases, the Ministry of Justice exercises its power by means of guidelines (...)[18]

Concepts for More Independence

Up to now, the professional associations of prosecutors in Germany have been the main proponents of a reform for the Prosecution Service with respect to its independence. The proposals for a new role of the Public Prosecution Service in Germany can be divided into two basic concepts.

First, it has been suggested to abolish any right of the Ministry of Justice to give instructions in individual cases.[19] Moreover, all personnel decisions and organisational questions concerning the Prosecution Service should be up to a new Board of Justice, and not to the Ministry anymore. According to this approach, the Board of Justice should consist of five judges and prosecutors. They should be elected by an Election Committee consisting of a majority of members of parliament in order to ensure a democratic legitimisation of the Justice Board.[20]

The second proposal goes much further: it has been suggested to abolish not only the external right of the Ministry of Justice to give instructions, but also the internal authority of the local head of the Prosecution Authority to give instructions in individual cases.[21] Thus, the Public Prosecutor should become as independent as judges are under German laws.

Although these concepts have been suggested by professional associations for about 20 years, the independence of the prosecution has never become a major topic on the agenda – neither among politicians nor academics. There have always been calls for more independence and debates on the best way to achieve this goal, but up to now these debates have been limited to a rather small group of professionals and academics.

Especially the large political parties have always been quite reluctant to support the proposals for a completely independent Prosecution Service and a system of self-administration in the justice system. For instance, in spring 2016, the German Judges Association asked all the parties represented in the state parliament of Rheinland-Pfalz for their position concerning the independence of prosecutors. Only two opposition parties supported the complete abolition of the government's right to give instructions to prosecutors in particular cases.[22] Thus, there is no political majority at the moment in favour of a clear separation between the Prosecution Service and the Ministry of Justice.

The lack of support for more independence of the German justice system is not really surprising, simply because there is no public pressure at all concerning this topic. Generally speaking, Germans are quite satisfied with their justice system. According to a survey conducted by the European Commission, Germany occupies fourth place in Europe with regard to the trust of the citizens in the justice system.[23] And for politicians, it seems to be too tempting to maintain the right to give orders to the Prosecution Service once they are in power.

Moreover, there are considerable concerns from a legal perspective. Politicians and some researchers argue that the power of the prosecution service – like every other power of the state in democratic countries – has to derive from democratically elected institutions.[24] According to this view, the Minister is accountable to Parliament for the work of the Prosecution Service on constitutional grounds. Hence, it should be a democratic logic that the Minister is entitled to supervise and to instruct the prosecutors. And in fact, I believe it is important to avoid the prosecution service becoming an autonomous state within a state.[25] This is necessary for constitutional reasons, but also in order to preserve the public trust into the justice system. But in order to meet this goal, it is not indispensable to stick to the Minister's right to give instructions in individual cases. Prosecutors are bound to the law and the principle of legality anyway. The crucial point is whether effective mechanisms of a legal control of prosecution decisions are in operation. Thus, it is rather a question of the prosecutor's accountability than of the Minister's right to give certain instructions to the Prosecution Service.

The European Impact

While there is no political majority in Germany to abolish the Minister's right to give directions at the moment, it might well be that the most important impetus will be an external one from the European level. Independence of prosecution decisions has become a major issue in the process that should result in the foundation of a European Prosecution Service, which should be responsible for the prosecution of offences affecting the financial interests of the Union. Since the Treaty of Lisbon in 2009, the establishment of a European Prosecution Authority had been a permanent object of negotiations between the EU member states. In October 2017, 20 member states agreed on a regulation implementing enhanced cooperation on the establishment of the European Public Prosecutor's Office. According to Art. 6 (1) of that regulation, the Prosecutor's Office (EPPO) "shall be independent" and its staff shall

> (…) neither seek nor take instructions from any person external to the EPPO, any Member State of the European Union or any institution, body, office or agency of the Union in the performance of their duties (…)[26]

Also the European Parliament has always emphasised that the envisaged authority should be "fully independent of national governments and the EU institutions and protected from political influence and pressure".[27]

Among the EU members, there seems to be a majority of states today that take it for granted that prosecutors act completely independent of the government.[28] The German law appears to be a rather exceptional case,[29] sometimes carefully criticised by EU institutions. Although the Council of Europe's Group of States against Corruption (GRECO) concluded in January 2015 that the judiciary and the prosecution service in Germany are of high quality and that the system ensures integrity and prevents corruption, the Group also referred critically to the right of Ministers of Justice to give instructions to public prosecutors in individual cases. Concerning the Prosecution Service, GRECO recommends, that "steps should be taken to ensure that the justice system is free from, and seen to be free from, political influence".[30]

At least, small steps have been taken in Germany towards more independence from the political level in recent years. And this is partly due to the relevant debate at the European level: until the beginning of the twenty-first century, the Heads of Prosecution Authorities (*Generalstaatsanwaelte*) in most states were employed as Political Civil Servants, with the consequence that they could be dismissed by the Minister at any time without any specific reason in order to ensure the Minister's influence on criminal policy. By 2010, all German states had changed this condition of employment so that the head of a prosecution authority has gained a little more independence from the particular government.

The Future of the Prosecution Service in Germany

What are the essential objectives to achieve for a Prosecution Service in a constitutional justice system? Prosecutors should

1. Do their work impartially
2. Enforce the law, independent of extraneous considerations, especially political and economic influences
3. Prosecution decisions should be perceived as just decisions, based on transparent criteria

Abolishing the Minister's right to give directions to the Prosecution Service in individual cases is not the only way to achieve these goals. Nevertheless, it is time for Germany to abolish this right, mainly because of political reasons. This step would improve the reputation of the prosecution system and the public trust in its impartiality. Thus, abandoning the Minister's right to give directions in individual cases would be in the interest of a criminal justice system in a democratic state, that strives for broad public acceptance. Although Ministers have relied very rarely on this right in the past, the few occasions when they did so have gained massive public attention. Individual directions, even if they are reasonable and in accordance with the law, leave the people with the impression that the administration of justice depends on the political will of the respective government.

Abolishing the Minister's power, however, is no guarantee for an independent Prosecution Service. Politically motivated influence is often practised with much subtlety and concealment, by means of official directives.[31] Leading prosecutors report that the Ministry of Justice has other means to make the government's position and expectations clear. Informal strategies like "asking" the prosecutor for frequent reports on a case, "discussing" the legal and political aspects with the prosecutors in charge and expressing the Minister's view to the Chief Prosecutor might be a gateway for undue influence that could be much more important than the legal relationship between the institutions. Especially if prosecutors have an interest in climbing the career ladder, informally expressed views of supervisors and representatives of the Ministry might be crucial factors in the decision-making process.

This is an inherent problem of every hierarchical organisation and it cannot be resolved by changing the law alone.[32] It requires more transparency in decision-making and effective procedures for the parties involved to control prosecution decisions. Furthermore, a free and independent media that is able to report critically on criminal justice decisions is essential to ensure a just decision-making process. Not least, we need self-confident prosecutors who show sufficient moral courage to resist any influences that are politically motivated – even though this resistance might not make their work any easier.

Government should, on the other hand, continue to give general directives to prosecution authorities. Most criminal justice systems are, like the German one, very much characterised by prosecutorial discretion. Discretion, however, needs certain criteria in order to ensure a – more or less – consistent and transparent delivery of justice. Some prosecutors criticise that the criminal justice systems in the different states have become "playgrounds for the Ministers of Justice".[33] That might be true sometimes, but it is questionable whether such a situation has to be regarded as a problem: the law and the legal system is inevitably the result of a political process, and the criminal justice system needs permanent reform. Criminal policy is nowadays – and should remain in the future – a matter of politics. If the law allows the use of discretion, democratically elected governments should be entitled to set priorities in the application of the criminal law, to issue guidelines, e.g. on the termination of proceedings in cases of minor crimes and on how the prosecution should deal with certain types of offences.

Concerning the internal structure of the Prosecution Service, it seems to be necessary to maintain a hierarchy in order to ensure a uniform application of the law. However, the Chief Prosecutors should only be entitled to control whether the subordinated prosecutors act in accordance with the law and relevant guidelines. Once a prosecutor has been involved in a case, the Head of the local Prosecution authority should not have the right to withdraw it from him or her anymore. The Chief Prosecutor's right to withdraw cases from a prosecutor in charge and to entrust it to another employee, as it currently exists in Germany (*Devolutionsrecht* and *Substitutionsrecht*), cannot be justified. It invites the Chief Prosecutor to exercise undue influence on the proceedings.

Nevertheless, it would not be appropriate to give prosecutors the complete independence of a judge, who is not supervised by anyone but the appeal court with regard to the content and lawfulness of his or her decisions.[34] Prosecution authorities are already powerful institutions in the criminal justice system. If individual prosecutors gain complete independence, their position in the criminal justice system will become even stronger and the difference between prosecutors and judges will be further diminished. Since prosecutors are not only responsible for the decision whether or not to charge someone, but also for the investigation process, they should be under the supervision of someone who is not directly involved in the particular case.

Finally, the decisions on hiring new prosecutors, internal promotions and the spending of money should remain with the Ministry of Justice. I do not believe that a change of these organisational issues would really improve the independence of prosecution decisions at large. Chronic problems concerning staff and financial resources will not be resolved because someone else has to deal with them.

Conclusions

I have tried to point out that criminal legislation, as well as the criminal procedure law, are increasingly characterised by discretion as a result of laws that are open to different interpretation and by the increasing importance of out-of-court decisions. The crucial point is not so much the relationship between Ministers and the Prosecution Service, but rather the fact that criminal laws allow a widespread use of discretion – and that prosecutors are almost compelled to make use of their discretionary power because the administration of criminal justice would be far too expensive and time-consuming otherwise. We should consider a genuine decriminalisation of certain types of behaviour instead of sticking to a system of decriminalisation by means of prosecutorial discretion that raises problems as to the criteria of decision-making and problems of accountability.

Democratic states have to guarantee that prosecutors are able to do their jobs impartially and free of undue political influences. The government's right to give direct orders concerning individual cases is a potential threat to this objective as well as to the reputation and public acceptance of a criminal justice system. Such a right, as it exists in Germany, should be abolished as soon as possible. Nevertheless, it is the function of elected governments to set the general course of criminal policy. Therefore, Ministers should be entitled to issue general guidelines to the Prosecution Service for dealing with certain types of offences. These guidelines are also necessary to ensure a minimum of uniformity in the application of the law.

When discussing prosecution systems, we should not just focus on the organisational and legal framework for prosecution services but also consider the criminal law. The root of the problem is the fact that the criminal law has become increasingly vague, and that the law gives a considerable amount of discretion – and subsequently power – to the prosecution. Diversion at the pre-trial stage has been a very successful strategy from a criminological perspective and has reduced the fiscal burden on criminal justice systems. Simultaneously, it has turned the prosecutor into a kind of pre-trial judge. With the increase of the prosecution's power, the public attention to and critique of its decisions has been increased as well. Decriminalisation of certain types of offences would be a more appropriate way of dealing with the high number of cases, which are usually not taken to court anyway.

Notes

1 *Sueddeutsche Zeitung*, 3 August 2015. www.sz.de/1.2592126.
2 *Suedeutsche Zeitung*, 4 August 2015. www.sz.de/1.2595895.
3 *Sueddeutsche Zeitung*, 20 May 2015. www.sz.de/1.2488240.
4 C Roxin and B Schuenemann, *Strafverfahrensrecht* (Muenchen, C.H. Beck, 2017) § 9 A II.
5 Verordnung ueber die Einfuehrung des muendlichen und oeffentlichen Verfahrens mit Geschworenen in Untersuchungssachen, 3 January 1849 (PrGS 1849).
6 Von Liszt, F., "Vortrag im Berliner Anwaltsverein am 23. Maerz 1901" *(1901)* 8 *Deutsche Juristen-Zeitung* 179, 180.
7 H-C. Schaefer, "Die Staatsanwaltschaft – ein politisches Instrument?" – inMichalke, R. *et al.* (eds) *Festschrift fuer Rainer Hamm* (Berlin: De Gruyter, 2008).
8 E. Schmidt, *Einfuehrung in die Geschichte der deutschen Strafrechtspflege* (Goettingen: Vandenhoek & Ruprecht, 1947), 295.
9 P. Collin, *Waechter der Gesetze oder Organ der Staatsregierung?* (Frankfurt am Main: Klostermann, 2000), 406; K. Pfoertner, "Die deutsche Staatsanwaltschaft: Marionetten der Politik?" (2008) *Kritische Vierteljahresschrift fuer Gesetzgebung und Rechtswissenschaft* 455, 456; E. Carsten/E. Rautenberg, *Die Geschichte der Staatsanwaltschaft in Deutschland bis zur Gegenwart* (Baden-Baden: Nomos, 2012), 515.
10 Data for the year 2015; Source: Statistisches Bundesamt (ed.), *Rechtspflege. Staatsanwaltschaften. Fachserie 10* (Wiesbaden, 2016) 26. "Cleared cases suitable for prosecution" do not include cases which were dropped because there was no sufficient evidence or because the case was connected to another criminal trial. Percentages do not add up to 100 due to rounding.
11 E. Kausch, *Der Staatsanwalt: Ein Richter vor dem Richter? Untersuchungen zum § 153a StPO* (Berlin: Duncker & Humblot, 1980).
12 § 257c Strafprozessordnung (StPO).
13 Schnoor, Giesen and Addicks argue that German prosecutors are never entitled to give personal data of a suspect to the media: Schnoor, C., T. Giesen and L. Addicks, "Mitteilungen der Staatsanwaltschaften an die Presse ohne Datenschutz" (2016) *Neue Zeitschrift fuer Strafrecht* 256, 263.
14 C. Danziger, *Die Medialisierung des Strafprozesses* (Berlin: Berliner Wissenschaftsverlag, 2009) 376 f.
15 V. Bugliosi, *The Prosecution of George W. Bush for Murder* (New York: Vanguard Press, 2008).
16 Der Tagesspiegel, 17 December 2014. www.tagesspiegel.de/politik/anzeigen-gegen-mitglieder-der-bush-regierung-folterpraktiken-der-cia-us-praesident-und-mitarbeiter-sollen-vor-gericht/11128678.html.
17 *Handelsblatt*, 29 October 2015. www.handelsblatt.com/12517612.html.
18 S. Huels, *Polizeiliche und staatsanwaltliche Ermittlungstätigkeit: Machtzuwachs und Kontrollverlust* (Berlin: Berliner Wissenschaftsverlag, 2007) 185.
19 Such a provision was introduced in 2013 in the French law; Art. 30 of the Code de Procedure Penale.
20 Suggestions of the professional association Deutscher Richterbund, *Zehn-Punkte-Papier zur Staerkung des Rechtsstaats* (Berlin: Deutscher Richterbund e.V., 2013) 2.

21 This has been suggested by the left-wing party *Die Linke*, the German Liberal Party *F.D.P.* and the *Neue Richtervereinigung*, an association of judges and prosecutors, see: www.neuerichter.de/details/artikel/article/plaedoyer-fuer-den-unabhaengigen-staatsanwalt-121.html.

22 According to a survey conducted by Deutscher Richterbund. www.drb.de/cms/index.php?id=939.

23 European Commission, *Flash Eurobarometer 385: Justice in the EU, Summary* (Brussels: European Commission, 2013) 4. www.ec.europa.eu/public_opinion/flash/fl_385_sum_en.pdf.

24 G. Andoor, "Abhaengige Staatsanwaelte: Und das ist auch gut so" (2015) *Legal Tribune Online* 8 August 2015, www.lto.de/persistent/a_id/16547/. H. Hund, "Deutsche Staatsanwaltschaften im Blickpunkt" (2015) *Juristen Alumni Trier*, www.uni-trier.de/fileadmin/fb5/ALU/Jahrheft_2013-14__1_.pdf.

25 Federico argues that this is what happened in Italy: G. di Federico, Prosecutorial independence and the democratic requirement of accountability in Italy (1998) *The British Journal of Criminology* 371, 384.

26 Council Regulation (EU) 2017/1939 of 12 October 2017, Article 6. www.db.eurocrim.org/db/en/doc/2107.pdf.

27 European Parliament Resolution, 29 April 2015.

28 E. Rautenberg, "Die Geschichte der Staatsanwaltschaft in Deutschland" (2014) *Neue Juristische Wochenschrift NJW-Aktuell* 12; Albrecht identifies a "common European concern" to ensure the independence of the prosecution process, although prosecutors are still dependent on the Executive in some European jurisdictions: P-A. Albrecht, "Sicherungsmechanismen fuer Autonomie und Unabhaengigkeit der Justiz" (2014) *Kritische Vierteljahresschrift fuer Gesetzgebung und Rechtsprechung* 387, 418.

29 M. Wilke, *Staatsanwaelte als Anwaelte des Staates?* (Goettingen: V&R unipress, 2015), 308.

30 Council of the European Union, *"Greco-report 2015"* (Brussels: Council of the European Union, 2015), 3. www.go.coe.int/jmE4E.

31 H-C. Schaefer, "Die Staatsanwaltschaft" (n 7).

32 Ibid.

33 C. Frank, "Grußwort zur Mitgliederversammlung" *3 Mitgliederzeitschrift des Vereins der Richter und Staatsanwaelte Baden-Wuerttemberg* (2014), 30, 31. www.richterverein-bw.de/medien/mitteilungen03-2014.pdf.

34 See also: Bundesministerium der Justiz (ed.), *Das Verhaeltnis von Gericht, Staatsanwaltschaft und Polizei im Ermittlungsverfahren, strafprozessuale Regeln und faktische (Fehl-?) Entwicklungen* (Berlin: Bundesministerium der Justiz, 2008) 41.

Bibliography

Albrecht, P-A. (2014) "Sicherungsmechanismen fuer Autonomie und Unabhaengigkeit der Justiz" *Kritische Vierteljahresschrift fuer Gesetzgebung und Rechtsprechung* 387.

Andoor, G (2015) "Abhaengige Staatsanwaelte: Und das ist auch gut so" *Legal Tribune Online 08.08.2015.*

Carsten, E. and E. Rautenberg (2012) *Die Geschichte der Staatsanwaltschaft in Deutschland bis zur Gegenwart* (Baden-Baden: Nomos-Verlag).

Collin, P. (2000) *"Waechter der Gesetze' oder "Organ der Staatsregierung"? Konzipierung, Einrichtung und Anleitung der Staatsanwaltschaft durch das preußische Justizministerium. Von den Anfaengen bis 1860* (Frankfurt am Main: Klostermann).

Council of Europe, Group of States against Corruption (Greco) (2015) *Evaluation Report Germany* (Strasbourg: Council of Europe).

Danziger, C. (2009) *Die Medialisierung des Strafprozesses. Eine Untersuchung zum Verhaeltnis von Medien und Strafprozess* (Berlin: Berliner Wissenschaftsverlag).

Di Federico, G. (1998) "Prosecutorial independence and the democratic requirement of accountability in Italy" *The British Journal of Criminology* 3: 371.

Frank, C. (2014) "Grußwort zur Mitgliederversammlung" *Mitgliederzeitschrift des Vereins der Richter und Staatsanwaelte Baden-Wuerttemberg* 3: 30.

Huels, S. (2007) *Polizeiliche und staatsanwaltliche Ermittlungstätigkeit: Machtzuwachs und Kontrollverlust* (Berlin: Berliner Wissenschaftsverlag).

Hund, H. (2015) "Deutsche Staatsanwaltschaften im Blickpunkt: Weisungsrecht der Politik, Medien, Verstaendigung etc." *Juristen Alumni Trier, Jahrheft 2013/14* 16.

Kausch, E. (1980) *Der Staatsanwalt: Ein Richter vor dem Richter? Untersuchungen zum § 153a StPO* (Berlin: Duncker & Humblot).

Pfoertner, K. (2008) "Die deutsche Staatsanwaltschaft: Marionetten der Politik? Unabhaengigkeit muss sein" *Kritische Vierteljahresschrift fuer Gesetzgebung und Rechtswissenschaft* 455.

Rautenberg, E. (2014) "Die Geschichte der Staatsanwaltschaft in Deutschland" *Neue Juristische Wochenschrift NJW-Aktuell*, 12.

Roxin, C. and B. Schuenemann (2017) "*Strafverfahrensrecht: Ein Studienbuch*" 29th edn (München: C.H. Beck).

Schaefer, H-C. (2008) "Die Staatsanwaltschaft – ein politisches Instrument?" – in Michalke, R., W. Köberer, J. Pauly and S. Kirsch (eds) *Festschrift fuer Rainer Hamm* (Berlin: De Gruyter), pp. 643–654.

Schnoor, C., T. Giesen and L. Addicks (2016) "Mitteilungen der Staatsanwaltschaften an die Presse ohne Datenschutz" *Neue Zeitschrift fuer Strafrecht* 256.

Wilke, M. (2015) *Staatsanwaelte als Anwaelte des Staates?* (Goettingen: V&R unipress).

14 Prosecutorial Independence and Effectiveness of the Nigerian Criminal Justice System

Adedeji Adekunle

Introduction

An independent prosecution system is no guarantee for an efficient criminal justice system where autonomy is not complemented with accountability. Constitutional prescriptions for autonomy of the Prosecutor or Attorney General often insulate the tenure of the prosecutor without necessarily addressing public interest and the duty of the prosecutor to act consistently with it.

The expectation that a prosecutor should act neutrally, implies that some mechanism of defining, monitoring and ensuring that neutrality is employed is in place. Less obvious is the requirement of accountability. A legal system based on respect for the rule of law also needs strong, independent and impartial prosecutors who are willing resolutely to investigate and prosecute suspected crimes regardless of the status of the suspect.

However, finding the appropriate balance between prosecutorial independence and accountability is challenging. Prosecutorial authorities must be sufficiently independent from external influence to permit the fair and impartial application of the law and prosecution policy. Yet prosecutors should be sufficiently transparent and accountable to the public to help ensure that prosecutorial authority is not abused.[1] One may then ask – what is the essential measure of independence for a prosecution service or what measure of accountability to society or political actors is necessary?

A review of international standards and state practice shows that a prosecution service must be able to provide neutral, non-political, non-arbitrary decision-making about the application of criminal law and policy to real cases. To ensure this, the institutional decisional independence of the entire prosecution service appears to be more important than the independence of the individual prosecutor. In this work therefore, we primarily explore the concepts of independence, accountability and security of tenure of a prosecutor in Nigeria in the context of the Nigerian legal system.

It is important to state at the outset that extant constitutional arrangements in Nigeria confer primacy on the Attorney General of the Federation (AGF) over federal offences.[2] By dint of his powers to initiate, take over and discontinue criminal proceedings, even those initiated by other prosecutorial bodies, the

AGF is undoubtedly the Chief prosecutor. There is need therefore to enquire what guides the exercise of these powers and what kind of relationship exists between the AGF and other agencies with powers of prosecution.

We also examine the arguments for the separation of the office of the Attorney General of the Federation (AGF) from the Minister of Justice particularly in light of recent constitutional proposals. The chapter will also examine the contention whether the Office of the Director of Public Prosecutions (DPP) should be under the office of the AG. It will further be contended in this chapter that independence or autonomy is not simply a question of security of tenure but also invites a review of budgetary and funding arrangements as well as objective oversight mechanisms.

Public Prosecutions in Nigeria

The Constitution of the Federal Republic of Nigeria, 1999, confers wide prosecutorial powers on the Attorney General of the Federation who is also the Minister of Justice. Under section 211 of the Constitution identical powers are also conferred on Attorneys General of the 36 states of the Federation in respect of state offences.

An Attorney General (state or federal) is therefore constitutionally empowered to institute, undertake, take over, continue or discontinue criminal proceedings depending on whether these are federal or state proceedings before any court in Nigeria.[3] Prosecutorial powers are also conferred on the specialised law enforcement agencies under their enabling statutes. Hitherto, police officers could routinely initiate prosecutions in any court on account of the Police Act[4] and the laws regulating Criminal Procedure in the states of the federation.

However recent legislation – the Administration of Criminal Justice Act 2015 – has restricted prosecutions at all levels to legal practitioners. While this has excluded lay police prosecutors from prosecutions, lawyers in the Police force may still undertake prosecutions subject to the prerogative of the AG to take over such prosecutions. The ACJA is however a federal Act and its scope limited to federal offences and criminal proceedings in the Federal Capital, Abuja and the federal courts. Interestingly, some state versions of ACJA have declined to restrict police prosecutions. There have also been some consequential adjustments in budgetary and manpower planning by the Federal and State Ministries of Justice to enable them effectively to take over these cases.

Office of the Attorney General

In Nigeria, the Offices of the Attorney General and Minister for Justice are fused and situated within the Ministry of Justice under the executive arm of Government.[5] This statutory provision implies that an appointee of the President performs the dual functions of Chief Law Officer/Prosecutor of the Federation and Minister of Justice. He therefore exercises the powers and functions of the prosecutor either personally or through delegated officials as well as coordinates the relationship between the Executive and Judicial arms of government in a manner that ensures the harmonious co-existence of the arms while maintaining their independence.[6]

The Ministry of Justice is the legal arm of the Federal Government of Nigeria, primarily concerned with handling cases before the judiciary that are initiated or defended by the government. It is headed by the AGF/Minister of Justice. Within the hierarchy of authority, the Permanent Secretary of the Ministry, who also doubles as the Solicitor-General of the Federation, is next in line after the AGF. The Ministry of Justice is structured into various departments with specific functions assigned accordingly such as Law Reporting, Citizens' Rights and in particular the Department of Public Prosecutions through which the prosecutorial powers of the AGF are exercised.

The Department of Public Prosecution is one of the mainstream departments in the Federal Ministry of Justice. Its primary functions include: proffering legal advice or opinion to the Nigeria Police and other law enforcement agencies, ministries and extra-ministerial departments on criminal matters; public prosecution of accused persons in all courts of competent jurisdiction; and instituting, taking over or discontinuing criminal action in courts of competent jurisdiction on behalf of the AGF.[7]

The Director of Public Prosecution of the Federation (DPPF) heads the department. The DPPF is a staff member of the Ministry of Justice and under the direct supervision of the AGF. The AGF therefore has the final authority on whether to institute, take over or discontinue any criminal proceedings. Such powers include taking over the prosecution, giving directions or altogether discontinuing the prosecution. This latter course, known as *nolle prosequi*, cannot be questioned by the court. When this power is used, the Attorney General has been described by the courts as a "master unto himself".[8]

The Attorney General's supervisory authority extends to prosecutions also undertaken by other prosecutorial bodies including prosecutions initiated by other law enforcement agencies like the Independent Anti-corruption Commission and the National Drug law Enforcement Agency. This power is no doubt far reaching and invites a consideration of what factors weigh on a decision whether to stop or take over prosecutions. Some indication of the factors that the AGF will consider before intervening in proceedings is provided under the Guidelines for Federal Prosecutors[9] which outlines steps that should be taken by all federal prosecutorial bodies before and during the prosecution of any matter. These guidelines highlight critical parameters to benchmark the public interest and materiality of a case in different situations. Thus an autonomous prosecuting service, by dint of the constitutional power over prosecutions, is still subject to the supervisory mandate of the Attorney General. Although control does not mean that the AGF should take over prosecutorial decisions of these agencies, his right to undertake selective or wholesale review of case files is not in doubt.[10] The exceptional case in which the Attorney General intervenes in such prosecutions and overrides the decision of such an agency is often justified on policy grounds or public interest. In some countries a strong press and public opinion may sufficiently moderate the level of political interference.[11]

Independence of the Prosecutor

The concept of Prosecutorial independence is not an end in itself; it is intended to put the prosecutor in a situation where he or she can take the right decision in a case without fear or favour, without being subjected to undue pressure from another source, whether it be the media, politicians, the police, a victim seeking revenge or even misguided public opinion. The subject cannot, of course, be looked at in isolation from broader considerations of the function of the prosecutor in upholding the rule of law, one of which is accountability, and these will also be discussed in this chapter.

In an earlier work[12] we proposed the following parameters as an ideal model of independence:

a The appointment and removal process must not expose the prosecutor(s) to political pressure or arbitrary decisions.
b The decisions of the prosecutor must in general be free from interference and be based on transparent and professional standards.
c The prosecutor must not be unnecessarily hampered by funding constraints and the agency must account directly to the legislature and not through some other agency.
d Prosecutors must, where there are other prosecuting agencies, operate under uniform and objective standards or code.

A prosecutor is therefore expected to carry out the fundamental duty of diligent prosecution independently, yet in the general public interest. It is apposite to note that it is the institutional independence of the entire prosecution service that is important and not the independence of the individual prosecutor who invariably is under the supervisory authority of a superior. This essentially means that independence of a prosecutor transcends the individual basis and must be viewed within an institutional framework.

Notwithstanding this, the individuals to be appointed or recruited as Attorney General and State Counsel respectively, must possess basic competence, integrity and good standing in society. It is necessary to distinguish between the interests of society and the interests of the state. Conducting an independent prosecution is in the interests of society; it is not for the benefit of the executive or of other state organisations. Therefore, the independence of prosecutors should also be seen as a tool to protect the interests of citizens.[13]

Institutional Location of the Prosecution and External Factors

To what extent do relations with other bodies and state functionaries, for example the executive and the legislature arms as well as the police and other investigative bodies, guarantee freedom from political or bureaucratic pressure? The independence of the prosecutor is a hollow concept without guaranteed financial and material resources. This entails the provision of the finance necessary to initiate and to carry out investigations, to prosecute offences in the courts and to properly carry out their other duties. This may also involve access to information, investigative tools and the availability of adequate support staff.

A prosecutorial organ may be properly defined as a state institution that complies with three basic criteria.[14] First is the competence and authority to investigate a crime (gathering information/evidence or instructing the police to gather such information/evidence). The second criterion is the discretionary power to indict or press charges and the third, representation of the interests of the public. Expectedly, such an organ with wide discretionary powers must be seen to be independent and accountable.

Prosecutorial independence is inevitably dependent on the location of the prosecutorial organ in the structure of government and also the rules governing appointment and career of the office. Institutional location may be such that the prosecutor is shielded from or exposed to political pressures from other branches of government.

A review of the prosecutorial systems of other jurisdictions shows that the prosecutorial organ may be located within the executive branch (as in the US, Mexico or Uruguay), within the judiciary (as in Italy, Colombia or Costa Rica), or it can be an autonomous institution (as in Chile, Guatemala or Switzerland).[15]

It has been argued that prosecutorial organs that are located within the executive branch are more likely subject to political pressures from the incumbent government, thus leaving prosecution of certain criminal cases dependent on the inclination or disposition of the government in power. In contrast, when the prosecutorial organ is located within the judiciary, public prosecutors are expected to enjoy the same degree of independence from government as judges do. In such case, overall prosecutorial independence would depend on judicial independence. And, finally, a prosecutorial organ designed as an autonomous state institution is expected to be less likely to misuse prosecutorial discretion due to pressures from external political forces.

Appointment and Tenure of the Prosecutor

Notwithstanding the constitutional provisions of appointing at least one Minister from every state of the Nigerian Federation,[16] the President has unfettered discretion to appoint and dismiss any Minister of the Federation. Thus, a ministerial appointment, beyond statutory requirements, is at the pleasure of the President with no definitive tenure prescribed by the Constitution. Section 147 (1) of the 1999 Constitution provides that "there shall be such offices of Ministers of the Government of the Federation as may be established by the President". The heads of such offices known as Ministers are then appointed by the President subject to the confirmation of nominations by the Legislature (Senate).[17]

Situating the above scenario within the Nigerian criminal justice system, it is noteworthy that the 1999 Constitution has explicit provisions for the Office of the AGF with the added requirement that the holder of the Office of the AGF shall also be a Minister of the Government.[18] Evidently therefore the Office of the AGF is located within the executive arm of government as the Ministry of Justice. The likelihood of political exposure and influence by the executive over the Attorney General/Minister of Justice appears quite high, considering that the Minister is a political appointee of the President like all other ministers. Consequently, with the executive having absolute authority over the career of the AGF/Minister, the likelihood that he will behave according to the preferences of the President is higher.

The knowledge that the office of AGF is not protected by specified tenure – meaning that the occupant can be dismissed at any time and for any reason – substantially waters down the independence of the office of the AGF as prosecutor. Very few occupants of the office can in such circumstances exercise their discretionary powers independent of the political inclinations of the executive, especially in the investigation and prosecution of political office holders or politically exposed persons.

Insecurity of tenure and its baleful effect on the independence of the prosecutor becomes quite significant given that the involvement of the legislature in the appointment of ministers, is permissible by the Constitution only in the process of appointing ministers including the AGF.[19] Thus, a decision to terminate the appointment of a minister may be exercised by the President without reference to any person or organ of government. It therefore appears that the independence of the AGF in his prosecutorial capacity will be better preserved if the legislature is also required to confirm any purported termination by the President. No member of cabinet enjoys such security of tenure under the present constitution. In fact such a proposal is contrary to the President's prerogative to hire and fire ministers under the Presidential system prescribed in the Constitution. It appears that in order to implement such a proposal, the Attorney General's office would have to be severed by constitutional amendment from that of the Minister of Justice. Arguments for such separation in Nigeria have been canvassed in recent years on the grounds that the fusion of the two offices facilitates abuse of power. Notably also, a Constitutional National Conference in 2014 recommended the separation of the office of the Minister of Justice from that of the Attorney General of the Federation (AGF) and further proposed that the AGF should be a career civil servant who would be less susceptible to political pressure in the discharge of duties, while the Minister of Justice would be appointed by the President as a member of cabinet.[20]

Also citing the need to insulate the very important office of the AGF from political impediments and interferences, the National Assembly passed the Constitution of the Federal Republic of Nigeria (Fourth Alteration) Act 2015 which, inter alia, sought to amend the constitution by establishing the Office of Minister of Justice separate from the Office of the AGF; prescribing the qualifications of an AGF; and guaranteeing the independence of the Office of the AGF through financial autonomy and security of tenure.[21] However, the bill was not signed by then President Goodluck Jonathan because it allegedly did not comply with the special majority requirements prescribed by section 9(3) of the Constitution.[22]

Mechanisms for Accountability and Efficiency

It must be noted that an absolutely unchecked prosecution service may result in inefficient use of resources, wide discretion and a lack of focus.[23] The key element therefore, is the ability of the prosecution to accomplish legitimate, publicly desirable goals and objectives, while effectively resisting improper interferences. In a democracy, the principle of accountability holds that government officials, whether elected or appointed, are responsible to the public for their decisions and actions. The concept of accountability is central to the idea of democratic governance based on the rule of law. In the absence of accountability, elections and the notion of the will of the people lose their meaning, and government has the potential to become arbitrary and self-serving.

The makers of the Nigerian Constitution in creating the office of the "Attorney General of the Federation" added the qualification that the occupant of the office shall be a "Minister of the Government", suggesting that at least in concept, these are two separable positions.[24] The Constitution therefore did not intend an Attorney General to be controlled by the Executive or the Federal Government but one whose mandate extends to all constituents of the Federation. It prescribes further that in the exercise of his constitutional powers the Attorney General shall have regard to public interest, the interest of justice and the need to prevent abuse of legal process.[25]

No doubt, the gravity of powers wielded by a prosecutor within the criminal justice system requires that the prosecutor should be accountable for the way in which the prosecutorial discretion is exercised.[26] However the Nigerian Constitution prescribes no measure for reviewing the Attorney General's decision when he acts outside the consideration of public good or the interest of justice. In the exercise of his powers for example, the AGF may discontinue a criminal proceeding. The power to discontinue, known as *nolle prosequi*, is not subject to any form of judicial scrutiny to determine the propriety or otherwise of the decision. This power as exercised by the AGF elevates him to the status of a "master unto himself" as stated by the court in *The State v Ilori.*[27] This suggests that nothing short of express constitutional amendment to subject to judicial review the decision of the AGF whether to prosecute a matter or not, or whether to discontinue criminal proceedings, will better meet the requirement for accountability of the prosecution in the interest of the public and reduce arbitrary decisions made by a public prosecutor.

Some Recent Developments in Nigeria

If judicial review is an unlikely tool of accountability, the question may be asked whether any other form of accountability measures can be brought to bear on the exercise of powers of the AGF. To what extent for example can a body of prosecutors undertake peer review of prosecutorial decisions? This appears to be the rationale for constituting the National Prosecution Coordination Committee

(NPCC)[28] albeit its mandate is limited to high profile cases that are of public interest as determined by the AGF.

Among other functions, the role of the NPCC is to advise the AGF on the exercise of his prosecutorial powers in Sections 150 and 174 of the 1999 Constitution, prepare a policy strategy document for the coordination of investigation and prosecution of high profile criminal cases in Nigeria and to also collate the list of such cases as well as assigning them to external prosecutors. The Committee is expected to scrutinise the proof of evidence and charges in high-profile criminal cases in the country before arraignment. In addition, it will receive and analyse reports from the investigation and prosecution teams engaged to handle such cases. It is doubtful whether in discharge of its advisory mandate, the NPCC can effectively supervise the AGF. In the first place the constitutional powers of the AGF are intact – he in fact chairs the NPCC, and apparently has a discretion in the choice of cases he refers to the Committee.

The NPCC appears to be motivated by the need to expedite the investigation and prosecution of "high profile cases". It remains to be seen if this objective will be achieved.[29] One regrettable aspect of the NPCC mandate is the institutionalisation of contracting out prosecutions to external lawyers. This is a grave derogation of the mandate of the office of the DPP and an inefficient use of services resourced and domiciled in the Federal Ministry of Justice. In our view this committee cannot therefore be seen as a check on the powers of the AGF, rather it appears to further reinforce the control and powers of the AGF over certain categories of prosecutions.[30]

A second perspective on control of prosecutorial discretion is provided by the relatively new Administration of Criminal Justice Act (ACJA 2015) which although it may not have gone as far as enabling judicial review prescribes safeguards and procedure that prosecutors, including the AGF, must conform to in the interest of an efficient criminal justice system. The ACJA 2015 aims to ensure that the system of administration of criminal justice in Nigeria is efficient in the management of criminal justice institutions, speedy dispensation of justice, protection of the society from crime and protection of the rights and interest of the suspect, the defendant and the victim.

With the ACJA 2015 there is a deliberate effort to transform the criminal justice system from its present state of retributive justice into a restorative justice system. The ACJA 2015 also addresses a wide range of issues that had prior to this time slowed down the criminal justice system, which in turn resulted in a poor output in terms of number of dispensed (either convicted, discharged or acquitted) criminal cases by the judiciary and an increased number of awaiting trial inmates. In addressing these issues the ACJA is divided into 49 parts addressing various fields of criminal justice administration. Although its application is for now limited to federal courts and institutions, many of the states of the Federation are in the process of enacting state versions of the Act. The ACJA 2015 impacts on the accountability of prosecutions in three main respects.

First, by virtue of section 106 of the Act, lay police prosecutors are excluded from undertaking prosecution of any offence. This effectively overrules a previous decision of the Supreme Court that affirmed that a lay police officer could undertake prosecution.[31] Section 106 of the Act however permits police officers who are lawyers to prosecute. Lay police prosecutors are required to hand over case files either to the Legal Department of the Police or the Federal Ministry of Justice. An immediate consequence of this provision is the increase in budgetary outlay for the recruitment and training of law officers in the Federal Ministry of Justice.

Second, the Attorney General or the Director of Public Prosecutions has an important role to play when it comes to instituting proceedings. One of the traditional roles is that of evaluating the material facts of a case investigated by the Police or security agency and advising on whether a prosecution should be instituted. ACJA 2015 prescribes in remand cases that such advice should issue within 14 days of receiving the case file.[32] The failure to comply with this timeline may result in the discharge of a suspect from remand.[33] This is to ensure that the time of the courts is not wasted on frivolous charges but that the court, prosecutors and defendants get on with serious business and expend resources on suspects with prima facie cases to answer.

Third, the ACJA 2015 preserves the prosecutor's discretion to accept a plea bargain but prescribes guidelines to prevent abuse especially as to what the prosecutor must consider before entering a plea bargain with the defendant. Hitherto diverse forms of discontinuance (more appropriately termed withdrawals) were permitted under Nigerian criminal procedural laws[34] although it is not always clear what the motives behind such withdrawals are. Lately there has been an increased propensity to resort to these provisions in order to enter into plea agreements with an accused person or a suspect.

Under section 270 of the ACJA 2015 the prosecutor may enter into a plea bargain after consultation with all the parties directly concerned including the victim of the offence.[35] A copy of the agreement must be sent to the AG after it has been reached. The court is not however bound to accept the agreement, as it may come to the conclusion that the sentence recommended is not proportional to the offence that the defendant pled guilty to.

The provisions of the ACJA 2015 show that it is possible to strike a balance between the requirements for independence and accountability without necessarily reviewing the Constitution or restructuring institutions. The present constitutional framework may not permit legislative supervision of the President's right to dismiss the AGF, but it certainly enables the legislature to prescribe, through laws, checks and safeguards on the exercise of prosecutorial powers.

The importance of legislative oversight in a Presidential system of government as a tool of accountability is also demonstrated by section 88 of the Constitution which enables the legislature to investigate the conduct of any public official with a view to exposing waste, corruption or inefficiency.[36] The importance of these provisions, coupled with the coercive powers of the legislature to compel attendance and obtain evidence, is often downplayed by the sensationalism that usually accompanies recourse to them by the legislature.[37] In our view these provisions, together with the routine interaction with the AGF, affords the legislature enough opportunity to effectively oversee prosecutorial functions.

Conclusion

This work examined the pertinent "ingredients" of independence that must be in place to ensure that the essential duty of the prosecution is achieved and finds that while there is the need for a certain level of autonomy for a sensitive office such as that of the "Chief Law Officer of the Federation", such autonomy must be complemented with accountability.

This buttresses the position that independence of a prosecutor transcends the individual basis and must be viewed within an institutional framework. There must be constitutional safeguards to ensure that prosecutors, independently and impartially, evaluate investigation reports and prosecute suspected crimes committed even if these crimes have been committed by persons holding political or sensitive offices.

This chapter also finds that prosecutorial independence is inevitably dependent on the location of the prosecutorial organ in the structure of government and also the rules governing appointment and career of the office. Institutional location may be such that the prosecutor is shielded or exposed to political pressures from other branches of government, which again raises the issue whether separating the office of the AGF from that of the Minister of Justice is the one-time solution for that balance. However, in our view insulating the tenure of the prosecutor or Attorney General without necessarily addressing the concept of public interest and the duty of the prosecutor to act consistently with it, does not solve the problem of accountability. The ACJA 2015 deals with this pertinent condition by prescribing safeguards and procedure that prosecutors, including the AGF, must conform to in the interest of an efficient criminal justice system. Its provisions show that it is possible to strike a balance between the requirements for independence and accountability without necessarily reviewing the Constitution or restructuring institutions.

We therefore make the following recommendations:

a The Administration of Criminal Justice Laws should be passed by all the states of Nigeria and uniformity with the basic safeguards that the ACJA provides should be maintained.

b There should be an avenue where the prosecution services explain their practices as well as their high-profile decisions in individual cases to the public, without adversely affecting victims' rights. This is to ensure openness and transparency, which will engender public confidence.

c The office of the Attorney General should be secured by tenure so that Attorneys-General do not exercise their power with apprehension and feel compelled to fall in line with the political inclinations of the executive to keep their office.

d The legislature should be required to confirm any purported termination of the incumbent AGF by the President. Corresponding provisions should be made for Attorneys-General of states.

e The National Prosecution Coordination Committee (NPCC), even with its ad hoc status, should have a level of independence from the office of the AGF if it is to carry out its stated functions free from political manipulation. In addition, rather than outsource cases the committee should aim at resourcing and tasking prosecutors in the Ministry of Justice to undertake prosecutions in accordance with the law and extant prosecutorial guidelines.

Notes

1 Martin Schönteich, "Strengthening Prosecutorial Accountability in South Africa" (2014) Institute for Security Studies Paper Series, 255 www.issafrica.org/uploads/paper255.pdf (accessed 22 June 2016).
2 State Offences are offences created by laws of the State in accordance with section 4(7) of the 1999 Constitution e.g. The State Criminal Code. Federal offences are created by Acts of the National Assembly pursuant to the legislative powers of the Federal Parliament reserved under section 4(2)–(4) of the 1999 Constitution of the Federal Republic of Nigeria (CFRN) Cap C23 Laws of the Federation of Nigeria (LFN) 2004.
3 S. 174 CFRN. These provisions are replicated for the states of the Federation.
4 Cap P19 LFN 2004.
5 Section 150, CFRN.
6 Federal Ministry of Justice, "The Ministry: Functions" www.justice.gov.ng/index.php/about-us/who-we-are/function (accessed 28 May 2016).
7 Federal Ministry of Justice, "The Ministry: Public Prosecutions" www.justice.gov.ng/index.php/about-us/departments/public-prosecution (accessed 28 May 2016).
8 *State v Ilori* (1983) 1 SCNLR 94.
9 *Prosecutors Guidelines Applicable To A Prosecutor Of A Federal Offence And Any Prosecution At A Federal Court Or Court Of The Federal Capital Territory (FCT). 2014.* (Prosecutors Guidelines) A Code of Conduct for Prosecutors is also in force. These instruments are accessible on www.justice.gov.ng/index.php/78-featured/105-code-of-conduct.
10 Although a recent attempt to review case files of an independent prosecutorial agency (EFCC) was initially resisted this view of the law eventually prevailed. See A. Adesomoju, "EFCC bows to AGF, Releases 103 high profile Cases" *The Punch* (Nigeria 3 September 2017) http://punchng.com/efcc-bows-to-agf-releases-103-high-profile-cases/ (accessed 26 February 2018).
11 See Lord Goldsmith Q.C. "Politics Public Interest and Prosecutions – A View by the Attorney-General" an address delivered on 20 November 2001 at the 13th Annual Tom Sargent Memorial Lecture – accessible online at www.attorneygeneral.gov.uk/attachments/TOM%20/SARGENT.doc ((accessed 30 June 2007).
12 A.O. Adekunle: "Rule of Law and Prosecutorial policy in Nigeria" in E.A. Azinge and B Owasanoye (eds), *Rule of law and Good Governance* (NIALS Lagos, 2010).
13 The European Network of Councils for the Judiciary (ENCJ), "Independence and Accountability of the Judiciary and of the Prosecution: Performance Indicators 2015" (ENCJ Report 2014–2015) Www.rechtspraak.nl/sitecollectiondocuments/ENCJ%20report.pdf (accessed 25 June 2016).
14 See Ann Van Aaken, Eli Salzberger and Stefan Voigt, "The Prosecution of Public Figures and the Separation of Powers: Confusion within the Executive – A Conceptual Framework" (2004) Constitutional Political Economy 15(3)261www.researchgate.net/publication/5144832_The_Prosecution_of_Public_Figures_and_the_Separation_of_Powers_Confusion_Within_the_Executive_Branch-A_Conceptual_Framework (accessed 21 June 2016).

15 Verónica Michel, "The Role of Prosecutorial Independence and Prosecutorial Accountability in Domestic Human Rights Trials" (2015) *Journal of Human Rights*, DOI: 10.1080/14754835.2015.1113864 http://dx.doi.org/10.1080/14754835.2015.1113864 (accessed 6 October 2016).
16 S. 147(3) CFRN.
17 S. 147(1) and (2)CFRN.
18 CRFN 1999. S. 150. See also S. 211 for corresponding provisions in relation to the Attorney General of a state.
19 CFRN 1999. S. 147.
20 See Chapter 6, para 6.9.1.1 of the Final Report of the National Conference (August 2014) p. 652.
21 www.thisdaylive.com/index.php/2016/07/10/time-to-separate-agf-from-minister-of-justice/ (accessed 7 November 2016).
22 see http:/placing.org/new/upload/PRESIDENTSVETOLETTERTONASS.pdf for a full text of the Presidents letter (accessed 3 December 2016).
23 Deji Adekunle, "Independent Prosecution Systems in Nigeria; Challenges and Prospects", Presented at Law Conference on Fostering Constitutionalism in Africa (Nairobi, 2007) www.ancl-radc.org.za/sites/default/files/Independent%20Prosecution%20Systems%20by%20Deji%20Adekunle.pdf (accessed 23 June 2016).
24 CFRN 1999. S. 150. However, as the earlier discussion on agitations for clearer demarcation of the offices show, this subtle distinction has not quite worked well in practice.
25 CFRN 1999 S174 (3).
26 D. Bugg, "Accountability, Independence and Ethics in the Prosecution Practice"; presented at The International Society for the Reform of Criminal Law 18th Annual Conference (Montreal, August 2004) www.cdpp.gov.au/news/accountability-independence-and-ethics-prosecution-practice (accessed 21 June 2016).
27 Note 8.
28 Channels TV 28 May 2016 "FG Sets Up National Panel For Prosecution Of High Profile Corruption Cases" www.channelstv.com/2016/05/28/fg-sets-up-national-panel-for-prosecution-of-high-profile-corruption-cases/ (accessed 21 June 2016.
29 The AGF has since directed agencies with prosecutorial powers to compile lists of pending suits currently being handled by them at various courts for proper classification so that cases that fall within the high-profile category will be taken over by the National Prosecution Coordination Committee (NPCC).
30 Note 10.
31 Federal Republic of Nigeria v Osahon *[2006] 5 NWLR (pt. 973) 361.*
32 Section 376 ACJA 2015.
33 Section 296 ACJA 2015.
34 Section 180 of the Criminal Procedure Act Cap C LFN2004.
35 Section 270 of the Administration of Criminal Justice Act (ACJA) provides for Plea Bargain. Subsection (2) guarantees the participation of the victim or his representatives to the effect that the prosecution may enter into plea bargaining with the defendant with the consent of the victim or his representative. Subsection (6) makes it mandatory that the Prosecution shall afford the victim or his representative the opportunity to make representations regarding the content of the agreement and the inclusion in the agreement order.
36 See section 128 for equivalent provisions in relation to the State legislatures.
37 An example is provided by the invitation by the Nigerian Senate to the Nigerian AGF over the initiation of fraud charges against the President and Deputy President of the Senate. See Vanguard of 1 July 2016 "Forgery: Senate walks out Buhari's aide, as AGF again shuns Senate summon" www.vanguardngr.com/2016/07/forgery-senate-walks-buharis-aide-agf-shuns-senate-summon/ (accessed 1 July 2016).

15 The Decision to Prosecute – The Accountability of Australian Prosecutors

Kellie Toole

Introduction

The prosecutor is a powerful figure, existing at a key intersection of state power and citizens' rights. Prosecutors' decisions on whether or not to prosecute in particular cases affect the life and liberty of criminal defendants, the reputation of the criminal justice system, and the social values articulated through the criminal law. A growing number of international scholars are seeking to better understand the role of the prosecutor, including the prosecutorial discretion and the implications of its exercise. The recurrent theme of the emerging scholarship is the need for prosecutors to be more accountable for their decisions to prosecute, so that the use of the prosecutorial discretion for improper purposes is discouraged, or at least identified and addressed (Luna and Wade, 2012b; Tonry, 2013). The international concerns raised the question of whether Australian prosecutors also need to be more accountable. To address this question, I considered the opportunities and incentives that enable and encourage the misuse of the prosecution internationally, and compared them to some key historical and contemporary characteristics of the Australian legal, political and social system.

The first part of this chapter introduces the concept of prosecutorial discretion, and the key prosecutorial accountability measures. The second part outlines the unique history, geography and population characteristics of Australia that are relevant to the development of the Australian prosecutorial system. The third part asserts, with reference to England, Japan and the USA, how unique Australian characteristics provide a bulwark against the concerns about the misuse of prosecutorial discretion raised in other countries. I conclude that in Australia, the opportunities for misuse of the prosecutorial discretion in the decision to prosecute are limited by the scale of the work in the offices of the Directors of Public Prosecutions (ODPPs), their centralisation and organisational culture, and the political and legislative framework within which they operate. I further conclude that the incentives for its misuse are minimised because career success as a prosecutor in Australia relies on the cautious use of the discretion, and does not demand an excessive adversarial approach to prosecuting. These features of the Australian criminal justice system combine to neutralise the concerns besetting overseas counterparts, rendering the international calls for urgent reform of prosecutorial accountability measures of limited relevance to Australia.

Discretion and Accountability

Discretion

The formal allocation of responsibility within the Australian criminal justice system is clear. State and territory parliaments pass criminal laws. Police investigate crimes and charge suspected criminals. The ODPPs prosecute serious crimes in the intermediate and higher courts, and the police prosecute most minor offences in the lower courts. The courts determine whether charges are proven or not, and impose penalty on defendants who are found guilty. Through the established division of roles, the legislative, executive and judicial branches of government fulfil distinct roles, and check and balance the exercise of the power of each. However, the ODPP is not expected or able to prosecute every case referred to it by the police. Rather, the discretion of prosecutors is inherent in the Anglo-Australian tradition. Sir Hartley Shawcross, the Attorney General of England and Wales between 1945 and 1951, made the classic pronouncement in 1951 that: "It has never been the rule in this country – and I hope it never will be – that suspected criminal offences must automatically be the subject of prosecution" (NSW Prosecutorial Guidelines, 2007: s 2.1.7). This principle was incorporated into Australian law, and is reflected in the current prosecutorial guidelines of every Australian jurisdiction. While the acceptance of the prosecutorial discretion is long-standing and widely accepted, its existence does generate certain concerns.

In 1885, A.V. Dicey identified the key feature of the rule of law as the "absolute supremacy or predominance of regular law as opposed to the existence of arbitrary power" (Dicey, 1975, p. 202). His reasoning was that "wherever there is discretion there is room for arbitrariness" (Dicey, 1975, p. 188). Dicey's proposition was subject to challenge over later decades. Sykes argued in 1935 that the "exercise of at least some discretionary power is implied in all government activities", and "'[d]iscretionary' does not necessarily mean 'arbitrary'" (Sykes, 1935, p. 57). However, restraint of the possession and exercise of discretionary power by government is widely considered a safeguard against the arbitrary exercise of power, and that attitude to discretion influences scholarly concern about the accountability of prosecutors.

Accountability

According to Bovens, in "contemporary political and scholarly discourse 'accountability' often serves as a conceptual umbrella that covers various other distinct concepts, such as transparency, equity, democracy, efficiency, responsiveness, responsibility and integrity [and] 'good governance'" (Bovens, 2007,

p. 449).[1] This chapter relies on the relatively narrow definition of accountability as a "concern for checks and oversight, for surveillance and institutional constraints on the exercise of power" (Schedler, 1999, p. 13). Calls for prosecutorial accountability are, in part, appeals for the provision of reliable and relevant information about prosecutions, which reflect a general demand for transparency regarding the activities of government (Kondo, 2002, p. 7). However, they also reflect particular concerns about the actual or potential use of prosecutorial discretion, including inadvertent misuse through workload pressure, inattention, lapse in judgment and/or inexperience; and deliberate misuse through an intention to affect an outcome or process of a prosecution for inappropriate or improper reasons. The deliberate misuse of the prosecutorial discretion could be motivated by factors such as the effect on the career prospects of a particular prosecutor, or on the fortunes of a particular political party.

Various measures are adopted across jurisdictions to achieve at least some level of prosecutorial accountability. The measures include bureaucratic mechanisms such as guidelines and policies, internal office review, and hierarchical structures for decision-making; judicial mechanisms including the control of court room processes and judicial review; direct accountability to the community through election of prosecutors by local constituencies; and political mechanisms, such as an Attorney General being responsible for oversight of prosecutorial decisions. However, this chapter focuses on the conditions underlying the need for accountability measures rather than on the mechanisms for prosecutorial accountability themselves. The following section outlines the combination of Australian geography and history that underpins the Australian prosecutorial system in ways that are relevant to the contemporary exercise of the prosecutorial discretion, and the consequent calls for greater prosecutorial accountability measures.

Australian Context

Geography

Australia is frequently defined by its geography. The "tyranny of distance" arising from its geographical remoteness from other Western countries is well documented (Blainey, 1966). Just as distinctive, but attracting less attention, is the national population and population distribution that results from its geography. It is the driest inhabited continent in the world (Department of Energy and Environment, undated), and supports a relatively small population of 24 million people (ABS, 2016). Despite the bush mythology essential to its national identity, Australia is highly urbanised, with 89 per cent of its population living in a city (United Nations, 2014, p. 48), and 64 per cent of that population is concentrated within one of the capital cities located in each of the eight states and territories (Hugo, 2013, pp. 73–75).

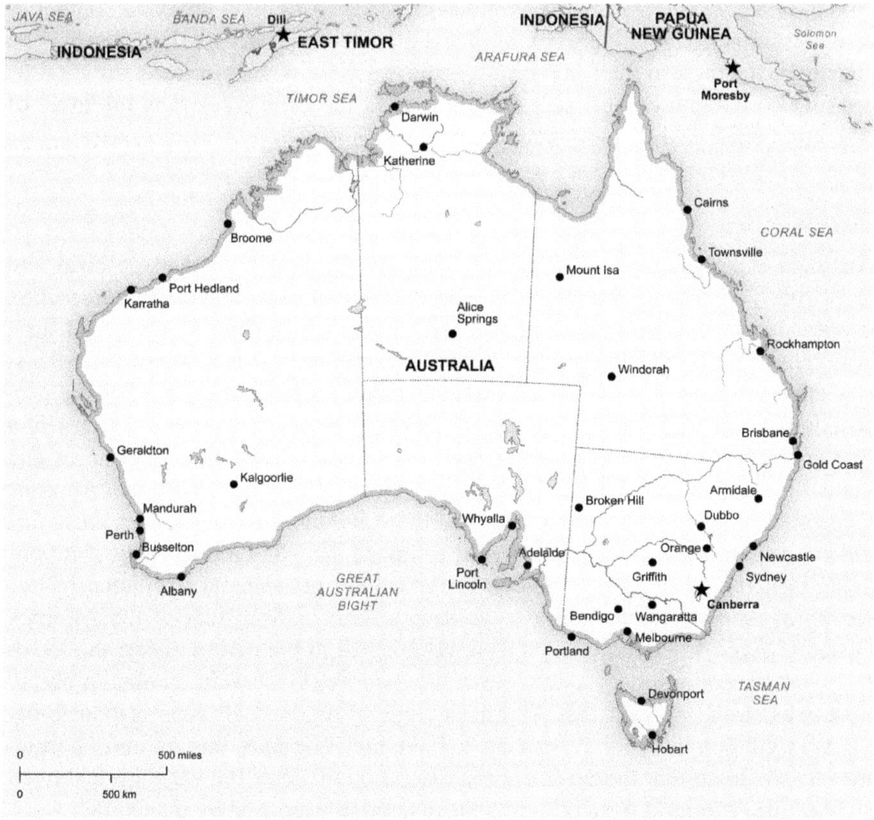

Figure 15.1 Map of Australia with National, State and Territory Capital Cities.

History

The modern Australian prosecutorial system retains the historical characteristics of political oversight by the Attorney General, and the political and legal autonomy of each jurisdiction.

Local Autonomy

The Federation of Australia was created in 1901 through the union of six separate self-governing British colonies. A strong degree of local independence and identity survived the union, and most criminal law was, and continues to be, enacted and enforced at the state and territory level.[2] The local enforcement of criminal offences enacted only for their particular jurisdiction, gives ODPPs a high level of autonomy over a limited range of criminal offences and offenders.

The low Australian population, concentrated in few highly dispersed and relatively independent urbanised coastal centres, has resulted in the development of a small number of relatively small, prosecutorial offices across the country. The enactment of the criminal law on the state or territory basis means the ODPPs are highly autonomous offices, but the size of the offices restricts the level of discretion exercised by individual prosecutors.

Attorney General

Australia inherited from England an Attorney General with dual political and legal roles, including responsibility for criminal prosecutions. The *Australian Courts Act 1828* (Imp) provided that until the establishment of the grand jury, criminal offences "shall be prosecuted by information, in the name of His Majesty's attorney general".[3] However, in NSW neither grand juries, nor private prosecutions, were viable given the penal nature of the settlement, and the lack of a free citizenry. Whereas in England, police, private individuals, grand juries and the DPP were also involved in criminal prosecutions, in NSW the Attorney General dominated prosecutions. Each of the subsequent colonies, even those that did not originate as convict settlements, followed the NSW model of prosecutions being undertaken by the Attorney General or by prosecutors appointed by the Governor, and whose authority to prosecute derived from that of the Attorney General.[4] Even when the ODPPs were established in the period during the 1970s to 1990s, the commitment to the role of the Attorney General in criminal prosecutions was strong enough that Attorneys General retained ultimate responsibility for prosecutions in every Australian jurisdiction. The later section on opportunities for the misuse of the prosecutorial discretion explores the way political oversight of the Attorneys General limits the discretion exercised by the ODPPs.

The following sections argue that the history and geography of Australia have affected the nature and operations of the ODPPs in ways that restrict the opportunities and incentives for the misuse of prosecutorial discretion. The unique characteristics of Australia are highlighted by comparisons with relevant features of England, Japan and the USA. These jurisdictions are used as comparators because they have attracted virulent criticism of the exercise of the prosecutorial discretion and vigorous calls for greater prosecutorial accountability, and also have striking local features that contrast with those of Australia.

Australian Safeguards

Opportunities

It is axiomatic that the improper exercise of prosecutorial discretion is contingent on prosecutors having the opportunity to misuse their discretion. The following section contends that the Australian prosecutorial system limits the opportunities for such misuse through the scale of the offices, their level of centralisation, organisational culture, political oversight and legislative environment.

Scale

The ODPPs each serve relatively small populations. NSW, the most populous state in Australia, serves a total population of 6,917,656 (ABS, 2011), while California, the most populous state in the USA, serves a population of 38,802,500 (United States Census Bureau, 2014). In addition, the police prosecute summary offences in most jurisdictions in Australia,[5] whereas most international prosecution services have a more onerous workload on account of being responsible for prosecuting both serious and minor offences. These factors combine to significantly reduce the workload of the ODPPs in comparison to their international counterparts.[6] For example, the state of NSW registered 18,135 prosecutions of serious crimes in the one-year period 2014–2015 (NSW DPP Annual Report, 2015, p. 10), and the Tasmanian office disposed of a total of 400 criminal matters in the same period (Tasmania DPP Annual Report, 2015, p. 4). The USA does not report on prosecutions in the same way as Australia, but the Los Angeles District Attorney's (DA's) Office alone (the largest prosecuting county in the country) handles approximately 71,000 serious crimes and 112,000 less serious crimes every year (County of Los Angeles, 2016).

The limited caseload of the ODPPs means the offices have relatively low staff numbers. California has 58 DAs running their own offices (California District Attorney's Association, 2015) and a total of 3904 prosecutors (Bies *et al.*, 2015, p. 22). NSW has one DPP, one central office, three suburban offices and six regional offices, and a total of 600 staff (including administrative staff) (Director of Public Prosecutions New South Wales, 2018). The following section on centralisation demonstrates how the Australian caseloads are also limited in comparison to the prosecution services of England, the USA and Japan.

Centralisation

The Australian model of one ODPP per jurisdiction sits in the middle of the international spectrum of levels of centralisation of prosecution services. For example, the USA has approximately 3000 prosecutorial offices run on a county-basis, and Japan and England and Wales jointly each have a single office.

Under the highly decentralised USA system, the prosecutorial function "is exercised independently of any other prosecuting authority … with each county district attorney having almost total autonomy" (Harris, 2012, p. 58). A multiplicity of county offices creates "fragmented, largely nonhierarchical decision-making, which raises equality issues due to the occasionally dramatic inconsistencies across cases and among parties", which are "seen as an acceptable price to be paid to respect local values and protect local autonomy" (Boerner, 2013 p. 188).

Countries that have centralised, national prosecution systems, face the opposite problem to the USA, because local decision makers are so far removed from the central prosecutor upon whose authority they are acting. In Japan, the Prosecutor General heads the Supreme Public Prosecutors Office in Tokyo and is responsible for the oversight of prosecutions across the country. However, the prosecutions are actually undertaken by 1,845 public prosecutors and 899 assistant prosecutors divided between eight High Public Prosecutors Offices, 50 Regional Public Prosecutors Offices with 203 district branches, and over 438 District Public Prosecutors offices (Public Prosecutor's Office, Japan, undated). Similarly, there is a single DPP responsible for prosecutions across England and Wales. As at March 2016, there were 2,131 prosecutors and 2,970 legal caseworkers covering 14 geographical areas across two countries (Crown Prosecution Service, 2017). In the year 2015–2016, the Crown Prosecution Service for England and Wales handled over half a million summary and indictable cases in the Magistrates Court, and almost 100,000 more serious cases in the Crown Court (Crown Prosecution Service, 2016).

The organisation of Australian prosecutions at the state and territory level, rather than at the national or county level, means prosecutors are neither without a central prosecuting authority, nor too far removed from one. The scale of the Australian offices enables a level of supervision of the exercise of prosecutorial discretion that is not possible internationally. The DPP can be personally involved in all cases of a certain type or level of seriousness or complexity, and can meet personally with complainants and prosecutors if that is deemed to be required.[7] The DPP of Western Australia gave evidence in 2016 before the Royal Commission into Institutional Responses to Child Sexual Abuse, that "one of the great benefits" of his office is that:

> Whilst we're in one of the biggest provinces in the world, there are nine floors in one building so I'm within 80 metres of any decision maker. The population of Perth is only 2 million, so we've got this great control.
>
> (Commonwealth of Australia, 2016, p. 92)[8]

The Deputy DPP of the Northern Territory similarly testified that: "We only have 45 prosecutors, so I have that direct contact with all of my prosecutors. If [a] complainant requires a meeting with myself then I conduct that meeting myself" (Commonwealth of Australia, 2016, p. 90).[9] Even in a relatively populous state like Victoria, the DPP advised that: "If I am in doubt about a case or I want some more information then I'll call them up and assemble them and we'll talk about it amongst the team" (Commonwealth of Australia, 2016, p. 95).[10]

Paradoxically, both decentralisation and nationalisation of prosecutions enable a level of individualism in decision-making that, at best, creates inconsistency and the perception of arbitrariness and, at worst, permits undetected, and unmonitored, deliberate misuse or injudicious use of prosecutorial discretion. The size and hierarchical internal structure of the Australian ODPPs limit the exercise of discretion by individual prosecutors and so avoids both of these problems.

Organisational Culture

The ODPPs rest on a principle dating back centuries, that prosecutors have an obligation to act as "Ministers of Justice" rather than zealous advocates (Plater, 2011). They are required to conduct all aspects of prosecutions, including making the decision to prosecute, in a manner fair to the court, all parties and the community generally, and not to single-mindedly pursue "winning" at trial by securing convictions. As discussed in more detail in the section below on incentives to misuse the prosecutorial discretion, these types of principles can be largely aspirational and difficult to enforce.

However, the involvement of the DPP in decision-making fosters a hierarchical organisational culture that is reflected at various levels throughout the ODPPs, and which supports the adherence to the principle of judicious use of the prosecutorial powers. Decisions on initiating and terminating proceedings are generally made only by prosecutors at a management level, and regular management meetings bring consistency to the decision-making processes across the offices. The difference between Australia and England, according to one Australian DPP at least, is the "paucity of the supervision, the management, the tiers" in England, compared to "multiple levels of management supervision" (Commonwealth of Australia, 2016, p. 103)[11] in Australia.

This hierarchical structure is compatible with, and further supported by, bureaucratic controls of rules and policies. Prosecutorial guidelines are supported by prosecutor-specific provisions of barrister and solicitor conduct rules, and rules and guidelines applicable to all government lawyers that impose requirements of fairness, integrity and commitment to the public interest. In addition, New South Wales, Victoria, Queensland, South Australia and the Australian Capital Territory have all adopted variants of the Commonwealth's Model Litigant Rules.[12]

By contrast, the American academic, David T. Johnson, interviewed American prosecutors and found a prevailing view that competent people should be hired and not supervised unduly, because the values of adaptability and innovation were more important than regularity and consistency. These attitudes resulted in limited internal controls and a lack of collective decision-making, (Johnson, 2002, pp. 141, 151, 153) which allow individuals to have a high level of individual discretion that creates risks of the misuse of prosecutorial discretion.

Political Oversight

The political oversight of the Australian prosecution system also acts as a check on the exercise of the prosecutorial discretion. While the Australian ODPPs conduct prosecutions, the Attorney General in each state and territory can either exercise prosecutorial powers concurrently with the DPP, or direct the DPP to take particular action on general matters of policy and/or in relation to specific cases.[13] While Attorneys General have used their prosecutorial powers sparingly, they have been prepared to direct or overrule DPPs in relation to both the decision to prosecute (Hine, 2010) and appeals of sentences[14] when media and public reaction indicate that the DPP's exercise of prosecutorial discretion did not reflect community expectations.

The Attorney General's oversight contrasts not only with the "almost complete power" of US DAs (Harris, 2012, pp. 59, 66), but also with the Japanese prosecutorial system, where prosecutors are so influential in the Ministry of Justice, that Johnson argues "the minister reigns while the prosecutors rule" (Johnson, 2002, pp. 119–120). This prosecutorial power reflects that, historically, the Supreme Court was an organ of the Ministry of Justice, and prosecutors controlled the budget, and the appointment and supervision of judges, and "frequently used these levers to pressure judges, thereby breaching again and again the principle of judicial independence" (Johnson, 2002, p. 61). After World War II, judges gained more independence, but the culture has not changed significantly and judges rarely challenge prosecutorial decisions (Ii, 2013, p. 460).

Legislative Environment

The legislative environment scaffolding the Australian prosecutorial role is the final check on the exercise of the prosecutorial discretion. Australia's legislation on the investigation and sentencing of criminal offences, in particular, bears indirectly, but powerfully, on the scope of the prosecutorial discretion. The Australian legislation does not facilitate the misuse of the discretion in the way legislation does, unintentionally, in the USA and Japan.

Sentencing

In the USA in the 1970s, a widespread perception emerged that judicial sentencing had become inconsistent and too lenient. This perception led to judges' sentencing discretion being curtailed through mandatory sentences, including life without parole for certain offences (Nellis, 2010, pp. 27–28), and repeat or habitual offender ("three strikes") laws (Pizzi, 2012: 189–194), that attracted lengthy mandatory prison terms (Nagorski, 2010, pp. 214–217). Ironically, the limitations placed on the sentencing discretion of judges led to a corresponding, unintended and largely unrecognised enhancement of the power of the prosecutors' charging discretion. Prosecutors are now able, and apparently willing, to derive a forensic advantage by "over-charging" or "bad faith charging". This process involves charging suspects with serious offences that attract high mandatory minimum sentences, and then negotiating "aggressive charge bargains" to less serious offences, with suspects who fear the consequences of going to trial on the original charges (Tonry, 2013, pp. 31–33). This unauthorised and highly criticised, but apparently common, tactic allows prosecutors to avoid the negative consequences of withdrawing cases or losing at trial (Turner, 2012, p. 105).

State and territory legislatures across Australia have also been influenced by "tough on crime" policies, which fuel regular public and parliamentary complaints about the leniency of judicial penalties for serious offending. Each jurisdiction has enacted some harsh mandatory sentences for particular offences or particular offenders. However, generally, sentencing is left to the discretion of judges and magistrates within the relatively wide scope afforded by penalty clauses in criminal statutes and codes (Rule of Law Institute of Australia, 2014). The limited number of mandatory sentences and repeat offender legislation restricts the opportunity for Australian prosecutors to misuse the prosecutorial discretion through the type of charge bargaining evident in the USA.

Investigative

Australia contrasts starkly with Japan regarding legislation governing the investigation of crime. The commitment in Australia to the strict delineation between the responsibility for investigating and prosecuting serious crimes is given effect though legislation setting out the functions and powers of the DPPs, and conferring investigative powers on the police in each jurisdiction. The differentiation reflects the principle that the separation of these functions is necessary to ensure the independence of both the police and the prosecutors.[15] The Japanese system does not adhere to the same principle.

Not only do Japanese prosecutors, unusually, have powers to investigate crimes, but those powers are extremely intrusive compared to those held by police in most jurisdictions, including Australia. In some cases, Japanese prosecutors can detain and interrogate a suspect for up to 23 days before deciding whether or not to charge them with an offence. During the detention period, there are few obligations to video-record the interrogation (Wachi, 2014, pp. 38, 674–675), and defence lawyers have limited pre-trial access to defendants, and restricted rights to attend interrogation sessions (Foote, 1992, pp. 380–382). In extreme, but not isolated, cases, prosecutors have been found to egregiously abuse their investigative powers in the service of their prosecutorial role. Prosecutors have been known to subject suspects to inducements, humiliations, lengthy and intense questioning, and threats and use of physical violence in order to elicit confessions and negate the need to proceed to trial. A comprehensive study of Japanese prosecution concluded that "[i]nvestigations are highly intrusive and sometimes coercive. Truth is fabricated, corrupted and concealed. Mistakes are made. Bias exists. Prosecutors are unaccountable and defense lawyers are all but impotent" (Johnson, 2002, p. 279). Criminal legislation in Australia balances the roles of the police, the prosecutors and the judiciary more effectively than in Japan or the USA, and in ways that limit the scope of the prosecutorial discretion available in making the decision to prosecute.

In Australia, the small, centralised offices with manageable caseloads are amenable to high levels of internal control that constrain the exercise of prosecutorial discretion. In combination with the legislative environment in which they operate, these factors minimise the opportunities for its misuse.

The existence of opportunity is insufficient to promote the systemic misuse of the prosecutorial discretion. If prosecutorial misuse is to become inherent or entrenched, or even common enough to generate concerns about levels of accountability, the system must contain incentives or motivations for prosecutors to take advantage of the available opportunities.

Incentives

This section identifies criteria for prosecutors' career progression, and the strength of the adversarial culture in which prosecutors work, as key factors that have been found to motivate prosecutors to misuse prosecutorial discretion in the USA and Japan. It compares those motivating factors to the equivalent conditions in Australia, and concludes that the situation in Australia does not act as an incentive to misuse prosecutorial discretion in the way that the situations in the comparator countries do.

Career Success and Reputation

In the USA, the incentive to misuse the discretion rests, primarily, in the pursuit of career success in a system where DAs are elected in an environment saturated with "tough on crime" politics. As anticipated in the section above on the organisational culture of the ODPPs, high principle governs criminal prosecution in both Australia and the USA. In Australia, the principle is expressed that the prosecutor is expected to be a Minister of Justice (Plater, 2011) because the Crown is "the fountain and head of justice and equity",[16] and "the State has created the courts and the legal system [so] it must set an example for the community which it leads and governs" (South Australian Crown Solicitor's Office, 2011, pp. 1–2). Similarly, the case law and DA Office policies in the USA hold that the role of a prosecutor is not that of "an ordinary party to a controversy, but one of a sovereignty whose obligation to govern impartially is as compelling as its obligation to govern at all".[17] However, the USA example demonstrates that compliance with this aspirational principle is affected by systemic incentives to adhere to or deviate from it. A motivator of conduct is the pursuit of professional success either within or outside of the prosecutorial system, and this depends, in turn, on how "success" is defined and rewarded within the system.

The USA DA is a high-profile elected position, and candidates are subject to vigorous public scrutiny from opponents and voters. The role attracts politically ambitious people seeking to "build a reputation on law and order as a precursor to a career in politics" (Harris, 2012, p. 59). The ability to use the prosecutorial role as a "stepping-stone to higher political offices – depend[s] on demonstrable 'success' in prosecuting crime" (Walther, 2000, p. 285), which is measured almost exclusively by reference to securing convictions. The pressures of electoral accountability in the context of a "tough on crime" policy agenda are routinely reported as undermining, rather than supporting, the adherence to obligations of sovereignty. United States of America prosecutors are "anchored in a contradiction" between the principles that underpin their position, and being subject to the "direct dependence on the electoral scrutiny of a public which fears crime and demands that officials get ever tougher with it" (Johnson, 2002, p. 29).

In a reversal of the pressure faced by prosecutors in the USA, the Japanese media and public are more likely to "focus on acquittals of those who were wrongfully charged than on failure to charge seemingly guilty suspects" (Turner, 2012, pp. 112–113). When defendants are acquitted at trial, prosecutors can face criticism for "sloppy investigations", "reckless practices" and "fascist intentions" (Johnson, 2002, p. 107). Allegations of this nature negatively affect prosecutors' careers (Turner, 2012, pp. 112–113), and the pressure can discourage the prosecution of defendants who might be acquitted, and allows self-interest to affect the judgment of whether or not to prosecute (Johnson, 2002, p. 239).

The prosecutorial systems of the USA and Japan take opposing approaches to measuring prosecutorial success or effectiveness, but they both emphasise trial outcomes in assessing prosecutor performance, and so both provide incentives to misuse prosecutorial discretion. Australia does not have inherent incentives to either aggressively pursue convictions or passively avoid acquittals. The system is neither divorced from electoral accountability nor a slave to it, because while DPPs need not fear electoral backlash over prosecutorial decisions, the oversight by the Attorney General requires them to reflect the expectations of the public. The type of conduct that affects career promotion, longevity and reputation within the criminal justice system is not measured by simple case metrics.

The Australian DPP is not a high-profile role, nor is it a common pathway to a political career. Where a prosecutor seeks career advancement outside of the prosecutorial system, it is typically for appointment to the judiciary, the private bar, or a senior government position such as the role of the Solicitor General. In evaluating and reporting on prosecutor performance, the annual reports of Australian ODPPs do sometimes note rates of acquittal at trial as well as other case resolution statistics. However, these criteria are subordinate to relationships, reputation, ethics and service to the community and the profession. Prominence is given to attendance and contribution at conferences and training courses; involvement in external committees, working parties and advisory groups; inter-agency cooperation especially with police, courts and the judiciary; community service; witness satisfaction; contribution to law reform; morale, pride and enthusiasm; assistance to royal commissions and other inquiries; and appointment as Queen's or Senior Counsel.[18] The system does not create incentives to exercise the prosecutorial discretion improperly, but rather contains incentives to adhere to the Minister of Justice role, which includes the moderate use of the discretion.

Adversarial Legal Culture

The incentives for the misuse of the prosecutorial discretion can extend beyond the deliberate choices of individual, ambitious prosecutors, and into the entrenched cultural expectations of the system in which they work. In the nineteenth century, the legal system of the USA developed a unique brand of "hyper-adversarialism"; a "belligerent", "brutally partisan process" that is "perhaps a manifestation of robust American individualism" (Luna and Wade, 2012a, p. 432). This system persists to the extent that, according to Tonry, the

> prevailing understanding in the rest of the developed world that prosecutors, like judges, should be apolitical, impartial, and unemotional does not exist. Many chief prosecutors are as much politicians as they are prosecutors. Even the best sometimes find political implications impossible to ignore in setting policies and priorities and in making decisions about individual cases. The worst give free rein to partisan and ideological considerations.
>
> (Tonry, 2013, p. 37)

The USA's adversarial system is a product of its unique history. The system has not developed in the same extreme way in Australia, and, as a result, the Minister of Justice role is not challenged as it is in the USA, and the prosecutorial discretion is far less susceptible to being misused in the service of adversarialism.

Conclusion

The wisdom of calls for prosecutorial accountability are manifest, given the nature and effects of the exercise of the prosecutorial discretion on whether or not to prosecute in particular cases. Australia is not a promised land where misuse of prosecutorial discretion is beyond contemplation. Its prosecution system needs to be subject to scrutiny, and serious consideration needs to be given to the adequacy of current prosecutorial accountability mechanisms. The concerns expressed about other jurisdictions may prove valuable in reflecting on the Australian prosecution system, and proposing reforms to it. However, the Australian system is shaped by its distinctive history, geography and politics. It is different to other prosecution systems, which have their own distinctive historical and contemporary features. The Australian conditions have generated a prosecution system operating in a policy and legal environment in which the opportunities for the improper exercise of prosecutorial discretion are minimised by their scale, organisational structure and culture, and by the political and legislative environment in which they operate. The system measures individual and institutional success by reference to broader considerations than case resolution metrics, which provides incentives for the judicious rather than the excessive or improper use of the prosecutorial discretion. It is, therefore, essential that prosecutorial accountability in Australia is considered in the context of its unique features, rather than as part of a general international movement arising from jurisdictions that are different in significant ways to one another and to Australia.

Notes

1 There is an extensive scholarship on public accountability, for example, Bovens, Mark *et al.* (eds), *The Oxford Handbook of Public Accountability* (Oxford University Press, 2014) and Dubnick, Melvin, "Seeking Salvation for Accountability", (Paper presented at the Annual Meeting of the American Political Science Association, Boston, 29 August–1 September 2002).

2 The Commonwealth prosecutes a range of offences relating under the *Crimes Act 1914; Criminal Code; Judiciary Act 1903; Migration Act 1958; Customs Act 1901; Corporations Act 2001.* See Commonwealth Director of Public Prosecutions, Australia's Federal Prosecution Service (2017) www.cdpp.gov.au/.

3 *Australian Courts Act 1828* (Imp) s 5.

4 R.R. Kidston, "The Office of Crown Prosecutor (More Particularly in New South Wales)" (1958) *Australian Law Journal* 32: 148.

5 New Zealand also maintains a police prosecution service: New Zealand Police, *Police Prosecution Service* (undated) www.police.govt.nz/about-us/structure/teams-units/police-prosecution-service.

6 Some ODPPs prosecute summary offences, but the populations and total case load are still small and amenable to internal oversight. In the reporting year 2014–2015, the Northern Territory finalised a total of 8,551 serious and minor matters: Northern Territory, *Director of Public Prosecutions Annual Report 2014–2015* (30 September 2015) 27, and the Australian Capital Territory finalised a total of 4,462: Australian Capital Territory, *Director of Public Prosecutions Annual Report 2014–2015* (6 October 2015) 54.

7 See, for example, Australian Capital Territory, *Director Of Public Prosecutions Annual Report 2014–2015* (6 October 2015) 7; Queensland, *Office of the Director Of Public Prosecutions, Director's Guidelines* (2015) ss 14, 17, 20, 24; Victoria, *Director Of Public Prosecutions Annual Report 2014–2015* (24 September 2015) 3; Office of the Director of Public Prosecutions for the State of Western Australia, *Annual Report 2014–2015* (17 September 2015) 10; Prosecution Guidelines of the Office of the Director of Public Prosecutions for New South Wales (2007) ss 7, 8, 9, 10; Northern Territory Office of the Director of Public Prosecutions, *Office of the Director of Public Prosecutions Guidelines* (2005) ss 4.2, 6.6 6.7, 6.10, 7.3, 7.8, 7.9, 7.11; Commonwealth of Australia, "Royal Commission into Institutional Responses into Child Sexual Abuse, *Public Hearing – Criminal Justice DPP Complaints and Oversight Mechanisms*" (2016) 68–112.

8 Joe McGrath, DPP, Western Australia.

9 Paul Usher, Deputy DPP, Northern Territory.

10 John Champion, DPP, Victoria.

11 Joe McGrath, DPP, Western Australia.

12 See, for example, the South Australian Crown Solicitor's Office, *Legal Bulletin 2: The Duties of the Crown as Model Litigant* (2011) 1–2. The complexity of the meaning of the Crown as a model litigant and the deficits in the current framework are discussed in Gabrielle Appleby, "The Government as Litigant" (2014) 37 *University of New South Wales Law Journal* 94.

13 *Director of Public Prosecutions Act 1990* (NT) ss 28–29; *Director of Public Prosecutions Act 1990* (ACT) s 20; *Director of Public Prosecutions Act 1984* (Qld) s 10A; *Director of Public Prosecutions Act 1986* (NSW) s 26; *Director of Public Prosecutions Act 1991* (WA) ss 27–28; *Director of Public Prosecutions Act 1991* (SA) s 9; *Nemer v Holloway and Others* (2003) 87 SASR 147, 165; *Public Prosecutions Act 1994* (Vic) s 10; *Director of Public Prosecutions Act 1973* (Tas) s 12; *Director of Public Prosecutions Act 1983* (Cth) ss 8, 10.

14 *Nemer v Holloway and Others* (2003) 87 SASR 147; *R v Watson; ex parte A-G (Qld)* [2009] QCA 279; *CMB v Attorney General (NSW)* (2015) 243 A Crim R 282.

15 The prosecution of summary offences by police in Australia raises questions of prosecutorial independence. See Christopher Christopher Corns, *Police Summary Prosecutions: The Past, Present and Future*, History of Crime, Policing and Punishment Conference, Australian Institute of Criminology in conjunction with Charles Sturt University, Canberra, 9–10 December 1999); Christopher Corns, *Public Prosecutions in Australia: Law Policy and Practice* (Thomson Reuters, 2014).
16 *Dyson v Attorney General* [1911] 1KB 410, 421.
17 *Berger v United States* 295 US78, 88 (1935).
18 Northern Territory, *Director of Public Prosecutions Annual Report 2014–2015* (30 September 2015) 9, 12–13, 21–26, 39; Australian Capital Territory, *Director of Public Prosecutions Annual Report 2014–2015* (6 October 2015) 1–16, 27–29; Victoria, *Director Of Public Prosecutions Annual Report 2014–2015* (24 September 2015) 1, 5–6, 8, 11, 21, 24, 27, 30; Queensland, *Office of the Director Of Public Prosecutions Annual Report 2014–2015* (undated) iii, 6, 17–18, 24, 29–30, 33; South Australia, *Director Of Public Prosecutions Annual Report 2014–2015* (undated) 5, 7–8, 15–23; New South Wales, *Office of the Director Of Public Prosecutions Annual Report 2014–2015* (undated) 3, 18, 20, 23–27; Tasmania, *Director Of Public Prosecutions Annual Report 2014–2015* (24 September 2015) 2–3; Office for the *Director Of Public Prosecutions for the State of Western Australia, Annual Report 2014–2015* (17 September 2015) 6–8, 13, 22, 24, 35–36, 40.

References

Appleby, G. (2014) "The Government as Litigant" *University of New South Wales Law Journal* 37: 94.

Australia, Commonwealth of (2016) "Royal Commission into Institutional Responses into Child Sexual Abuse", *Public Hearing – Criminal Justice DPP Complaints and Oversight Mechanisms.*

Australian Bureau of Statistics (2011) *Data and Analysis* www.abs.gov.au/websitedbs/censushome.nsf/home/data?opendocument&navpos=200.

Australian Bureau of Statistics (2016) *Population Clock* (19 September) www.abs.gov.au/ausstats/abs@.nsf/0/1647509ef7e25faaca2568a900154b63?OpenDocument.

Australian Government, Department of Environment and Energy (n.d.) *Outback Australia – The Rangelands* www.environment.gov.au/land/rangelands.

Bies, K.J., I.M. Deporto, D.G. Long, M.S. McKoy, D.A. Mukamal and D.A. Sklansky (2015) *Stuck in the '70s: The Demographics of California Prosecutors: A Report* (Stanford Criminal Justice Center).

Blainey, G. (1966) *The Tyranny of Distance: How Distance Shaped Australia's History* (Melbourne, Australia: Sun Books).

Boerner, D. (2013) "Prosecution in Washington State" – in Tonry, M. (ed.) *Prosecutors and Politics: A Comparative Perspective* (Chicago, IL: University of Chicago Press), p. 187.

Bovens, M. (2007) "Analysing and Assessing Accountability: A Conceptual Framework" *European Law Journal* 13: 447.

California District Attorney's Association (2015) *District Attorney Roster* www.cdaa.org/district-attorney-roster.

Corns, C. (1999) *Police Summary Prosecutions: The Past, Present and Future* (History of Crime, Policing and Punishment Conference, Australian Institute of Criminology in conjunction with Charles Sturt University, Canberra).

Crown Prosecution Service (2017) *Facts about the CPS* www.cps.gov.uk/about/facts.html.

Crown Prosecution Service, Annual Report and Accounts 2015–16 (30 June 2016) Annex D.

Department of Economic and Social Affairs, Population Division (2014) *World Urbanization Prospects: The 2014 Revision, Final Report* (United Nations).

Dicey, A.V. (1975) *Introduction to the Law of the Constitution* 10th edn (Oxford: Oxford University Press).

District Attorney, County of Los Angeles Office (2016) *Office Overview* da.co.la.ca.us/about/office-overview.

Foote, D.H. (1992) "The Benevolent Paternalism of Japanese Criminal Justice" *California Law Review*: 317.

Harris, D.A. (2012) "The Interaction and Relationship between Prosecutors and Police Officers in the United States, and How This Affects Police Reform Efforts" – in Luna, E. and M. Wade (eds) *The Prosecutor in Transnational Perspective* (Oxford: Oxford University Press), p. 20.

Hine, B. (2010) "Office of The State Coroner, Finding of Inquest into the Death of Mulrunji" (14 May).

Hugo, G. (2013) "Population Distribution and Internal Migration" –in Pincus, J. and G. Hugo (eds) *A Greater Australia: Population, Policies And Governance* (Committee for Economic Development of Australia).

Ii, T. (2013) "Japan's Judicial System May Change, But Its Fundamental Nature Says Virtually the Same: Recent Japanese Reforms on the Judicial Appointment and Evaluation" *Hastings International and Comparative Law Journal* 36: 459.

Johnson, D.T. (2002) *The Japanese Way of Justice: Prosecuting Crime in Japan* (Oxford: Oxford University Press).

Kondo, S. (2002) "Fostering Dialogue to Strengthen Good Governance" – in Organisation For Economic Co-Operation and Development (OECD) *Public Sector Transparency and Accountability: Making It Happen* (OECD), p. 7.

Luna, E. and M. Wade (2012a) "Looking Back and at the Challenges Ahead" – in Luna, E. and M. Wade (eds) *The Prosecutor in Transnational Perspective* (Oxford: Oxford University Press), p. 424.

Luna, E. and M. Wade (2012b) *The Prosecutor in Transnational Perspective* (Oxford: Oxford University Press).

Nagorski, A. (2010) "Arguments against the Use of Recidivist Statutes That Contain Mandatory Minimum Sentences" *University of Saint Thomas Journal of Law and Public Policy* 5: 214.

Nellis, A. (2010) "Throwing Away the Key: The Expansion of Life without Parole Sentences in the United States" *Federal Sentencing Reporter* 23: 27.

New South Wales (n.d.) *Office of the Director of Public Prosecutions Annual Report 2014–2015*, pp. 3, 18, 20, 23–27.

Office of the Director of Public Prosecutions, New South Wales (2018) *About the DPP* www.odpp.nsw.gov.au/about-the-odpp

Pizzi, W.T. (2012) "A Perfect Storm: Prosecutorial Discretion in the United States" – in Luna, E. and M. Wade (eds) *The Prosecutor In Transnational Perspective* (Oxford: Oxford University Press), p. 189.

Plater, D. (2011) *The Changing Role of the Modern Prosecutor: Has the Notion of the "Minister of Justice" Outlived its Usefulness?* (PhD Thesis, University of Tasmania).

Policy of the Director of Public Prosecutions for Victoria (2017).

Prosecution Guidelines of the Office of the Director of Public Prosecutions for New South Wales (2007).

Public Prosecutor's Office (n.d.) *Organization of Prosecutor's Office* www.kensatsu.go.jp/soshiki_kikou/index.htm.

Rule of Law Institute of Australia (2014) *Mandatory Sentencing* www.lawcouncil.asn.au/lawcouncil/index.php/law-council-media/news/352-mandatory-sentencing-debate.

Schedler, A. (1999) "Conceptualizing Accountability" –in Schedler, A., L. Diamond and M.F. Plattner (eds) *The Self-Restraining State: Power and Accountability in New Democracies* (Boulder, CO: Lynne Rienner Publishers), p. 13.

South Australian Crown Solicitor's Office (2011) *Legal Bulletin 2: The Duties of the Crown as Model Litigant.*

Sykes, E.I. (1935) "The Rule of Law in the Modern World" 1 *Res Judicatae* 56.

Tasmania (2015) *Director of Public Prosecutions Annual Report 2014–2015* (24 September), pp. 2–3.

Tonry, M. (2013) "Prosecutors and Politics in Comparative Perspective" – in Tonry, M. (ed.) *Prosecutors and Politics: A Comparative Perspective* (Chicago, IL: University of Chicago Press), p. 12.

Turner, J.I. (2012) "Prosecutors and Bargaining in Weak Cases: A Comparative View" – in Luna, E. and M. Wade (eds) *The Prosecutor In Transnational Perspective* (Oxford: Oxford University Press), p. 102.

United States Census Bureau (2014) *State & County QuickFacts* quickfacts.census.gov/qfd/states/06000.html.

Wachi, T.K. Watanabe, K. Yokota, Y. Otsuka, H. Kuraishi and M. Lamb (2014) "Police Interviewing Styles and Confessions in Japan" *Psychology, Crime & Law* 673.

Walther, S. (2000) "The Position and Structure of the Prosecutor's Office in the United States" *European Journal of Crime Criminal Law and Criminal Justice* 8(3): 283.

16 Regulating the Prosecutorial Role in Wrongful Convictions

Kent Roach[1]

Introduction

Prosecutors are getting much attention in the burgeoning scholarship on wrongful convictions. Reflecting the origins of the innocence movement, much of this literature is American. A 2013 meta-study of nine other studies found only 63 cases in which prosecutors were sanctioned for 3,625 acts of misconduct in the US federal and state systems.[2] One of those nine studies discovered over 700 judicial findings of prosecutorial misconduct but only ten cases of prosecutors being disciplined by the bar. Moreover, one prosecutor who had withheld exculpatory evidence that caused a man to serve 22 years for a murder he did not commit was not disciplined because of the lack of clear and convincing evidence. He was elected to serve as his county's district attorney while the wrongly convicted man died in prison.[3] Stories such as these help explain calls for courts and legal regulators to sanction prosecutors who have contributed to or caused wrongful convictions.

As in other fields, such as medicine, much can be learned from studying errors such as wrongful convictions. The first part of this chapter will suggest that understanding the complex role of prosecutors with respect to wrongful convictions can provide important insights into the prosecutor's role. It will distinguish between direct and indirect prosecutorial contributions to wrongful convictions. Prosecutors play a direct role with respect to failures to disclose evidence to the accused, but they more often play a more indirect role in not preventing police, witness or forensic error that also cause wrongful convictions.

The indirect role that prosecutors play in most wrongful convictions will inform the second part of the chapter. It will provide a taxonomy of regulatory strategies for prosecutors to prevent and correct wrongful convictions. A distinction will be made between "hard strategies" that focus on external regulation in the form criminal, civil or regulatory sanctions and "softer strategies" that focus on self-regulation in the form of education, ethical reform, reputational losses and organizational reform and culture. Although much popular discourse and professional literature is focused on hard sanctions[4] it will be suggested that softer strategies[5] may be especially valuable in addressing the indirect contribution of prosecutors to wrongful convictions.

The final part will argue that the optimal approach to addressing the prosecutorial role in wrongful convictions will combine elements of both hard and softer strategies. Using the Canadian experience with wrongful convictions as a case study, it will suggest that the use of softer strategies including education, public inquiries and reputational harms can have some success in raising prosecutorial awareness and changing prosecutorial behaviour. At the same time, the Canadian approach can be criticized for not disciplining prosecutors who have played a role in wrongful convictions and for not embracing systemic reforms that may decrease the risk of wrongful convictions but also make prosecutions more difficult. This may be changing with a recent case that imposed a massive civil liability award because of prosecutorial misconduct that contributed to a wrongful conviction.[6] Canada may be moving to a regime that uses both hard and softer strategies to influence the significant powers that prosecutors have to prevent and correct wrongful convictions. This may be a positive development that brings Canada's approach in line with John Braithwaite's influential theories of responsive regulation,[7] but the optimal mix of hard and softer strategies may remain illusive and will depend on context.

The Causes of and Prosecutorial Role in Wrongful Convictions

There is a growing literature on wrongful convictions written by both social scientists and academic lawyers. This literature provides some important insights into the role and performance of prosecutors. At the same time, some caveats are in order. Much of the literature is American and may not transfer well into other common law systems.[8] Many American prosecutors are elected, while in other common law countries they are almost always appointed and in civilian countries they may be career state officials, sometimes associated with the judiciary. In addition, the time lag between a wrongful conviction and its correction is often significant. This means that much of the literature on the prosecutorial role in wrongful convictions may be examining prosecutorial conduct that occurred decades ago.

The American Registry of Wrongful Convictions

The American Registry of Wrongful Convictions has 2,138 wrongful convictions registered up to December 2017. It defines wrongful convictions as cases where the accused is exonerated as innocent. Of the cases, 57 per cent involved perjury, 52 per cent involved "official misconduct", 29 per cent involved mistaken eyewitness identification, 24 per cent involved false or misleading forensic evidence and 12 per cent involved false confessions.[9] These figures record the frequently overlapping or concurrent causes of wrongful convictions. Most of these wrongful convictions do not involve DNA exonerations. The DNA exonerations have higher percentages of cases involving false forensics, mistaken eyewitness identification and false confessions than the broader data set in the

American Registry.[10] This probably means that the American Registry is more likely than DNA data sets to pick up cases where prosecutors have contributed to wrongful convictions.

The registry unfortunately does not break down the role of prosecutors with respect to "official misconduct". Fortunately, a study of the registry as of October 2013 (when official misconduct was classified as a contributing factor in 47 per cent of all cases) found that prosecutorial misconduct was the predominant factor in only 6 per cent of all cases that were in the registry at the time. In that category of cases, 57 cases involved the prosecutor withholding exculpatory evidence, seven cases involved the prosecutor misleading the trier of fact, five cases involved the prosecutor knowingly offering perjured or false testimony, four cases involved prosecutors coercing a defendant, three involved retaliatory charges and one case involved discriminatory selection of a jury.

The failure of a prosecutor to disclose exculpatory evidence is the most common and most direct form of prosecutorial contribution to wrongful convictions. Indeed a failure to disclosure exculpatory evidence could potentially attract criminal prosecution for obstruction of justice, successful due process challenges, civil liability and professional sanctions including disbarment.

In an additional 18 per cent of all cases in the registry, the authors of the 2013 study found that prosecutorial misconduct was a contributing factor to the wrongful conviction.[11] Such contributing factors include calling misleading evidence or offering steep inducements for guilty pleas that place pressure even on the innocent to plead guilty. In any event, this study suggests that prosecutors were a material or contributing factor in 24 per cent of all registered wrongful convictions in 2013. This suggests that prosecutors play a significant, but not necessarily dominant role, in many wrongful convictions.

Prosecutors, Charging Decisions and Guilty Pleas

An obvious question with respect to most wrongful convictions is, why did the prosecutor proceed with the charge in the first place? It is important, however, not to be fixated with hindsight. In most common law jurisdictions, the standard for laying charges is quite low. Preliminary judicial review of prosecutions generally defers questions of credibility and weight to the trier of fact. In most cases, the police present the prosecutor with a case against the accused that does not include alternative suspects and theories of the case.[12]

Civilian jurisdictions where prosecutors supervise investigations[13] may be better at ensuring the accuracy of initial charging decisions though there is also the danger that prosecutors who are actively involved in investigations will be less able to act as a check on police investigations. In common law systems, courts and disciplinary bodies will be reluctant to review charging decisions, which are generally seen as lying at the heart of prosecutorial discretion.

The low hurdles of most pre-trial screens are not well-aligned with high-volume criminal justice systems where most accused plead guilty. Until quite recently, many have assumed that most wrongful convictions would arise from contested trials. This assumption has been undermined by the increasing recognition that a significant number of wrongly convicted persons plead guilty. As of February 2016, guilty pleas accounted for 16 per cent of the exonerations in the American registry and the number is growing as they represented 74 of 166 exonerations recorded in 2016.[14] In Canada, there is also growing recognition that a significant number of wrongful convictions have arisen from guilty pleas.[15]

The prosecutorial role in guilty plea wrongful convictions requires study. Some prosecutors who accept guilty pleas from the innocent may not be guilty of misconduct. They may be responding to caseload pressures and they may not be in a position to appreciate all of the weaknesses of their evidence or of defences that the accused might develop.[16] Other prosecutors, however, may have offered attractive plea bargains to avoid having dubious evidence tested in court.

Prosecutors and Disclosure

The failure of prosecutors to disclose exculpatory evidence to the defence is the most obvious form of prosecutorial misconduct that contributes to wrongful conviction. At the same time, not all disclosure violations are black and white. Although disclosure violations are frequently litigated in both the United States and Canada, courts frequently find disclosure violations to be harmless and confirm convictions.[17] Although prosecutors have ethical and legal obligations to disclose material in their possession, they cannot disclose material that the police did not collect or include in their file. Another of the lessons of wrongful convictions is that police, especially in high profile cases, do not always follow alternative leads or explanations of what happened. The influence that prosecutors have to prevent such forms of tunnel vision will vary from jurisdiction to jurisdiction and may be greater in civilian systems where prosecutors supervise or even conduct the investigation. Prosecutorial involvement in police investigations has the potential to act as a check on tunnel vision, but it can also make the prosecutor prey to the same tunnel vision. Having an independent prosecutor review police charges can act as a check on tunnel vision, but the intensity of such prosecutorial reviews may vary with resources and local practice.

Prosecutors and Witnesses

The US registry identifies mistaken witness identification as a factor in 29 per cent of wrongful convictions with witness perjury and false accusations being a factor in 57 per cent of wrongful convictions.[18] It is difficult to hold prosecutors responsible for eyewitness who make genuine mistakes and identify the wrong perpetrator. Even in such cases, however, prosecutors play an indirect role. They may be able to influence police identification practices. They are also in a position to control the positive confirmation they provide to witnesses in contested cases who may have to testify multiple times in a prosecution. Prosecutors also could consent to allowing the defence to use expert evidence about the frailties of eyewitness identification, especially with respect to cross-racial misidentifications that have played such an important role in American DNA exonerations.

With respect to witnesses who lie or make false accusations, prosecutors may play a more direct role. They may offer possible accomplices to the accused such robust incentives that they produce a real danger of false testimony. They may also call jail-house informers to provide testimony against the accused. At the very least, it will be important for prosecutors to record and disclose to the accused the incentives they provide to witnesses.

Prosecutors and False Confessions

About 12 per cent of cases in the American registry involve false confessions.[19] The prosecutorial role with respect to such confessions is generally indirect. To be sure, prosecutors should vet confessions for accuracy and consistency with the evidence. At the same time, false confessions can seem quite reliable if they include "hold back" details of the crime that the police have consciously or inadvertently provided to the suspect.

Prosecutors can play a role with respect to police practices that may induce false confessions. For example, prosecutors can insist on interrogations being recorded and they can ensure that the police do not place undue pressures that may induce a false confession.

Prosecutors and Forensic Evidence

False or misleading forensic evidence is a factor in 24 per cent of the cases in the American registry.[20] There have been some documented and shocking cases where prosecutors have relied on and sometimes sought out forensic experts in the face of evidence that they were not properly trained and had provided unreliable expert opinion evidence in the past.[21] At the same time, many cases where forensic evidence contributes to wrongful convictions may not be quite as stark with prosecutors playing a more indirect role. Prosecutors may rely on past judicial acceptance of forensic evidence and their own lack of expertise to simply continue to offer forensic evidence that may not be reliable. Even those who are critical of such prosecutor conduct, tend to argue that prosecutors have ethical as opposed to legal obligations to take more steps to ensure the reliability of the forensic evidence that they present in criminal cases.[22]

There is a growing consensus that many of the identification comparison sciences that the criminal justice system routinely relies upon, including fingerprinting, fire identification and even forensic pathology identifying causes of death, are based on an underdeveloped science.[23] Fundamental change that may take a generation or more is required to increase our knowledge of reliability. Prosecutors have an important role to play with respect to this necessary change, but an indirect one.

Summary

This section provided a summary overview of the causes of wrongful convictions that will be of most assistance to those not familiar with the growing literature on the topic. The focus has been on the role that the prosecutor plays with respect to wrongful convictions. The general conclusion has been that while prosecutors bear direct responsibility for some wrongful convictions, most notably those where they have failed to disclose exculpatory evidence and when they offer plea bargains as a means to avoid testing dubious evidence, in many other cases prosecutors play a more indirect role.

Intentional prosecutorial misconduct causes some wrongful conviction but the prosecutorial role with respect to police, witness and forensic error as well as systemic causes is more indirect. Prosecutors act as gatekeepers to the criminal justice system for witnesses who lie and for forensic experts who are wrong. As Peter Joy has observed "the prosecutor is the first line of defense against many of the common factors that lead to wrongful convictions".[24] In this way, prosecutors are in an excellent position to influence practices that produce wrongful convictions even when they are not directly responsible for those practices.

Increased evidence about the causes of wrongful convictions should be of interest to those who study prosecutors because it affirms the central but constrained and dependent role that the prosecutor plays in the criminal justice system. Wrongful convictions may not be typical of all cases, but the growing number of wrongful convictions that have originated with guilty pleas brings them closer to the usual range of cases. All of this evidence suggests that while prosecutors are not the direct cause of most wrongful convictions, they play a significant indirect role with respect to most of the causes of wrongful convictions.

A Taxonomy of Hard and Softer Strategies to Regulate Prosecutorial Conduct

This part of the chapter provides an analytical taxonomy of different strategies to deal with the prosecutorial role in wrongful convictions. Hard ex-post accountability measures that impose criminal, civil or professional sanctions on prosecutors will be examined first. Although difficult to apply, these strategies may be warranted in cases where prosecutorial misconduct has been the direct cause of wrongful convictions.

Next, so-called softer and self-regulatory measures that relate to education, ethics, rewards, reputational loss and organizational structures and cultures will be examined. These strategies may be helpful in responding to cases where prosecutors are the direct cause of wrongful convictions, but also in other cases where they play a more indirect role.

Hard Accountability Measures

Criminal Sanctions

Prosecutors could be guilty of obstruction of justice or as accessories to perjury if they knowingly presented false evidence to a court. Prosecutions of prosecutors are, however, rare. They would encounter formidable problems of proof because crimes based on obstruction and perjury generally require proof of high levels of criminal fault.[25] Once prosecutors become criminal suspects, they have the same due process rights including rights not to cooperate in investigations as other suspects.

Civil Liability

The prospects for holding prosecutors civilly liable are not strong in any country but especially in the US where prosecutors enjoy absolute immunity from civil liability with respect to matters related to the prosecutorial process including even knowledge of a witness's falsehoods and knowing refusal to disclose material evidence.[26] American prosecutors also enjoy a robust qualified immunity with respect to other matters such as advising the police.[27] The rationale for such immunities is that the fear of individual liability will over-deter individual prosecutors. At the same time, the US Supreme Court has even rejected holding a prosecutorial agency civilly liable for failing properly to train and supervise prosecutors after repeated disclosure violations.[28] These immunities reflect concerns that floodgates of litigation would open wide, especially given unique American rules that can make it essentially costless to sue officials even if the suit is dismissed.

Civil fault only needs to be established on a balance of probabilities whereas criminal fault must be established beyond a reasonable doubt and prosecutors who are sued civilly are subject to mandatory discovery. Nevertheless even in jurisdictions that more readily allow prosecutors to be sued civilly than the United States, a plaintiff often has to establish high levels of fault such as malice[29] or gross negligence.[30]

Another alternative to damages are costs orders in cases where prosecutors have engaged in practices that have imposed needless costs on the accused. Cost awards are generally not made in criminal cases, but under the 1998 Hyde Amendment[31] in the United States, they can be awarded in cases of misconduct. Costs can also be awarded in Canada, but generally they require a finding of gross negligence in violating the accused's human rights.[32] In many cases, prosecutors held personally liable for damages or costs will be indemnified by their employer, undercutting some of the deterrent effects of civil sanctions.

Professional Discipline

Prosecutors as lawyers are subject to professional discipline by legal regulators. The US Congress enacted a law in 1998 that provided that federal prosecutors would be subject to the same disciplinary rules as other lawyers.[33] The law was spearheaded by Congressman Joseph McDade (R-Pa) after he was indicted by federal prosecutors, but acquitted by a jury. In Canada, the Supreme Court affirmed in 2002 that a prosecutor could be subject to professional discipline by a law society for misconduct including failures to make disclosure. At the same time, the Court cautioned against disciplinary review of the exercise of core prosecutorial discretion relating to matters such as charging decisions.[34]

A number of American commentators have argued that increased professional discipline has a greater potential than criminal or civil discipline to apply to prosecutorial conduct that contributes to wrongful convictions. They emphasize that some ethical rules relating to disclosure and other matters are designed to ensure that prosecutors act in a fair and impartial manner. They also stress that professional discipline as an administrative matter requires less proof of fault than criminal prosecutions or civil lawsuits.[35]

The advantages of professional discipline over criminal or civil liability may, however, be more theoretical than real. Empirical studies suggest that prosecutors are rarely disciplined for misconduct.[36] A 2009 New York Bar Task Force on wrongful convictions found no disciplinary actions taken against prosecutors despite disclosure violations being involved in about half of the wrongful convictions in the state.[37] In Canada, there is no record of the prosecutor subsequently being disciplined for alleged late disclosure violations in the landmark 2002 case that established that prosecutors were amenable to discipline by the bar.[38] An Ontario study found that prosecutors were only the subject of disciplinary hearings in nine of 2200 cases over 23 years.[39]

Summary

Although it may be desirable to improve some of the hard prosecutorial accountability mechanisms, the low use of criminal, civil or administrative discipline in cases where prosecutors contribute to wrongful convictions suggest that other remedies are needed. At the same time, some shocking and egregious cases of prosecutorial misconduct in some wrongful conviction cases helps explain why much of the American literature and discourse demands punitive measures.[40]

Softer Accountability Measures

Many of the leading scholars on prosecutors have concluded that the ethics and integrity of individual prosecutors are more important than legal sanctions that they may suffer for engaging in misconduct. For example, Professor John Edwards concluded that prosecutorial independence ultimately depended on the integrity of those who hold the office of Attorney General.[41] In 2009, the late Marc Rosenberg drew similar conclusions even while documenting the dramatic rise of the availability of external judicial and law society regulation of prosecutorial behaviour in Canada.[42] Barry Scheck, one of the co-founders of the Innocence Project, has argued that the frequent failure of criminal, civil or administrative discipline of prosecutors in the United States suggests that "if only by default … internal regulation" may be the best way to reform prosecutorial practices. Scheck also argues that there are "concrete reasons to be optimistic that this approach will be both practical and effective".[43]

Education

Prosecutors are unlikely to take steps to correct or prevent wrongful convictions if they believe that wrongful convictions are extremely rare events. Bruce Macfarlane, who served as a senior prosecutor in Canada, has stressed the importance of continuing education of prosecutors in changing attitudes and making them more willing to accept that wrongful convictions have occurred.[44] He points to an almost 200-page research report released by an official group of senior prosecutors in Canada in 2004 and updated in 2011 as evidence of how Canadian prosecutors have become more aware of the causes of wrongful convictions.[45] There is a tendency in some quarters to dismiss education as just talk and window dressing, but it can equip prosecutors with knowledge and provide role models who have acted to prevent or correct wrongful convictions.

Public Inquiries

Much of the education materials used by prosecutors in Canada about wrongful convictions (as well as judges, defence lawyers and others) comes from seven public inquiries that have since 1989 been conducted in Canada into wrongful convictions. These inquiries are a hybrid institution appointed at the discretion of the executive but generally headed by sitting or retired judges. They typically have generous budgets to conduct hearings and commission research. Canadian inquiries are constitutionally precluded from making conclusions of either civil or criminal liability.[46] Nevertheless, they have not hesitated to reach conclusions that prosecutors have acted improperly in the wrongful convictions that they examined and to make recommendations directed at prosecutors.

Reputational Harms

Prosecutors are professionals who understandably value their reputations. The conclusions of various public inquiries about prosecutorial conduct can have a significant effect on reputations. Canada's second commission of inquiry into a wrongful conviction concluded that a senior prosecutor who up to that time had a legendary reputation had in the course of a wrongful conviction suffered from "tunnel vision in the most staggering proportions".[47] Another of the Canadian inquiries found that the conduct of three senior prosecutors who participated in a number of disclosure violations "fell below then existing professional standards expected of lawyers and agents of the Attorney General".[48] On the one hand, none of the three was subject to subsequent professional discipline illustrating the failure of "hard" disciplinary sanctions. On the other hand, their reputations were adversely affected by conclusions reached in the inquiry by a widely respected retired judge. In some cases, investigative media reports may also impose reputational harms on prosecutors who have been involved in wrongful convictions. Reputational harms may be effective "softer" sanctions that do not depend on formal findings that prosecutors have breached relevant criminal, civil or professional disciplinary standards.

Rewards

If reputational harms function as a "softer" stick then rewards function as carrots for professionals. Daniel Medwed has observed that prosecutors in Santa Clara County California who have assisted in revealing wrongful convictions earn "prizes and public recognition".[49] This finding is particularly striking given that the available evidence suggests that Californian prosecutors are highly unlikely to be sanctioned for their role in wrongful convictions. More generally, many employers rely more on rewards than sanctions to influence the behaviour of professionals.[50]

Ethical Reform and Leadership

In many jurisdictions, the ethical rules concerning prosecutors remain quite vague and have not been updated to contain lessons learned from wrongful convictions. Ontario's rules of professional conduct contained detailed provisions relating to fees, property, marketing and withdrawal of services but, when it comes to the prosecutor, simply has only the following anodyne rule:

> **5.1–3** When acting as a prosecutor, a lawyer shall act for the public and the administration of justice resolutely and honourably within the limits of the law while treating the tribunal with candour, fairness, courtesy, and respect.[51]

Even leaving aside whether prosecutors will be disciplined under this vague rule, such bare bones rules miss an opportunity to educate and persuade lawyers about their ethical duties. There are also concerns that rules of professional conduct have not kept up with new disclosure and other obligations of prosecutors.[52]

In 2008, the American Bar Association amended Rule 3.8 of the Model Rules of Professional Conduct to require investigations when "a prosecutor knows of new, credible and material evidence creating a reasonable likelihood that a convicted defendant did not commit an offence of which the defendant was convicted". This rule, however, has only been adopted in a few states and been criticized for its "lack of teeth and limited implementation".[53] At the same time, it should be recognized that ethical reforms have a potential to change practices even when they are not used to impose disciplinary sanctions.

Organizational Culture and Innovation

In the United States, informal and often localized organizational changes within prosecutor's offices seem to be playing a more important role in the correction of wrongful conviction than formal legal changes. Data from the American registry reveals that conviction integrity units in prosecutorial offices played a role in 269 exonerations between 2003 and 2017 even though there are only 33 such units in the decentralized American prosecutorial system.[54]

Internal Guidelines

Another form of self-regulation is the use of internal administrative policies by prosecutors. Prosecutors are bureaucrats and internal policy guidelines can play an important role in structuring the exercise of discretion and making it more transparent. The desk-book that guides the Public Prosecution Service of Canada now includes a chapter on the prevention of wrongful convictions that covers the main causes of wrongful conviction including guilty pleas.[55]

Summary

Self-regulation and internal reforms by prosecutors hold much promise both because of the difficulty of external regulation that imposes sanctions and because of the reality that prosecutors often play only an indirect and contributing role to wrongful conviction. Education, rewards and ethical leadership can inspire prosecutors to encourage police and forensic reforms that may decrease the risk of wrongful convictions. Because they must be applied in a fair manner, sanctions can only address cases of proven prosecutorial misconduct.

At the same time, it would be wrong to suggest that there is always a dichotomy between hard and softer forms of regulations. They can interact. For example, changes to ethical rules can lead by example, but they could also be used in disciplinary proceedings against prosecutors. Prosecutors may fear reputational harms, but these may follow from the imposition of formal sanctions as well as from the findings of public inquiries or the investigative media. Finally, education and sanctions can be mutually re-enforcing because the more widespread knowledge is about the causes of wrongful convictions, the more willing judges and disciplinary bodies may be to impose sanctions for prosecutorial conduct that contributes to wrongful convictions.

Combining Hard and Softer Strategies to Better Prevent and Correct Wrongful Convictions

One distinct trend, perhaps magnified in high punishment societies such as China[56] and the United States,[57] is enthusiasm for the notion that prosecutors should be disciplined for their role in wrongful convictions. Such approaches are influenced by broad punitive trends in society.[58]

Punishment may be warranted in the case of proven prosecutorial misconduct and the threat of punishment may also make prosecutors more amenable to softer strategies such as education, organizational reform and ethical leadership. Nevertheless, the evidence examined in the first part of this chapter suggests that prosecutors will only be directly responsible for a minority of wrongful convictions. At the same time, however, prosecutors continue to play a central gatekeeper role in the criminal justice system. They are perhaps the criminal justice actors in the best position to prevent and correct wrongful convictions.

The optimal regulatory system will likely combine credible threats of hard sanctions that can be applied to the worst cases and more pervasive use of softer strategies that have the potential to make prosecutors take proactive steps to prevent and correct wrongful convictions. Such an approach to regulating prosecutorial conduct is consistent with John Braithwaite's theory of responsive regulation.[59] Braithwaite's theory revolves around a regulatory pyramid with persuasion at the base, with escalating use of regulatory, civil or criminal sanctions when persuasion fails. It also calls for de-escalation from sanctions when organizations respond positively and take steps to prevent the targeted harm.

Braithwaite's pyramid recognizes the costs in terms of resources, time and resistance, in applying formal sanctions. It also recognizes that less coercive approaches have the potential to tap into both the virtue and expertise of the regulated to take proactive steps beyond the legal minimum to prevent the targeted harm. At the same time, his approach does not rely on the good will of the regulated because it has a place for harsher sanctions that are designed to deter misconduct and when necessary incapacitate those who have proven unwilling or unable to change their behaviour.

Although some may be attracted to a sanctions-based approach, given the vast powers and frequent impunity of prosecutors, such an approach will only be applicable in a minority of cases where direct and provable prosecutorial misconduct causes wrongful convictions. Even in such cases, prosecutors will often be able to use their resources and employ judicial deference to their exercise of prosecutorial discretion to escape sanctions. In addition, a sanctions dominated approach could result in prosecutors becoming more adversarial and defensive when confronted with alleged wrongful conclusions and this could make them more reluctant voluntarily to correct wrongful convictions. Prosecutors might also interpret conclusions that they are not legally liable for conduct with approval of the conduct even though changes in their conduct could have many benefits.

The precise mix of hard and softer strategies will vary in different jurisdictions and over time. Reliance on softer and internal approaches as opposed to external discipline may also depend in part on prosecutorial cultures and even the personalities of prosecutors. This suggests that internal and softer strategies may be more fragile and dynamic and less transparent than external and harder strategies. In the end, the optimal approach to reform will combine internal self-regulation with some degree of external regulation that encourages prosecutors to act as ministers of justice concerned about avoiding and correcting wrongful convictions.

A Canadian Example of Combined Hard and Soft Strategies

In a significant number of cases, Canadian prosecutors have assisted in the correction of wrongful convictions. To this extent, the idea of the prosecutor as a minister of justice more concerned with truth than wins is alive.[60] At the same time, until recently the Canadian approach could be criticized for failing to impose hard sanctions on Canadian prosecutors who have played a direct role in wrongful convictions. For example, Mel Green argued in 2004 that "it is a constant source of discouragement that no Canadian prosecutor ... have ever been held accountable for his or her misdeeds (including continuing instances of material non-disclosure) in the course of a wrongful conviction prosecution".[61]

Why have Canadian prosecutors become relatively receptive to the reality of wrongful conviction despite the absence of hard sanctions for their role in them? As I have argued more fully elsewhere, the seven Canadian public inquiries held into wrongful convictions since 1989 have played an extremely important role.[62] The Canadian inquiries lack powers to draw conclusions of criminal or civil liability[63] and only one of them has even considered whether prosecutors should be referred for professional discipline before ultimately concluding that such referrals were not warranted.[64] That said, both the hearings and reports of the inquiries are well publicized and a number of prosecutors have suffered significant reputational harms because of how they answered questions at inquiries and adverse conclusions about their behaviour drawn in inquiry reports.

The Canadian inquiries should not be romanticized. Many of their recommendations related to systemic reforms to lessen the risk of wrongful convictions have not been implemented This suggests that while softer strategies, including the education and reputational harms produced by the inquiries, may make prosecutors more amenable to correcting wrongful convictions, governments and prosecutors may still reject systemic reforms that will make the criminal justice system less efficient. For example, Canada still lacks a legislated framework for both identifications and interrogations even though such reforms have been proposed.[65] Prosecutors have been willing to form committees to vet the use of jailhouse informers, but they have not extended such vetting to other incentivized witnesses that may also be prone to lie.[66] In general, Canada lags behind the United States and even Australia in adopting legislative reforms to prevent and correct wrongful convictions. In other words, there is a distinction between the prosecutorial ability to correct revealed wrongful convictions and a reluctance to engage in systemic reforms that may also decrease rightful convictions.

There are some signs that Canada may be becoming more willing to use hard sanctions against prosecutors. A 2015 Supreme Court of Canada decision established that the state as an entity could be held responsible for damages under the Canadian Charter of Rights and Freedoms when prosecutors knew or ought to have known that non-disclosure of material would infringe the accused's right to full answer and defence.[67] The "softer" Canadian approach that relies on inquiries and self-regulation by prosecutors is gaining a harder edge, at least with respect to civil liability.

In the summer of 2016, this harder edge became a reality when a Canadian trial judge awarded $8 million in damages to Ivan Henry who was wrongly convicted of a series of sexual assaults in the early 1980s and spent almost 27 years in custody.[68] Most of the damages ($7.5 million) was awarded in order to vindicate and deter the violation of Mr. Henry's constitutional rights to disclosure. The total award received by Mr. Henry is not out of line with cash settlements voluntarily paid by Canadian governments for similar wrongful convictions. Nevertheless, it is unprecedented as a court order award on the basis of civil fault. The government has announced that it will not appeal the award.

It is an open question what effect the Henry award will have on future prosecutorial conduct. Some might argue that it will deter the type of disclosure violations that led to the award. At the same time, deterrence is speculative and perhaps ephemeral. There can also be a perverse form of deterrence. A prosecutor who had worked on the original file as a junior lawyer played a key role in bringing the possibility that Mr. Henry was wrongly convicted to the attention of more senior officials. Consistent with softer regulatory strategies, the lawyer was rewarded for her whistle-blowing conduct. Alas it is possible that someone who feared professional discipline, a civil lawsuit or criminal prosecution might have been more reluctant to correct a wrongful conviction. One would like to think that ethical prosecutors would prioritize the liberty and reputational interests of the wrongfully convicted over their own interests, but one cannot be certain in this regard. This example affirms that the optimal mix of hard and soft strategies to regulating prosecutorial conduct that contributes to wrongful convictions may remain illusive.

Conclusion

The growing scholarship on wrongful convictions should be of interest to those who study prosecutors. Prosecutors can play a dominant causal role with respect to wrongful convictions especially when they fail to disclose exculpatory evidence to the accused. That said, the literature also suggests that prosecutors will play a more indirect role in many more wrongful convictions by serving as a gatekeeper for police, witnesses and forensic experts who all may make direct contributions to wrongful convictions. The prosecutor often acts as a critical and sometimes the only mediating actor between police, witnesses and forensic experts with the criminal justice system.

The often indirect role that prosecutors play in wrongful convictions, combined with incentives, skills and resources that they have to defend themselves, helps explain why the record of imposing criminal, civil or professional disciplinary sanctions on prosecutors is so weak. This has led me to suggest that softer and self-regulatory strategies including education and ethical reform hold more promise.

Consistent with John Braithwaite's theory of responsive regulation, both hard and soft strategies have a role to play in regulating prosecutorial behaviour. Canada may be following this approach as it is supplementing the softer strategies of education and public inquiries with harder strategies such as civil liability. The optimal mix of hard and softer strategies will depend on the particular context and the amenability of prosecutors to self-regulation.

Notes

1 I thank the Pierre Trudeau Foundation for its generous support of my work and Philip Stenning for helpful comments on an earlier version of this chapter as well as all of the organizers and participants of the Onati conference where an earlier version of this chapter was presented.
2 Centre for Prosecutor Integrity *An Epidemic of Prosecutor Misconduct* (Centre for Prosecutor Integrity: Rockville MD, 2013) at Appendix B.
3 Kathleen Ridolfi and Maurice Possley *Preventive Error: A Report on Prosecutorial Misconduct 1997–2009* (Northern California Innocence Project, Santa Clara, 2010) 4–5.
4 Daniel Medwed "The Zeal Deal: Prosecutorial Resistance to Post-Conviction Claims of Innocence" (2004) 84 *Boston Univ. L.Rev.* 125; Melvyn Green "Crown Culture and Wrongful Convictions: A Beginning" (2005) 29 *CR* (6th) 262; Jerome Kennedy "Crown Culture and Wrongful Convictions" (2016) 63 *CLQ* 415.
5 See for example Alafair Burke "Improving Prosecutorial Decision Making: Some Lessons of Cognitive Science" (2006) 47 *Wm and Mary L.Rev.* 1587; Stephanos Bibas "Prosecutorial Regulation versus Prosecutorial Accountability" (2009) 157 *U.Pa. L.Rev.* 959; Bruce MacFarlane "Wrongful Convictions: Drilling Down to Understand Distorted Decision-Making by Prosecutors" (2016) 63 *CLQ* 439.
6 *Henry v. British Columbia* 2016 BCSC 1038.
7 John Braithwaite *Responsive Regulation and Restorative Justice* (Oxford: Oxford University Press, 2002).
8 Eric Colvin "Convicting the Innocent: A Critique of Theories of Wrongful Convictions" (2009) 20 *Criminal Law Forum* 173.
9 National Registry of Wrongful Convictions "% of Exonerations by Contributing Factor" at www.law.umich.edu/special/exoneration/Pages/ExonerationsContribFactorsByCrime.aspx (accessed 8 December, 2017).
10 Brandon Garrett *Convicting the Innocent* (Cambridge, MA: Harvard University Press, 2011).
11 Charles MacLean, James Berles and Adam Lamparello "Stop Blaming the Prosecutors: The Real Causes of Wrongful Convictions and Rightful Exonerations" (2015) 44 *Hofstra L.Rev* 151, 157–159.
12 Daniel Medwed *Prosecution Complex* (New York: New York University Press, 2012) 23.
13 This is not the case in all civilian jurisdictions. See Julia Jansson in this volume.
14 "Exonerations in 2016" at www.law.umich.edu/special/exoneration/Documents/Exonerations_in_2016.pdf (accessed 19 December 2017).
15 Amanda Carling "A Way to Reduce Indigenous Overrepresentation: Prevent False Guilty Plea Wrongful Convictions" (2017) 64 *CLQ* 415.
16 On the problem of battered women who may have valid self-defence claims being pressured into pleading guilty to avoid murder convictions see Kent Roach "The Wrongful Conviction of Indigenous People in Australia and Canada" (2015) 17 *Flinders L.J.* 203, 210–222.
17 Brandon Garrett *Convicting the Innocent* (Cambridge, MA: Harvard University Press, 2011) at 200–202.
18 "% of Exonerations by Contributing Factor" at www.law.umich.edu/special/exoneration/Pages/ExonerationsContribFactorsByCrime.aspx (accessed 14 January 2018).

19 Ibid.
20 Ibid.
21 Paul Giannnelli and Kevin McMunigal "Prosecutors, Ethics and Expert Witnesses" (2007) *Fordham L. Rev* 76: 1493.
22 Gary Edmond "(Ad)ministering Justice: Expert Evidence and the Professional Responsibilities of Prosecutors" (2013) *UNSWLJ* 37: 921.
23 *National Academy of Science Report on the Forensic Sciences* (Washington, DC: National Academy of Sciences, 2009).
24 Peter Joy "The Relationship between Prosecutorial Misconduct and Wrongful Convictions: Shaping Remedies for a Broken System" [2006] *Wisconsin L. Rev* 399, 406.
25 See *R. v. Kirkham* (1998) 126 CCC (3d) 397 (Sask Q.B.) acquitting a prosecutor of two counts of obstruction of justice in relation to collecting information about jurors not disclosed to the defence. The prosecutor was subsequently suspended by the Law Society for 6 months. *Law Society of Saskatchewan v. Kirkham* [1999] LSDD No. 19.
26 *Imber v. Pachtman* 424 U. 409, 425 (1976).
27 *Burns v. Reed* 500 US 478, 493 (1991).
28 *Connick v. Thompson* 131 SCt 1350 (2011).
29 *Nelles v. The Queen* [1989] 2 SCR 170 (recognizing tort of malicious prosecution).
30 *Henry v. British Columbia* [2015] 2 SCR 214 (recognizing ability to sue for human rights violations related to non-disclosure by prosecutor but requiring proof of gross negligence).
31 18 USC 3006A.
32 Costs to the accused are ordered in Canada as an alternative constitutional to more drastic remedies such as stays of proceedings and exclusion of evidence but generally when there has been "a marked and unacceptable departure from the reasonable standards expected of the prosecution". *R. v. Dunedin Construction* [2001] 3 SCR 575, [87].
33 28 USC 430B.
34 *Krieger v. Law Society of Alberta* [2002] 3 SCR 372.
35 Ellen Yaroshefsky "Wrongful Convictions: It is Time to Take Prosecution Discipline Seriously" (2004) 8 *DCLR*. 275; Angela Davis *Arbitrary Justice: The Power of the American Prosecutor* (Oxford: Oxford University Press, 2007) at 463–464; Daniel Medwed *Prosecution Complex* supra at 31.
36 Fred Zacharias "The Professional Discipline of Prosecutors" (2001) *NCLRev* 78: 721.
37 New York Bar Association *Final Report of the New York Bar's State Bar Association's Task Force on Wrongful Convictions* (Albany: New York Bar Association, 2009) at 20.
38 David Layton and Michel Proulx *Ethics and the Criminal Law* 2nd edn (Toronto: Irwin Law, 2015) ch 12.
39 Jennifer Pagliaro, Jayme Poisson, "Ontario fails to track complaints against Crown Attorneys" *Toronto Star*, 16 December 2014 at www.thestar.com/news/queenspark/2014/12/16/ontario_fails_to_track_complaints_against_crown_attorneys.html (accessed 21 December 2017).
40 Alafair Burke "Talking About Prosecutors" (2010) *Cardozo L.Rev*. 31: 2119.
41 J.Ll. J. Edwards *Walking the Tightrope of Justice* (Halifax, NS: Queens Printer, 1989), 133.
42 Marc Rosenberg "The Attorney General and the Administration of Criminal Justice" (2009) *Queens LJ* 34: 813.
43 Barry Scheck "Professional and Conviction Integrity Programs: Why We Need Them, Why the will Work and Models for Creating Them" (2010) *Cardozo L.Rev*. 31: 2215, 2215; Barry Scheck "Conviction Integrity Units Reconsidered" (2017) *Ohio St. Crim L.J.* 14: 705, 750.
44 Bruce Macfarlane "Wrongful Convictions: Drilling Down to Understand Distorted Decision-Making by Prosecutors" supra.

45 Report of the Federal/Provincial/Territorial Heads of Prosecutions Subcommittee on the Prevention of Wrongful Convictions – Fall 2011 at www.ppsc-sppc.gc.ca/eng/pub/ptj-spj/.
46 *Starr v. Houlden* [1990] 1 SCR 1366.
47 *Report of the Kaufman Commission on Proceedings Involving Guy Paul Morin* (Toronto: Queens Printer, 1998), 489–489.
48 *Commission of Inquiry into Certain Aspects of the Trial and Conviction of James Driskell* (Toronto: Queens Printer, 2007), 110–111.
49 Medwed *Prosecution Complex* supra at 133.
50 M.L. Friedland *Sanctions and Rewards in the Legal System* (Toronto: University of Toronto Press, 1989).
51 Law Society of Upper Canada Rules of Professional Conduct at www.lsuc.on.ca/printlist.aspx?id=671&langtype=1033.
52 Layton and Proulx *Ethics and Canadian Criminal Law* supra at 624–626.
53 Medwed *Prosecution Complex* supra at 135.
54 Exonerations in 2017 at www.law.umich.edu/special/exoneration/Documents/ExonerationsIn2017.pdf.
55 Public Prosecution Service of Canada Deskbook Chapter 2.4 Prevention of Wrongful Convictions 2 March 2014 at www.ppsc-sppc.gc.ca/eng/pub/fpsd-sfpg/fps-sfp/tpd/p2/ch04.html.
56 Na Jiang *Wrongful Convictions in China* (Berlin: Springer, 2016). My claim both with respect to the US and China is not that prosecutors are routinely sanctioned, but that such hard strategies are stressed over softer strategies of self-regulation or systemic reforms. See "China Resists Harshly Punishing Those Responsible for Wrongful Convictions" *New York Times* 3 Feb 2016 (complaints that "demerits" entered against prosecutors, police and judges involved in a wrongful conviction were not severe enough) (accessed 2 January 2018).
57 "Ex Prosecutor in Texas Punished for a Wrongful Conviction" *New York Times* 9 Nov, 2013 (ten days jail and 500 hours of community service for contempt of court in not revealing exculpatory evidence. Even in this case, however, the reputational loss of the former prosecutor being disgraced and having to resign a judgeship were probably more severe than the punishment imposed for his criminal conduct) (accessed 2 January 2018).
58 David Garland *The Culture of Control* (Chicago, IL: University of Chicago Press, 2001).
59 John Braithwaite *Responsive Regulation and Restorative Justice* (Oxford: Oxford University Press, 2002) ch. 2.
60 For more description of these cases see Kent Roach "Wrongful Convictions in Canada" (2012) *U of Cincinnati L.Rev.* 80: 1465.
61 Mel Green "Crown Culture and Wrongful Convictions" supra at 273.
62 Kent Roach "Comparative Reflections on Miscarriages of Justice in Australia and Canada" (2015) *Flinders L.J.* 17: 381.
63 *Starr v. Houlden* [1990] 1 SCR 1366.
64 Commission of Inquiry into Certain Aspects of the Trial and Conviction of James Driskell supra.
65 Report of the Federal/Provincial/Territorial Heads of Prosecutions Subcommittee on the Prevention of Wrongful Convictions – Fall 2011 at www.ppsc-sppc.gc.ca/eng/pub/ptj-spj/ at ch 7 (henceforth FPT Report) ch 6.
66 Ibid., ch 7.
67 *Henry v. British Columbia* [2015] 2 SCR 214.
68 *Henry v. British Columbia* 2016 BCSC 1038.

17 Conclusion

Victoria Colvin and Philip Stenning

Our goal with this volume has been to explore the understudied role of the prosecutor across different jurisdictions. In these concluding remarks, we undertake two tasks. The first is to explore the main conclusions drawn from individual chapters and from across the collection as a whole. As this has been an exploratory volume, our second task is to identify areas of omission and to propose a future research agenda for ongoing study of the roles of the prosecutor. Reviewing developments in the evolution of the role of prosecutor across many common and civil law jurisdictions, as the chapters of this book have done, provides a revealing window on emerging global trends that cannot be perceived from looking at any one individual jurisdiction.

Some important current trends and issues emerge clearly from the chapters. The most notable of these is the growing power of prosecutors in both common law and civil law jurisdictions. Increasingly, prosecutors influence the outcome of cases through the exercise of discretion in pre-trial processes. This is particularly the situation in common law systems, but is becoming a factor in civil law jurisdictions as well. Further, as Bronitt notes, prosecutors are increasingly being given tools to resolve potentially criminal allegations outside of the formal court process, and therefore without the protections of a system requiring proof of guilt and conviction prior to sanctions.

Related to this is what appears in so many of these jurisdictions to be an accountability deficit with respect to the exercise of prosecutorial power. This reflects the difficulty that is experienced in many jurisdictions in finding the right balance between the political independence and the political accountability of prosecutors, the latter being too often sacrificed in pursuit of the former. As the chapters by Blengino, Jasch and Wandall make clear, this is an issue that is not peculiar to common law jurisdictions. There is no simple answer to what mechanisms are most appropriate or what level of oversight best strikes the balance. As Toole notes, prosecution occurs in a highly jurisdictionally specific context. In some common law countries, the courts have recently begun to step in to address this accountability deficit by increasing their willingness to subject prosecutorial decision-making to judicial review and oversight. But many commentators remain to be convinced that such judicial accountability is an adequate substitute for effective political and public accountability in democratic states.

As several of the chapters in the book illustrate, prosecution systems are evolving to meet challenges that are either new or newly recognized. These include better meeting the needs of victims, protecting suspects from wrongful convictions, addressing the challenges of particular kinds of offending (drug courts, domestic violence courts, etc.), and involving "the community" more directly and actively in the processes for responding to offending. During the last 40 years or so, there have been attempts in many jurisdictions, often led by prosecutors themselves, both to adapt the criminal prosecution process, and to explore alternatives to it, to better address these challenges. These include not only restorative justice processes such as family group conferencing, but also truth and reconciliation commissions, in which prosecutors play much less central roles than they do in conventional criminal prosecution processes.

The development of international criminal tribunals and the International Criminal Court during the last 30 years has, as O'Brien discusses in her chapter, posed new challenges for prosecutors, not least of which has been to preserve some political independence, and the appearance of it, in the exercise of their prosecutorial authority. The development of the prosecutorial role in these international fora is still very much a work in progress.

There remain multiple areas where further research – in particular comparative research – is needed. First, the conventional belief has been that it is the procedural context of prosecutors – specifically whether they are operating in civil or common law jurisdictions – that most explains the differences in their historical and emerging roles, practices and relationships. What the chapters in the book collectively illustrate, however, is how much knowledge and policy transfer, or "borrowing", there has been between these two major legal systems as far as the role of prosecutors is concerned, during the last 50 years or so. There is also borrowing between jurisdictions within each of the two systems, with the result that there is almost as much variation within each of these systems as there is between them. This highlights the need for further comparative research to illuminate the nature and reasons for these differences in greater depth.

Related to this, of course, is the relative absence within the extant English-language literature of accounts of the evolving roles of prosecutors in other legal systems, such as Islamic sharia-law systems in countries such as Iran, and in one-party communist countries such as China (see e.g. Fujin, 1998). Unfortunately, that is a deficit this book has not been able to address. While we did try to include a chapter by a scholar from China in the book, unfortunately we were not successful in doing so. We were also not able to attract scholars from other non-democratic countries to contribute to the book. Accordingly, we have not been able to get a reading on how prosecutorial roles are developing in countries in which prosecutors may be subject to strong political direction, or where the prosecutorial role is seen through lenses other than those of the liberal democratic tradition.

The chapters in the book are also dominated by experience in countries in Europe and North America and other "Western" jurisdictions such as Australia.

Despite our efforts to attract scholars from Africa, South America and Asia, jurisdictions in these areas of the world are under-represented in this collection and remain so in the English-language literature more generally. This has meant that apart from some of the chapters by scholars in Australia, and Professor Adekunle's chapter on Nigeria, the impact of colonial legacies in shaping the roles of prosecutors has not been explored in detail in this book. Further research is needed into how the role of the prosecutor has been influenced by the ways in which imperial practices and approaches have been adapted, and in some cases abandoned, to suit the circumstances and political cultures of such countries in colonial and post-colonial times. In particular, the emerging acknowledgement of the cultural specificities and the aspirations of Indigenous peoples and how this affects the work of prosecutors in the criminal justice system is an area requiring further scholarly consideration.

Finally, what emerges from the book as a whole is the shortage of systematic empirical research on the role of prosecutors and their relationships with other key actors in the criminal prosecution process (police, defence lawyers, judges and magistrates, and victims, complainants and witnesses). This reflects the fact that the literature on prosecutors is still very much dominated by legal scholars, despite the emerging interest of social scientists in this area of research during the last 30 or 40 years, especially in common law jurisdictions. Yet without more empirical research, we will not be able to adequately understand the actual roles that prosecutors play in the criminal process, as opposed to the roles set out for them in laws and official policies, and in professional traditions and conventions. It will be social science funding agencies that will have the greatest opportunity to address this deficit in the current research literature on prosecutors.

At the beginning of the twenty-first century, the institution of the prosecutor is at a cross-roads worldwide. We began our Introduction to this book with the observation that the prosecutor is a figure both powerful and enigmatic. As the former factor increases, often in unpredictable ways, it is imperative that we work to reduce the latter. This collection has attempted to make the prosecutor less of an enigma, but there remains much to be done.

Reference

Fujin, G. (1998) "The Position and Role of Chinese Procuratorial Organs in Criminal Justice" – in UNAFEI *Resource Material Series No. 53* (Tokyo: UNAFEI) – accessible online at www.unafei.or.jp/english/pdf/RS_No53/No53_19PA_Fujin.pdf – This series includes papers on prosecutors' roles in many other Asian countries, as well as in two African and two Central American countries.

Index